P9-DXH-623

Decisions of the United States Supreme Court

1991-92 TERM

---

by
The Editorial Staff
United States Supreme Court Reports,
Lawyers' Edition

IIII®

Lawyers Cooperative Publishing
Aqueduct Building, Rochester, New York 14694

PREFACE

This volume is designed to serve as a quick-reference guide to the work of the United States Supreme Court during its 1991–1992 Term. Its important features are described below.

The Court's Personnel. A list of the Justices of the Supreme Court is accompanied by photographs and biographical sketches of each Justice serving during the Term.

Survey of the Term. A succinct narrative statement outlines the high spots of the Term.

Summaries of Decisions. Every important decision of the Supreme Court is individually summarized. These summaries (reprinted from Vols. 116–120 L Ed 2d) describe the manner in which the case came before the Court, the facts involved and issues presented, the holding of the Court and the reasons supporting that holding, the name of the Justice who wrote the opinion of the majority, and the names and views of those of the Justices who concurred or dissented.

The Summaries are printed in the order in which the cases were decided by the Court. Notations to Summaries indicate the volume and page at which the full opinion of the Court may be found in the official reports (US) published by the Federal Government, and the privately published United States Supreme Court Reports, Lawyers' Edition (L Ed 2d), and Supreme Court Reporter (S Ct).

Following each Summary is a listing of the attorneys who argued in behalf of the litigants.

Glossary. A glossary of common legal terms defines, in simple, nontechnical language, various legal words and phrases frequently used in the Supreme Court's decisions.

Table of Cases. A complete Table of Cases makes possible the location of the Summary of any case through the name of a party litigant.

Index. A detailed, alphabetical word index makes possible the location of the Summary of any case by consulting the index entries for appropriate factual and conceptual terms.

THE COURT'S PERSONNEL

JUSTICES

OF THE

SUPREME COURT OF THE UNITED STATES

_____

1991–92 Term

_____

Chief Justice
HON. WILLIAM H. REHNQUIST

Associate Justices
HON. BYRON R. WHITE

HON. HARRY A. BLACKMUN

HON. JOHN P. STEVENS

HON. SANDRA DAY O'CONNOR

HON. ANTONIN SCALIA

HON. ANTHONY M. KENNEDY

HON. DAVID H. SOUTER

HON. CLARENCE THOMAS

BIOGRAPHIES OF THE JUSTICES

Chief Justice Rehnquist was born in Milwaukee, Wisconsin, on October 1, 1924, the son of William B. and Margery P. Rehnquist. He married Natalie  Cornell in 1953. They have three children, James, Janet, and Nancy.

Chief Justice Rehnquist attended public schools in Shorewood, Wisconsin, and received his B.A. degree, with great distinction, and an M.A. degree from Stanford University in 1948. He also earned an M.A. degree from Harvard University in 1950, and then returned to Stanford University, where he received his LL.B. degree in 1952.

From 1952 to 1953, he served as law clerk for Justice Robert H. Jackson, Supreme Court of the United States. From 1953 to 1969, Chief Justice Rehnquist engaged in private practice in Phoenix, Arizona, and in 1969, he was appointed Assistant Attorney General, Office of Legal Counsel, by President Nixon.

Chief Justice Rehnquist served in the United States Army Air Corps in this country and overseas from 1943 to 1946, and was discharged with the rank of sergeant.

Chief Justice Rehnquist was nominated to the position of Associate Justice of the United States

Supreme Court by President Nixon on October 21, 1971, and took office on January 7, 1972. On June 17, 1986, he was nominated Chief Justice by President Reagan, and on September 26, 1986, he was sworn in as Chief Justice.

Chief Justice Rehnquist's professional activities have included membership in the American Bar Association, the Arizona Bar Association, the Maricopa County (Arizona) Bar Association (President, 1963), the National Conference of Lawyers and Realtors, the National Conference of Commissioners of Uniform State Laws, and the Council of the Administrative Conference of the United States.

Justice White was born in Ft. Collins, Colorado, on June 8, 1917, the son of Alpha Albert White and

Maud Burger White. He married Marion Lloyd Stearns on June 15, 1946. They have two children, Charles Byron and Nancy Pitkin.

Justice White attended elementary and high schools at Wellington, Colorado. He graduated from the University of Colorado in 1938 with a B.A. degree, and attended Oxford University, Oxford, England, as a Rhodes Scholar, from January, 1939 until October, 1939. From October, 1939 to October, 1941, and from February, 1946 to November, 1946, he attended Yale University Law School, receiving an LL.B. degree, magna cum laude.

Justice White volunteered for service in the United States Navy in July 1941, served in the Pacific as a naval intelligence officer during World War II, and was honorably discharged as a Lieutenant, U.S.N.R., in 1946.

Upon graduation from Yale, Justice White served from 1946 to 1947 as law clerk to Chief Justice Vinson, Supreme Court of the United States.

In 1947, he joined the law firm of Lewis, Grant, Newton, Davis and Henry (now Davis, Graham and Stubbs), in Denver, Colorado. He became a partner and remained with that firm until January 1961, when he was appointed Deputy Attorney General of the United States by President Kennedy.

Justice White was nominated by President Kennedy as Associate Justice of the Supreme Court of the United States on April 3, 1962, and took his seat on April 16, 1962.

He is a member of the American Bar Association and the Colorado Bar Association.

Justice Blackmun was born in Nashville, Illinois, on November 12, 1908, the son of Corwin M. and

Theo H. Blackmun. He married Dorothy E. Clark on June 21, 1941. They have three daughters: Nancy Clark, Sally Ann, and Susan Manning.

After attending Van Buren Grade School and Mechanic Arts High School in St. Paul, Minnesota, Justice Blackmun attended Harvard College, where, in 1929, he received his A.B. degree, summa cum laude. He earned his LL.B. degree from Harvard Law School in 1932.

He then served for two years as law clerk for Judge John B. Sanborn of the United States Court of Appeals for the Eighth Circuit.

In 1934, he joined the law firm then known as Dorsey, Colman, Barker, Scott & Barber, in Minneapolis, Minnesota. He became a general partner of that firm in 1943 and remained with it until 1950. During this same period he was also an instructor at St. Paul College of Law (now William Mitchell College of Law) (1935–1941), and taught at the University of Minnesota Law School (1945–1947).

In 1950 he became resident counsel of the Mayo Clinic in Rochester, Minnesota, and held that position until 1959, when he was appointed a judge of the United States Court of Appeals for the Eighth Circuit by President Eisenhower.

Justice Blackmun was nominated by President Nixon as Associate Justice of the United States Supreme Court on April 14, 1970, and took his seat on June 9, 1970.

He is a member of the American Bar Association, the Minnesota State Bar Association, the Third

Judical District (Minnesota) Bar Association, the
Olmsted County, Minnesota, Bar Association, and
the American Judicature Society.

Justice Stevens was born in Chicago, Illinois, on April 20, 1920. He is married to Maryan Mulholland Stevens and has four children, John Joseph, Kathryn Stevens Tedlicka, Elizabeth Jane, and Susan Roberta.

Justice Stevens received an A.B. degree from the University of Chicago in 1941 and a J.D. degree, magna cum laude, from Northwestern University School of Law in 1947.

During the 1947–1948 Term of the United States Supreme Court, he was a law clerk to Justice Wiley Rutledge, and in 1949, he was admitted to practice law in Illinois. In 1951 and 1952, Justice Stevens was Associate Counsel to the Subcommittee on the Study of Monopoly Power of the Judiciary Committee of the United States House of Representatives, and from 1953 to 1955 he was a member of the Attorney General's National Committee to Study Anti-trust Law. From 1970 to 1975 he served as a Judge of the United States Court of Appeals for the Seventh Circuit.

Justice Stevens served in the United States Navy from 1942 to 1945.

Justice Stevens was appointed to the position of Associate Justice of the United States Supreme Court by President Ford on December 1, 1975, and took his seat on December 19, 1975.

Justice Stevens is a member of the Illinois Bar Association, Chicago Bar Association, Federal Bar Association, American Law Institute, and American Judicature Society.

Justice O'Connor was born in El Paso, Texas, on March 26, 1930, the daughter of Harold A. Day and

 Ada Mae Wilkey Day. She married John Jay O'Connor III in 1952. They have three children, Scott, Brian, and Jay.

Justice O'Connor graduated from Stanford University in 1950 with a B.A. degree, magna cum laude. She earned her LL.B. degree at Stanford in 1952.

Justice O'Connor served as a deputy county attorney in San Mateo County, California, from 1952 to 1953, and as a civilian attorney for the Quartermaster Market Center in Frankfurt, Germany, from 1954 to 1957. She was in the private practice of law in Maryvale, Arizona, from 1958 to 1960, and served as an Assistant Attorney General in Arizona from 1965 to 1969.

Justice O'Connor was a member of the Arizona State Senate from 1969 to 1975. She was a judge of the Maricopa County Superior Court in Phoenix, Arizona, from 1975 to 1979, and served on the Arizona Court of Appeals from 1979 to 1981.

Justice O'Connor was appointed to the position of Associate Justice of the United States Supreme Court by President Reagan on July 7, 1981, and took office on September 25, 1981.

Justice Scalia was born on March 11, 1936 in Trenton, New Jersey. He married Maureen McCarthy, September 10, 1960.  They have nine children: Ann Forrest, Eugene, John Francis, Catherine Elisabeth, Mary Clare, Paul David, Matthew, Christopher James, and Margaret Jane.

Justice Scalia attended Georgetown University and University of Fribourg (Switzerland), receiving his A.B. degree in 1957. He earned his LL.B. degree in 1960 from Harvard University.

Justice Scalia was admitted to the Ohio Bar, 1962, and the Virginia Bar, 1970. He was in private practice with Jones, Day, Cockley and Reavis, Cleveland, Ohio, from 1961 to 1967.

He served as general counsel, Office of Telecommunications Policy, Executive Office of the President, 1971 to 1972; chairman, Administrative Conference of the United States, 1972 to 1974; Assistant Attorney General, Office of Legal Counsel, U. S. Department of Justice, 1974 to 1977.

Justice Scalia was a professor of law at the University of Virginia from 1967 to 1974, a scholar in residence at the American Enterprise Institute in 1977, visiting professor of law at Georgetown University in 1977, professor of law at the University of Chicago from 1977 to 1982, and visiting professor of law at Stanford University from 1980 to 1981.

From 1982 to 1986, Justice Scalia served as a Judge of the United States Court of Appeals for the District of Columbia Circuit. He was nominated by President Reagan as Associate Justice of the United States Supreme Court, and he took the oath of office on September 26, 1986.

Justice Kennedy was born in Sacramento, California, on July 23, 1936. He married Mary Davis on

June 29, 1963, and they have three children, Justin Anthony, Gregory Davis, and Kristin Marie.

Justice Kennedy attended Stanford University and the London School of Economics, receiving a B.A. from Stanford in 1958. He then earned an LL.B. from Harvard Law School in 1961. From 1960 to 1961, he was on the board of student advisors, Harvard Law School.

Justice Kennedy was admitted to the California bar in 1962 and the United States Tax Court bar in 1971. From 1961 to 1963, he was an associate at Thelen, Marrin, Johnson & Bridges, San Francisco, then practiced as a sole practitioner in Sacramento from 1963 to 1967, and was a partner in Evans, Jackson & Kennedy, Sacramento, from 1967 to 1975. He was nominated to be a judge of the United States Court of Appeals for the Ninth Circuit by President Ford, and took the oath of office on May 30, 1975. In addition, Justice Kennedy has been a professor of constitutional law at McGeorge School of Law, University of the Pacific, from 1965 to 1988.

He has served in the California Army National Guard, 1961; the Judicial Conference of the United States Advisory Panel on Financial Disclosure Reports and Judicial Activities (subsequently renamed the Advisory Committee on Codes of Conduct), 1979 to 1987; and the board of the Federal Judicial Center, 1987 to 1988. He has been on the Committee on Pacific Territories, 1979 to 1988, and was

named chairman 1982. He is a member of the
American Bar Association, Sacramento County Bar
Association, State Bar of California, and Phi Beta
Kappa.

Justice Kennedy was nominated by President
Reagan as an Associate Justice of the Supreme
Court, and took the oath of office on February 18,
1988.

Justice Souter was born in Melrose, Massachusetts on September 17, 1939, the son of Joseph Alexander and Helen Adams Hackett Souter.

He graduated from Harvard College in 1961 with an A.B. degree. After two years as a Rhodes Scholar, Justice Souter received an A.B. in Jurisprudence from Oxford University in 1963. He earned an LL.B. degree from Harvard Law School in 1966 and an M.A. degree from Oxford University in 1989.

Justice Souter was an associate at the law firm of Orr and Reno in Concord, New Hampshire from 1966 to 1968. He then became an Assistant Attorney General of New Hampshire. In 1971, he became Deputy Attorney General, and in 1976, Attorney General of New Hampshire. Justice Souter was named Associate Justice of the Superior Court of New Hampshire in 1978. In 1983, he was appointed as an Associate Justice of the Supreme Court of New Hampshire.

On May 25, 1990, Justice Souter became a Judge of the United States Court of Appeals for the First Circuit. He was nominated by President Bush as an Associate Justice of the United States Supreme Court, and he took his seat on October 9, 1990.

Justice Souter is a member of the National Association of Attorneys General, the New Hampshire Bar Association, and the American Bar Association.

Justice Thomas was born in Pinpoint, Georgia on June 23, 1948. He married Virginia Lamp on May

30, 1987, and has one child, Jamal Adeen.

Justice Thomas attended Conception Seminary and Holy Cross College, receiving an A.B. degree, cum laude, from Holy Cross in 1971. He earned a J.D. degree from Yale Law School in 1974.

He was admitted to the Missouri Bar in 1974, and after serving as Assistant Attorney General of Missouri from 1974 to 1977, he was an attorney for the Monsanto Company from 1977 to 1979.

Justice Thomas served as a legislative assistant to Senator John C. Danforth of Missouri from 1979 to 1981, before serving as Assistant Secretary for Civil Rights for the United States Department of Education from 1981 to 1982 and Chairman of the United States Equal Employment Opportunity Commission from 1982 to 1990.

On March 12, 1990, Justice Thomas became a Judge of the United States Court of Appeals for the District of Columbia Circuit. He was nominated by President Bush as Associate Justice of the United States Supreme Court, and he took the oath of office on October 23, 1991.

SURVEY OF THE 1991-92–TERM

by

Gary Knapp, M.B.A., J.D.

---

§ 1. Generally; statistics

The Supreme Court's 1991-92 Term began on October 7, 1991. The court took a recess from June 29, 1992 until October 5, 1992, at which time the 1991-92 Term adjourned.

On October 23, 1991, Justice Clarence Thomas became a member of the Supreme Court, assuming the seat that had been left vacant by the retirement of Justice Thurgood Marhall in the summer of 1991.

Statistics released by the Office of the Clerk of the Supreme Court reveal that 6,770 cases appeared on the court's docket for the 1991-92 Term. Of these, 901 cases were carried over from the prior term, and 5,869 were docketed during the 1991-92 Term.

Of the 6,770 cases on the docket during the 1991-92 Term, 5,630 nonoriginal cases were disposed of by (1) the court's denial of review, (2) the court's dismissal, or (3) withdrawal. Another 74 nonoriginal cases were summarily decided. A total of 876 cases, including 11 original cases, were not acted upon, or remained undisposed of.

There were 196 cases available for argument during the 1991-92 Term, of which cases 127 were argued and 3 were dismissed or remained without argument, leaving 66 cases still available for argument.

Of the 127 cases which were argued, 120 were disposed of by signed opinion, 3 were disposed of by per curiam opinion, and 4 were set for reargument.

§ 2. Landmark decisions

During the 1991-92 Term, the Supreme Court handed down a number of well-publicized landmark decisions. Statutory restrictions on the availability of abortion continued to present publicly controversial issues for the court. It was held that, under the due process clause of the Federal Constitution's Fourteenth Amendment, (1) certain provisions of a Pennsylvania abortion statute—including requirements of informed consent, a 24-hour waiting period, and parental consent—were valid, but (2) provisions requiring spousal notification prior to an abortion were invalid (Planned Parenthood of

Southeastern Pennsylvania v Casey (1992, US) 120 L Ed 2d 674, 112 S Ct 2791, infra § 3).

In another decision that was of major public interest, the court held that (1) the Federal Cigarette Labeling and Advertising Act of 1965 (15 USCS §§ 1331-1340, later amended) did not pre-empt state civil, common-law damages claims with respect to cigarette smoking; and (2) the 1965 Act's successor, the Public Health Cigarette Smoking Act of 1969 (15 USCS §§ 1331-1340, later amended), pre-empted some but not all such state-law claims (Cipollone v Liggett Group, Inc. (1992, US) 120 L Ed 2d 407, 112 S Ct 2608, infra § 16).

During the 1991-92 Term, the Supreme Court was called upon to determine the effect, on a variety of issues, of the free speech clause of the Federal Constitution's First Amendment. In a highly publicized case, it was held that a city's bias-motivated crime ordinance, which banned the display of symbols—including a burning cross—that aroused anger in others on the basis of race, color, creed, religion, or gender, was facially invalid under the free speech clause (R. A. V. v St. Paul (1992, US) 120 L Ed 2d 305, 112 S Ct 2538, infra § 21). The court also held that (1) an airport terminal operated by a public authority is a nonpublic forum, and thus a ban on solicitation at such a terminal need only satisfy a reasonableness standard to satisfy the free speech clause, and (2) a regulation which prohibited repetitive solicitation of money in the interior of an airport terminal operated by a public authority was reasonable, and thus did not violate the clause, where solicitation was permitted on the sidewalks outside terminal buildings (International Soc. for Krishna Consciousness, Inc. v Lee (1992, US) 120 L Ed 2d 541, 112 S Ct 2701, infra § 7), but (3) a regulation which prohibited the repetitive distribution of literature within an airport terminal operated by a public authority violated the free speech clause (Lee v International Soc. for Krishna Consciousness, Inc. (1992, US) 120 L Ed 2d 669, 112 S Ct 2709, infra § 7). Moreover, the court held that a New York statute was inconsistent with the free speech clause, where the statute (1) provided that an entity contracting with a criminal accused for the production of a book or other work describing the crime must pay to the state's crime victims board any moneys owed to the accused under the contract, and (2) required the board to deposit such funds in an escrow account for payment to victims of the crime and to the accused's other creditors (Simon & Schuster, Inc. v Members of New York State Crime Victims Bd. (1991, US) 116 L Ed 2d 476, 112 S Ct 501, infra § 20).

Issues involving public schools were considered by the Supreme court in a number of cases during the 1991-92 Term. In a case that received significant coverage by the news media, the court held that the inclusion of an invocation and a benediction by a member of the clergy as part of an official public school graduation ceremony is forbidden by the Federal Constitution's First Amendment prohibition of the establishment of religion (Lee v Weisman (1992, US) 120 L Ed 2d 467, 112 S Ct 2649, infra § 48). In connection with a public high school student's action against a county school district under Title IX of the Education Amendments of 1972 (20 USCS §§ 1681-1688), it was held that a damages remedy was available in an action to enforce Title IX, where the student alleged that she had been subjected to gender-based discrimination, including sexual intercourse with a male teacher

(Franklin v Gwinnett County Public Schools (1992, US) 117 L Ed 2d 208, 112 S Ct 1028, infra § 52). Moreover, the court decided two cases involving school desegregation. In one case, the Supreme Court held, with respect to a particular Georgia school district which had once been segregated by law and was operating under a desegregation decree, that a Federal District Court did not, as a matter of law, lack discretion to permit the school district to regain control over student assignment, transportation, physical facilities, and extracurricular activities, while retaining court supervision over the areas of faculty and administrative assignments and the quality of education, where full compliance had not been demonstrated (Freeman v Pitts (1992, US) 118 L Ed 2d 108, 112 S Ct 1430, infra § 49). In the other case, the Supreme Court held that (1) a state's adoption and implementation of race-neutral admissions policies were insufficient by themselves to demonstrate that the state had complied with its duty, under the equal protection clause of the Federal Constitution's Fourteenth Amendment and Title VI of the Civil Rights Act of 1964 (42 USCS § 2000d), to dismantle the state's prior dual, racially segregated public university system; and (2) in particular, several surviving aspects of Mississippi's prior dual, public university system remained suspect (United States v Fordice (1992, US) 120 L Ed 2d 575, 112 S Ct 2727, infra § 49).

The court issued several decisions during the 1991-92 Term concerning governmental actions at various stages of the criminal law process. It was held that the Federal Government had failed, as a matter of law, to establish that rather than being entrapped, an individual who was accused of violating 18 USCS § 2252(a)(2)(A), which prohibits the

receipt through the mails of sexually explicit depictions of children, was predisposed to receive such
materials through the mails (Jacobson v United
States (1992, US) 118 L Ed 2d 174, 112 S Ct 1535,
infra § 15). Furthermore, the Supreme Court held
that (1) the forcible abduction from Mexico to the
United States of a Mexican citizen who had been
indicted on federal criminal charges did not violate
a United States-Mexico extradition treaty (31 UST
5059, TIAS No. 9656), and, therefore, (2) the fact
of the accused's forcible abduction did not prohibit
the accused's trial in a Federal District Court for
alleged violations of the criminal law of the United
States (United States v Alvarez-Machain (1992, US)
119 L Ed 2d 441, 112 S Ct 2188, infra § 25). The
Supreme Court also held that the use of excessive
force by prison officers against a prisoner may
constitute cruel and unusual punishment in violation
of the Federal Constitution's Eighth Amendment,
even though the prisoner does not suffer serious
injury (Hudson v McMillian (1992, US) 117 L Ed 2d
156, 112 S Ct 995, infra § 44), and that the refusal
of an Illinois trial court in a capital murder case to
inquire on voir dire, as requested by the defense,
whether potential jurors would automatically impose
the death penalty if the defendant was convicted,
violated the due process clause of the Federal Constitution's Fourteenth Amendment (Morgan v Illinois (1992, US) 119 L Ed 2d 492, 112 S Ct 2222,
infra § 51).

In an antitrust case, the court held that a photocopier manufacturer was not entitled to a summary
judgment dismissing claims by independent service
organizations that the manufacturer had (1) tied the
sale of service for the copiers to the sale of parts, in
violation of § 1 of the Sherman Act (15 USCS § 1),

and (2) monopolized and attempted to monopolize the sale of service and parts for the copiers, in violation of § 2 of the Act (15 USCS § 2) (Eastman Kodak Co. v Image Technical Services, Inc. (1992, US) 119 L Ed 2d 265, 112 S Ct 2072, infra § 10).

A pension plan's antialienation provision, which was required for tax qualification under § 206(d)(1) of the Employee Retirement Income Security Act of 1974 (29 USCS § 1056(d)(1)), was held to constitute a transfer restriction under "applicable nonbankruptcy law," and thus to allow exclusion of a debtor's interest in the plan from the property of the bankruptcy estate under 11 USCS § 541(c)(2) (Patterson v Shumate (1992, US) 119 L Ed 2d 519, 112 S Ct 2242, infra § 13).

In two cases decided during the 1991-1992 Term, the Supreme Court held that particular state regulation concerning the disposal of hazardous waste violated the Federal Constitution's commerce clause (Art I, § 8, cl 3). In one case, the regulation found invalid was a disposal fee imposed by Alabama on hazardous waste generated out of state, but not on waste generated within the state (Chemical Waste Management, Inc. v Hunt (1992, US) 119 L Ed 2d 121, 112 S Ct 2009, infra, § 60). In the other case, the regulation found invalid was a Michigan statute barring a private landfill owner from accepting solid waste originating outside the county in which the landfill was located (Ft. Gratiot Sanitary Landfill, Inc. v Michigan Dept. of Natural Resources (1992, US) 119 L Ed 2d 139, 112 S Ct 2019, infra § 60). In an additional case involving the disposal of hazardous waste, the Supreme Court held that certain provisions of the Low-Level Radioactive Waste Policy Amendments Act of 1985 (42 USCS § 2021b et seq.) violated the Federal Constitution, but were severable from other provisions of the Act which did not violate the Federal Constitution (New York v United States (1992, US) 120 L Ed 2d 120, 112 S Ct 2408, infra § 60).

Several cases involving state taxation were decided by the court during the 1991-92 Term. The court held, with respect to a mail-order house that had no physical nexus with North Dakota and whose only connection with North Dakota customers was by common carrier or mail, that North Dakota's imposition on the mail-order house of the duty to collect use taxes (1) did not violate the due process clause of the Federal Constitution's Fourteenth Amendment, but (2) did violate the Federal Constitution's commerce clause (Art I, § 8, cl 3) (Quill Corp. v North Dakota (1992, US) 119 L Ed 2d 91, 112 S Ct 1904, infra § 54). In addition, the Supreme Court held that Kansas' income tax, in taxing benefits received from the United States by military retirees, but not taxing benefits received by state and local government retirees, was inconsistent with federal retention of employee tax immunity in 4 USCS § 111, which retention was coextensive with the prohibition against discriminatory taxes embodied in the federal constitutional doctrine of intergovernmental tax immunity (Barker v Kansas (1992, US) 118 L Ed 2d 243, 112 S Ct 1619, infra § 55).

It was held that a provision of the Veterans' Reemployment Rights Act (38 USCS § 2024(d)) does not implicitly limit the length of military service after which a member of the Armed Forces retains a right to civilian reemployment (King v St. Vincent's Hosp. (1991, US) 116 L Ed 2d 578, 112 S Ct 570, infra § 59).

Finally, in an important decision concerning local elections, the court held that changes in the decisionmaking powers of the elected members of Alabama county commissions were not changes with respect to voting and, thus, were not subject to the preclearance requirements of § 5 of the Voting Rights Act (42 USCS § 1973c) (Presley v Etowah County Com. (1992, US) 117 L Ed 2d 51, 112 S Ct 820, infra § 22).

§ 3. Abortion

The Supreme Court held that, under the due process clause of the Federal Constitution's Fourteenth Amendment, (1) certain provisions of a Pennsylvania abortion statute—including requirements of informed consent, a 24-hour waiting period, and parental consent—were valid, but (2) provisions requiring spousal notification prior to an abortion were invalid. [Planned Parenthood of Southeastern Pennsylvania v Casey (1992, US) 120 L Ed 2d 674, 112 S Ct 2791.]

§ 4. Admiralty and maritime law

The court held that 33 USCS § 933(g)—a Longshore and Harbor Workers' Compensation Act (LHWCA) provision that under certain circumstances, if a third-party claim is settled without the written approval of the worker's employer, all future benefits are forfeited—applied to a worker whose employer, at the time of such a settlement, was neither paying compensation to the worker nor was yet subject to an order to pay compensation under the LHWCA. [Estate of Cowart v Nicklos Drilling Co. (1992, US) 120 L Ed 2d 379, 112 S Ct 2589.]

It was held that, even though "ship repairman" is an occupation enumerated in the Longshore and Harbor Workers' Compensation Act (33 USCS §§ 901 et seq.), a ship repairman may qualify under certain circumstances as a "seaman" under the Jones Act (46 USCS Appx § 688), and thus be entitled to bring a personal injury suit under the Jones Act. [Southwest Marine, Inc. v Gizoni (1991, US) 116 L Ed 2d 405, 112 S Ct 486.]

§ 5. Adoption Assistance and Child Welfare Act

It was held that a provision of the Adoption Assistance and Child Welfare Act of 1980 (42 USCS § 671(a)(15)) was not enforceable in a private action under either (1) 42 USCS § 1983, or (2) a suit brought directly under the Act. [Suter v Artist M. (1992, US) 118 L Ed 2d 1, 112 S Ct 1360.]

§ 6. Airline fares

The court held that enforcement, through state consumer-protection laws, of restrictions on the advertising of airline fares was pre-empted by a provision of the Airline Deregulation Act of 1978 (49 USCS Appx § 1305(a)(1)). [Morales v Trans World Airlines, Inc. (1992, US) 119 L Ed 2d 157, 112 S Ct 2031.]

§ 7. Airport terminals

The Supreme Court held that (1) an airport terminal operated by a public authority is a non-public forum, and thus a ban on solicitation at such a terminal need only satisfy a reasonableness standard to satisfy the free speech guarantee of the Federal Constitution's First Amendment, and (2) a regulation which prohibited repetitive solicitation of money in the interior of an airport terminal operated by a public authority was reasonable, and thus did not violate the free speech guarantee, where solicitation was permitted on the sidewalks outside terminal buildings. [International Soc. for Krishna

Consciousness, Inc. v Lee (1992, US) 120 L Ed 2d 541, 112 S Ct 2701.]

However, the court held that a regulation which banned the repetitive distribution of literature within airport terminals operated by a public authority violated the Federal Constitution's First Amendment free speech guarantee. [Lee v International Soc. for Krishna Consciousness, Inc. (1992, US) 120 L Ed 2d 669, 112 S Ct 2709.]

§ 8. Aliens and immigration

The Supreme Court held that Exemption 6 of the Freedom of Information Act (5 USCS § 552(b)(6))—exempting from disclosure personnel and similar files of which the disclosure would constitute a clearly unwarranted invasion of personal privacy—authorized the deletion of names and other identifying information from United States State Department reports containing summaries of confidential, individual interviews with Haitian nationals who had been involuntarily returned to Haiti after attempting to emigrate illegally to the United States. [United States Dept. of State v Ray (1991, US) 116 L Ed 2d 526, 112 S Ct 541.]

Another case involving aliens held that an Immigration and Naturalization Service rule (8 CFR § 103.6(a)(2)(ii))—generally requiring that the bond on which an excludible alien is released, pending a deportability determination, contain a condition forbidding unauthorized employment—was consistent with the authority of the United States Attorney General, under § 242(a) of the Immigration and Nationality Act (8 USCS § 1252(a)). [INS v National Center for Immigrants' Rights, Inc. (1991, US) 116 L Ed 2d 546, 112 S Ct 551.]

In each of two cases involving the possibility of asylum for an alien, the court's holding was unfavorable to the alien. In one case, the court held that the United States Attorney General did not abuse his discretion in denying an alien's motion to reopen deportation proceedings—where the alien, who was a member of the Provisional Irish Republican Army, (1) had previously conceded his deportability and designated Ireland as the country to which he should be deported, and (2) asserted as new evidence supporting his motion to reopen the proceedings the implementation of a previously ratified treaty permitting his extradition from Ireland to the United Kingdom—either on the basis that the alien had failed to adduce new material evidence, or on the basis that the alien had not satisfactorily explained his previous withdrawal of his claims for asylum and withholding of deportation and thus had waived such claims. [INS v Doherty (1992, US) 116 L Ed 2d 823, 112 S Ct 719.] In the other case, it was held that an attempt by Guatemalan guerrillas to coerce a Guatemalan individual into military service did not necessarily constitute persecution on account of political opinion so as to make the individual eligible for asylum as a refugee in the United States. [INS v Elias-Zacarias (1992, US) 117 L Ed 2d 38, 112 S Ct 812.]

For a case involving attorneys' fees awards for deportation proceedings, see § 11, infra.

§ 9. American National Red Cross

It was held that the "sue and be sued" provision (36 USCS § 2) of the federal corporate charter of the American National Red Cross conferred original jurisdiction on the federal courts over all cases to which the Red Cross was a party, so that the Red

Cross could remove from a state court to a federal court any state-law action which the Red Cross was defending. [American Nat. Red Cross v S. G. (1992, US) 120 L Ed 2d 201, 112 S Ct 2465.]

§ 10. Antitrust law

The Supreme Court held that a photocopier manufacturer was not entitled to a summary judgment dismissing claims by independent service organizations that the manufacturer had (1) tied the sale of service for the copiers to the sale of parts, in violation of § 1 of the Sherman Act (15 USCS § 1), and (2) monopolized and attempted to monopolize the sale of service and parts for the copiers, in violation of § 2 of the Act (15 USCS § 2). [Eastman Kodak Co. v Image Technical Services, Inc. (1992, US) 119 L Ed 2d 265, 112 S Ct 2072.]

Reviews by Montana and Wisconsin of fee rates for title searches, examinations, and settlements—which rates (1) were collectively set by title insurance companies through private ratings bureaus, and (2) under state law, would go into effect unless vetoed by state officials—were held not to be sufficiently active to satisfy the "active supervision" requirement of the state-action doctrine, which would immunize the companies from federal antitrust liability. [FTC v Ticor Title Ins. Co. (1992, US) 119 L Ed 2d 410, 112 S Ct 2169.]

§ 11. Attorneys' fees

It was held that the Equal Access to Justice Act (5 USCS § 504, 28 USCS § 2412) does not authorize the award of attorneys' fees for administrative deportation proceedings before the Immigration and Naturalization Service. [Ardestani v INS (1991, US) 116 L Ed 2d 496, 112 S Ct 515.]

The court held that, in awarding attorneys' fees under § 7002(e) of the Solid Waste Disposal Act (42 USCS § 6972(e)) or § 505(d) of the Federal Water Pollution Control Act (33 USCS § 1365(d)), a court may not enhance the award above the lodestar amount in order to reflect the fact that the party's attorneys were retained on a contingent fee basis. [Burlington v Dague (1992, US) 120 L Ed 2d 449, 112 S Ct 2638.]

§ 12. Bankruptcy—generally

The Supreme Court held that a Federal District Court did not have authority, in a bankruptcy case, to enjoin Federal Reserve Board proceedings against a debtor bank holding company for alleged banking-law violations. [Board of Governors of Federal Reserve System v MCorp Financial, Inc. (1991, US) 116 L Ed 2d 358, 112 S Ct 459.]

It was held that a debtor in bankruptcy was not entitled, under 11 USCS § 506(d), to "strip down" a creditor's lien on real property to the judicially determined value of the collateral. [Dewsnup v Timm (1992, US) 116 L Ed 2d 903, 112 S Ct 773.]

A trustee appointed to liquidate and distribute property, as part of a consolidated Chapter 11 bankruptcy plan for corporate debtors and an individual debtor, was held to be required, with respect to federal income taxes that became due after the appointment of the trustee, (1) under 26 USCS § 6012(b)(3), to file a tax return and pay tax due on income attributable to the corporate debtor's property, as the assignee of the property of a corporation, and (2) under 26 USCS § 6012(b)(4), to file a tax return and pay tax due on income attributable to the individual debtor's property, as the fiduciary of a trust. [Holywell Corp. v Smith (1992, US) 117 L Ed 2d 196, 112 S Ct 1021.]

It was held that a Federal Court of Appeals has jurisdiction, under 28 USCS § 1292, to review the appeal of an interlocutory order issued by a Federal District Court sitting as a bankruptcy appellate court. [Connecticut Nat. Bank v Germain (1992, US) 117 L Ed 2d 391, 112 S Ct 1146.]

Moreover, the court held that a bankruptcy trustee was barred from contesting, after the expiration of the 30-day period for filing objections under Bankruptcy Rule 4003(b), the validity of an exemption claimed by a debtor under 11 USCS § 522(*l*), even where the debtor had no colorable basis for claiming the exemption. [Taylor v Freeland & Kronz (1992, US) 118 L Ed 2d 280, 112 S Ct 1644.]

§ 13. —Transfers

Two cases decided during the Supreme Court's 1991-1992 Term pertained to the avoidance of transfers under 11 USCS § 547(b). In one case, it was held that payments on long-term debt may qualify for the "ordinary course of business" exception (11 USCS § 547(c)(2)) to a bankruptcy trustee's power under 11 USCS § 547(b) to avoid preferential transfers. [Union Bank v Wolas (1991, US) 116 L Ed 2d 514, 112 S Ct 527.] In the other case, the court held that, for purposes of determining whether a transfer is voidable under 11 USCS § 547(b)(4)(A) as occurring within 90 days of the filing of a bankruptcy petition, the transfer of a check occurs on the date that the drawee bank honors the check. [Barnhill v Johnson (1992, US) 118 L Ed 2d 39, 112 S Ct 1386.]

The Supreme Court held that no provision of law established an unequivocal textual waiver of the

United States Government's sovereign immunity from a bankruptcy trustee's claims for monetary relief, where the trustee was seeking to void a payment to the Internal Revenue Service. [United States v Nordic Village, Inc. (1992, US) 117 L Ed 2d 181, 112 S Ct 1011.]

The court also held that a pension plan's antialienation provision, which was required for tax qualification under § 206(d)(1) of the Employee Retirement Income Security Act of 1974 (29 USCS § 1056(d)(1)), constituted a transfer restriction under "applicable nonbankruptcy law," and thus allowed exclusion of a debtor's interest in the plan from the property of the bankruptcy estate under 11 USCS § 541(c)(2). [Patterson v Shumate (1992, US) 119 L Ed 2d 519, 112 S Ct 2242.]

§ 14. Child abuse actions

The court held that (1) there is a domestic relations exception to federal courts' diversity jurisdiction under 28 USCS § 1332, but (2) the exception did not permit a Federal District Court to abstain from exercising diversity jurisdiction over a woman's child-abuse tort action for damages against her former husband and his female companion. [Ankenbrandt v Richards (1992, US) 119 L Ed 2d 468, 112 S Ct 2206.]

§ 15. Child pornography

The Supreme Court held that the Federal Government had failed, as a matter of law, to establish that rather than being entrapped, an individual who was accused of violating 18 USCS § 2252(a)(2)(A), which prohibits the receipt through the mails of sexually explicit depictions of children, was predisposed to receive such materials through the mails.

[Jacobson v United States (1992, US) 118 L Ed 2d 174, 112 S Ct 1535.]

§ 16. Cigarette smoking claims

The court held that (1) the Federal Cigarette Labeling and Advertising Act of 1965 (15 USCS §§ 1331-1340, later amended) did not pre-empt state-law damages claims with respect to cigarette smoking; and (2) the 1965 Act's successor, the Public Health Cigarette Smoking Act of 1969 (15 USCS §§ 1331-1340, later amended), pre-empted some but not all such state-law claims. [Cipollone v Liggett Group, Inc. (1992, US) 120 L Ed 2d 407, 112 S Ct 2608.]

§ 17. Civil procedure sanctions

It was held that a Federal District Court was authorized to impose sanctions pursuant to Rule 11 of the Federal Rules of Civil Procedure, even though the District Court was later determined to lack subject matter jurisdiction. [Willy v Coastal Corp. (1992, US) 117 L Ed 2d 280, 112 S Ct 1076.]

§ 18. Conspiracy

The Supreme Court held that the due process clause of the Federal Constitution's Fifth Amendment did not require that a general guilty verdict on a federal multiple-object conspiracy charge had to be set aside if the evidence was inadequate to support a conviction as to one of the objects. [Griffin v United States (1991, US) 116 L Ed 2d 371, 112 S Ct 466.]

The court held that the double jeopardy clause of the Federal Constitution's Fifth Amendment does not bar a federal prosecution for conspiracy, where some overt acts were based on substantive offenses

SURVEY §21

for which the defendant was previously convicted
[United States v Felix (1992, US) 118 L Ed 2d 25,
112 S Ct 1377.]

§ 19. County taxation

The Indian General Allotment Act of 1887 (25
USCS §§ 331 et seq.) was held (1) to permit a
county to impose an ad valorem tax on reservation
land patented in fee pursuant to the Act, but (2) not
to allow the county to enforce its excise tax on sales
of such land. [County of Yakima v Confederated
Tribes & Bands of Yakima Indian Nation (1992, US)
116 L Ed 2d 687, 112 S Ct 683.]

§ 20. Crime victims

The court held that a New York statute was
inconsistent with the Federal Constitution's First
Amendment free speech guarantee, where the statute (1) provided that an entity contracting with a
criminal accused for the production of a book or
other work describing the crime must pay to the
state's crime victims board any moneys owed to the
accused under the contract, and (2) required the
board to deposit such funds in an escrow account
for payment to victims of the crime and to the
accused's other creditors. [Simon & Schuster, Inc. v
Members of New York State Crime Victims Bd.
(1991, US) 116 L Ed 2d 476, 112 S Ct 501.]

§ 21. Cross burning

The Supreme Court held that a city's bias-motivated crime ordinance, which banned the display of
symbols—including a burning cross—that aroused
anger in others on the basis of race, color, creed,
religion, or gender, was facially invalid under the
Federal Constitution's First Amendment free speech

guarantee. [R. A. V. v St. Paul (1992, US) 120 L Ed 2d 305, 112 S Ct 2538.]

§ 22. Elections and voting rights

It was held that Illinois election laws—as construed by the Supreme Court of Illinois to (1) disqualify a "new" political party's entire slate of candidates for election to political offices in a certain county, and (2) prohibit the new party from using an "established" party's name—violated the new party's candidates' rights, under the Federal Constitution's First Amendment, of access to the county ballot. [Norman v Reed (1992, US) 116 L Ed 2d 711, 112 S Ct 698.]

The court held that changes in the decisionmaking powers of the elected members of Alabama county commissions were not changes with respect to voting and, thus, were not subject to the preclearance requirements of § 5 of the Voting Rights Act (42 USCS § 1973c). [Presley v Etowah County Com. (1992, US) 117 L Ed 2d 51, 112 S Ct 820.]

Two cases decided during the Supreme Court's 1991-1992 Term involved the issue whether the Federal Constitution's Article I, § 2, clause 3—which requires that seats in the United States House of Representatives be apportioned among the states "according to their respective Numbers"—was violated by certain congressional reapportionment procedures following the 1990 census. In one case, the court held that reapportionment according to the "method of equal proportions" authorized by 2 USCS § 2a did not violate Article I, § 2. [United States Dept. of Commerce v Montana (1992, US) 118 L Ed 2d 87, 112 S Ct 1415.] In the other case, in addition to holding that the allocation, by the Secretary of Commerce, of federal employees stationed overseas to their home states, for purposes of reapportionment, did not violate Article I, § 2, clause 3, the court held that the Secretary's allocation (1) did not violate the Federal Constitution's Fourteenth Amendment, which requires that the persons in each state be counted in apportioning representatives, and (2) was not a "final agency action" reviewable under the judicial review provision of the Administrative Procedure Act (5 USCS § 7040). [Franklin v Massachusetts (1992, US) 120 L Ed 2d 636, 112 S Ct 2767.]

The Supreme Court held that a Tennessee statute, which prohibited the solicitation of votes and the display or distribution of campaign literature within 100 feet of the entrance to a polling place, did not violate the Federal Constitution's First and Fourteenth Amendments. [Burson v Freeman (1992, US) 119 L Ed 2d 5, 112 S Ct 1846.]

Moreover, the court held that a Hawaii statute that prohibited write-in voting did not violate the rights of the state's voters under the Federal Constitution's First and Fourteenth Amendments, where the state's electoral scheme provided constitutionally sufficient ballot access. [Burdick v Takushi (1992, US) 119 L Ed 2d 245, 112 S Ct 2059.]

§ 23. Endangered species

The Supreme Court held that a provision of the Department of the Interior and Related Agencies Appropriations Act of 1990 (PL 101-121)—which was to the effect that the Act's other provisions met the requirements of earlier statutes on which specified pending cases involving logging and the endangered spotted owl were based—did not violate the Federal Constitution's Article III, which vests federal judicial power in the federal courts. [Robertson v Seattle Audubon Soc. (1992, US) 118 L Ed 2d 73, 112 S Ct 1407.]

Environmental groups were held to lack standing to challenge a regulation interpreting § 7(a)(2) of the Endangered Species Act (16 USCS § 1536(a)(2)) as not applying to actions taken in foreign nations. [Lujan v Defenders of Wildlife (1992, US) 119 L Ed 2d 351, 112 S Ct 2130.]

§ 24. Extortion

It was held that a public official's affirmative act of inducement, such as a demand, was not a necessary element of the Hobbs Act offense of extortion "under color of official right" (18 USCS § 1951(b)(2)). [Evans v United States (1992, US) 119 L Ed 2d 57, 112 S Ct 1881.]

§ 25. Extradition treaties

The Supreme Court held that (1) the forcible abduction from Mexico to the United States of a Mexican citizen who had been indicted on federal criminal charges did not violate a United States-Mexico extradition treaty (31 UST 5059, TIAS No. 9656), and, therefore, (2) the fact of the accused's forcible abduction did not prohibit the accused's trial in a Federal District Court for alleged violations of the criminal law of the United States. [United States v Alvarez-Machain (1992, US) 119 L Ed 2d 441, 112 S Ct 2188.]

§ 26. Federal taxation—income

The court held that a target corporation's professional expenses incurred in the course of a friendly takeover of the corporation did not qualify for a federal income tax deduction under § 162(a) of Internal Revenue Code (26 USCS § 162(a)) as ordinary and necessary business expenses, where the transaction produced significant benefits to the corporation extending beyond the tax year in question. [INDOPCO, Inc. v Commissioner (1992, US) 117 L Ed 2d 226, 112 S Ct 1039.]

The Supreme Court held that backpay received in settlement of claims under Title VII of the Civil Rights Act of 1964 (42 USCS §§ 2000e et seq.) was not excludible from gross income under § 104(a)(2) of the Internal Revenue Code (26 USCS § 104(a) (2)) as damages for personal injuries. [United States v Burke (1992, US) 119 L Ed 2d 34, 112 S Ct 1867.]

See Holywell Corp. v Smith (1992, US) 117 L Ed 2d 196, 112 S Ct 1021, supra § 12, in which a trustee appointed to liquidate and distribute property, as part of a consolidated Chapter 11 bankruptcy plan for corporate debtors and an individual debtor, was held to be required, with respect to federal income taxes that became due after the appointment of the trustee, (1) under 26 USCS § 6012(b)(3), to file a tax return and pay tax due on income attributable to the corporate debtor's property, as the assignee of the property of a corporation, and (2) under 26 USCS § 6012(b)(4), to file a tax return and pay tax due on income attributable to the individual debtor's property, as the fiduciary of a trust.

§ 27. —Firearms

The court held that the National Firearms Act (NFA) (26 USCS §§ 5801 et seq.) could not be construed to require a gun manufacturer—who packaged as a unit a pistol and kit that could be used to quickly convert the pistol into a rifle with either a 21-inch barrel or a 10-inch barrel—to pay, with respect to the packaged unit, the tax imposed under 26 USCS § 5821 for "making" a firearm. [United States v Thompson/Center Arms Co. (1992, US) 119 L Ed 2d 308, 112 S Ct 2102.]

§ 28. Federal Tort Claims Act

Secret Service agents were held to be entitled to qualified immunity in a lawsuit, brought under the Federal Tort Claims Act (28 USCS §§ 2671 et seq.), involving an alleged unlawful arrest, where the agents had reasonable grounds to believe that the arrestee had threatened the President. [Hunter v Bryant (1991, US) 116 L Ed 2d 589, 112 S Ct 534.]

It was held that 28 USCS § 2674—which precludes liability of the United States, under the Federal Tort Claims Act (28 USCS §§ 2671 et seq.), for punitive damages—did not bar the recovery of damages under the Act for future medical expenses and loss of enjoyment of life, because only damages legally considered punitive under traditional common-law principles are barred under the Act. [Molzof v United States (1992, US) 116 L Ed 2d 731, 112 S Ct 711.]

§ 29. Foreign Sovereign Immunities Act

It was held that a Federal District Court, under the commercial exception in the Foreign Sovereign Immunities Act of 1976 (28 USCS §§ 1602 et seq.), was authorized to assert jurisdiction over a breach-of-contract claim against the Republic of Argentina and its central bank concerning Argentina's alleged default on certain public bonds. [Republic of Argentina v Weltover, Inc. (1992, US) 119 L Ed 2d 394, 112 S Ct 2160.]

§ 30. Grand jury evidence

The Supreme Court held that a United States Court of Appeals had exceeded its authority by imposing a rule under which a prosecutor must present to a grand jury substantial exculpatory evidence that is in the prosecutor's possession. [United States v Williams (1992, US) 118 L Ed 2d 352, 112 S Ct 1735.]

For a case involving the admissibility of grand jury testimony under hearsay provisions of the Federal Rules of Evidence, see § 32, infra.

§ 31. Habeas corpus

The court held that, with respect to the admission of evidence to prove "battered child syndrome" at the California murder trial of an accused for allegedly killing his infant daughter, (1) a Federal Court of Appeals which set aside the accused's conviction exceeded the limited scope of federal habeas corpus review of state convictions, where the Court of Appeals relied in part upon a conclusion that the evidence was incorrectly admitted pursuant to California law; and (2) neither the introduction of the evidence nor the jury instruction as to the use of the evidence violated the due process clause of the Federal Constitution's Fourteenth Amendment. [Estelle v McGuire (1991, US) 116 L Ed 2d 385, 112 S Ct 475.]

The Supreme Court denied a request for a writ of mandamus to compel a Federal Court of Appeals to issue a decision, on a second habeas corpus petition from a state of Washington prisoner who had been sentenced to death, where the state had failed to object to an order delaying the decision. [Re Blodgett (1992, US) 116 L Ed 2d 669, 112 S Ct 674.]

It was held that, where a federal habeas corpus petitioner challenges a state court conviction on the ground that material facts were not adequately developed in the state proceedings, the petitioner, in order to be entitled to an evidentiary hearing, generally must show (1) cause for the petitioner's failure to develop the facts, and actual prejudice resulting from such failure; or (2) that a fundamental miscarriage of justice would result from failure to hold a federal evidentiary hearing. [Keeney v Tamayo-Reyes (1992, US) 118 L Ed 2d 318, 112 S Ct 1715.]

The court held that evidence against an accused was (1) sufficient to support the accused's state-court grand larceny conviction, and (2) thus required the denial of the accused's petition for federal habeas corpus relief based on a claim of insufficiency of the evidence. [Wright v West (1992, US) 120 L Ed 2d 225, 112 S Ct 2482.]

It was also held that an accused who had been convicted and sentenced to death in a Louisiana trial had not satisfied the "actual innocence" standard—which would have allowed review of the accused's successive and abusive claims challenging the death sentence despite the accused's failure to satisfy the normal cause-and-prejudice requirement for such a review—and was thus not entitled to federal habeas corpus consideration of the claims challenging the sentence. [Sawyer v Whitley (1992, US) 120 L Ed 2d 269, 112 S Ct 2514.]

The rule of prior United States Supreme Court decisions—holding certain aggravating-circumstances provisions of state capital sentencing statutes to be unconstitutionally vague—was held to be retroactively available to support federal habeas corpus relief for an accused whose death sentence had become final before such decisions were rendered. [Stringer v Black (1992, US) 117 L Ed 2d 367, 112 S Ct 1130.]

§ 32. Hearsay rules

The Supreme Court held that the admission of testimony against an accused under Illinois hearsay exceptions for spontaneous declarations and medical-treatment statements did not violate the confrontation clause of the Federal Constitution's Sixth Amendment. [White v Illinois (1992, US) 116 L Ed 2d 848, 112 S Ct 736.]

The court held that Rule 804(b)(1) of the Federal Rules of Evidence—which provides that the hearsay rule does not exclude former testimony by an unavailable declarant if the party against whom such testimony is offered had an opportunity and "similar motive" to develop such testimony—did not allow the admission of grand jury testimony of a witness invoking the privilege against self-incrimination under the Federal Constitution's Fifth Amendment, absent a showing of similar motive. [United States v Salerno (1992, US) 120 L Ed 2d 255, 112 S Ct 2503.]

§ 33. Immunity from civil rights action

It was held that a state judge was immune from a 42 USCS § 1983 suit for money damages for the alleged use of excessive force by police officers in bringing a public defender into the judge's courtroom for purposes of a pending case pursuant to the judge's alleged order. [Mireles v Waco (1991, US) 116 L Ed 2d 9, 112 S Ct 286.]

The Supreme Court held that state officials, rather than being immune from personal liability for damages under 42 USCS § 1983 based upon actions taken in their official capacities, are subject to such liability, where the § 1983 actions are brought against the officials in their individual capacities. [Hafer v Melo (1991, US) 116 L Ed 2d 301, 112 S Ct 358.]

The court also held that private defendants who are charged with 42 USCS § 1983 liability for invoking state replevin, garnishment, and attachment statutes later declared unconstitutional are not entitled to qualified immunity from a § 1983 suit that is available to public officials. [Wyatt v Cole (1992, US) 118 L Ed 2d 504, 112 S Ct 1827.]

§ 34. Incompetence to stand trial

It was held that a California statute, which required that a criminal defendant who alleged that he or she was incompetent to stand trial prove such incompetence by a preponderance of the evidence, did not violate the due process clause of the Federal Constitution's Fourteenth Amendment. [Medina v California (1992, US) 120 L Ed 2d 353, 112 S Ct 2572.]

§ 35. In forma pauperis proceedings

Leave to proceed in forma pauperis was denied under Supreme Court Rule 39.8 to individuals whose frequent in forma pauperis petitions to the Supreme Court had been rejected without recorded dissent. [Zatko v California (1991, US) 116 L Ed 2d 293, 112 S Ct 355.]

The Supreme Court held that a Federal District Court's dismissal of an in forma pauperis action as factually frivolous under 28 USCS § 1915(d) is (1) appropriate when the alleged facts rise to the level of the irrational or the wholly incredible, and (2) reviewable on appeal under an abuse-of-discretion standard. [Denton v Hernandez (1992, US) 118 L Ed 2d 340, 112 S Ct 1728.]

§ 36. Insanity acquittees

It was held that a Louisiana statute under which an insanity acquittee who had been confined to a mental institution would not be released until the acquittee was able to demonstrate that the acquittee was not dangerous—regardless of whether the acquittee then suffered from any mental illness—violated the due process clause of the Federal Constitution's Fourteenth Amendment. [Foucha v Louisiana (1992, US) 118 L Ed 2d 437, 112 S Ct 1780.]

§ 37. Intrastate coal purchases

The court held that an Oklahoma statute requiring coal-fired electric utilities in Oklahoma to burn a mixture containing at least 10 percent Oklahoma-mined coal violated the Federal Constitution's commerce clause (Art I, § 8, cl 3). [Wyoming v Oklahoma (1992, US) 117 L Ed 2d 1, 112 S Ct 789.]

§ 38. Jury selection

In two cases decided during the Supreme Court's 1991-92 Term which involved the use of peremptory challenges in jury selection, the court held in one case [Trevino v Texas (1992, US) 118 L Ed 2d 193, 112 S Ct 1547] that under the circumstances of the particular case, an accused's objection, under the equal protection clause of the Federal Constitution's Fourteenth Amendment, to a state's race-based use of peremptory challenges—which objection occurred prior to the Supreme Court's decision in Batson v Kentucky (1986) 476 US 79, 90 L Ed 2d 69, 106 S Ct 1712, requiring the prosecution to present race-neutral justification for its peremptory challenges—had been preserved for review by the Supreme Court, and in the other case [Georgia v McCollum (1992, US) 120 L Ed 2d 33, 112 S Ct 2348] that the equal protection clause prohibited Georgia criminal defendants from engaging in purposeful racial discrimination in their exercise of peremptory challenges.

§ 39. Labor relations

It was held that (1) a union member who sued his local union for money damages under Title I of the Labor Management Reporting and Disclosure Act (29 USCS §§ 401 et seq.) was entitled to a jury trial; and (2) under § 301(a) of the Labor Management Relations Act of 1947 (29 USCS § 185(a)), a Federal District Court had jurisdiction over the breach-of-contract suit brought by the member against the local for claimed violations of the constitution of an international union and the bylaws of the local, where the member alleged that the constitution and bylaws constituted contracts between the international and the local. [Wooddell v International Brotherhood of Electrical Workers, Local 71 (1991, US) 116 L Ed 2d 419, 112 S Ct 494.]

The Supreme Court held that a store owner, who was a joint owner of a shopping plaza parking lot, had not committed an unfair labor practice under § 8(a)(1) of the National Labor Relations Act (29 USCS § 158(a)(1)) by barring nonemployee union organizers from the parking lot. [Lechmere, Inc. v NLRB (1992, US) 117 L Ed 2d 79, 112 S Ct 841.]

For cases involving maritime workers as employees, see § 4, supra; for a case involving pensions and retirement funds, see § 41, infra; for a case involving veterans' reemployment rights, see § 59, infra; for a case involving workers' compensation, see § 61, infra; and for cases involving workplace safety and health, see § 62, infra.

§ 40. Notice of appeal

It was held that an informal brief filed with a Federal Court of Appeals within the time allowed by Rule 4 of the Federal Rules of Appellate Procedure (FRAP) for filing a notice of appeal is, if the brief conveys the information required by FRAP Rule 3, effective as a notice of appeal under Rule 3, which requires that such a notice be filed with a Federal District Court. [Smith v Barry (1992, US) 116 L Ed 2d 678, 112 S Ct 678.]

§ 41. Pensions and retirement funds

The term "employee," as it appears in § 3(6) of the Employee Retirement Income Security Act (29 USCS § 1002(6))—which defines the term as any individual employed by an employer—was held to incorporate traditional agency-law criteria for identifying master-servant relationships. [Nationwide Mut. Ins. Co. v Darden (1992, US) 117 L Ed 2d 581, 112 S Ct 1344.]

§ 42. Permit fees for use of public property

A county ordinance empowering the county administrator to adjust permit fees for use of public property, based on the amount of hostility likely to be created by the content of speech, was held to violate the Federal Constitution's First Amendment. [Forsyth County v Nationalist Movement (1992, US) 120 L Ed 2d 101, 112 S Ct 2395.]

§ 43. Port construction

The court held that the Secretary of the Army had discretion, under § 10 of the Rivers and Harbors

Appropriation Act (33 USCS § 403), to condition the approval of an Alaskan city's port construction on Alaska's disclaimer of a federal-state boundary change. [United States v Alaska (1992, US) 118 L Ed 2d 222, 112 S Ct 1606.]

§ 44. Prisons and prisoners

The Supreme Court held that a clear showing of a grievous wrong evoked by new and unforeseen conditions is not required, under Federal Civil Procedure Rule 60(b), for a Federal District Court to modify a consent decree stemming from institutional reform litigation. [Rufo v Inmates of Suffolk County Jail (1992, US) 116 L Ed 2d 867, 112 S Ct 748.]

It was held that the use of excessive force by prison officers against a prisoner may constitute cruel and unusual punishment in violation of the Federal Constitution's Eighth Amendment, even though the prisoner does not suffer serious injury. [Hudson v McMillian (1992, US) 117 L Ed 2d 156, 112 S Ct 995.]

A federal prisoner, who allegedly had been subjected to cruel and unusual punishment in violation of the Federal Constitution's Eighth Amendment, was held not to be required to exhaust the Federal Bureau of Prisons' internal grievance procedure before initiating a Bivens action solely for money damages. [McCarthy v Madigan (1992, US) 117 L Ed 2d 291, 112 S Ct 1081.]

For cases involving habeas corpus proceedings by prisoners, see § 31, supra.

§ 45. Racketeer Influenced and Corrupt Organizations Act

It was held that the Securities Investor Protection Corporation was unable to maintain a civil suit, under a Racketeer Influenced and Corrupt Organizations Act provision (18 USCS § 1964(c)), against a participant in an alleged stock manipulation conspiracy that allegedly disabled broker-dealers from meeting obligations to customers, where the conspiracy did not proximately cause the claimed injury. [Holmes v Securities Investor Protection Corp. (1992, US) 117 L Ed 2d 532, 112 S Ct 1311.]

§ 46. Railroads

The Supreme Court held that the Federal Employers' Liability Act (45 USCS §§ 51-60) created a cause of action, enforceable in a state court, against a state-owned railroad. [Hilton v South Carolina Public Rys. Com. (1991, US) 116 L Ed 2d 560, 112 S Ct 560.]

The court also held that the Interstate Commerce Commission did not exceed its authority, under 45 USCS § 562(d)(1), in requiring one railroad to convey a particular segment of track to the National Railroad Passenger Corporation (Amtrak), for the purpose of reconveying the segment to a second railroad, in connection with an agreement with the second railroad, whereby the second railroad would maintain the segment and would grant Amtrak and the first railroad trackage rights. [National R. Passenger Corp. v Boston & Maine Corp. (1992, US) 118 L Ed 2d 52, 112 S Ct 1394.]

§ 47. Reconsideration of court order

It was held that, under 18 USCS § 3731 and under Rule 4(b) of the Federal Rules of Appellate Procedure, the Federal Government's 30-day appeal period with respect to a Federal District Court order denying the government's motion to reconsider a

prior order suppressing evidence in a pending criminal trial had begun to run on the date of the order
denying reconsideration. [United States v Ibarra
(1991, US) 116 L Ed 2d 1, 112 S Ct 4.]

§ 48. Religion in public schools

The court held that the inclusion of an invocation
and a benediction by a member of the clergy as part
of an official public school graduation ceremony is
forbidden by the Federal Constitution's First
Amendment prohibition of the establishment of
religion. [Lee v Weisman (1992, US) 120 L Ed 2d
467, 112 S Ct 2649.]

§ 49. School desegregation

The Supreme Court held that, with respect to a
particular Georgia school district which had once
been segregated by law and was operating under a
desegregation decree, a Federal District Court did
not, as a matter of law, lack discretion to permit the
school district to regain control over student assignment, transportation, physical facilities, and extracurricular activities, while retaining court supervision over the areas of faculty and administrative
assignments and the quality of education, where full
compliance had not been demonstrated. [Freeman v
Pitts (1992, US) 118 L Ed 2d 108, 112 S Ct 1430.]

The court also held that (1) a state's adoption and
implementation of race-neutral admissions policies
were insufficient by themselves to demonstrate that
the state had complied with its duty, under the
equal protection clause of the Federal Constitution's
Fourteenth Amendment and Title VI of the Civil
Rights Act of 1964 (42 USCS § 2000d), to dismantle
the state's prior dual, racially segregated public

university system; and (2) in particular, several surviving aspects of Mississippi's prior dual, public university system remained suspect. [United States v Fordice (1992, US) 120 L Ed 2d 575, 112 S Ct 2727.]

§ 50. Sentencing—generally

It was held that under 18 USCS § 3742, a reviewing court is authorized, in appropriate circumstances, to affirm a sentence imposed by a Federal District Court, where the District Court's departure, under 18 USCS § 3553(b), from the sentencing range prescribed by the Federal Sentencing Guidelines was based on both valid and invalid factors. [Williams v United States (1992, US) 117 L Ed 2d 341, 112 S Ct 1112.]

The Supreme Court held that with respect to the sentencing of a juvenile in federal court, a Juvenile Delinquency Act provision (18 USCS § 5037(c)(1) (B))—which requires that the length of official detention in certain circumstances be limited to the maximum term of imprisonment if the juvenile had been tried and convicted as an adult—refers to the maximum sentence that could be imposed if the juvenile were being sentenced after application of the Federal Sentencing Guidelines (18 USCS Appx Ch 1-7). [United States v R. L. C. (1992, US) 117 L Ed 2d 559, 112 S Ct 1329.]

It was held that under 18 USCS § 3585(b), which gives a defendant convicted of a federal crime the right to receive credit for certain time spent in official detention before the defendant's sentence begins, the appropriate credit is to be computed by the United States Attorney General after a defendant has begun to serve his or her sentence, rather than by a Federal District Court at the time of sentencing. [United States v Wilson (1992, US) 117 L Ed 2d 593, 112 S Ct 1351.]

In addition, the Supreme Court held that (1) under 18 USCS § 3553(e) and § 5K1.1 of the Federal Sentencing Guidelines—which provisions authorize a Federal District Court, upon a motion by the government, to impose a sentence on a federal defendant below a statutory or Guidelines minimum to reflect the defendant's substantial assistance to the government—the government's refusal to file such a motion is subject to judicial review for constitutional violations, but (2) the defendant in the case at hand had raised no claim to such review. [Wade v United States (1992, US) 118 L Ed 2d 524, 112 S Ct 1840.]

For cases involving the use of habeas corpus proceedings to review sentencing, see § 31, supra.

§ 51. —Death penalty

It was held that the introduction, at a capital sentencing proceeding, of evidence as to the accused's membership in a white racist prison gang violated the Federal Constitution's First Amendment, where the evidence had no relevance to the issues being decided in the proceeding. [Dawson v Delaware (1992, US) 117 L Ed 2d 309, 112 S Ct 1093.]

The state of California's application to vacate a stay of an accused's execution by cyanide gas was granted by the Supreme Court, where the accused had not challenged the method of execution in prior petitions filed in federal courts. [Gomez v United States Dist. Court (1992, US) 118 L Ed 2d 293, 112 S Ct 1652.]

The Supreme Court held that a Nevada court's judgment upholding a defendant's homicide conviction and death sentence would be reversed and remanded, where the defendant claimed that the forced administration of an antipsychotic drug to the defendant during trial violated the defendant's rights under the Federal Constitution's Sixth and Fourteenth Amendments. [Riggins v Nevada (1992, US) 118 L Ed 2d 479, 112 S Ct 1810.]

An application for a stay of execution was denied by the Supreme Court, where a Federal District Court had found that alleged exculpatory evidence produced by the defense in a death penalty case did not amount to a colorable claim of innocence. [Coleman v Thompson (1992, US) 119 L Ed 2d 1, 112 S Ct 1845.]

The Supreme Court held that the death sentence imposed upon a convicted murderer by a Florida trial court (1) was not rendered invalid under the Federal Constitution's Eighth Amendment by (a) the trial judge's weighing of the allegedly vague "especially heinous, atrocious, or cruel" aggravating factor, or (b) instructions to the advisory jury on a "cold, calculated and premeditated" aggravating factor, which was found by a Florida appellate court to be unsupported by the evidence; but (2) was rendered invalid by the trial judge's explicit weighing of the "coldness" factor, where the appellate court did not perform harmless-error analysis. [Sochor v Florida (1992, US) 119 L Ed 2d 326, 112 S Ct 2114.]

It was held that the refusal of an Illinois trial court in a capital murder case to inquire on voir dire, as requested by the defense, whether potential jurors would automatically impose the death penalty if the defendant was convicted, violated the due process clause of the Federal Constitution's Fourteenth Amendment. [Morgan v Illinois (1992, US) 119 L Ed 2d 492, 112 S Ct 2222.]

It was also held that the imposition of a death sentence by a Florida trial court violated the Federal Constitution's Eighth Amendment, where (1) the jury that rendered at the sentencing hearing an advisory verdict recommending the death sentence had been instructed on an unconstitutionally vague aggravating circumstance, and (2) the sentencing court was required under state law to give great weight to the jury's recommendation. [Espinosa v Florida (1992, US) 120 L Ed 2d 854, 112 S Ct 2926.]

As to review of death sentences in habeas corpus proceedings, see § 31, supra.

§ 52. Sex discrimination

The court held, in connection with a public high school student's action against a county school district under Title IX of the Education Amendments of 1972 (20 USCS §§ 1681-1688), that a damages remedy was available in an action to enforce Title IX, where the student alleged that she had been subjected to gender-based discrimination, including sexual intercourse with a male teacher. [Franklin v Gwinnett County Public Schools (1992, US) 117 L Ed 2d 208, 112 S Ct 1028.]

§ 53. Speedy trial

It was held that the Federal Government's negligent 8½-year delay between an accused's indictment and arrest violated the accused's Sixth Amendment right to a speedy trial, despite the lack of a showing of actual prejudice. [Doggett v United States (1992, US) 120 L Ed 2d 520, 112 S Ct 2686.]

§ 54. State taxation—generally

The court held, with respect to a mail-order house that had no physical nexus with North Dakota and whose only connection with North Dakota customers was by common carrier or mail, that North Dakota's imposition on the mail-order house of the duty to collect use taxes (1) did not violate the due process clause of the Federal Constitution's Fourteenth Amendment, but (2) did violate the Federal Constitution's commerce clause (Art I, § 8, cl 3). [Quill Corp. v North Dakota (1992, US) 119 L Ed 2d 91, 112 S Ct 1904.]

It was held that the equal protection clause of the Federal Constitution's Fourteenth Amendment was not violated by the California Constitution's real property tax system, which system generally assesses property on its value at the time of acquisition, rather than on the property's current value. [Nordlinger v Hahn (1992, US) 120 L Ed 2d 1, 112 S Ct 2326.]

§ 55. —Income

The Supreme Court held that Kansas' income tax, in taxing benefits received from the United States by military retirees, but not taxing benefits received by state and local government retirees, was inconsistent with federal retention of employee tax immunity in 4 USCS § 111, which retention was coextensive with the prohibition against discriminatory taxes embodied in the federal constitutional doctrine of intergovernmental tax immunity. [Barker v Kansas (1992, US) 118 L Ed 2d 243, 112 S Ct 1619.]

It was held that (1) the "unitary business principle" governs states' federal constitutional power to tax nondomiciliary corporations' income, and (2) New Jersey violated the due process clause of the

Federal Constitution's Fourteenth Amendment and the Constitution's commerce clause (Art I, § 8, cl 3), with respect to a multijurisdictional nondomiciliary corporation doing business in the state, by taxing capital gains that were earned by the corporation from the sale of its interest in an unrelated business enterprise. [Allied-Signal, Inc. v Director, Div. of Taxation (1992, US) 119 L Ed 2d 533, 112 S Ct 2251.]

The court held that an Iowa statute imposing a business tax on the income of corporations doing business in the state facially discriminated against foreign commerce, and therefore violated the Federal Constitution's foreign commerce clause (Art I, § 8, cl 3), where the statute (1) allowed a deduction for dividends which a corporation received from its domestic subsidiaries, but not for those received from its foreign subsidiaries, and (2) did not allow a parent corporation a credit for taxes paid to a foreign country on the earnings underlying dividends received from a foreign subsidiary. [Kraft General Foods, Inc. v Iowa Dept. of Revenue & Finance (1992, US) 120 L Ed 2d 59, 112 S Ct 2365.]

Moreover, the court held that a state was not prohibited under 15 USCS § 381(a)—which precludes a state from taxing income derived from interstate commerce within the state where the only business activities within the state consist of "solicitation of orders" for tangible goods—from imposing a net income tax on a gum manufacturer, where the manufacturer's in-state activities included the replacement, supply, and storage of gum. [Wisconsin Dept. of Revenue v William Wrigley, Jr., Co. (1992, US) 120 L Ed 2d 174, 112 S Ct 2447.]

§ 56. Taking of property

It was held that a rent control ordinance regulating mobile homes, when viewed in the context of a California statute which limited the bases on which owners of mobile home parks could terminate the tenancy of a mobile home owner, did not constitute a physical "taking" under the Federal Constitution's Fifth Amendment. [Yee v Escondido (1992, US) 118 L Ed 2d 153, 112 S Ct 1522.]

The Supreme Court held that (1) a state cannot justify its regulations which deprive real property owners of all economically beneficial use of their land, consistent with the takings clause of the Federal Constitution's Fifth Amendment, on the ground that harmful or noxious uses of property can be proscribed by government regulation without compensation, and (2) thus, a South Carolina court had applied the wrong standard in determining whether a state beachfront management statute, by barring construction, effected a "taking" of property under the Fifth Amendment. [Lucas v South Carolina Coastal Council (1992, US) 120 L Ed 2d 798, 112 S Ct 2886.]

§ 57. Trademark infringement

Inherently distinctive trade dress was held to be protectable from infringement, under federal trademark law (15 USCS § 1125(a)), without proof of secondary meaning. [Two Pesos, Inc. v Taco Cabana, Inc. (1992, US) 120 L Ed 2d 615, 112 S Ct 2753.]

§ 58. Venue

The Supreme Court held that the equal protection clause of the Federal Constitution's Fourteenth Amendment was not violated by Montana venue rules which (1) required a suit against a Montana corporation to be brought in only the county where the corporation had its principal place of business, but (2) permitted a suit against a foreign corporation to be brought in any county. [Burlington N. R. Co. v Ford (1992, US) 119 L Ed 2d 432, 112 S Ct 2184.]

§ 59. Veterans' rights

It was held that a provision of the Veterans' Reemployment Rights Act (38 USCS § 2024(d)) does not implicitly limit the length of military service after which a member of the Armed Forces retains a right to civilian reemployment. [King v St. Vincent's Hosp. (1991, US) 116 L Ed 2d 578, 112 S Ct 570.]

§ 60. Waste disposal

The Supreme Court held that (1) the Environmental Protection Agency (EPA) was authorized by the Clean Water Act (33 USCS §§ 1251 et seq.) to issue a permit authorizing a sewage treatment plant in Arkansas to discharge effluent into a stream, based on a finding that the discharges which reached Oklahoma's waters would not cause a detectable violation of Oklahoma's water quality standards; and (2) a United States Court of Appeals exceeded the legitimate scope of judicial review of an agency determination when it invalidated the EPA's issuance of the permit on the ground that the EPA had misinterpreted Oklahoma's water quality standards. [Arkansas v Oklahoma (1992, US) 117 L Ed 2d 239, 112 S Ct 1046.]

The court held that Congress did not waive the Federal Government's sovereign immunity from liability for civil fines imposed by a state for past violations of either (1) the Clean Water Act (33 USCS §§ 1251 et seq.); or (2) the Resource Conservation and Recovery Act of 1976 (42 USCS §§ 6901 et seq.). [United States Dept. of Energy v Ohio (1992, US) 118 L Ed 2d 255, 112 S Ct 1627.]

It was also held that (1) provisions of the Low-Level Radioactive Waste Policy Amendments Act of 1985 (42 USCS §§ 2021b et seq.) which induced states to provide for the disposal of low-level radioactive waste generated within their borders through monetary incentives (42 USCS § 2021e(d)) and access incentives (42 USCS § 2021e(e)(2)) were valid; and (2) a provision of the Act which required states or regional compacts to "take title" and assume liability for such waste under certain circumstances (42 USCS § 2021e(d)(2)(C)) violated the Federal Constitution's Tenth Amendment, but was severable from remainder of Act. [New York v United States (1992, US) 120 L Ed 2d 120, 112 S Ct 2408.]

In two cases decided during the 1991-1992 Term, the Supreme Court held that particular state regulation concerning the disposal of hazardous waste violated the Federal Constitution's commerce clause (Art I, § 8, cl 3). In one case, the regulation found invalid was a disposal fee imposed by Alabama on hazardous waste generated out of state, but not on waste generated within the state. [Chemical Waste Management, Inc. v Hunt (1992, US) 119 L Ed 2d 121, 112 S Ct 2009.] In the other case, the regulation found invalid was a Michigan statute barring a private landfill owner from accepting solid waste originating outside the county in which the landfill was located. [Ft. Gratiot Sanitary Landfill, Inc. v Michigan Dept. of Natural Resources (1992, US) 119 L Ed 2d 139, 112 S Ct 2019.]

See Gade v National Solid Wastes Management Assn. (1992, US) 120 L Ed 2d 73, 112 S Ct 2374, infra § 62, in which it was held that Illinois statutes which required the licensing of hazardous waste equipment operators and laborers working at hazardous waste cleanup sites, and which imposed certain initial and continuing requirements as to license applicants in both categories, were preempted by the Occupational Safety and Health Act (29 USCS §§ 651 et seq.) to the extent that such statutes established occupational safety and health standards for training those who work with hazardous wastes.

See also Burlington v Dague (1992, US) 120 L Ed 2d 449, 112 S Ct 2638, supra § 11, wherein the court held that, in awarding attorneys' fees under § 7002(e) of the Solid Waste Disposal Act (42 USCS § 6972(e)) or § 505(d) of the Federal Water Pollution Control Act (33 USCS § 1365(d)), a court may not enhance the award above the lodestar amount in order to reflect the fact that the party's attorneys were retained on a contingent fee basis.

§ 61. Workers' compensation

The court held that a Michigan statute requiring employers retroactively to repay workers' compensation benefits that had been withheld in reliance on a Michigan "benefits coordination" statute did not violate (1) the Federal Constitution's contract clause (Art I, § 10), or (2) the due process clause of the Federal Constitution's Fourteenth Amendment. [General Motors Corp. v Romein (1992, US) 117 L Ed 2d 328, 112 S Ct 1105.]

§ 62. Workplace safety and health

The Supreme Court held that 42 USCS § 1983 does not provide a remedy for a city employee who is fatally injured in the course of his employment as a result of the city's customary failure to train or warn its employees about known hazards in the workplace, because such a failure does not violate the due process clause of the Federal Constitution's Fourteenth Amendment. [Collins v Harker Heights (1992, US) 117 L Ed 2d 261, 112 S Ct 1061.]

It was held that Illinois statutes which required the licensing of hazardous waste equipment operators and laborers working at hazardous waste cleanup sites, and which imposed certain initial and continuing requirements as to license applicants in both categories, were pre-empted by the Occupational Safety and Health Act (29 USCS §§ 651 et seq.) to the extent that such statutes established occupational safety and health standards for training those who work with hazardous wastes. [Gade v National Solid Wastes Management Assn. (1992, US) 120 L Ed 2d 73, 112 S Ct 2374.]

SUMMARIES OF DECISIONS

UNITED STATES, Petitioner

v

ALEJANDRO GARCIA IBARRA

502 US —, 116 L Ed 2d 1, 112 S Ct 4

Decided October 15, 1991.

Decision: Federal Government's 30-day appeal period held to have begun to run on date of Federal District Court's order denying motion to reconsider prior order suppressing evidence in pending criminal trial.

SUMMARY

Under 18 USCS § 3731, the Federal Government may appeal a Federal District Court order suppressing evidence which the government proposes to use in a pending criminal case, provided that the appeal (1) is taken within 30 days after the decision has been rendered, and (2) is diligently prosecuted. Also, Rule 4(b) of the Federal Rules of Appellate Procedure provides that when an appeal by the government is authorized by statute, the notice of appeal shall be filed in the District Court within 30 days after the entry of the order appealed from. In a federal narcotics trial in which the Federal Government proposed to use certain evidence obtained as a result of a search, the United States District Court for the District of Wyoming—noting that the government had abandoned a "continuing consent"

1

theory to justify the search—rejected other arguments and granted the accused's motion to suppress
the evidence (725 F Supp 1195). The government
filed with the District Court a motion for reconsideration on the sole basis of a reassertion of the
continuing consent theory, but the District Court
denied the motion (731 F Supp 1037). The government then noticed an appeal 76 days after the initial
suppression order, but less than 30 days after the
denial of the motion for reconsideration. The
United States Court of Appeals for the Tenth Circuit, dismissing the appeal as untimely, expressed
the view that, because the motion had sought reconsideration of a previously disavowed theory, the
motion did not "toll" the 30-day period to appeal
which began to run on the date of the initial order
(920 F2d 702).

The United States Supreme Court granted the
Federal Government's petition for certiorari,
granted the respondent accused's motion to proceed in forma pauperis, vacated the judgment of the
Court of Appeals, and remanded the case to the
Court of Appeals for further proceedings. In a per
curiam opinion expressing the unanimous view of
the court, it was held that under § 3731 and under
Rule 4(b), the 30-day period began to run on the
date of the District Court's order denying the motion for reconsideration, because (1) as a general
rule, a motion for rehearing in a criminal case, like a
motion for rehearing in a civil case, renders an
otherwise final decision of a District Court not final
until the District Court decides the petition for
rehearing, (2) even though petitions to reconsider
based on previously abandoned grounds may not be
apt to fare well, and even though some motions to
reconsider are so totally lacking in merit that the

virtues of the general rule are not realized by delaying the 30-day period, there is no certain way of deciding in advance which motions for reconsideration have the requisite degree of merit, and thus it is better that all such motions be subsumed under the general rule, (3) for purposes of the general rule, the motion in question was a sufficiently "true" motion for reconsideration, where the motion sought to reconsider a question decided in the case in order to effect an alteration of the rights adjudicated, (4) there was no assertion that the government's abandonment and reassertion of the theory was done in bad faith, and (5) only a single motion for reconsideration was filed.

RAYMOND MIRELES, Petitioner

v

HOWARD WACO

502 US —, 116 L Ed 2d 9, 112 S Ct 286

Decided October 21, 1991.

Decision: State judge held immune from 42 USCS
§ 1983 suit for money damages for alleged use
of excessive force by police officers in bringing
public defender into courtroom pursuant to
judge's alleged order.

SUMMARY

A county public defender filed a 42 USCS § 1983
suit for money damages in the United States District
Court for the Central District of California against a
California state judge and two police officers, and
alleged that (1) after the public defender failed to
appear for an initial call of the judge's morning
calendar, the judge ordered the police officers to
seize the public defender forcibly and with excessive
force and bring him into the judge's courtroom; (2)
the officers by means of unreasonable force and
violence removed the public defender from another
courtroom and brought him into the judge's courtroom; and (3) the judge knowingly approved and
ratified each of the officers' acts. The judge, however, moved to dismiss the complaint as to him for
failure to state a claim upon which relief could be
granted. The District Court agreed, dismissed the
claim against the judge, and entered final judgment
as to him, on the ground of "complete judicial
immunity." On appeal, the United States Court of

Appeals for the Ninth Circuit, in reversing, expressed the view that if the judge had requested and authorized the use of excessive force, then the judge would not have been acting in his judicial capacity and would not be immune from suit (934 F2d 214).

The United States Supreme Court granted the judge's petition for certiorari, and reversed the judgment of the Court of Appeals. In a per curiam opinion expressing the view of REHNQUIST, Ch. J., and WHITE, BLACKMUN, O'CONNOR, and SOUTER, JJ., it was held that, even though the allegations of the public defender's complaint were taken as true for purposes of reviewing the judge's motion to dismiss, the judge was immune from a § 1983 suit for money damages, because (1) the judge's alleged actions were taken in his judicial capacity, where (a) under the state's law, a judge's direction to court officers to bring before him a person who is in the courthouse was a function normally performed by a judge, (b) the public defender, who was called into the courtroom for purposes of a pending case, was dealing with the judge in the judge's judicial capacity, (c) although a judge's direction to police officers to carry out a judicial order with excessive force was not a function normally performed by a judge, the relevant inquiry was to look to the particular act's relation to a general function normally performed by a judge, that is, the function of directing police officers to bring before the court counsel in a pending case, and (d) the fact that the judge's order was carried out by police officers did not transform his acts from "judicial" to "executive" in character; and (2) even though the judge acted in excess of his authority if he authorized and ratified the officers' alleged use of excessive force, such an action, taken in the very aid of the judge's jurisdiction over a

5

matter before him, could not be said to have been taken in the absence of all jurisdiction.

STEVENS, J., dissenting, expressed the view that, accepting the allegations of the complaint as true in order to review the motion to dismiss, (1) the judge's alleged order to bring the public defender into his courtroom was an action taken in a judicial capacity; but (2) the judge's alleged order to commit a battery on the public defender was not an action taken in a judicial capacity, as such an order had no relation to a function normally performed by a judge; and (3) the fact that both orders were alleged to have occurred as part of the same communication did not enlarge the judge's immunity.

SCALIA, J., joined by KENNEDY, J., dissenting, expressed the view that (1) he was unsure whether the disposition of the court or the disposition favored by STEVENS, J., was correct; (2) the case ought not to have been decided without briefing and argument; and (3) in any event, the petition for certiorari ought to have been denied, as the factual situation presented by the case was so extraordinary that the case did not warrant the expenditure of the court's time.

———————

VLADIMIR ZATKO

v

CALIFORNIA (No. 91-5052)

———

VLADIMIR ZATKO

v

UNITED STATES DISTRICT COURT FOR THE NORTHERN DISTRICT OF CALIFORNIA (No. 91-5111)

———

VLADIMIR ZATKO

v

UNITED STATES DISTRICT COURT FOR THE NORTHERN DISTRICT OF CALIFORNIA (No. 91-5166)

———

VLADIMIR ZATKO

v

UNITED STATES (No. 91-5167)

———

JAMES L. MARTIN

v

SALLY MRVOS (No. 91-5244)

———

JAMES L. MARTIN

v

EDWARD C. SMITH et al. (No. 91-5246)

———

JAMES L. MARTIN

v

DELAWARE LAW SCHOOL OF WIDENER
UNIVERSITY, INC., et al. (No. 91-5307)

———

JAMES L. MARTIN

v

JOHN D. WALMER et al. (No. 91-5331)

———

JAMES L. MARTIN

v

STEPHEN W. TOWNSEND et al. (No. 91-5332)

———

JAMES L. MARTIN

v

SUPREME COURT OF NEW JERSEY
(No. 91-5401)

———

VLADIMIR ZATKO

v

CALIFORNIA (No. 91-5416)

———

JAMES MARTIN

v

BAR OF THE DISTRICT OF COLUMBIA COURT
OF APPEALS (No. 91-5476)

JAMES MARTIN

v

DANIEL HUYETT (No. 91-5583)

VLADIMIR ZATKO

v

UNITED STATES DISTRICT COURT FOR THE
NORTHERN DISTRICT OF CALIFORNIA
(No. 91-5594)

VLADIMIR ZATKO

v

UNITED STATES DISTRICT COURT FOR THE
NORTHERN DISTRICT OF CALIFORNIA
(No. 91-5692)

VLADIMIR ZATKO

v

CALIFORNIA (No. 91-5730)

VLADIMIR ZATKO

v

CALIFORNIA (No. 91-5732)

502 US —, 116 L Ed 2d 293, 112 S Ct 355

Decided November 4, 1991.

Decision: Leave to proceed in forma pauperis denied, under Supreme Court Rule 39.8, for individuals whose frequent in forma pauperis petitions had been rejected without recorded dissent.

SUMMARY

Motions to proceed in forma pauperis in the United States Supreme Court were made by one person with respect to nine cases and by a second person with respect to eight cases. During a period of 10 years, the first person had filed with the Supreme Court 73 petitions, including 34 within the last 2 of those 10 years, while during the same periods, the second person had filed with the Supreme Court 45 and 15 petitions, respectively. In every filing, the court had permitted the petitioners to proceed in forma pauperis and had denied the petitions without recorded dissent.

In a per curiam opinion expressing the view of REHNQUIST, Ch. J., and WHITE, O'CONNOR, SCALIA, KENNEDY, and SOUTER, JJ., the court invoked Supreme Court Rule 39.8—which authorizes denial of leave to proceed in forma pauperis with respect to frivolous or malicious filings—to deny the petitioners leave to proceed in forma pauperis, because (1) the petitioners had repeatedly and extremely abused the integrity of the court's process through frequent

10

frivolous filings, (2) the court's goal of fairly dispensing justice is compromised when it is forced to devote its limited resources to the processing of repetitious and frivolous filings, and (3) it is vital that the right to file in forma pauperis not be encumbered by those who would abuse the integrity of the court's process by frivolous filings.

STEVENS, J., joined by BLACKMUN, J., dissented, expressing the view that, rather than having applied Rule 39.8 to deny the petitioners leave to proceed in forma pauperis, the court should have denied certiorari, because (1) the symbolic effect of the court's effort to draw distinctions among the multitude of frivolous petitions—conveyance of the message that the court did not have have an overriding concern about equal access to justice for both the rich and poor—was powerful, and (2) by branding the petitioners under Rule 39.8, the court increased the chances that the petitioners' future petitions would not be evaluated with the attention they deserve.

THOMAS, J., did not participate.

———

BARBARA HAFER, Petitioner

v

JAMES C. MELO, Jr., et al.

502 US —, 116 L Ed 2d 301, 112 S Ct 358

Argued October 15, 1991.
Decided November 5, 1991.

Decision: State officials held subject to personal liability for damages under 42 USCS § 1983 based on official acts, where § 1983 actions were brought against officials in their individual capacities.

SUMMARY

Employees of the Pennsylvania Auditor General's Office, based on their dismissals from their jobs by the Auditor General, filed against the Auditor General actions under 42 USCS § 1983, which provides that any "person" acting under color of state law in violating another's federal rights is liable to the injured party. Some of the employees sought monetary damages, while others sought both monetary damages and reinstatement. The United States District Court for the Eastern District of Pennsylvania dismissed all the § 1983 actions. The District Court held that the actions were barred because, under the United States Supreme Court's decision in Will v Michigan Dept. of State Police (1989) 491 US 58, 105 L Ed 2d 45, 109 S Ct 2304—in which it was held that state officials acting in their official capacities are not "persons" subject to liability under § 1983—the Auditor General could not be held liable for employment decisions made in her official

capacity as Auditor General. Reversing the judgment of the District Court, the United States Court
of Appeals for the Third Circuit (1) as to claims for
reinstatement brought against the Auditor General
in her official capacity, rested on the Supreme
Court's statement in Will that state officials, sued
for injunctive relief in their official capacities, are
"persons" subject to liability under § 1983; and (2)
as to monetary claims, held that the employees
could maintain § 1983 individual-capacity suits
against the Auditor General, because (a) the employees sought damages from the Auditor General
in her personal capacity, and (b) she had acted
under color of state law in dismissing the employees.

On certiorari, the United States Supreme Court
affirmed. In an opinion by O'CONNOR, J., expressing
the unanimous view of the eight participating members of the court, it was held that the Auditor
General could be held personally liable to the employees for damages under 42 USCS § 1983, because (1) with respect to the court's holding in Will
that state officials acting in their official capacities
are not "persons" subject to liability under § 1983,
the phrase "acting in their official capacities" is best
understood as a reference to the capacity in which
an official is sued rather than the capacity in which
the official inflicts the alleged injury, (2) state officials, sued in their individual capacities, are "persons" under § 1983, and (3) the Federal Constitution's Eleventh Amendment, which immunizes states
from suits in federal courts, does not bar suits
brought against state officials in their individual
capacities under § 1983.

THOMAS, J., did not participate.

COUNSEL

Jerome R. Richter argued the cause for petitioner. William Goldstein argued the cause for respondents.

———————

BOARD OF GOVERNORS OF THE FEDERAL
RESERVE SYSTEM OF THE UNITED STATES,
Petitioner

v

MCORP FINANCIAL, INC., et al. (No. 90-913)

———

MCORP, et al., Petitioners

v

BOARD OF GOVERNORS OF THE FEDERAL
RESERVE SYSTEM OF THE UNITED STATES
(No. 90-914)

502 US —, 116 L Ed 2d 358, 112 S Ct 459

Argued October 7, 1991.
Decided December 3, 1991.

Decision: Federal District Court held not to have
authority, in bankruptcy case, to enjoin Federal
Reserve Board proceedings against debtor bank
holding company for alleged banking law violations.

SUMMARY

The Board of Governors of the Federal Reserve
System, alleging that a bank holding company had
violated the Board's "source of strength" regulation
(12 CFR § 225.4(a)(1)) by engaging in unsafe and
unsound banking practices that jeopardized the
financial condition of the company's subsidiary
banks, commenced an administrative proceeding
against the company and issued temporary cease
and desist orders (1) barring the company from

15

declaring or paying dividends or from dissipating any of its nonbank assets without prior Board approval, and (2) requiring the company to use all of its assets to provide capital support to subsidiary banks. After the company's request for financial assistance was denied by the Federal Deposit Insurance Corporation, and after the company's creditors filed an involuntary bankruptcy petition, the company filed voluntary petitions under Chapter 11 of the Bankruptcy Code (11 USCS §§ 1101-1174) in the United States Bankruptcy Court for the Southern District of Texas. The Board subsequently commenced a second administrative proceeding alleging that the company had violated § 23A of the Federal Reserve Act (12 USCS § 371c) by causing two of its subsidiaries to extend unsecured credit to an affiliate. The company filed a complaint in the Bankruptcy Court seeking (1) a declaration that both administrative proceedings had been automatically stayed pursuant to 11 USCS § 362(a), or (2) an injunction against further prosecution of those proceedings without the prior approval of the Bankruptcy Court. The adversary proceeding was transferred to the United States District Court for the Southern District of Texas, which entered a preliminary injunction halting the Board's proceedings and restraining the Board from exercising its authority over bank holding companies to effect a reorganization of the company and its subsidiaries except through participation in the bankruptcy proceedings (101 BR 483). The United States Court of Appeals for the Fifth Circuit, having determined that 12 USCS § 1818(i) deprives Federal District Courts of jurisdiction to enjoin the Board's administrative proceedings if the Board's actions do not exceed its statutory authority, (1) vacated the District Court's injunction with respect to the proceeding under § 23A, but (2) remanded the case to the District Court with instructions to enjoin the Board from further prosecution of the charges under § 225.4(a) (1), as the Court of Appeals found that the "source of strength" regulation exceeded the Board's statutory authority (900 F2d 852).

On certiorari, the United States Supreme Court (1) affirmed the judgment of the Court of Appeals with respect to the Board's proceeding under § 23A, and (2) reversed the judgment of the Court of Appeals with respect to the Board's proceeding under § 225.4(a)(1). In an opinion by STEVENS, J., expressing the unanimous view of the eight participating members of the court, it was held that the District Court lacked jurisdiction to enjoin either regulatory proceeding, as (1) 12 USCS § 1818(i)(1) precludes judicial review of Board actions except through challenges to a temporary Board order, petitions for review of a final Board order, or enforcement actions initiated by the Board; (2) the Board's planned actions against the company, although constituting a continuation of administrative proceedings and as such apparently subject to the automatic stay under 11 USCS § 362(a)(1) upon filing of the company's bankruptcy petition, fell within an exemption (11 USCS § 362(b)(4)) for proceedings to enforce a governmental unit's police or regulatory power, and the application of that exemption did not depend on the validity of the administrative or enforcement action in question; (3) the company was not protected by 11 USCS § 362(a)(3) or § 362(a)(6), because the possibility that the Board's proceedings might conclude with orders affecting the Bankruptcy Court's control of company assets was not sufficient to justify the

17

operation of the stay against proceedings exempted by § 362(b)(4); (4) the preclusive language of § 1818(i)(1) is not qualified or superseded by 28 USCS § 1334(b), which authorizes District Courts to exercise concurrent jurisdiction with other courts over certain bankruptcy-related civil proceedings, because (a) the Board is not a court, and (b) prosecution of Board proceedings, prior to entry of a final order and prior to the commencement of any enforcement action, is unlikely to impair the Bankruptcy Court's exclusive jurisdiction over estate property protected by 28 USCS § 1334(d); and (5) a precedent asserted as allowing judicial review of any agency actions that allegedly exceed the agency's statutory authority is inapposite with regard to proceedings under § 225.4(a)(1), because that precedent involved a statute which, unlike 12 USCS § 1818, did not expressly provide for judicial review.

THOMAS, J., did not participate.

COUNSEL

Jeffrey P. Minear argued the cause for the Federal Reserve Board in Nos. 90-913 and 90-914.

Alan B. Miller argued the cause for MCorp, et al. in Nos. 90-913 and 90-914.

DIANE GRIFFIN, Petitioner

v

UNITED STATES

502 US —, 116 L Ed 2d 371, 112 S Ct 466

Argued October 7, 1991.
Decided December 3, 1991.

Decision: Due process held not to require that general guilty verdict on federal multiple-object conspiracy charge be set aside if evidence is inadequate to support conviction as to one object.

SUMMARY

A federal grand jury investigating an alleged narcotics operation returned a multicount indictment, one count of which charged a woman not otherwise named in the indictment, as well as two other individuals, with conspiring to defraud an agency of the Federal Government in violation of 18 USCS § 371. The conspiracy was alleged to have had two objects: (1) impairing the efforts of the Internal Revenue Service (IRS) to collect taxes, and (2) impairing the efforts of the Drug Enforcement Administration (DEA) to ascertain forfeitable assets. During trial before a Federal District Court, the prosecution presented evidence which implicated the woman in the object of defrauding the IRS, but failed to present evidence connecting the woman to the object of defrauding the DEA. The District Court denied the woman's requests to (1) instruct the jury that she could be convicted only if the jury found that she was aware of the IRS object of the

19

conspiracy, and (2) submit special interrogatories requiring the jury to identify the object of which the jury believed that the woman had had knowledge. The jury returned a general verdict of guilty against the woman on the conspiracy to defraud count. In affirming the woman's conviction, the United States Court of Appeals for the Seventh Circuit rejected her argument that the general verdict could not stand because it left in doubt whether the jury had convicted her of conspiring to defraud the IRS, for which there was sufficient proof, or of conspiring to defraud the DEA, for which, as the prosecution conceded, there was not sufficient proof (913 F2d 337).

On certiorari, the United States Supreme Court affirmed. In an opinion by SCALIA, J., joined by REHNQUIST, Ch. J., and WHITE, STEVENS, O'CONNOR, KENNEDY, and SOUTER, JJ., it was held that (1) in a federal prosecution, the due process clause of the Federal Constitution's Fifth Amendment does not require that a general guilty verdict on a multiple-object conspiracy charge be set aside if the evidence is inadequate to support conviction as to one of the objects, because (a) the historical practice fails to support such a requirement, given that it was settled law in England before the Declaration of Independence, and in the United States long afterwards, that a general jury verdict was valid so long as it was legally supportable on one of the submitted grounds, even though that practice gave no assurance that a valid ground, rather than an invalid one, was actually the basis for the jury's action, and (b) despite some decisions departing from that rule, there is no precedent in which the Supreme Court has set aside a general verdict because one of the possible bases of conviction was neither unconstitutional nor even illegal, but merely unsupported by sufficient evidence; and (2) although it would generally be preferable, where the evidence is insufficient to support an alternative legal theory of liability, for the trial court to give an instruction removing that theory from the jury's consideration, the refusal to do so does not provide an independent basis for reversing an otherwise valid conviction.

BLACKMUN, J., concurred in the judgment, (1) expressing the view that the woman had not made out a violation of the due process clause, inasmuch as she had not presented any sustained constitutional argument whatsoever; (2) agreeing with the Supreme Court that it would generally be preferable for the trial court to remove unsupported theories from the jury's consideration; and (3) commending to the prosecution the alternative safeguards of (a) charging the two objectives in separate counts, or (b) agreeing to the request for special interrogatories.

THOMAS, J., did not participate.

COUNSEL

Michael G. Logan argued the cause for petitioner. William C. Bryson argued the cause for respondent.

WAYNE ESTELLE, Warden, Petitioner

v

MARK OWEN McGUIRE

502 US —, 116 L Ed 2d 385, 112 S Ct 475

Argued October 9, 1991.

Decided December 4, 1991.

Decision: Introduction of evidence to prove "battered child syndrome" at California murder trial for allegedly killing infant, and jury instruction as to evidence's use, held not to violate due process.

SUMMARY

At the California trial of an accused who was charged with second-degree murder for allegedly killing his infant daughter, the trial court allowed the introduction of evidence of prior rib and rectal injuries of the daughter to prove "battered child syndrome," which syndrome is said to indicate that a child found with serious, repeated injuries has not suffered those injuries by accidental means. The trial court's jury instructions as to the evidence's use included an instruction that the evidence was received and might be considered only for the limited purpose of determining if the evidence tended to show matters including a clear connection between the other two "offenses" and the one of which the accused was charged, so that it might logically be concluded that if the accused committed other offenses, the accused also committed the crime charged. The accused was found guilty. On direct review, the California Court of Appeal, in affirming the accused's conviction, concluded that proof of the daughter's prior injuries to establish battered child syndrome was proper under California law. The California Supreme Court denied review. The accused then filed a habeas corpus petition in the United States District Court for the Northern District of California, which denied relief. On appeal, the United States Court of Appeals for the Ninth Circuit, in reversing and in setting aside the accused's conviction, expressed the view that (1) the prior injury evidence had been erroneously admitted to establish battered child syndrome, because (a) no evidence linked the accused to the prior injuries, and (b) no claim had been made at trial that the daughter had died accidentally; (2) the trial court's instruction on the evidence's use allowed a finding of guilt based simply on a judgment that the accused had committed the prior bad acts; and (3) the evidence's admission, in conjunction with the instruction, rendered the accused's trial arbitrary and fundamentally unfair, in violation of the due process clause of the Federal Constitution's Fourteenth Amendment (902 F2d 749).

On certiorari, the United States Supreme Court reversed. In an opinion by REHNQUIST, Ch. J., joined by WHITE, BLACKMUN, SCALIA, KENNEDY, and SOUTER, JJ., and joined in part (as to holdings 1 and 2 below) by STEVENS and O'CONNOR, JJ., it was held that (1) the Court of Appeals exceeded the limited scope of federal habeas corpus review of state convictions under 28 USCS § 2241, where the Court of Appeals relied in part on a conclusion that the evidence of the daughter's prior rib and rectal injuries had been incorrectly admitted pursuant to California law; (2) the introduction of that evidence did not so infuse the trial with unfairness as to deny

23

due process of law, under the Fourteenth Amendment, where (a) under California law as to second-degree murder, the prosecution was required to prove that the daughter's death had been caused by the accused's intentional act, (b) proof of the daughter's battered child status helped to do that, for the evidence, although not linked by any direct evidence to the accused, demonstrated that the daughter's death had been the result of an intentional act by someone, and not an accident, and (c) even though the accused did not raise the defense of accidental death at trial, the prosecution had to prove all the offense's elements beyond a reasonable doubt, and the evidence of battered child syndrome was relevant to show intent; (3) even if the jury instruction as to the use of the prior injury evidence was incorrect under state law, such fact was not a basis for federal habeas corpus relief; and (4) while the challenged instruction was not so clear as it might have been, the instruction did not so infuse the trial with unfairness as to deny due process of law, because there was not a reasonable likelihood that the jury applied the instruction in a way that violated the Constitution, given that (a) the most likely interpretation of the two-offenses phrase was that it referred to the prior rib and rectal injuries, (b) the if-committed phrase left it to the jury to determine whether the accused committed the prior acts, (c) to the extent that the jury may have believed that the accused committed the prior acts and used that as a factor in deliberation, there was sufficient evidence to sustain such a jury finding by a preponderance of the evidence, and (d) with respect to the claim that the instruction allowed the jury to base a determination of guilt upon a conclusion that the accused

24

committed the prior acts and therefore had a propensity to commit that type of crime, there was not a reasonable likelihood that the jury would have concluded that the instruction, read in the context of other instructions, authorized the use of propensity evidence pure and simple.

O'CONNOR, J., joined by STEVENS, J., concurring in part and dissenting in part, expressed the view that (1) the evidence of battered child syndrome was relevant, because (a) the state had to prove that the accused had intended to kill his daughter, and (b) the evidence that the daughter was a battered child was probative of causation and intent; but (2) the trial court's instruction as to the use of the prior injury evidence was erroneous under the due process clause, because the instruction may have relieved the state of its burden of proving the identity of the daughter's murderer beyond a reasonable doubt, for the instruction (a) encouraged the jury to assume that the accused had inflicted the prior injuries, and (b) then directed the jury to conclude that the prior abuser was the murderer; and (3) the case ought to be remanded for a determination whether the instruction error was harmless.

THOMAS, J., did not participate.

COUNSEL

Dane R. Gillette argued the cause for petitioner.
Ann Hardgrove Voris argued the cause for respondent.

SOUTHWEST MARINE, INC., Petitioner

v

BYRON GIZONI

502 US —, 116 L Ed 2d 405, 112 S Ct 486

Argued October 15, 1991.
Decided December 4, 1991.

Decision: Maritime worker whose occupation of ship repairman was listed in Longshore and Harbor Workers' Compensation Act (33 USCS § 902(3)) held not precluded from being "seaman" under Jones Act (46 USCS Appx § 688).

SUMMARY

The Longshore and Harbor Workers' Compensation Act (LHWCA) (33 USCS §§ 901-950) provides the exclusive remedy against an employer for an injured maritime worker who meets the statutory definition of "employee" (33 USCS § 905(a)). Under the LHWCA, an "employee" is any person engaged in maritime employment, including a ship repairman and other enumerated occupations (33 USCS § 902(3)), but "employee" does not include "a master or member of a crew of any vessel" (33 USCS § 902(3)(G)). A corporation which operated a ship repair facility in San Diego, California owned several floating platforms which were used to move materials and to support ship repairmen which the corporation employed. The platforms, which were not navigable in themselves, were moved about by tugboats and put into place alongside vessels under repair at berths or in drydock at the corporation's shipyard or a nearby naval station. A ship repair-

man, who was employed by the corporation as a
rigging foreman, suffered disabling injuries when his
foot broke through a thin wooden sheet which
covered a hole in the deck of the platform on which
he was working. The employee submitted a claim
for, and received, medical and compensation benefits from the corporation pursuant to the LHWCA.
Subsequently, the employee sued the corporation in
the United States District Court for the Southern
District of California and alleged that he was a
"seaman" within the meaning of the Jones Act (46
USCS Appx § 688) who had been injured as a result
of the corporation's negligence. The corporation
moved for summary judgment, on the grounds that
(1) the employee was not a Jones Act seaman, in
view of the nature of the platforms and the nature
of the employee's duties; and (2) the employee was
a harbor worker, who as such was precluded from
bringing his Jones Act claim because the LHWCA
was the exclusive remedy of a covered "employee"
against an employer. The District Court granted the
corporation's summary judgment motion on both
grounds. On appeal, the United States Court of
Appeals for the Ninth Circuit, reversing, expressed
the view that (1) questions of fact existed as to the
employee's seaman status; and (2) insofar as the
LHWCA by its terms, as provided in § 902(3)(G),
did not cover "a master or member of a crew of any
vessel"—which phrase was the equivalent of "seaman" under the Jones Act—employees whose work
involved ship repair were not necessarily restricted
to a remedy under the LHWCA (909 F2d 385).

On certiorari, the United States Supreme Court
affirmed. In an opinion by WHITE, J., expressing the
unanimous view of the eight participating members
of the court, it was held that (1) a maritime worker

27

whose occupation was one of those enumerated in the LHWCA definition of "employee" nevertheless might be entitled to bring suit as a "seaman" under the Jones Act; (2) a maritime worker was limited to LHWCA remedies only if no genuine issue of fact existed as to whether the worker was a seaman under the Jones Act; and (3) not all ship repairmen lack the requisite connection, as a matter of law, to a vessel in navigation to qualify for status as "seamen" for purposes of the Jones Act.

THOMAS, J., did not participate.

COUNSEL

George J. Tichy, II argued the cause for petitioner.

Preston Easley argued the cause for respondent.

Robert A. Long, Jr. argued the cause for the United States, as amicus curiae, supporting respondent.

GUY WOODDELL, Jr., Petitioner

v

INTERNATIONAL BROTHERHOOD OF
ELECTRICAL WORKERS, LOCAL 71, et al.

502 US —, 116 L Ed 2d 419, 112 S Ct 494

Argued October 16, 1991.
Decided December 4, 1991.

Decision: Right to jury trial held applicable to
union member's LMRDA claim; § 301(a) of
LMRA held to grant federal jurisdiction over
member's claim that local violated international
union's constitution.

SUMMARY

Title I of the Labor-Management Reporting and
Disclosure Act of 1959 (LMRDA) (29 USCS §§ 401
et seq.) grants specified rights to union members.
Also, § 301(a) of the Labor Management Relations
Act of 1947 (LMRA) (29 USCS § 185(a)) grants
Federal District Courts jurisdiction over suits for
violation of contracts between an employer and a
labor organization representing employees in an
industry affecting commerce as defined in the
LMRA, or between any such labor organizations. A
member of a local union of an international brotherhood brought suit against the local and its officers
in a District Court, and sought injunctive relief, lost
wages and benefits, additional compensatory damages, punitive damages, and attorneys' fees. The
member's complaint included claims to the effect
that (1) the member's rights protected by the
LMRDA had been violated, in that (a) he had alleg-

29

edly been discriminated against in job referrals
because of his opposition to proposed union policy,
and (b) he had allegedly been denied his right to a
fair hearing during internal disciplinary proceedings
by the local; and (2) there had been violations of
the international's constitution and the local's bylaws with respect to matters including job referrals,
which violations were allegedly breaches of contract
redressable under § 301(a), for the international's
constitution and the local's bylaws allegedly constituted contracts between the international and the
local. The District Court, however, in the course of
acting on two summary judgment motions filed by
defendants, dismissed all claims against all defendants. On appeal, the United States Court of Appeals for the Sixth Circuit reversed the dismissal of
the LMRDA job-referral claim, but (1) otherwise
affirmed the District Court's decision, including the
District Court's holding that the member had no
right to have his LMRDA claim tried to a jury; and
(2) with respect to the § 301(a) breach-of-contract
claim, expressed the view that § 301(a) did not
authorize such an action to be brought by an individual union member (907 F2d 151).

On certiorari, the United States Supreme Court
reversed the judgment of the Court of Appeals and
remanded the case for further proceedings. In an
opinion by WHITE, J., expressing the unanimous
view of the eight participating members of the
court, it was held that (1) under the Federal Constitution's Seventh Amendment, the union member
was entitled to a jury trial on his LMRDA claim for
money damages, because (a) the injunctive relief
sought was incidental to the damages, (b) the claim
for lost wages could not be treated as restitutionary
30

incident to an order reinstating the member to a job from which the member had been terminated, as the damages sought were for pay for jobs to which the union had allegedly failed to refer the member, and (c) actions under the LMRDA are closely analogous to personal injury actions; and (2) the District Court had subject-matter jurisdiction, under the between-labor-organizations provision in § 301(a), over the member's breach of contract claim, because (a) the member's personal standing to bring the suit was not disputed, (b) the member charged that the international's constitution and the local's bylaws constituted contracts between two labor organizations—that is, the international and the local—within the meaning of § 301(a), where, among other factors, the international's constitution included a rule which required the international's approval of all local bylaws, (c) union constitutions are an important form of contract between labor organizations, (d) members of a collective bargaining unit are often the beneficiaries of union constitutions, and, when they are, they may bring suit on these contracts under § 301(a), (e) if such a suit by a union member was not allowed under § 301(a), then the same contract terms might be given different meanings based solely on the identity of the party suing, (f) the allowance of such suits did not signal an unwarranted intrusion on state contract law that Congress could not have intended, and (g) even though such suits had been allowed by a number of lower federal courts for up to 10 years, there was no evidence that the federal courts had been overwhelmed by trivial litigation in this area.

THOMAS, J., did not participate.

COUNSEL

Theodore E. Meckler argued the cause for petitioner.

Frederick G. Cloppert, Jr. argued the cause for respondents.

SIMON & SCHUSTER, INC., Petitioner

v

MEMBERS OF THE NEW YORK STATE CRIME
VICTIMS BOARD et al.

502 US —, 116 L Ed 2d 476, 112 S Ct 501

Argued October 15, 1991.
Decided December 10, 1991.

Decision: New York statute, requiring that criminal's income from books or other works describing crime be escrowed and made available
to victims of crime, held inconsistent with Federal Constitution's First Amendment.

SUMMARY

In order to prevent criminals—such as the serial
killer who was popularly known as "the Son of
Sam"—from profiting from their notoriety while
their victims remained uncompensated, the state of
New York enacted a statute in 1977 which (1)
provided that an entity contracting with a person
accused or convicted of a crime for the production
of a book or other work describing the crime was
required to pay to the New York crime victims
board any moneys owed to that person under the
contract, and (2) required the board to deposit such
funds in an escrow account for payment to (a) any
victim of the crime who, within 5 years of the
account's establishment, brought a civil action leading to recovery of a judgment against the accused or
convicted person, and (b) to the person's other
creditors. The statute defined "person convicted of
a crime" to include any person who had voluntarily

33

and intelligently admitted the commission of a crime for which such person was not prosecuted. The statute applied to works on any subject, provided that they expressed the accused or convicted person's thoughts, feelings, opinions, or emotions regarding the person's crime, however tangentially or incidentally. In 1981, a publisher agreed to pay both a writer and an admitted organized crime figure for a book about the crime figure's life. The book, which became a bestseller, described the crime figure's participation in a variety of crimes. In 1986, after the crime victims board became aware of the book, the board ordered the publisher to suspend all future payments to the crime figure. The board subsequently (1) determined that the publisher had violated the statute, (2) ordered the crime figure to turn over the payments he had already received, and (3) ordered the publisher to turn over all money payable to the crime figure at the time or in the future. The publisher, bringing suit under 42 USCS § 1983 in the United States District Court for the Southern District of New York against the members of the board, sought declaratory and injunctive relief. The District Court, finding the statute consistent with the Federal Constitution's First Amendment, granted summary judgment to the board members (724 F Supp 170). The United States Court of Appeals for the Second Circuit affirmed (916 F2d 777).

On certiorari, the United States Supreme Court reversed. In an opinion by O'CONNOR, J., joined by REHNQUIST, Ch. J., and WHITE, STEVENS, SCALIA, and SOUTER, JJ., it was held that the statute was inconsistent with the First Amendment, because (1) regardless of whether the First Amendment "speaker" was the author or the publisher, the statute singled out

34

speech on a particular subject for a financial burden that the state placed on no other speech and no other income; (2) although the state had a compelling interest in insuring that victims of crime were compensated by those who harmed them, in insuring that criminals did not profit from their crimes, and in using the profits of criminals' crimes to compensate victims, and although it could be assumed that the income escrowed under the statute represented the fruits of crime, the state had little if any interest in limiting such victim compensation to the proceeds of the criminal's speech about the crime; and (3) the statute was not narrowly tailored but rather was significantly overinclusive as a means of insuring victim compensation from the profits of crime, in that the statute reached a wide range of literature that did not enable a criminal to profit from a crime while a victim remained uncompensated.

BLACKMUN, J., concurring in the judgment, expressed the view that the statute was underinclusive as well as overinclusive.

KENNEDY, J., concurring in the judgment, expressed the view that (1) the fact that the content of the speech regulated by the statute had the full protection of the First Amendment was itself a full and sufficient reason for holding the statute unconstitutional; and (2) it was unnecessary and incorrect to ask whether the state could show that the statute was necessary to serve a compelling state interest and was narrowly drawn to achieve that end, since the "compelling interest" test should not be applied to content-based restrictions on speech.

THOMAS, J., did not participate.

COUNSEL

Ronald S. Rauchberg argued the cause for petitioner.

Howard L. Zwickel argued the cause for respondents.

––––––––––

RAFEH-RAFIE ARDESTANI, Petitioner

v

IMMIGRATION AND NATURALIZATION
SERVICE

502 US —, 116 L Ed 2d 496, 112 S Ct 515

Argued October 8, 1991.
Decided December 10, 1991.

Decision: Equal Access to Justice Act (5 USCS § 504, 28 USCS § 2412) held not to authorize award of attorneys' fees for administrative deportation proceedings before Immigration and Naturalization Service.

SUMMARY

The Equal Access to Justice Act (EAJA) (5 USCS § 504, 28 USCS § 2412) permits a prevailing party in an "adversary adjudication" before a federal administrative agency to recover attorneys' fees from the Federal Government. A provision of the EAJA (5 USCS § 504(b)(1)(C)(i)) defines an "adversary adjudication" as an adjudication "under section 554" of Title 5 (5 USCS § 554), which section delineates the scope of proceedings governed by the formal adjudication requirements of the Administrative Procedure Act (APA) (5 USCS §§ 556, 557) and sets forth some of those requirements. An alien sought asylum in the United States for fear of persecution on return to her home country, Iran. Although the United States Department of State informed the Immigration and Naturalization Service (INS) that the alien's fear of persecution was well founded, the INS denied the asylum application and issued an order to show cause why the alien should not be deported. At the deportation hearing, the alien successfully renewed her application for asylum. The immigration judge, having determined that the alien was the prevailing party in the adjudication and that the INS' position had not been substantially justified, granted the alien's application for attorneys' fees under the EAJA. The INS appealed the fees award to the Board of Immigration Appeals (BIA). The BIA, vacating, denied the award on the ground that administrative deportation hearings were not within the scope of the EAJA. The United States Court of Appeals for the Eleventh Circuit, denying the alien's petition for review, similarly held that the EAJA does not apply to deportation hearings (904 F2d 1505).

On certiorari, the United States Supreme Court affirmed. In an opinion by O'CONNOR, J., joined by REHNQUIST, Ch. J., and WHITE, SCALIA, KENNEDY, and SOUTER, JJ., it was held that (1) deportation proceedings are not adversary adjudications "under section 554" and thus do not fall within the category of proceedings for which the EAJA authorizes the award of attorneys' fees, given that (a) in order for proceedings to fall "under section 554," such proceedings must be subject to or governed by § 554 and thus must be governed by the procedures mandated by the APA, (b) any ambiguities in the EAJA's legislative history are insufficient to undermine this understanding of the phrase "under section 554," and (c) deportation proceedings are governed by the procedures prescribed by the Immigration and Nationality Act of 1952 (8 USCS §§ 1101 et seq.) rather than by the APA, notwithstanding that the regulations governing immigration proceedings conform closely to the procedures required for formal adjudication under the APA; and (2) although the broad purposes of the EAJA would be served by making the EAJA applicable to deportation proceedings, the plain language of the EAJA —coupled with the requirement that waivers of sovereign immunity be strictly construed in favor of the United States—prevented such an extension of the EAJA.

BLACKMUN, J., joined by STEVENS, J., dissenting, expressed the view that the alien was entitled to an award of attorneys' fees, given that (1) the EAJA's definition of the term "adversary adjudication" could be read to support the applicability of the EAJA to deportation proceedings, and (2) such an interpretation was confirmed by the legislative history and strongly favored by the purposes of the EAJA.

THOMAS, J., did not participate.

COUNSEL

David N. Soloway argued the cause for petitioner. Lawrence G. Wallace argued the cause for respondent.

UNION BANK, Petitioner

v

HERBERT WOLAS, Chapter 7 Trustee for the
Estate of ZZZZ BEST CO., INC.

502 US —, 116 L Ed 2d 514, 112 S Ct 527

Argued November 5, 1991.
Decided December 11, 1991.

Decision: Payments on long-term debt held to qualify for ordinary course of business exception
under 11 USCS § 547(c)(2) to bankruptcy trustee's power to avoid preferential transfers.

SUMMARY

Less than 7 months after borrowing $7 million
from a bank, a company filed a voluntary petition
under Chapter 7 of the Bankruptcy Code (11 USCS
§§ 701-766). During the 90 days prior to the filing
of its petition, the company made two interest
payments to the bank totaling approximately $100,-
000 and paid a loan commitment fee of about
$2,500. The trustee of the debtor company's estate
filed a complaint against the bank in the United
States Bankruptcy Court for the Central District of
California, which complaint sought the recovery of
those payments as preferential transfers under 11
USCS § 547(b). The Bankruptcy Court, however, (1)
found that the loans in question had been made in
the ordinary course of business or financial affairs of
both the company and the bank; (2) found that the
payments in question had been made according to
ordinary business terms and in the ordinary course
of business; (3) concluded that the payments fell

within the exception to the trustee's avoiding powers provided by 11 USCS § 547(c)(2); and therefore
(4) entered summary judgment in favor of the bank.
The United States District Court for the Central
District of California affirmed (1989 US Dist LEXIS
17500). The United States Court of Appeals for the
Ninth Circuit, however, reversed, as it held that the
ordinary course of business exception to avoidance
of preferential transfers was not available to long-
term creditors (921 F2d 968).

On certiorari, the United States Supreme Court
reversed and remanded. In an opinion by STEVENS,
J., expressing the unanimous view of the court, it
was held that payments on long-term debt may
qualify for the ordinary course of business exception
to a trustee's power to avoid preferential transfers,
because (1) there is no language in § 547(c)(2)
distinguishing between long-term and short-term
debt; (2) given the clarity of the statutory text, the
trustee's burden of persuasion was exceptionally
heavy; (3) even if Congress had adopted the present
provisions of § 547(c)(2), which prior to a 1984
amendment had applied only to payments made
within 45 days of the date that the debt was incurred, to redress specific problems of specific
short-term creditors, Congress redressed those
problems by entirely deleting the time limitation; (4)
it was not clear that § 547(c)(2) merely codified the
judicially crafted "current expense" rule applied
prior to enactment of the Bankruptcy Code of 1978;
and (5) even if availability of § 547(c)(2) to long-
term creditors did not directly further the policy of
equal treatment for creditors, which was one of two
basic policies underlying § 547, such availability (a)
did further the other basic policy of discouraging
creditors from racing to the courthouse to dismem-

ber the debtor, and (b) might indirectly further the goal of equal distribution.

SCALIA, J., concurred, expressing regret that the legislative history and policy arguments made by the trustee had to be addressed with regard to a statute devoid of any language that could be thought to distinguish between long-term and short-term debt.

COUNSEL

John A. Graham argued the cause for petitioner. Herbert Wolas argued the cause for respondent.

———————

UNITED STATES DEPARTMENT OF STATE,
Petitioner

v

MICHAEL D. RAY et al.

502 US —, 116 L Ed 2d 526, 112 S Ct 541

Argued October 9, 1991.
Decided December 16, 1991.

Decision: Exemption 6 of FOIA held to authorize deletion of names and other identifying information from reports of interviews with Haitian nationals returned to Haiti after attempting illegal emigration.

SUMMARY

Exemption 6 of the Freedom of Information Act (FOIA) (5 USCS § 552(b)(6)) provides that FOIA disclosure requirements do not apply to "personnel and medical files and similar files the disclosure of which would constitute a clearly unwarranted invasion of personal privacy." A number of Haitian nationals had been involuntarily returned to Haiti after attempting to emigrate illegally to the United States. The United States State Department, in order to monitor compliance with an assurance by the Haitian Government that such returnees would not be subject to prosecution for illegal departure, conducted confidential interviews with a sample of such returnees, and all but one or two in the sample reported that they had not been harassed or prosecuted since their return. A Florida lawyer represented other Haitian nationals who were (1) seeking political asylum in the United States, and (2) attempting to prove, in immigration proceedings, that Haitians who emigrated illegally would face a well-founded fear of persecution if they returned. The lawyer and three of his clients made a series of FOIA requests, and the State Department's response included the release of 17 reports containing summaries of individual interviews with such returnees under the monitoring program, but the Department redacted—that is, deleted—the names and other identifying information from the reports before release. The lawyer and the clients then filed a FOIA suit in the United States District Court for the Southern District of Florida, and sought the redacted information. Although the Department cited Exemption 6, the District Court's rulings included an order to produce the redacted information, as the court expressed the view that any invasion of privacy for the "mere" act of disclosure of names and addresses was (1) "de minimis" and little more than speculation, and (2) clearly outweighed by the public interest in the safe relocation of returned Haitians (725 F Supp 502). On appeal, the United States Court of Appeals for the Eleventh Circuit, in affirming the District Court's order under somewhat different reasoning, expressed the view that (1) there were significant privacy interests at stake, where (a) the requesters wanted the redacted information in order to contact the returnees directly and to question them about their treatment by the Haitian Government, and (b) the returnees had been promised confidentiality; but (2) such privacy interests were outweighed by the public interest in learning whether the Federal Government (a) was adequately monitoring Haiti's compliance with its obligation not to persecute returnees, and (b) was honest to the public in stating that Haiti was adhering to its obligation; and (3) although the redacted information would not, in and of itself, tell the requesters anything about Haiti's treatment of returnees or the Federal Government's honesty, the indirect benefit of giving the requesters a means to locate the returnees and to cross-examine them provided a public value that required disclosure (908 F2d 1549).

On certiorari, the United States Supreme Court reversed. In an opinion by STEVENS, J., joined by REHNQUIST, Ch. J., and WHITE, BLACKMUN, O'CONNOR, and SOUTER, JJ., as to holding 1 below, and expressing the unanimous view of the eight participating members of the court as to holdings 2-4 below, it was held that Exemption 6 authorized the redaction of the names and other identifying information from the 17 reports, because (1) the interest in protecting the privacy of the redacted information was substantial, where (a) disclosure would publicly link particular, named individuals with highly personal information in the reports' summaries, (b) disclosure would publicly identify the interviewees as people who cooperated with the Department investigation, and thus subject the interviewees to possible embarrassment or retaliatory action, and (c) the assurances of confidentiality had special significance, in view of the possibility that interviewees given such assurances might have been willing to discuss private matters that the interviewees would not otherwise have exposed to the public, the risk of mistreatment of the interviewees, and the requesters' plan to make direct contact with the interviewees once identified; (2) although the public interest in knowing whether the Department had adequately monitored Haiti's compliance was cognizable under FOIA, that interest was adequately served by disclosure of the redacted summaries, and thus disclosure of the unredacted documents would constitute a clearly unwarranted invasion of the interviewees' privacy; (3) with respect to the claim that direct contact with identified interviewees would result in a "derivative use" of the redacted information to obtain additional information outside government files, there was no need to address whether a derivative use theory would ever justify disclosure of information about private individuals, because nothing in the record suggested that a second set of interviews with the already interviewed returnees would produce any relevant information that was not set forth in the documents already produced; and (4) with respect to the claimed interest in ascertaining the reports' veracity, there was not a scintilla of evidence, either in the documents themselves or elsewhere in the record, that tended to impugn the integrity of the reports.

SCALIA, J., joined by KENNEDY, J., concurring in part and concurring in the judgment, expressed the view that (1) the court did not refute the persuasive contention that consideration of "derivative uses," whether to establish a public interest or to establish an invasion of privacy, was impermissible under Exemption 6; and (2) since derivative use on the public-interest side and derivative use on the privacy-invasion side went together, the court should have been consistent in its abstention from deciding the derivative use question, and should not have discussed, with respect to the invasion of privacy, such matters as the possibility of retaliatory action or the requesters' plan to make direct contact with identified interviewees; but (3) the assertion of Exemption 6 had to be sustained, because (a) disclosure of the unredacted documents would constitute an invasion of personal privacy, through disclosure of the fact that particular persons had agreed, under a pledge of confidentiality, to report to a foreign power—that is, the United States—concerning the conduct of the persons' own—that is, the Haitian—government, and (b) the public interest had been adequately served by disclosure of the redacted summaries.

THOMAS, J., did not participate.

COUNSEL

Kent L. Jones argued the cause for petitioner.
Michael Dean Ray argued the cause for respondents.

IMMIGRATION AND NATURALIZATION
SERVICE, et al., Petitioners

v

NATIONAL CENTER FOR IMMIGRANTS'
RIGHTS, INC., et al.

502 US —, 116 L Ed 2d 546, 112 S Ct 551

Argued November 13, 1991.
Decided December 16, 1991.

Decision: INS rule generally requiring that bond on
which excludible alien is released, pending deportability determination, contain condition forbidding unauthorized employment held not facially invalid.

SUMMARY

Section 242(a) of the Immigration and Nationality
Act (8 USCS § 1252(a)) authorizes the Attorney
General of the United States to arrest excludible
aliens and, pending a determination of their deportability, either to hold them in custody or to release
them on a bond containing conditions prescribed by
the Attorney General. Several individuals and organizations filed suit against the Immigration and
Naturalization Service (INS) alleging that 8 CFR
§ 103.6(a)(2)(ii)—an INS regulation which is entitled
Condition against unauthorized employment and
requires that a condition barring employment be
included in an excludible alien's release bond issued
pending a deportability determination, unless the
District Director for the INS determines that employment is appropriate—was facially invalid. After
the United States District Court for the Central

District of California entered a nationwide preliminary injunction against enforcement of the regulation, and the United States Court of Appeals for the
Ninth Circuit affirmed in part (743 F2d 1365), the
District Court, on remand, (1) granted summary
judgment for the individuals and organizations on
the ground that the regulation was beyond the
Attorney General's authority, and (2) certified a
class consisting of everyone who had been or might
be denied the right to work pursuant to the regulation. After the Court of Appeals again affirmed (791
F2d 1351), and the Supreme Court of the United
States vacated the Court of Appeals' judgment and
remanded for further consideration (481 US 1009,
95 L Ed 2d 489, 107 S Ct 1881), the District Court
held that the regulation was invalid as exceeding the
Attorney General's authority under § 1252(a). The
Court of Appeals affirmed, holding that under the
statute, (1) a bond had to relate either to securing
an alien's appearance at a hearing or to protecting
the nation against danger from active subversives,
and (2) bond conditions could be imposed on only
an individualized basis (913 F2d 1350).

On certiorari, the United States Supreme Court
reversed and remanded. In an opinion by STEVENS,
J., expressing the unanimous view of the court, it
was held that the regulation was consistent with the
Attorney General's authority under § 1252(a), because (1) the regulation did not contemplate the
inclusion of no-work conditions in bonds issued to
aliens who were authorized to work, since (a) the
reference in the regulation's text to "employment"
should be read as a reference to "unauthorized
employment" in the regulation's title, (b) the government consistently had maintained that the regulation implicated only a bond condition barring

49

unauthorized employment, and (c) the conclusion that the regulation did not contemplate no-work conditions concerning aliens who were authorized to work was further supported by the (i) regulation's language excluding the condition upon a determination that employment was appropriate, (ii) the agency's comments when the regulation was promulgated, and the agency's operating instructions, indicating that permanent resident aliens were not subject to the condition, and (iii) absence of evidence that the INS has imposed the condition on any such alien, (2) the regulation, being wholly consistent with the established concern of immigration law of preserving jobs for American workers, was squarely within the scope of the Attorney General's statutory authority, and (3) when properly construed and when viewed in the context of various INS procedures which, when taken together, were designed to insure that aliens detained and bonds issued under the regulation would receive individualized determinations, the regulation provided the individualized determinations contemplated in § 1252(a).

COUNSEL

Stephen J. Marzen argued the cause for petitioners.

Peter A. Schey argued the cause for respondents.

KENNETH HILTON, Petitioner

v

SOUTH CAROLINA PUBLIC RAILWAYS
COMMISSION

502 US —, 116 L Ed 2d 560, 112 S Ct 560

Argued October 8, 1991.
Decided December 16, 1991.

Decision: Federal Employers' Liability Act (45
USCS §§ 51-60) held to create cause of action,
enforceable in state court, against state-owned
railroad.

SUMMARY

In Parden v Terminal R. of Alabama State Docks
Dept. (1964) 377 US 184, 12 L Ed 2d 233, 84 S Ct
1207, the United States Supreme Court held that
the Federal Employers' Liability Act (FELA) (45
USCS §§ 51-60)—which provides in part (45 USCS
§ 51) that any "common carrier by railroad" engaged in interstate commerce is liable for injuries to
its employees resulting from the negligence of other
employees, officers, or agents of the carrier—authorized suits against state-owned railways. An employee of the South Carolina Public Railways Commission, which Commission was a state agency operating as a common carrier in interstate commerce,
alleged that he had been injured in the scope and
course of his employment as a result of the Commission's negligence, and he brought suit against
the Commission under the FELA in a Federal District Court. The action was dismissed and refiled in
a state trial court after the Supreme Court held in

51

Welch v Texas Dept. of Highways & Public Transp.
(1987) 483 US 468, 97 L Ed 2d 389, 107 S Ct 2941,
that the Jones Act (46 USCS Appx § 688), which
incorporated the remedial scheme of the FELA, did
not abrogate the states' immunity from suit in federal court under the Federal Constitution's Eleventh
Amendment. The state trial court, however, dismissed the employee's complaint on the ground that
the FELA did not authorize actions for money
damages against state agencies even in a state forum, as the court found that the Parden ruling had
been severely limited by subsequent Supreme Court
decisions and was no longer good law. The Supreme Court of South Carolina affirmed, relying on
its decision in another case in which it had interpreted the decision in Will v Michigan Dept. of
State Police (1989) 491 US 58, 105 L Ed 2d 45, 109
S Ct 2304, as holding that a statute will not be
interpreted to create a cause of action against a
state for money damages unless it contains unmistakably clear language showing that Congress had
intended to do so.

On certiorari, the United States Supreme Court
reversed and remanded. In an opinion by KENNEDY,
J., joined by REHNQUIST, Ch. J., and WHITE, STE-
VENS, and SOUTER, JJ., it was held that the FELA
creates a cause of action, enforceable in state court,
against a state-owned railroad, because the policies
in favor of adhering to the Parden decision far
outweigh those suggesting departure from that precedent, given that (1) workers' compensation laws in
many states specifically exclude railroad workers
from their coverage because of the assumption that
the FELA provides adequate coverage for those
workers, and overruling Parden would thus require
those states to re-examine their statutes, meanwhile

putting at risk all employees and employers who have acted on the assumption that they were covered; (2) overruling Parden would also throw into doubt previous United States Supreme Court decisions holding that the entire federal scheme of railroad regulation applies to state-owned railroads; (3) it is not accurate to characterize the Welch decision as having considered and rejected the above arguments for adhering to the Parden precedent, because the Welch decision did not address the concern that conferring immunity from state court suit would strip FELA and Jones Act protection from state employees; (4) the Welch decision is not determinative of the issue in the case at hand, because the Eleventh Amendment does not apply in state courts; (5) the issue thus becomes a pure question of statutory construction, where the doctrine of stare decisis is most compelling; (6) the Will decision did not import the entirety of the Supreme Court's Eleventh Amendment jurisprudence into the area of statutory construction; and (7) the rule requiring a "clear statement" of congressional intent to impose liability on a state, though useful in interpreting legislation, need not be applied to the FELA because the rule does not prevail over the doctrine of stare decisis as applied to a longstanding statutory construction implicating important reliance interests.

BLACKMUN, J., concurred in the judgment.

O'CONNOR, J., joined by SCALIA, J., dissented, expressing the view that (1) stare decisis dictated that the court follow the clear statement rule established by the Will and Welch decisions, rather than reviving the substantially discredited Parden decision; (2) the clear statement rule is not a mere canon of statutory interpretation but derives from the Federal Constitution itself, and protects the balance of power between the states and the Federal Government; (3) it is not assumed that states waive their right to challenge an abrogation of their traditional authority merely because they have acquiesced in, or even relied upon, longstanding congressional regulation; (4) the clear statement rule applies to the FELA, because the FELA provides for a cause of action for damages and because states have traditionally regulated their liability to damages suits, but the rule would not apply to other congressional regulation of state railroads, because states have not traditionally regulated interstate railroads; and (5) the concern that state railway employees would be without a remedy should not determine the result in this case, as states could allow other compensation schemes to fill the void if the FELA is held inapplicable to such cases.

THOMAS, J., did not participate.

COUNSEL

Robert J. Beckham argued the cause for petitioner.

Keating L. Simons, III argued the cause for respondent.

———

WILLIAM "SKY" KING, Petitioner

v

ST. VINCENT'S HOSPITAL

502 US —, 116 L Ed 2d 578, 112 S Ct 570

Argued October 16, 1991.
Decided December 16, 1991.

Decision: Provision of Veterans' Reemployment Rights Act (38 USCS § 2024(d)) held not to limit length of military service after which member of Armed Forces retains right to civilian reemployment.

SUMMARY

A provision of the Veterans' Reemployment Rights Act (38 USCS § 2024(d)) states that (1) an employee shall upon request be granted a leave of absence to perform active duty for training or inactive duty training in the Armed Forces of the United States; and (2) such an employee is to be permitted to return to the employee's position with such seniority, status, pay, and vacation as the employee would have had if the employee had not been absent for such purpose. A hospital employee who was a member of the Alabama National Guard applied to become Command Sergeant Major in the Active Guard/Reserve program and thereby undertook to serve a 3-year, full-time tour of duty. After the employee was selected for this position, he so notified his employer and requested a leave of absence from his job. The employer denied the leave request on the ground that a 3-year leave was unreasonable and thus beyond the guarantee of

§ 2024(d). Subsequently, the employer brought a declaratory judgment action in the United States District Court for the Northern District of Alabama to settle the issue whether § 2024(d) provided reemployment rights after tours of duty as long as the one in question. The District Court, rendering declaratory judgment for the employer, held that (1) a reasonableness standard applied in determining whether the employee had a right to receive a leave of absence under § 2024(d); and (2) the request for a 3-year leave of absence was per se unreasonable. The United States Court of Appeals for the Eleventh Circuit affirmed (901 F2d 1068).

On certiorari, the United States Supreme Court reversed and remanded. In an opinion by SOUTER, J., expressing the unanimous view of the eight participating members of the court, it was held that § 2024(d) did not implicitly limit the length of military service after which a member of the Armed Forces retains a right to civilian reemployment, given that (1) even though the Supreme Court, if it were free to tinker with the statutory scheme, could reasonably accord some significance to the burdens imposed on both employers and workers in the case of long leaves of absence, the fact that the text of § 2024(d) placed no explicit limit on the length of a tour after which an Armed Forces member may enforce reemployment rights, while other subsections of § 2024, protecting other classes of service personnel, expressly limited the periods of their protection, implied that the simplicity of § 2024(d) was deliberate, consistent with a plain meaning to provide a benefit without conditions on length of service; (2) even if the express durational limitations of the other subsections unsettled the significance of the drafting of § 2024(d), the Supreme Court would ultimately read § 2024(d) in favor of the employee under the canon that provisions for benefits to members of the Armed Services are to be construed in the beneficiaries' favor; and (3) differences of treatment among the various classes of service personnel protected by various companion provisions of § 2024(d) were not to be understood to create a hierarchy of reemployment rights under which reservists subject to training duty within the meaning of § 2024(d) would receive less protection than inductees, enlistees, and others who were covered by other provisions.

THOMAS, J., did not participate.

COUNSEL

Amy L. Wax argued the cause for petitioner.
Harry L. Hopkins argued the cause for respondent.

_____

BRIAN V. HUNTER and JEFFREY JORDAN,
Petitioners

v

JAMES V. BRYANT, Jr.

502 US —, 116 L Ed 2d 589, 112 S Ct 534

Decided December 16, 1991.

Decision: Secret Service agents held entitled to qualified immunity in lawsuit involving alleged unlawful arrest where agents had reasonable grounds to believe that arrestee had threatened President.

SUMMARY

At two offices of a California university, an individual delivered copies of a rambling letter which, among other things, referred to a plot by "Mr. Image," who was described as "Communist white men within the National Council of Churches," to assassinate the President of the United States, who was then traveling in Germany. After university police telephoned the United States Secret Service, a Secret Service agent interviewed university employees and was informed that the individual who delivered the letter (1) had stated that "[h]e should have been assassinated in Bonn," (2) had spoken of "bloody coups" and "assassination," and (3) had said something about "across the throat" while moving his hand horizontally across his throat to simulate a cutting action. The agent and one of his colleagues then visited the address on the letter, where the individual gave them permission to enter his apartment. The individual admitted writing and delivering the letter, but he refused to identify "Mr. Image," to answer questions about his feelings toward the President, or to state whether he intended to harm the President; and he answered questions about "Mr. Image" in a rambling manner. Given permission to search the apartment, the agents found the original of the letter and thereafter arrested the individual for making threats against the President in violation of 18 USCS § 871(a). The individual was arraigned before a magistrate and held without bond until the complaint against him was dismissed on the government's motion 14 days later. The individual then brought an action including Bivens claims against the agents, which claims alleged in part that the agents had violated the individual's rights under the Federal Constitution's Fourth Amendment by arresting the individual without probable cause and without a warrant. After dismissing all other defendants and claims, the District Court denied the agents' motion for summary judgment on qualified immunity grounds with respect to the arrest claims. The United States Court of Appeals for the Ninth Circuit, affirming, held that the agents (1) were entitled to qualified immunity for arresting the individual without a warrant, but (2) had not sustained the burden of establishing qualified immunity on the claim that they had arrested the individual without probable cause, because their reason for the arrest—their belief that "Mr. Image" could be a pseudonym for the individual himself—was not the most reasonable reading of the individual's letter, and summary judgment based on lack of probable cause is proper only if there is only one reasonable conclusion a jury could reach (903 F2d 717).

Granting certiorari, the United States Supreme Court reversed and remanded. In a per curiam opinion expressing the views of REHNQUIST, Ch. J., and WHITE, BLACKMUN, O'CONNOR, and SOUTER, JJ., it was held that (1) the Court of Appeals' statement of the law was wrong because that statement (a) routinely placed the question of immunity in the hands of the jury, whereas immunity ordinarily should be decided long before trial, and (b) looked to whether a more reasonable interpretation of the events could be constructed after the fact rather than whether the agents acted reasonably under settled law in the circumstances; (2) the agents were entitled to immunity if a reasonable officer could have believed that probable cause existed to arrest the individual; and (3) even assuming that the agents, along with the magistrate, erred in concluding that probable cause existed to arrest the individual, the agents nevertheless would be entitled to qualified immunity because their decision was reasonable, even if mistaken.

SCALIA, J., concurred in the judgment, expressing the view that (1) the Court of Appeals had purported to be applying the standard now required by the Supreme Court, but had erred in finding that this standard was not met on the facts before it, and (2) it is worthwhile to establish that such an error will not be allowed to stand with respect to those who guard the life of the President.

STEVENS, J., dissented, expressing the view that (1) the Court of Appeals had properly stated the applicable law; (2) the question presented is whether a reasonable, trained law enforcement officer could have concluded that the evidence available to the agents at the time they arrested the individual constituted probable cause to believe that he had committed the crime of threatening the President's life; and (3) though the confusing set of facts relating to the individual's letter might have justified a trained officer's concluding that a mentally unstable person might pose a threat to the President, the agents did not establish that a reasonable officer could have concluded that he had sufficient evidence to support a finding of probable cause at the time of the individual's arrest.

KENNEDY, J., dissented, expressing the view that the case did not lend itself to summary disposition and should be set for full briefing and oral argument, given (1) the fact that two Justices disagree with the proposition that the Court of Appeals misstated the law, and (2) the precedential weight that later courts would accord to all the questions presented in the case and addressed by the Supreme Court in express terms or by clear implication.

THOMAS, J., did not participate.

———

In Re JAMES BLODGETT, Superintendent,
Washington State Penitentiary, et al., Petitioners

502 US —, 116 L Ed 2d 669, 112 S Ct 674

Decided January 13, 1992.

Decision: Mandamus to compel Federal Court of
Appeals to issue decision, on second habeas
corpus petition by state prisoner condemned to
death, denied where state failed to object to
order delaying decision.

SUMMARY

An accused was convicted in a Washington state
trial court in 1982 on multiple counts of murder
and was sentenced to death. After his conviction
and sentence were affirmed on direct appeal (103
Wash 2d 1, 691 P2d 929) and the United States
Supreme Court denied certiorari (471 US 1094, 85
L Ed 2d 526, 105 S Ct 2169), the accused in 1985
filed a habeas corpus petition in the United States
District Court for the Western District of Washington. The District Court denied the petition, the
United States Court of Appeals for the Ninth Circuit
affirmed (829 F2d 1453), and the Supreme Court, in
1988, denied certiorari (488 US 948, 102 L Ed 2d
369, 109 S Ct 380). In March 1989, the accused
filed a second habeas corpus petition in the same
District Court, which denied a stay or other relief
days later. The Court of Appeals, however, granted
the accused an indefinite stay of execution, and the
case was argued and submitted in June 1989. No
decision was forthcoming, and in 1990 the Court of
Appeals did not respond either to inquiries from the

state attorney general or to the accused's motion to withdraw certain issues from consideration. In July 1990, the accused filed a personal restraint petition in state court, his third state action for collateral relief. In February 1991, the Court of Appeals noted the accused's motion to withdraw issues, requested a report on the status of the state court proceedings, vacated its submission of the case, and did not act on a request that the case be resubmitted. In March 1991, the state's highest court denied the personal restraint petition. In June 1991, the accused advised the Court of Appeals that he wished to discharge his counsel and proceed pro se and that he would file a third habeas corpus petition in the District Court. In August 1991, the Court of Appeals granted the motion to relieve counsel, directed the accused to file his third habeas corpus petition, and stated that it would wait for the District Court's ruling on that petition before taking further action. Finally, in October 1991, the state attorney general filed with the Supreme Court a petition for a writ of mandamus to direct the Court of Appeals to issue its decision on the second habeas corpus petition. The Court of Appeals' response indicated that (1) the submission of the case had been vacated in February 1991 because the appeal would have become moot if the state courts had granted the personal restraint petition, (2) the court wished to avoid piecemeal appeals by awaiting the District Court's decision on the third habeas corpus petition, and (3) consolidation of the last two petitions was consistent with the objective of the Circuit's Death Penalty Task Force, which sought to eliminate successive habeas corpus petitions.

Granting the accused leave to proceed in forma pauperis, the United States Supreme Court denied the state's petition for a writ of mandamus. In a per curiam opinion expressing the views of REHNQUIST, Ch. J., and WHITE, O'CONNOR, SCALIA, KENNEDY, SOUTER, and THOMAS, JJ., it was held that (1) the Supreme Court would decline to issue a writ of mandamus to the Court of Appeals—although the Supreme Court (a) was concerned that the state had sustained severe prejudice by the 2½-year stay of execution, (b) found no plausible explanation or reason for the Court of Appeals' delay prior to the accused's personal restraint petition, and (c) found grounds to question both the necessity and the propriety of the Court of Appeals' August 1991 order—because the state had not objected to the August 1991 order, whereas the state, as a predicate for extraordinary relief, should have asked the Court of Appeals to vacate or modify that order before coming to the Supreme Court for relief, given the requirement of Rule 20.1 of the Supreme Court Rules that, in order to justify the granting of an extraordinary writ, it must be shown that adequate relief cannot be obtained in any other form or from any other court; (2) denial of the writ was without prejudice to the state's right to again seek mandamus relief or to request any other extraordinary relief by motion or petition if unnecessary delays or unwarranted stays occurred in the Court of Appeals' disposition of the matter; and (3) in view of the delay that had already occurred, any further postponements or extensions of time would be subject to a most rigorous scrutiny if the state filed a further and meritorious petition for relief.

STEVENS, J., joined by BLACKMUN, J., concurred in the judgment, expressing the view that the state's petition for mandamus should have been denied summarily, because (1) in only the most extraordinary circumstances would it be appropriate for the Supreme Court to issue a writ of mandamus to require a Federal Court of Appeals to render its decision in a case under advisement; (2) the Court of Appeals' response provided a completely satisfactory explanation for its July 1990 decision to defer ruling on the merits of the second habeas corpus petition pending state court disposition of the personal restraint petition, namely, the desire to avoid piecemeal litigation and to address all of the accused's claims in a single ruling; (3) since that explanation alone was sufficient to mandate denial of the state's petition, there was no occasion for the Court of Appeals to explain its delay prior to July 1990; and (4) the state had failed to comply with Rule 20.1.

WILLIAM LEWIS SMITH, Petitioner

v

WAYNE S. BARRY et al.

502 US —, 116 L Ed 2d 678, 112 S Ct 678

Argued December 2, 1991.
Decided January 14, 1992.

Decision: Informal brief filed in Federal Court of
Appeals held effective as notice of appeal under
Rule 3 of Federal Rules of Appellate Procedure,
if filing of brief is timely and conveys information required by Rule 3.

SUMMARY

Rule 3 of the Federal Rules of Appellate Procedure (FRAP) requires (1) that a notice of appeal be
filed within the time allowed by FRAP Rule 4, and
(2) that such a notice (a) specify the party or parties
taking the appeal, (b) designate the judgment, order, or part thereof appealed from, and (c) name
the court to which the appeal is taken. A Maryland
state prison inmate filed, in the United States District Court for the District of Maryland, a 42 USCS
§ 1983 action alleging that several prison officials
had violated the inmate's rights under the Federal
Constitution's Eighth Amendment. After a verdict in
favor of most of the officials but against two of
them, the two officials filed a motion for judgment
notwithstanding the verdict, and the inmate, without
consulting his attorney, filed, with the United States
Court of Appeals for the Fourth Circuit, a notice of
appeal that, because it was filed while the motion

for judgment notwithstanding the verdict was pending, was invalid under Rule 4. Despite the invalidity of the notice, the Clerk of the Court of Appeals sent to all parties copies of the court's "informal brief," which was used in pro se appeals and which contained questions about the parties' legal positions. After the District Court denied the motion for judgment notwithstanding the verdict, and before the Rule 4 deadline for filing a notice of appeal, the inmate returned his informal brief to the Court of Appeals. Holding that a brief could never qualify as a notice of appeal required under Rule 3, the Court of Appeals dismissed the inmate's appeal for want of jurisdiction (919 F2d 893).

On certiorari, the United States Supreme Court reversed the judgment of the Court of Appeals and remanded the case for further proceedings. In an opinion by O'CONNOR, J., joined by REHNQUIST, Ch. J., and WHITE, BLACKMUN, STEVENS, KENNEDY, SOUTER, and THOMAS, JJ., it was held that the inmate's informal brief would be effective as a notice of appeal under Rule 3, if the brief conveyed the information required by Rule 3, because (1) papers at technical variance with Rule 3 may be treated as the functional equivalent of what the Rule requires; (2) the notice afforded by a document determines its sufficiency as a notice of appeal; (3) although the FRAP envision that a notice of appeal and the appellant's brief will be separate filings, (a) Rule 3(c) provides that an appeal shall not be dismissed for informality of form or title of the notice of appeal, and (b) proper briefing is not a jurisdictional requirement under the FRAP; and (4) although Rule 3(a) directs that an appeal be filed with a District Court, Rule 4(a)(1) provides that a notice of appeal that is mistakenly filed in a Court of

Appeals shall be deemed filed in a District Court on the day it is received in the Court of Appeals.

SCALIA, J., concurred in the judgment, expressing the view that, without relying on the theory that the inmate's brief was the functional equivalent of a notice of appeal, the judgment was supported by Rule 3(c)'s provision that an appeal shall not be dismissed for informality of form or title of the notice of appeal.

COUNSEL

Steven H. Goldblatt argued the cause for petitioner.

David H. Bamberger argued the cause for respondents.

_____

COUNTY OF YAKIMA, et al., Petitioners

v

CONFEDERATED TRIBES AND BANDS OF THE
YAKIMA INDIAN NATION (No. 90-408)

———

CONFEDERATED TRIBES AND BANDS OF THE
YAKIMA INDIAN NATION, Petitioner

v

COUNTY OF YAKIMA and DALE A. GRAY,
Yakima County Treasurer (No. 90-577)

502 US —, 116 L Ed 2d 687, 112 S Ct 683

Argued November 5, 1991.
Decided January 14, 1992.

Decision: Indian General Allotment Act of 1887 (25
USCS §§ 331 et seq.) held to permit county ad
valorem tax on fee-patented reservation land,
but not to allow county excise tax on sales of
such land.

SUMMARY

The Indian General Allotment Act of 1887, as
amended (25 USCS §§ 331 et seq.), empowered the
President of the United States to allot most tribal
lands to individual tribe members without the consent of the Indian nations involved; § 5 of the Act
(25 USCS § 348) provided that each allotted parcel
would be held by the United States in trust for at
least 25 years before a fee patent, free of any
encumbrance, would be issued to the Indian allottee, and § 6 of the Act (25 USCS § 349) provided

that upon receipt of a fee patent, an allottee would be subject to state laws, and that the Secretary of Interior could issue an allottee a fee patent prior to the expiration of the 25-year trust period, after which issuance all restrictions as to sale, encumbrance, or taxation of the allotted land would be removed. Although the Indian Reorganization Act of 1934 (25 USCS §§ 461 et seq.) halted further allotments and extended indefinitely the existing trust periods for allotted Indian lands, the Reorganization Act imposed no restraints on alienation or encumbrance of lands that already had been fee-patented under the Allotment Act. As a result of patents distributed during the allotment era, 20 percent of the Yakima Indian Reservation, which is located almost entirely within Yakima County in the state of Washington, is owned in fee by the Yakima Indian Nation, individual Indians, or non-Indians. When the county, which, pursuant to state law, imposed ad valorem taxes on real property in the county and excise taxes on the sales of such property, sought to foreclose on the reservation's fee lands for which ad valorem and excise taxes were past due, the Yakima Nation brought an action for declaratory and injunctive relief, contending that federal law prohibited these taxes on fee-patented lands held by the tribe or its members. The United States District Court for the Eastern District of Washington entered summary judgment for the tribe and entered an injunction prohibiting imposition or collection of taxes on the lands. The United States Court of Appeals for the Ninth Circuit (1) held that the excise tax was impermissible, but that the ad valorem tax was impermissible only if it had a demonstrably serious impact on the the tribe's political integrity, economic security, or health and welfare, and (2) remanded the case to the District Court to determine whether the tax had such an impact (903 F2d 1207).

On certiorari, the United States Supreme Court affirmed the judgment of the Court of Appeals and remanded the case for further proceedings. In an opinion by SCALIA, J., joined by REHNQUIST, Ch. J., and WHITE, STEVENS, O'CONNOR, KENNEDY, SOUTER, and THOMAS, JJ., it was held that the Allotment Act (1) permitted the county to impose the ad valorem tax, because (a) the Act authorized state taxation of fee-patented lands, (b) the tax constituted taxation of land within the meaning of the Act, and was therefore prima facie valid, and (c) the tribe did not have a protectable interest against imposition of the tax on tribe members, since the case involved not a proposed extension of the tribe's inherent powers, but an asserted restriction of the state's congressionally conferred powers; but (2) did not allow the county to impose the excise tax, because (a) the § 6 language referring to the taxation of land explicitly authorized only "taxation of . . . land," not "taxation with respect to land," "taxation of transactions involving land," or "taxation based on the value of land," and (b) since it was reasonable to interpret the language as not including a tax upon the sale of real estate, prior Supreme Court cases required the court to interpret § 6 for the benefit of the tribe.

BLACKMUN, J., concurring in part and dissenting in part, (1) agreed that the county could not impose excise taxes on Indian-owned fee-patented lands; but (2) expressed the view that the county also could not impose ad valorem taxes on such lands, because (a) the Allotment Act did not evince unmistakably clear intent to allow taxation of such lands, and (b) many intervening statutes reflected current

71

and longstanding federal policies weighing decisively against the court's finding that Congress had intended the states to tax Indian-held lands.

COUNSEL

Jeffrey C. Sullivan argued the cause for petitioners and cross-respondents.

Robert Wayne Bjur argued the cause for respondent and cross-petitioner.

Edwin S. Kneedler argued the cause, as amicus curiae, supporting respondent and cross-petitioner.

BARBARA J. NORMAN, et al., Petitioners

v

DOROTHY REED et al. (No. 90-1126)

COOK COUNTY OFFICERS ELECTORAL
BOARD, et al., Petitioners

v

DOROTHY REED et al. (No. 90-1435)

502 US —, 116 L Ed 2d 711, 112 S Ct 698

Argued October 7, 1991.
Decided January 14, 1992.

Decision: Illinois election laws, as construed to bar
new party from running county candidates for
lack of 25,000 petition signatures in each electoral district, held to violate First Amendment.

SUMMARY

Under Illinois statutes, organizers of a new political party must (1) canvass the electoral area where
they wish to run candidates; (2) when running
candidates for statewide office, obtain the signatures
of 1 percent of the voters at the last statewide
election or 25,000 voters, whichever is less; and (3)
when running candidates solely for offices within a
political subdivision of the state, circulate petitions
containing a complete list of candidates for all
offices to be filled in the subdivision at large, and
obtain signatures (a) from 5 percent of the voters at
the last election in the subdivision or 25,000 voters,
whichever is less, or (b) if the subdivision is divided

into separate districts from which some officers are elected, from 5 percent of the voters at the last election in each district or 25,000 voters, whichever is less. Also, an Illinois statute provides that new political parties may not bear the same name as any established party. A group of citizens sought (1) to expand the Harold Washington Party (HWP), which was already an established party in the city of Chicago, throughout Cook County—which was divided into one Chicago city district and one suburban district, each of which was large enough to require 25,000 signatures on new-party nominating petitions—and (2) to run candidates for at-large, city-district, and suburban-district county board seats in 1990. The citizens gathered 44,000 signatures from the city district, but only 7,800 signatures from the suburban district. Interested voters filed objections to the HWP petitions with the county electoral board, but the electoral board ruled that (1) the citizens were not barred from running for county offices under the HWP name because of the fact that a party of the same name already existed in the city, especially since the most recent HWP mayoral candidate had authorized the county candidates to use the party name; (2) the failure to collect 25,000 signatures from the suburban district disqualified the HWP from running candidates for suburban-district county board seats, but not for city-district and at-large seats; and (3) the HWP's failure to designate candidates for county judicial offices did not disqualify the entire HWP slate for county offices. The Circuit Court of Cook County, Illinois (1) affirmed the electoral board's ruling as to use of the HWP name, but (2) held that either the lack of sufficient signatures in the suburban district or the failure to designate judicial candidates was sufficient grounds to disqualify the entire HWP slate of candidates. On review, the Supreme Court of Illinois held, in a brief written order, that (1) the citizens were prohibited from using the HWP name, and (2) the failure to obtain sufficient signatures in the suburban district disqualified the entire slate of candidates.

On certiorari, the United States Supreme Court affirmed in part, reversed in part, and remanded the case for further proceedings. In an opinion by SOUTER, J., joined by REHNQUIST, Ch. J., and WHITE, BLACKMUN, STEVENS, O'CONNOR, and KENNEDY, JJ., it was held that (1) even though the election was over, the controversy was not moot; (2) the interpretation of the party-name rule as barring candidates from running for county offices under the name of the HWP was broader than necessary to advance electoral order and accordingly violated the citizens' right of political association under the Federal Constitution's First Amendment; (3) the interpretation of the petition requirements as disqualifying all of the HWP county candidates because of the lack of sufficient signatures from the suburban district also violated the citizens' First Amendment rights as not being the least restrictive means of advancing the state's interest in limiting ballot access to parties with demonstrated public support; (4) however, requiring the candidates for the suburban-district seats to obtain 25,000 signatures from the suburbs did not unduly burden their right to run for those seats under the HWP name, and the citizens could not cite obtaining the required signatures in the city district as a sufficient condition for running candidates in the suburban district; and (5) the constitutionality of the circuit court's ruling that the HWP candidates were also disqualified due to the lack of candidates for judicial offices would not be considered, because the Illinois Supreme Court had not addressed and decided that issue.

SCALIA, J., dissented, expressing the view that, given the absence of any challenge to the constitutionality of the statutory requirement that new parties run a complete slate of candidates in each district, there was no basis for ruling that the state cannot require 25,000 signatures for each district election in order for the HWP to run candidates for county office.

THOMAS, J., did not participate.

COUNSEL

Robert E. Pincham, Jr. argued the cause for petitioners in No. 90-1126.

Kenneth L. Gillis argued the cause for petitioners in No. 90-1435.

Gregory A. Adamski argued the cause for respondents.

SHIRLEY M. MOLZOF, Personal Representative of
the Estate of ROBERT E. MOLZOF, Petitioner

v

UNITED STATES

502 US —, 116 L Ed 2d 731, 112 S Ct 711

Argued November 4, 1991.
Decided January 14, 1992.

Decision: Federal Tort Claims Act ban on awards of
punitive damages (28 USCS § 2674) held to
apply to only damages legally considered punitive under traditional common-law principles.

SUMMARY

After a patient at a Veterans' Administration hospital in Wisconsin suffered irreversible brain damage and was left permanently comatose as a result
of negligence by hospital employees, the patient's
guardian ad litem filed an action on the patient's
behalf in a Federal District Court, which action
sought to recover damages from the United States
under the Federal Tort Claims Act (FTCA) (28
USCS §§ 2671-2680). The United States admitted
liability, and the case proceeded to a bench trial on
the issue of damages. The District Court (1) ordered the hospital to continue its free medical
services for the patient at the existing level of care,
(2) awarded damages of $75,750 for supplemental
care not provided by the hospital—physical and
respiratory therapy and doctor visits, (3) refused to
award damages for medical care that would dupli-
cate the free medical services being provided by the
hospital, and (4) declined to award damages for the

patient's loss of enjoyment of life. The patient died after the District Court's final judgment was entered, and his widow was substituted as plaintiff in her capacity as personal representative of his estate. The United States Court of Appeals for the Seventh Circuit affirmed the District Court's judgment, as the Court of Appeals—noting that the FTCA barred awards of punitive damages (28 USCS § 2674), and defining punitive damages as any damages in excess of those necessary to compensate victims or their survivors for the pecuniary loss suffered by reason of the tort—held that (1) since the government had provided free medical care to the patient and the widow appeared satisfied with that care, any additional award for future medical expenses would be punitive in effect and therefore was barred under § 2674, and (2) even assuming that a comatose patient can recover damages for loss of enjoyment of life under Wisconsin law, such damages could not redress the patient's loss and therefore were also barred as punitive (911 F2d 18).

On certiorari, the United States Supreme Court reversed the judgment of the Court of Appeals and remanded the case for further proceedings. In an opinion by Thomas, J., expressing the unanimous view of the court, it was held that (1) § 2674 bars the recovery of only what are legally considered "punitive damages" under traditional common-law principles—that is, damages which are intended to act as punishment for intentional or egregious conduct—and does not limit the United States' liability to compensatory damages for actual pecuniary losses; and (2) the damages for loss of enjoyment of life and for future medical expenses sought by the patient's estate were not punitive damages under the common law or under § 2674, because (a) their

78

recovery did not depend on any proof that the defendant had engaged in intentional or egregious misconduct, and (b) their purpose was not to punish.

COUNSEL

Daniel A. Rottier argued the cause for petitioner.
Christopher J. Wright argued the cause for respondent.

IMMIGRATION AND NATURALIZATION
SERVICE, Petitioner

v

JOSEPH PATRICK DOHERTY

502 US —, 116 L Ed 2d 823, 112 S Ct 719

Argued October 16, 1991.
Decided January 15, 1992.

Decision: Attorney General's denial of alien's motion to reopen deportation proceedings held not abuse of discretion.

SUMMARY

An alien who was a citizen of both Ireland and the United Kingdom, and who was a member of the Provisional Irish Republican Army, was tried in a Northern Ireland court for the murder of a British army officer in Northern Ireland. After escaping from prison and being convicted in absentia, the alien entered the United States illegally. The Immigration and Naturalization Service (INS) located him and began deportation hearings against him. At a hearing before an immigration judge in September 1986, the alien conceded deportability and, pursuant to 8 USCS § 1253(a), designated Ireland as the country to which he should be deported. In conjunction with this designation, the alien withdrew an application he had made for asylum and for withholding of deportation. The immigration judge, rejecting a challenge by the INS to the designation, ordered that the alien be deported to Ireland. The Board of Immigration Appeals (BIA) affirmed the deportation order in March 1987. The Federal Government appealed the BIA's determination to the

Attorney General. While the deportation order was being reviewed, the alien filed a motion to reopen his deportation proceedings on the ground that an extradition act implemented by Ireland in December 1987, under which the alien could be extradited from Ireland to the United Kingdom, constituted new evidence which required reopening of his claims for asylum and withholding of deportation under an INS regulation (8 CFR § 3.2) which provides that motions to reopen in deportation proceedings shall not be granted unless it appears that evidence sought to be offered is material and was not available and could not have been discovered or presented at the former hearing. The Attorney General, reversing the BIA's determination, (1) rejected the alien's designation of Ireland, (2) ordered the alien deported to the United Kingdom, and (3) remanded the alien's motion to reopen. On remand, the BIA granted the motion on the ground that the alien had produced new material evidence. On appeal, the BIA's decision to reopen was reversed by the Attorney General on the grounds that (1) the 1987 extradition act was not new evidence warranting reopening, given that the treaty upon which the act was based had been signed 6 months before the alien withdrew his asylum and withholding of deportation claims in 1986; (2) by withdrawing those claims, the alien had waived them; and (3) the alien's involvement in serious nonpolitical crimes in Northern Ireland made him statutorily ineligible for withholding of deportation and undeserving of the discretionary relief of asylum. On appeal, the United States Court of Appeals for the Second Circuit reversed the Attorney General's order that denied the motion to reopen, on the ground that the denial was an abuse of discretion (908 F2d 1108).

On certiorari, the United States Supreme Court reversed. REHNQUIST, Ch. J., announced the judgment of the court, and in a part of his opinion which constituted the opinion of the court and which was joined by WHITE, BLACKMUN, O'CONNOR, and KENNEDY, JJ., it was held that the Attorney General did not abuse his discretion in denying the alien's motion to reopen the deportation proceedings, either on the basis that the alien had failed to adduce new material evidence, or on the basis that the alien had not satisfactorily explained his previous withdrawal of the claims for asylum and withholding of deportation and thus had waived such claims. Also, REHNQUIST, Ch. J., joined by WHITE, BLACKMUN, and O'CONNOR, JJ., expressed the view that it was within the Attorney General's discretion to decide that neither the denial of the alien's designation nor the change in Irish extradition law qualified as new material evidence to support reopening. In addition, REHNQUIST, Ch. J., joined by KENNEDY, J., expressed the view that the Attorney General did not abuse his discretion by holding that (1) the alien had waived his claims for asylum and withholding of deportation by deliberately withdrawing such claims in the initial proceedings in order to obtain a tactical advantage, and (2) under applicable regulations, those claims could have been submitted in the initial proceedings even though they were inconsistent with other claims made by the alien.

SCALIA, J., joined by STEVENS and SOUTER, JJ., concurring in the judgment in part and dissenting in part, expressed the view that (1) the Attorney General's broad discretion to deny asylum justified his refusal to reopen the proceedings so that the alien might apply for that relief, but a similar rationale was not applicable to the denial of reopening for the withholding of deportation claim; (2) there was no waiver or procedural default with respect to the withholding of deportation claim; (3) the Attorney General abused his discretion in decreeing that, for reasons unrelated to the merits of the withholding of deportation claim, the alien would not be allowed reopening to apply for that relief; and (4) the case should have been remanded to the United States Court of Appeals for a detailed review of the factual record in order to determine whether the alien was statutorily ineligible for withholding of deportation.

THOMAS, J., did not participate.

COUNSEL

Maureen E. Mahoney argued the cause for petitioner.

Mary Boresz Pike argued the cause for respondent.

RANDALL D. WHITE, Petitioner

v

ILLINOIS

502 US —, 116 L Ed 2d 848, 112 S Ct 736

Argued November 5, 1991.
Decided January 15, 1992.

Decision: Admission of testimony against accused
under Illinois hearsay exceptions for spontaneous declarations and medical-treatment statements held not to violate Sixth Amendment's
confrontation clause.

SUMMARY

At the Illinois trial of an accused on charges
arising out of an alleged sexual assault on a child,
the child never testified, as (1) the state attempted
on two occasions to call the child as a witness, but
in each instance the child experienced emotional
difficulty and left without testifying; and (2) the
defense made no attempt to call the child as a
witness. The trial court neither made, nor was asked
to make, a specific finding that the child was unavailable to testify. Over the defense's objections,
however, the trial court, under the state's hearsay
exceptions for spontaneous declarations and for
statements made in the course of securing medical
treatment, permitted testimony by the child's baby-
sitter, the child's mother, an investigating officer, an
emergency room nurse, and a doctor, regarding
prior, out-of-court statements made by the child to
these individuals about the alleged assault. The
accused was found guilty of aggravated criminal

sexual assault, residential burglary, and unlawful restraint. On appeal, the Appellate Court of Illinois, Fourth District, in affirming the accused's conviction, ruled that (1) the trial court acted within its discretion under state law in admitting the child's hearsay statements; and (2) the admission of the statements did not violate the accused's right, under the confrontation clause of the Federal Constitution's Sixth Amendment, to confront the witnesses against him (198 Ill App 3d 641, 555 NE2d 1241). The Illinois Supreme Court denied discretionary review.

On certiorari, the United States Supreme Court affirmed. In an opinion by REHNQUIST, Ch. J., joined by WHITE, BLACKMUN, STEVENS, O'CONNOR, KENNEDY, and SOUTER, JJ., it was held that (1) the Sixth Amendment's confrontation clause applies to more out-of-court statements admitted under an accepted hearsay exception than those few statements in the character of ex parte affidavits—that is, where the circumstances surrounding the statements suggest that the statements were made for the principal purpose of accusing or incriminating a defendant—because such a narrow reading of the confrontation clause, which would virtually eliminate the clause's role in restricting the admission of hearsay testimony, is foreclosed by the Supreme Court's prior decisions, which have consistently sought to steer a middle course that recognizes that hearsay rules and the confrontation clause are generally designed to protect similar values and stem from the same roots; but (2) the confrontation clause does not require that before a criminal trial court, under the hearsay exceptions for spontaneous declarations and for statements made in the course of securing medical treatment, permits the prosecution to present testimony against an accused regarding a declarant's prior, out-of-court statements, either the prosecution must produce the declarant or the trial court must find that the declarant is unavailable, because (a) these two hearsay exceptions are firmly rooted, (b) the out-of-court statements admitted under the two exceptions are not themselves made in the course of a prior judicial proceeding, and have substantial probative value that cannot be duplicated simply by the declarant's later testifying in court, and (c) the establishment of a generally applicable unavailability rule would have few practical benefits while imposing pointless litigation costs; and (3) there is no basis under the confrontation clause to import a necessity requirement—to the effect that any confrontation restrictions must be necessary to protect a child's physical and psychological well-being—for in-court procedures once a child witness is testifying, to the much different context of a child's prior, out-of-court declarations admitted under established exceptions to the hearsay rule.

THOMAS, J., joined by SCALIA, J., concurring in part and concurring in the judgment, expressed the view that (1) the Supreme Court reached the correct result under the court's precedents; but (2) the court unnecessarily rejected in dicta the suggestion that the confrontation clause in general may not regulate the admission of hearsay evidence; (3) it would be possible to interpret the confrontation clause with a formulation to the effect that the federal constitutional right of confrontation (a) extends to any witness who actually testifies at trial, but (b) is implicated by extrajudicial statements only insofar as they are contained in formalized testimonial materials, such as affidavits, depositions, prior testimony, or confessions; and (4) such a formulation would (a) greatly simplify the inquiry in the hearsay context, and (b) avoid the problem posed by the court's current focus on hearsay exceptions that are "firmly rooted" in the common law.

COUNSEL

Gary R. Peterson argued the cause for petitioner.

Arleen C. Anderson argued the cause for respondent.

Stephen L. Nightingale argued the cause, as amicus curiae, supporting the respondent.

ROBERT C. RUFO, Sheriff of Suffolk County, et
al., Petitioners

v

INMATES OF THE SUFFOLK COUNTY JAIL et
al. (No. 90-954)

———

THOMAS C. RAPONE, Commissioner of
Correction of Massachusetts, Petitioner

v

INMATES OF THE SUFFOLK COUNTY JAIL et
al. (No. 90-1004)

502 US —, 116 L Ed 2d 867, 112 S Ct 748

Argued October 9, 1991.
Decided January 15, 1992.

Decision: Clear showing of grievous wrong evoked
by new and unforeseen conditions, held not
required, under Federal Civil Procedure Rule
60(b), to modify consent decree stemming from
institutional reform litigation.

SUMMARY

In 1971, inmates at a county jail in Suffolk
County, Massachusetts sued the county sheriff, the
state commissioner of corrections, the mayor of the
city of Boston, and nine city councilors, claiming
that inmates not yet convicted of the crimes charged
against them were being held at the jail under
conditions that violated the Federal Constitution.
Based on its holding that conditions at the jail were
constitutionally deficient, the United States District
88

Court for the District of Massachusetts permanently enjoined the government officials from housing a pretrial detainee in a cell with another inmate after a certain date, and from housing any pretrial detainees at the jail after a certain later date (360 F Supp 676). In 1978, the United States Court of Appeals for the First Circuit ordered that the jail be closed unless a plan was presented to create a constitutionally adequate facility for pretrial detainees in the county (573 F2d 98). In response to this order, the District Court was presented with a plan that formed the basis for a consent decree that was entered by the District Court in 1979. The decree, which called for construction of a new county jail that would provide inmates with single-occupancy cells, based the planned capacity of the new jail on a projected decline in inmate population. The case was later litigated in the state courts, and the government officials were ordered by the Supreme Judicial Court of Massachusetts to increase the planned capacity of the jail in response to the fact that the inmate population, rather than declining as projected, had increased (394 Mass 624, 477 NE2d 361). Afterward, the District Court, in 1985, modified the consent decree to permit the capacity of the new jail to be increased in any amount so long as the jail was designed for single-cell occupancy. Subsequently, while the jail was under construction, the county sheriff, based on the increase in the population of pretrial detainees, moved, under Rule 60(b) of the Federal Rules of Civil Procedure—which authorizes a court to relieve a party from a final judgment, order, or proceeding for certain reasons, which reasons are specified (1) in Rule 60(b)(5) as (a) satisfaction, release, or discharge of the judgment, (b) reversal or vacation of a prior judgment

89

on which the judgment is based, or (c) inequitability of continued prospective application of the judgment, and (2) in Rule 60(b)(6), as any other reason justifying such relief—to modify the consent decree to allow double bunking in some of the jail's cells. Holding that Rule 60(b)(5) codified the standard under which nothing less than a clear showing of grievous wrong evoked by new and unforeseen conditions should lead to a change in what was decreed after years of litigation with the consent of all concerned, and that the sheriff has failed to make a case for modification under the "grievous wrong" standard or under Rule 60(b)(6), the District Court refused to grant the requested modification (734 F Supp 561). The Court of Appeals affirmed the judgment of the District Court without elaboration (915 F2d 1557).

On certiorari, the United States Supreme vacated and remanded for further proceedings. In an opinion by WHITE, J., joined by REHNQUIST, Ch. J., and SCALIA, KENNEDY, and SOUTER, JJ., it was held that (1) the "grievous wrong" standard did not apply to requests under Rule 60(b) to modify consent decrees stemming from institutional reform litigation; (2) a District Court should exercise flexibility in considering such requests, because (a) the Rule, by providing that, on such terms as are just, a party may be relieved from a final judgment or decree where it is no longer equitable that the judgment have prospective application, permitted a flexible standard, (b) the recent upsurge in institutional reform litigation had made the ability of a District Court to modify a decree in response to changed circumstances all the more important, (c) since institutional reform consent decrees often remained in place for extended periods of time, the likelihood of significant changes occurring during the life of a decree was increased, (d) the experience of the Federal District Courts and Courts of Appeals in implementing and modifying such decrees had demonstrated that a flexible approach was often essential to achieving the goals of reform litigation, and (e) a flexible standard would not destroy the utility of consent decrees; and (3) under the flexible standard, a party, such as the sheriff, seeking modification of an institutional reform consent decree had to establish that a significant change in facts or law warranted revision of the decree, and that the party's proposed modification was suitably tailored to the changed circumstance.

O'CONNOR, J., concurred, expressing the view that (1) the Supreme Court's review of the District Court's decision concerning modification of the consent decree should examine primarily the District Court's method of exercising its substantial discretion rather than the District Court's result, (2) the District Court had abused its discretion by imposing on its discretion limits that did not legally exist, and (3) portions of the Supreme Court's opinion might be read to place on the District Court's discretion constraints that were as misplaced as the ones with which the District Court had fettered itself.

STEVENS, J., joined by BLACKMUN, J., dissenting, expressed the view that the District Court had not abused its discretion in refusing to modify the consent decree, because (1) the District Court's finding that the overcrowding problem faced by the sheriff was neither new nor unforeseen was amply supported by the record, (2) the strong public interest in protecting the finality of court decrees always counsels against modifications, and (3) allowing the requested modification would undermine a central purpose of the decree, which purpose was a prohibition against double celling.

THOMAS, J., did not participate.

COUNSEL

Chester A. Janiak argued the cause for petitioners in No. 90-954.

John T. Montgomery argued the cause for petitioners in No. 90-1004.

Max D. Stern argued the cause for respondents.

ALETHA DEWSNUP, Petitioner

v

LOUIS L. TIMM et al.

502 US —, 116 L Ed 2d 903, 112 S Ct 773

Argued October 15, 1991.

Decided January 15, 1992.

Decision: Debtor in bankruptcy held not entitled under 11 USCS § 506(d) to "strip down" creditor's lien on real property to judicially determined value of collateral.

SUMMARY

A couple took out a loan for $119,000, which loan was accompanied by a deed of trust granting the creditors a lien on two parcels of farmland owned by the couple. The couple defaulted on the loan, and 2 years later the creditors issued a notice of default. Before a foreclosure sale could take place, the couple filed two successive petitions for reorganization under Chapter 11 of the Bankruptcy Code (11 USCS §§ 1101-1174), each of which was dismissed, and then filed a petition for liquidation under Chapter 7 of the Bankruptcy Code (11 USCS §§ 701-766); and the pendency of these bankruptcy proceedings prevented the creditors from proceeding with the foreclosure sale. The couple subsequently filed an adversary proceeding in the United States Bankruptcy Court for the District of Utah, which proceeding sought to avoid the portion of the creditors' lien which exceeded the fair market value of the land, pursuant to 11 USCS § 506(d)—which provided that a lien was void to the extent that it

93

secured a claim against the debtor that was not an "allowed secured claim"—on the theory that the excess portion of the lien was not an allowed secured claim within the meaning of 11 USCS § 506(a), which provided that an "allowed claim" secured by a lien on property in which the estate has an interest is a "secured claim" to the extent of the value of the creditor's interest in the estate's interest in such property. The Bankruptcy Court denied the requested relief, as the court (1) assumed that the land in question had been or would be abandoned by the bankruptcy trustee, since the couple otherwise would not have standing to bring such a proceeding, and (2) concluded that the land was not property in which the estate had an interest and therefore was not covered by § 506(d) (87 BR 676). The United States District Court for the District of Utah summarily affirmed the Bankruptcy Court's judgment of dismissal with prejudice; and the United States Court of Appeals for the Tenth Circuit affirmed the judgment of the District Court on the ground that the estate had no interest in the abandoned property (908 F2d 588).

On certiorari, the United States Supreme Court affirmed. In an opinion by BLACKMUN, J., joined by REHNQUIST, Ch. J., and WHITE, STEVENS, O'CONNOR, and KENNEDY, JJ., it was held that the couple could not "strip down" the creditors' lien to the value of the collateral, under the circumstances presented, because (1) the contrasting positions taken by the parties and amici curiae in argument before the Supreme Court demonstrate that § 506 and its relationship to other provisions of the Bankruptcy Code embrace some ambiguities; (2) although the court, if it were writing on a clean slate, might be inclined to agree that the words "allowed secured claim" must take the same meaning in § 506(d) as in § 506(a), Congress must have enacted the Code with a full understanding of the prior rule that liens pass through bankruptcy unaffected, and, given the ambiguity in the text, the court was not convinced that Congress intended to depart from that rule; and (3) although not without difficulty, the best of the several suggested approaches to interpreting § 506 was that the words "allowed secured claim" in § 506(d) need not be read as an indivisible term of art defined by reference to § 506(a) but should be read term-by-term to refer to any claim that was, first, "allowed"—as the claim in the case at hand had been pursuant to 11 USCS § 502—and second, "secured," thereby voiding liens only when the claims they secure have not been allowed.

SCALIA, J., joined by SOUTER, J., dissented, expressing the view that (1) the phrase "allowed secured claim" in § 506(d) clearly referred to the allowed "secured claim" described in § 506(a); (2) the interpretation of "allowed secured claim" endorsed by the Supreme Court rendered § 506(d)'s phrase "[t]o the extent that a lien secures a claim" mere surplusage; (3) the reasoning of the Court of Appeals was fallacious because the application of § 506(a), and hence of § 506(d), cannot be undone if and when the estate ceases to have an interest in property in which it had an interest at the outset of the bankruptcy proceeding; (4) the Supreme Court's view that the conflicting interpretations of § 506 demonstrated the ambiguity of the statute would make any litigated statute ambiguous; and (5) pre-Bankruptcy Code practice has never been held to be determinative in the face of contradictory statutory text.

THOMAS, J., did not participate.

COUNSEL

Timothy B. Dyk argued the cause for petitioner.

Richard G. Taranto argued the cause for respondents.

Ronald J. Mann argued the cause for the United States, as amicus curiae, supporting respondents.

STATE OF WYOMING, Plaintiff

v

STATE OF OKLAHOMA

502 US —, 117 L Ed 2d 1, 112 S Ct 789

Argued November 4, 1991.
Decided January 22, 1992.

Decision: Oklahoma statute requiring coal-fired electric utilities to burn mixture containing at least 10 percent Oklahoma-mined coal held to violate Federal Constitution's commerce clause (Art I, § 8, cl 3).

SUMMARY

Although the state of Wyoming does not itself sell coal, it assesses a severance tax, based on the fair market value of extracted coal, on those who extract coal from land in Wyoming. From 1981 through 1986, virtually 100 percent of the coal purchased by four Oklahoma electric utilities, of which three were privately owned and one was a state agency, had been extracted from Wyoming by the mining companies that sold the coal to the utilities. After the January 1, 1987 effective date of an Oklahoma statute requiring coal-fired electric utilities in Oklahoma to burn a mixture containing at least 10 percent Oklahoma-mined coal, the utilities reduced their purchase of Wyoming-mined coal in favor of Oklahoma-mined coal, and Wyoming's 1987 and 1988 severance tax revenues were more than $500,-000 per year lower than they had been prior to 1987. Wyoming filed in the United States Supreme Court an original bill of complaint seeking (1) a

97

declaration that the Oklahoma statute violated the Federal Constitution's commerce clause (Art I, § 8, cl 3), and (2) a permanent injunction against enforcement of the statute. After several Supreme Court decisions and orders as to various issues in the case, a Special Master who had been appointed by the court recommended findings of fact and conclusions of law generally supporting Wyoming's motion for summary judgment and rejecting Oklahoma's motion for summary judgment. The Special Master issued a report recommending that the court (1) hold that (a) Wyoming had standing to sue, (b) the case was appropriate to the court's original jurisdiction, and (c) because the statute discriminated against interstate commerce on its face and in practical effect, and because the discrimination was not justified by any purpose advanced by Oklahoma, the statute violated the commerce clause; and (2) either dismiss the action as it related to the Oklahoma-owned utility without prejudice to Wyoming to assert its claim in an appropriate forum, or, alternatively, find the statute severable to the extent that it could constitutionally be applied to that utility.

On exceptions to the report of the Special Master, the Supreme Court adopted the Special Master's recommended findings of fact and, with one exception, his recommended conclusions of law; denied Oklahoma's motion for summary judgment; granted Wyoming's motion for summary judgment; stated that a judgment and decree enjoining enforcement of the state statute would be entered; and retained continuing jurisdiction over the case. In an opinion by WHITE, J., joined by BLACKMUN, STEVENS, O'CONNOR, KENNEDY, and SOUTER, JJ., it was held that (1) Wyoming had standing to bring the complaint, because (a) the case involved a substantial direct injury in the form of a loss of specific tax revenues, and (b) the loss fairly could be traced to the Oklahoma statute; (2) the case was appropriate for the court's discretionary exercise of its original jurisdiction, because Wyoming had raised a claim of sufficient seriousness and dignity to make such an exercise obligatory, since (a) Wyoming's challenge under the commerce clause precisely implicated serious and important concerns of federalism fully in accord with the purposes and reach of the court's original jurisdiction, (b) Wyoming's claim was substantial and touched on a direct injury to the state, (c) there were no assurances that Wyoming's interests under the Constitution would find another forum for appropriate hearing and full relief, and (d) the amount in controversy was not too small to support the exercise of jurisdiction; and (3) the Oklahoma statute was invalid under the commerce clause, because (a) the statute discriminated, facially and in practical effect, against interstate commerce, (b) Oklahoma had failed to justify the statute in terms of the local benefits flowing from it and the unavailability of nondiscriminatory alternatives adequate to preserve those benefits, and (c) the Federal Power Act's "saving clause" (16 USCS § 824(b)(1)), which reserved to the states the regulation of local retail electric rates, did not make permissible the Oklahoma statute's discriminatory impact on the movement on Wyoming coal in interstate commerce.

SCALIA, J., joined by REHNQUIST, Ch. J., and THOMAS, J., dissented, expressing the view that (1) the court's rejection, at two points in the proceedings prior to the appointment of the Special Master, of Oklahoma's assertion that Wyoming lacked standing to challenge the Oklahoma statute did not impede the court from considering that assertion when it was made as an exception to the Special Master's report; (2) Wyoming had not established the "injury in fact" required for standing under Article III; and (3) even if Wyoming had established an injury in fact, it did not have standing to bring the suit, because the injury complained of did not fall within the zone of interests sought to be protected by the commerce clause.

THOMAS, J., joined by REHNQUIST, Ch. J., and SCALIA, J., dissented, expressing the view that, even if Wyoming had standing to challenge the Oklahoma statute, the court should have declined to exercise its original jurisdiction over the case, because (1) Wyoming's alleged injury was entirely derivative of private Wyoming mining companies' reduced sales to Oklahoma utilities, and (2) Wyoming had advanced no reason why the mining companies did not or could not themselves challenge the statute in another, more convenient, forum.

COUNSEL

Neal Leader argued the cause for plaintiff.
Mary B. Guthrie argued the cause for defendant.

IMMIGRATION AND NATURALIZATION
SERVICE, Petitioner

v

JAIRO JONATHAN ELIAS-ZACARIAS

502 US —, 117 L Ed 2d 38, 112 S Ct 812

Argued November 4, 1991.
Decided January 22, 1992.

Decision: Guatemalan guerrillas' attempt to coerce
Guatemalan into military service held not necessarily to constitute persecution on account of
political opinion so as to make Guatemalan
eligible for asylum in United States.

SUMMARY

A Guatemalan native was apprehended for entering the United States without inspection, and the
Immigration and Naturalization Service brought
proceedings to deport him. The Guatemalan conceded his deportability, but requested asylum as a
refugee under §§ 101(a)(42) and 208(a) of the Immigration and Nationality Act (8 USCS §§ 1101(a)
(42), 1158(a)). In support of his request, the Guatemalan testified that (1) two armed, uniformed guerrillas had come to his home in Guatemala and asked
him and his parents to join with them; (2) when he
and his parents refused, the guerrillas had asked
why, had said that they would be back, and had told
the family that they should think it over; (3) he did
not want to join the guerrillas because they were
against the government and because he was afraid
that the government would retaliate against his
family; and (4) he had left Guatemala because he

was afraid that the guerrillas would return. The
Immigration Judge concluded that the Guatemalan
had failed to demonstrate persecution or a well-
founded fear of persecution on account of race,
religion, nationality, membership in a particular
social group, or political opinion within the terms of
§ 101(a)(42), and thus was not eligible for asylum.
The Board of Immigration Appeals (BIA) summarily
dismissed the Guatemalan's appeal on procedural
grounds, and denied his motion to reopen the
deportation proceeding so that he could submit new
evidence that the guerrillas had twice returned to
his home in continued efforts to recruit him. However, the United States Court of Appeals for the
Ninth Circuit, treating the BIA's second ruling as an
affirmance on the merits of the Immigration Judge's
decision, reversed, as the court held that acts of
conscription by a nongovernmental group constitute
persecution on account of political opinion and that
the Guatemalan had a well-founded fear of such
conscription (921 F2d 844).

On certiorari, the United States Supreme Court
reversed the judgment of the Court of Appeals. In
an opinion by SCALIA, J., joined by REHNQUIST,
Ch. J., and WHITE, KENNEDY, SOUTER, and THOMAS,
JJ., it was held that a guerrilla organization's attempt to coerce a person into performing military
service does not necessarily constitute persecution
on account of political opinion within the meaning
of § 101(a)(42), and that the determination of the
BIA in the case at hand, therefore, should have
been upheld, because (1) in order to reverse the
BIA's determination, a reviewing court would have
to find that the evidence (a) not only supported but
compelled the conclusion that the Guatemalan's
refusal to join the guerrillas was a form of expres-

sive conduct that constituted the statement of a
political opinion, and (b) compelled the further
conclusion that the Guatemalan had a well-founded
fear that the guerrillas would persecute him because
of that political opinion; (2) a person resisting
forced recruitment by guerrillas is not thereby expressing a political opinion hostile to the guerrillas,
and the record in the case at hand (a) showed that
the Guatemalan had had a nonpolitical motive for
refusing to join the guerrillas, and (b) did not show
—even if this would suffice—that the guerrillas had
erroneously believed that the Guatemalan's refusal
was politically based; (3) even if the evidence compelled the conclusion that the Guatemalan had held
a political opinion, he would have to establish that
the record also compelled the conclusion that the
guerrillas would persecute him because of that opinion rather than because of his refusal to fight with
them, a point which he had not established with the
necessary degree of clarity; and (4) the fact that the
guerrillas had had a political motive for seeking
recruits did not render the forced recruitment a
persecution on account of political opinion but
instead went far to refute the proposition that the
Guatemalan feared persecution on account of political opinion.

STEVENS, J., joined by BLACKMUN and O'CONNOR,
JJ., dissented, expressing the view that (1) the record in this case was more than adequate to support
the conclusion that the Guatemalan's refusal to join
the guerrillas was a form of expressive conduct that
constituted a statement of political opinion within
the meaning of the Act; and (2) the guerrillas'
implied threat to take or kill the Guatemalan if he

103

did not change his position therefore constituted threatened persecution on account of political opinion.

COUNSEL

Maureen E. Mahoney argued the cause for petitioner.

James Robertson argued the cause for respondent.

———

LAWRENCE C. PRESLEY, Appellant

v

ETOWAH COUNTY COMMISSION et al.
(No. 90-711)

———

ED PETER MACK and NATHANIEL GOSHA, III,
Appellants

v

RUSSELL COUNTY COMMISSION et al.
(No. 90-712)

502 US —, 117 L Ed 2d 51, 112 S Ct 820

Argued November 12, 1991.
Decided January 27, 1992.

Decision: Changes in decisionmaking powers of elected members of Alabama county commissions held not to be changes with respect to voting subject to preclearance requirements of § 5 of Voting Rights Act (42 USCS § 1973c).

SUMMARY

In the two Alabama counties of Etowah and Russell, voters elected county commissions whose principal function was to supervise and control the maintenance, repair, and construction of county roads. Prior to 1986, the Etowah County Commission consisted of five members elected at large, with four of the members required to reside in separate districts which also functioned as road districts; and, while the commission voted collectively on the division of funds among those districts, spending priorities within each district were controlled by the resident commissioners. However, in 1987—after the Etowah County Commission was restructured, pursuant to a federal court's consent decree, to consist of six members elected by the voters of separate districts, and after two new commissioners, one of them black, were elected—the four holdover commissioners passed a resolution placing all moneys for road repair, maintenance, and improvement in a common fund, to be used countywide according to need rather than allocated among the districts. In Russell County, prior to 1979, the rural members of the county commission—then consisting of three members elected at large from rural residency districts and two members elected at large from an urban residency district—had individual authority over road repair and maintenance; but a corruption scandal was followed by the passage of a 1979 resolution removing that authority and delegating all such functions to a county engineer who was appointed by and accountable to the commission as a whole. In 1986, with the implementation of a district-by-district election scheme, Russell County elected its first black commissioners in modern times. The Etowah and Russell County resolutions, and an Alabama statute implementing the Russell County resolution, were never submitted to the federal courts or to the United States Department of Justice for preclearance pursuant to § 5 of the Voting Rights Act of 1965 (42 USCS § 1973c). The newly elected black commissioners from both counties filed a single complaint in the United States District Court for the Middle District of Alabama, which complaint alleged racial discrimination in violation of the Federal Constitution and various federal statutes including § 5. The District Court, however, ruled that neither the Etowah County "common fund" resolution nor the adoption of the county engineer system in Russell County were subject to preclearance under § 5.

On appeal, the United States Supreme Court affirmed. In an opinion by KENNEDY, J., joined by REHNQUIST, Ch. J., and O'CONNOR, SCALIA, SOUTER, and THOMAS, JJ., it was held that (1) the preclearance requirements of § 5 do not apply to changes which affect only the distribution of power among officials, and specifically do not apply to the Etowah County Commission's "common fund" resolution, because (a) the resolution has no connection to voting procedures, (b) the resolution has no bearing on the substance of voting power, and (c) an argument that the resolution is a covered change under § 5, on the theory that the enactment of the resolution leaves each commissioner with less individual power and therefore diminishes the value of votes cast for the commissioners, would work an unconstrained expansion of § 5's coverage, as innumerable state and local enactments having nothing to do with voting affect the power of elected officials; and (2) the adoption of the county engineer system in Russell County is not a change covered by § 5, because (a) the transfer of operations to the county engineer is not a change involving the manner of voting, candidacy requirements and qualifications, or the composition of the electorate, and (b) although the delegation of authority to an appointed official is arguably similar to the replacement of an elected official with an appointed one, a type of change which has been held to be covered by § 5, (i) the county commission is still subject to election by the voters and still retains substantial authority, and (ii) though the commissioner's direct authority was reduced, such alteration in an elected official's powers is not in itself a rule governing voting within the scope of § 5.

STEVENS, J., joined by WHITE and BLACKMUN, JJ., dissented, expressing the view that (1) any resolution that reallocates decisionmaking power by means of transferring authority from an elected district representative to an official or group controlled by the majority has a potential for discrimination against the constituents in the disadvantaged districts and is therefore subject to § 5, a rule that would require preclearance of both the Russell County resolution and the Etowah County resolution; and (2) at the very least, the reallocation of decisionmaking authority of an elective office that occurs after the victory of a black candidate, and after the entry of a consent decree designed to give black voters an opportunity to have representation on an elective body, is covered by § 5, a rule that would require preclearance of the Etowah County resolution.

COUNSEL

Edward Still argued the cause for appellants.

Robert A. Long, Jr. argued the cause for the United States, as amicus curiae, supporting the appellants.

Paul M. Smith argued the cause for appellees.

LECHMERE, INC., Petitioner

v

NATIONAL LABOR RELATIONS BOARD

502 US —, 117 L Ed 2d 79, 112 S Ct 841

Argued November 12, 1991.

Decided January 27, 1992.

Decision: Store owner held not to have committed unfair labor practice under § 8(a)(1) of National Labor Relations Act (29 USCS § 158(a)(1)) by barring nonemployee union organizers from parking lot.

SUMMARY

A retail store was located in a shopping plaza within the metropolitan area of Hartford, Connecticut. All of the store's 200 employees lived in the Hartford metropolitan area; none of them lived on the store owner's property. The store owner was a joint owner of the shopping plaza's parking lot, which was separated from a public highway by a 46-foot-wide grassy strip, almost all of which was public property. In a campaign to organize the store employees, a union inserted a full-page advertisement in a Hartford newspaper, but the advertisement drew little response. Subsequently, union organizers who were not store employees entered the parking lot and placed handbills on the windshields of cars parked in a corner of the lot that was used mostly by the store employees. Each time this occurred, store personnel asked the organizers to leave and the handbills were removed. The organizers relocated to the grassy strip, from where they displayed

picket signs over a period of 7 months. The organizers were able to secure the names and addresses
of 41 employees, approximately 20 percent of the
total. The union sent four mailings to these employees and made some attempts to contact them by
phone or by home visits. These efforts resulted in
only one signed union authorization card. Alleging
that the store owner had violated § 8(a)(1) of the
National Labor Relations Act (NLRA) (29 USCS
§ 158(a)(1)) by barring the organizers from the
parking lot, the union filed an unfair labor practice
charge with the National Labor Relations Board
(NLRB). An administrative law judge ruled in the
union's favor. The NLRB, affirming, (1) applied a
standard under which (a) the employees' rights
under § 7 of the NLRA (29 USCS § 157)—which
guarantees employees the right of self-organization
—were balanced against the store owner's property
rights, and (b) the availability of reasonably effective
alternative means of communication was considered;
(2) found that the union had no such alternative
means available; and (3) held that the store owner
was required by § 7 to grant access to the organizers. On appeal, the United States Court of Appeals
for the First Circuit denied the store owner's petition for review and enforced the NLRB's order (914
F2d 313).

On certiorari, the United States Supreme Court
reversed the Court of Appeals' judgment and denied enforcement of the NLRB's order. In an opinion by THOMAS, J., joined by REHNQUIST, Ch. J., and
O'CONNOR, SCALIA, KENNEDY, and SOUTER, JJ., it was
held that (1) under § 7 of the NLRA, an employer
cannot be compelled to allow distribution of union
literature by nonemployee organizers on the employer's property, unless the location of the plant
110

and the living quarters of the employees place the employees beyond the reach of reasonable union efforts to communicate with them through the usual channels; (2) the store owner was not required by § 7 to allow distribution of union literature by non-employee union organizers on store property, and thus the store owner did not commit an unfair labor practice under § 8 of the NLRA by barring the organizers from the parking lot, given that (a) the fact that the employees did not reside on the store owner's property meant that they were presumptively not beyond the reach of the union's message, (b) the fact that the employees lived in a large metropolitan area did not, in itself, render the employees inaccessible so as to justify trespass by the organizers on the store owner's property, and (c) under the circumstances, the existence of unique obstacles frustrating the union's access to the employees was not established; and (3) the NLRB's conclusion that there was no reasonable, effective alternative means available for the union to communicate its message to the employees rested on erroneous legal foundations and could not be accepted by the Supreme Court.

WHITE, J., joined by BLACKMUN, J., dissenting, expressed the view that (1) circumstances other than inaccessibility of employees may warrant the entry of nonemployee union organizers into an employer's parking lot under §§ 7 and 8(a)(1) of the NLRA; (2) no prior showing regarding reasonable alternatives should be required as a precondition to any inquiry that balances employees' § 7 rights and the employer's property rights; (3) the Supreme Court, announcing in NLRB v Babcock & Wilcox Co. (1956) 351 US 105, 100 L Ed 975, 76 S Ct 679, that nonemployee organizers are treated less favorably under § 7 than employees, wrongly failed to defer to the NLRB's contrary position; and (4) the Supreme Court should have deferred, in the case at hand, to the NLRB's construction of § 7 and the NLRB's conclusion that the union had no reasonable alternatives.

STEVENS, J., dissenting, expressed the view that (1) the Court of Appeals' judgment should have been affirmed for the first two reasons stated by WHITE, J.; and (2) the majority's strict construction of NLRB v Babcock and Wilcox Co., supra, was not consistent with subsequent Supreme Court cases; but (3) the central holding in the Babcock and Wilcox case—rejecting the NLRB's view that the rules applicable to union organizing draw no distinction between employees and nonemployees— was correct and was not inconsistent with the current law of deference to administrative agencies.

COUNSEL

Robert P. Joy argued the cause for petitioner.

Michael R. Dreeben argued the cause for respondent.

————————

KEITH J. HUDSON, Petitioner

v

JACK McMILLIAN et al.

503 US —, 117 L Ed 2d 156, 112 S Ct 995

Argued November 13, 1991.
Decided February 25, 1992.

Decision: Prisoner held able to maintain claim of cruel and unusual punishment under Federal Constitution's Eighth Amendment based on officers' excessive use of force not resulting in serious injury.

SUMMARY

An inmate in a Louisiana state penitentiary sued three corrections security officers under 42 USCS § 1983 in the United States District Court for the Middle District of Louisiana. Claiming that the officers had violated the cruel and unusual punishment clause of the Federal Constitution's Eighth Amendment, the inmate alleged that (1) one officer, after arguing with the inmate, punched the inmate in the mouth, eyes, chest, and stomach while another officer held the inmate in place and kicked and punched him from behind, (2) the third officer, who was the supervisor on duty, watched the beating but merely told the other officers "not to have too much fun," and (3) as a result of the beating, the inmate suffered minor bruises and swelling of his face, mouth, and lip, and the blows also loosened the inmate's teeth and cracked his partial dental plate. The parties consented to disposition of the case by a United States Magistrate, who found that the first

113

two officers had used force when there was no need
to do so and that the supervising officer had expressly condoned their actions. The inmate was
awarded damages of $800. On appeal, the United
States Court of Appeals for the Fifth Circuit reversed on the grounds that (1) prisoners who allege
use of excessive force in violation of the Eighth
Amendment must prove significant injury, and (2)
although the officers' use of force was objectively
unreasonable and clearly excessive and occasioned
unnecessary and wanton infliction of pain, the inmate could not prevail on his claim because his
injuries were minor and required no medical attention (929 F2d 1014).

On certiorari, the United States Supreme Court
reversed. In an opinion by O'CONNOR, J., joined by
REHNQUIST, Ch. J., and WHITE, KENNEDY, and
SOUTER, JJ., and joined in part (except for point 1
below) by STEVENS, J., it was held that (1) for
purposes of establishing whether prison officials
have inflicted unnecessary and wanton pain and
suffering on a prisoner so as to violate the prisoner's rights under the cruel and unusual punishment
clause, where the officials are accused of using
excessive physical force, the core judicial inquiry is
whether force was applied (a) in a good-faith effort
to maintain or restore discipline, or (b) maliciously
and sadistically to cause harm; (2) in order to
establish a violation of the cruel and unusual punishment clause based on a claim of excessive use of
force by prison officers, a prisoner who shows unnecessary and wanton infliction of pain is not required to show serious injury, given that (a) the
absence of serious injury, although relevant to the
inquiry as to whether the use of force violated the
Eighth Amendment, does not end that inquiry, and

114

(b) contemporary standards of decency are always violated when prison officials maliciously and sadistically use force to cause harm, regardless of whether significant injury is evident; and (3) the blows allegedly directed at the inmate by the security officers were not de minimis for Eighth Amendment purposes, and the extent of the inmate's alleged injuries provided no basis for dismissal of the inmate's claim against the officers under 42 USCS § 1983.

STEVENS, J., concurring in part and concurring in the judgment, expressed the view that (1) the "unnecessary and wanton infliction of pain" standard, rather than the "malicious and sadistic" standard, should be applied to determine whether injuries to prisoners that are inflicted absent a prison disturbance constitute cruel and unusual punishment; (2) the officers' attack on the inmate in the case at hand resulted in the infliction of unnecessary and wanton pain; and (3) although reliance on the malicious and sadistic standard in the case at hand was misplaced, even this more demanding standard was met.

BLACKMUN, J., concurring in the judgment, (1) agreed that the Eighth Amendment does not require a showing of significant injury in the excessive-force context, and (2) expressed the view that (a) the malicious and sadistic standard should not be extended to all allegations of excessive force, even outside the context of a prison riot, (b) a significant injury requirement was not necessary to curb the number of court filings by prison inmates, and (c) the court's opinion did not limit injury cognizable under the Eighth Amendment to physical injury.

THOMAS, J., joined by SCALIA, J., dissenting, expressed the view that (1) a use of force that causes only insignificant harm to a prisoner is not cruel and unusual punishment; (2) the Eighth Amendment applies to only a narrow class of deprivations involving serious injury inflicted by prison officials acting with a culpable state of mind; (3) there was no justification for applying the malicious and sadistic standard to all excessive force cases, without regard to the constraints facing prison officials; and (4) the appropriate federal constitutional inquiry in the case at hand would have been whether any available state remedies were adequate under the due process clause of the Fourteenth Amendment.

COUNSEL

Alvin J. Bronstein argued the cause for petitioner.

John G. Roberts, Jr. argued the cause for the United States, as amicus curiae, in support of the petitioner.

Harry McCall, Jr. argued the cause for respondents.

UNITED STATES, Petitioner

v

NORDIC VILLAGE, INC., DAVID O. SIMON,
Trustee

503 US —, 117 L Ed 2d 181, 112 S Ct 1011

Argued December 9, 1991.
Decided February 25, 1992.

Decision: Sovereign immunity of United States held
not unequivocally waived with respect to bankruptcy trustee's claim against Internal Revenue
Service for monetary relief.

SUMMARY

After a corporation filed a petition for relief
under Chapter 11 of the Bankruptcy Code (11
USCS §§ 1101-1174), an officer and shareholder of
the corporation drew a $26,000 check on the corpo-
rate account and used $20,000 of that money to
obtain a cashier's check payable to the Internal
Revenue Service (IRS). As directed, the IRS applied
these funds against the officer's individual tax liability. The bankruptcy trustee appointed for the corporation subsequently commenced an adversary proceeding in the United States Bankruptcy Court for
the Northern District of Ohio, which proceeding
sought to recover, among other transfers, the $20,-
000 paid by the officer to the IRS. Determining that
the officer's unauthorized postpetition transfer could
be avoided under 11 USCS § 549(a) and recovered
from the IRS under 11 USCS § 550(a), the Bankruptcy Court entered judgment against the IRS in
the amount of $20,000. The United States District

Court for the Northern District of Ohio affirmed.
The United States Court of Appeals for the Sixth
Circuit, in affirming, rejected a defense, raised for
the first time on appeal, that sovereign immunity
barred the judgment entered against the government, as the court found that the sovereign immunity of the United States had been waived by 11
USCS § 106(c)—which states that notwithstanding
any assertion of sovereign immunity, (1) any provision of the Bankruptcy Code which contains the
terms "creditor," "entity," or "governmental unit"
applies to governmental units, and (2) a determination by the court of an issue arising under a Code
provision binds governmental units (915 F2d 1049).

On certiorari, the United States Supreme Court
reversed. In an opinion by SCALIA, J., joined by
REHNQUIST, Ch. J., and WHITE, O'CONNOR, KEN-
NEDY, SOUTER, and THOMAS, JJ., it was held that
neither § 106(c) nor any other provision of law
establishes an unequivocal textual waiver of the
United States Government's immunity from a bankruptcy trustee's claims for monetary relief, as (1)
§ 106(c), though expressly waiving sovereign immunity, fails to establish unambiguously that the waiver
extends to monetary claims, as (a) the language of
§ 106(c) is susceptible of at least two interpretations
that do not authorize monetary relief, and (b) legislative history has no bearing on the ambiguity point;
(2) 28 USCS § 1334(d), which grants the Federal
District Court in which a bankruptcy case is initiated
exclusive jurisdiction over the property of the
debtor and the estate, does not thereby empower a
Bankruptcy Court to compel the United States to
return any property that passes into the estate upon
commencement of the bankruptcy proceeding; (3) a
Bankruptcy Court's in rem jurisdiction does not
118

override sovereign immunity, and the premise for such an argument was missing in the case at hand because the Bankruptcy Court below did not purport to exercise in rem jurisdiction; and (4) resort to the principles of trust law was of no help to the trustee under the circumstances presented.

STEVENS, J., joined by BLACKMUN, J., dissented, expressing the view that (1) the literal text of § 106(c) unquestionably foreclosed the defense of sovereign immunity in the case at hand; (2) the legislative history unambiguously demonstrates that Congress intended § 106(c) to be read literally; and (3) the court's insistence on clear statements of waiver with respect to sovereign immunity, which is merely a judgemade doctrine, burdens the Congress with unnecessary re-enactment of provisions that are already plain enough when read literally, and imposes substantial and unfortunate costs on litigants, the legislature, and the public at large.

COUNSEL

Richard H. Seamon argued the cause for petitioner.

Marvin A. Sicherman argued the cause for respondent.

HOLYWELL CORPORATION, et al., Petitioners

v

FRED STANTON SMITH, etc., et al. (No. 90-1361)

———

UNITED STATES, Petitioner

v

FRED STANTON SMITH et al. (No. 90-1484)

503 US —, 117 L Ed 2d 196, 112 S Ct 1021

Argued December 4, 1991.
Decided February 25, 1992.

Decision: Trustee liquidating and distributing property as part of plan under Chapter 11 of Bankruptcy Code held required, as to income attributable to property, to file federal income tax returns and pay tax.

SUMMARY

Corporate debtors and an affiliated individual debtor each filed bankruptcy petitions under Chapter 11 of the Bankruptcy Code (11 USCS §§ 1101 et seq.). The Bankruptcy Court for the Southern District of Florida consolidated the cases, and, prior to confirmation of a Chapter 11 reorganization plan, the debtors represented their own bankruptcy estates as debtors in possession. In August 1985, creditors approved a consolidated reorganization plan that placed all property of the debtors' estates into a trust, provided for appointment of a trustee to liquidate the property and distribute it to the creditors, and permitted the debtors to remain in
120

business. The plan said nothing about whether the trustee had to file federal income tax returns with respect to income attributable to the property or had to pay any income tax due as a result of such income. The United States did not object to the plan's confirmation, and the plan took effect on October 10, 1985. One of the corporate debtors filed for the fiscal year ending July 31, 1985 a federal income tax return that included capital gains derived from the postbankruptcy sale of certain property of the debtors' estates. The debtor asked the trustee to pay the taxes owed on this income. Although the estates subsequently derived income that included capital gains and interest, neither the corporate debtors nor the trustee filed federal income tax returns for any fiscal year ending after July 31, 1985. Over the opposition of the United States and the debtors, the Bankruptcy Court granted the trustee's request for a declaratory judgment that the trustee had no duty under the federal income tax laws to file income tax returns or pay income tax (85 BR 898). The United States District Court for the Southern District of Florida, in an unreported opinion, affirmed the Bankruptcy Court judgment, and the United States Court of Appeals for the Eleventh Circuit affirmed the District Court judgment (911 F2d 1539).

On certiorari, the United States Supreme Court reversed. In an opinion by THOMAS, J., expressing the unanimous view of the court, it was held that the trustee (1) had a duty to file federal income tax returns and pay income tax (a) with respect to income attributable to the corporate debtors' property, under 26 USCS § 6012(b)(3), which required the assignee of the property of a corporation to file a federal income tax return concerning the property, and under 26 USCS § 6151(a), which provided that the person required to file a federal income tax return had to pay the tax shown on the return to be due, because the trustee was an assignee of the corporate debtors' property under § 6012(b)(3), since (i) the trustee met the usual ordinary and legal definition of the word "assignee," and (ii) § 6012(b)(3) applied when a corporation transferred all or substantially all of its property and required an assignee to file a return "whether or not" the assigned property or business was being operated, and (b) with respect to income attributable to the individual debtor's property, under 26 USCS § 6012(b)(4), which required the fiduciary of a trust to file a federal income tax return concerning the trust, and under § 6151(a), because the trustee was the fiduciary of a trust of the individual under § 6012(b)(4), since (i) the trust created by the plan fit the 26 CFR § 301.7701-4(d) description of a liquidating trust, and (ii) the plan assigned the property of the individual debtor's estate to the trustee and gave the trustee powers consistent with the 26 USCS § 7701(a)(6) definition of a "fiduciary"; and (2) had to perform this duty despite the plan's failure to require the trustee to file income tax returns or pay any income taxes, because § 1141(a) of the Bankruptcy Code (11 USCS § 1141(a)), which stated that the provisions of a confirmed plan bound any creditor, did not preclude the United States, as a creditor, from seeking payment of any taxes, since the United States was not seeking from the trustee any taxes that became due prior to the trustee's appointment, where 11 USCS § 101(10) defined "creditor" as used in § 1141(a) as an entity with various kinds of preconfirmation claims.

122

COUNSEL

Kent L. Jones argued the cause for petitioners.
Herbert Stettin argued the cause for respondents.

CHRISTINE FRANKLIN, Petitioner

v

GWINNETT COUNTY PUBLIC SCHOOLS and
WILLIAM PRESCOTT

503 US —, 117 L Ed 2d 208, 112 S Ct 1028

Argued December 11, 1991.
Decided February 26, 1992.

Decision: Damages remedy held available in sex
discrimination action under Title IX of Education Amendments of 1972 (20 USCS §§ 1681-
1688).

SUMMARY

Title IX of the Education Amendments of 1972
(20 USCS §§ 1681-1688) forbids sex discrimination
under any education program or activity receiving
federal financial assistance. A student in a high
school operated by the Gwinnett County school
district in Georgia filed a complaint in the United
States District Court for the Northern District of
Georgia against the school district under Title IX.
In her complaint, the student alleged that (1) she
was subjected to continual sexual harassment and
abuse, including coercive intercourse, by a male
teacher at the school, (2) teachers and administra-
tors were aware of the teacher's conduct but took
no action to halt it, and (3) the school closed its
investigation of the teacher's conduct after the
teacher resigned on the condition that all matters
pending against him be dropped. The District Court
dismissed the complaint on the ground that Title IX

did not authorize an award of damages, and, on appeal, the United States Court of Appeals for the Eleventh Circuit affirmed (911 F2d 617).

On certiorari, the United States District Court reversed and remanded. In an opinion by WHITE, J., joined by BLACKMUN, STEVENS, O'CONNOR, KENNEDY, and SOUTER, JJ., it was held that a money damages remedy is available for an action brought to enforce Title IX, given that (1) there is a traditional presumption in favor of the availability of any appropriate relief for violation of a federal right; (2) in the years before and after Congress enacted Title IX, the Supreme Court regarded the denial of a remedy as the exception rather than the rule; (3) analysis of the text and history of the Civil Rights Remedies Equalization Amendment of 1986 (42 USCS § 2000d-7) and the Civil Rights Restoration Act of 1987 (PL 100-259, 102 Stat 28)—which statutes were enacted to amend Title IX after the Supreme Court had announced that there is an implied private right of action to enforce Title IX—leads to the conclusion that Congress did not intend to limit the remedies available in a suit brought under Title IX; (4) application of the presumption in favor of appropriate relief with respect to Title IX actions does not violate separation of powers principles by unduly expanding the federal courts' power into a sphere properly reserved to the executive and legislative branches; (5) the fact that Title IX may have been enacted pursuant to Congress' power under the spending clause does not mean that the presumption in favor of all appropriate remedies should not apply to private actions under Title IX; and (6) the assertion that the remedies permissible under Title IX should be limited to backpay and prospective relief conflicts with sound logic.

SCALIA, J., joined by REHNQUIST, Ch. J., and THOMAS, J., concurring in the judgment, expressed the view that (1) when rights of action are judicially implied, categorical limitations on their remedial scope may properly be judicially implied as well, but (2) the Civil Rights Remedies Equalization Amendment of 1986 must be read as an implicit acknowledgment that damages are available in private actions under Title IX.

COUNSEL

Joel I. Klein argued the cause for petitioner.

Albert M. Pearson, III argued the cause for respondents.

Stephen L. Nightingale argued the cause for the United States, as amicus curiae.

INDOPCO, INC., Petitioner

v

COMMISSIONER OF INTERNAL REVENUE

503 US —, 117 L Ed 2d 226, 112 S Ct 1039

Argued November 12, 1991.
Decided February 26, 1992.

Decision: Professional expenses incurred by target corporation in course of friendly takeover held not deductible by corporation as ordinary and necessary business expenses under § 162(a) of Internal Revenue Code (26 USCS § 162(a)).

SUMMARY

As a result of a friendly takeover during August 1978, a publicly held corporation became a wholly owned subsidiary of a larger corporation. In connection with the takeover, the subsidiary engaged the services of an investment banking firm and a law firm. The investment banking firm charged the subsidiary a total of $2,225,586, the law firm charged the subsidiary a total of $505,069, and the subsidiary, in connection with the takeover, spent $150,-962 for miscellaneous items, such as accounting, printing, proxy solicitation, and Securities and Exchange Commission fees. On its federal income tax return for its short taxable year ending in August 1978, the subsidiary claimed a deduction for the investment banking expenses but did not deduct the legal or miscellaneous expenses. After the Commissioner of Internal Revenue disallowed the claimed deduction, the subsidiary, asserting the right to deduct the investment expenses, the legal expenses, and the miscellaneous expenses, sought redetermination in the United States Tax Court. In a decision that was based primarily on the long-term benefits that accrued to the subsidiary from the takeover, the Tax Court ruled that the expenses were capital in nature and therefore not deductible under § 162(a) of the Internal Revenue Code (26 USCS § 162(a)) on the 1978 return as ordinary and necessary business expenses (93 TC 67). Rejecting the subsidiary's contention that, because the disputed expenses did not create or enhance a separate and distinct additional asset, they could not be capitalized and therefore were deductible under § 162, the United States Court of Appeals for the Third Circuit affirmed the Tax Court judgment (918 F2d 426).

On certiorari, the United States Supreme Court affirmed. In an opinion by BLACKMUN, J., expressing the unanimous view of the court, it was held that the investment banking expenses, legal expenses, and miscellaneous expenses did not qualify as ordinary and necessary business expenses deductible by the subsidiary under § 162(a), because (1) the record in the case amply supported the lower courts' findings that the takeover produced significant benefits to the subsidiary that extended beyond its 1978 tax year, where (a) reports by the subsidiary and the investment banker indicated that such benefits would occur, (b) following the takeover, the subsidiary no longer was subject to the substantial shareholder-relations expenses, such as reporting and disclosure obligations, proxy battles, and derivative suits, that a publicly traded corporation incurs, and (c) the takeover also allowed the subsidiary, in the interest of administrative convenience and simplicity, to eliminate previously authorized but unissued preferred shares of stock and to reduce the total

128

number of authorized common shares from 8,000,-
000 to 1,000; (2) the expenses bore the indicia of
capital expenditures and were to be treated as such,
where (a) in disallowing deductions for professional
expenses in a wide variety of cases concerning
corporate structure, courts had characterized an
expenditure as capital in nature because its purpose
was related to a corporation's operations and better-
ment for longer than the current taxable year, and
(b) the rationale behind those decisions applied
equally to the expenses in question; and (3) the fact
that the expenses did not create or enhance a
separate and distinct additional asset was not controlling.

COUNSEL

Richard J. Hiegel argued the cause for petitioner.
Kent L. Jones argued the cause for respondent.

ARKANSAS, et al., Petitioners

v

OKLAHOMA et al. (No. 90-1262)

———

ENVIRONMENTAL PROTECTION AGENCY,
Petitioner

v

OKLAHOMA et al. (No. 90-1266)

503 US —, 117 L Ed 2d 239, 112 S Ct 1046

Argued December 11, 1991.
Decided February 26, 1992.

Decision: EPA's issuance of discharge permit to
sewage plant, based on finding that discharges
would not cause detectable violation of downstream state's water quality standards, held authorized by Clean Water Act.

SUMMARY

An Arkansas city, in an application to the United
States Environmental Protection Agency (EPA),
sought a permit for the city's new sewage treatment
plant under the National Pollution Discharge Elimination System (NPDES). The EPA, pursuant to
§ 402(a)(1) of the Clean Water Act (33 USCS
§ 1342(a)(1)), issued a permit which (1) authorized
the plant to discharge up to half of its effluent into a
stream whose waters ultimately entered a river
which flowed into Oklahoma, but (2) imposed various conditions, including a provision that the permit
would be modified if a pending study determined

that more stringent limitations were necessary to insure compliance with Oklahoma's water quality standards. Oklahoma authorities, challenging the permit before the EPA, alleged that the plant's discharge violated Oklahoma standards prohibiting any degradation of water quality in the river in question. An administrative law judge (ALJ) affirmed the issuance of the permit on the ground that the discharge would not have an "undue impact" on Oklahoma waters; but the EPA's Chief Judicial Officer (CJO), remanding for application of a different standard of review, interpreted Oklahoma's ban on degradation of the river in question as allowing the permit to be upheld if the record showed by a preponderance of the evidence that the authorized discharges would not cause an actual detectable violation of Oklahoma water quality standards. On remand, the ALJ made detailed factual findings and determined that the CJO's standard had been met. The CJO sustained the issuance of the permit. However, the United States Court of Appeals for the Tenth Circuit, on judicial review, reversed the issuance of the permit, as the court (1) interpreted the Act as providing that a proposed source may not be permitted where it would discharge effluent that would contribute to conditions currently constituting a violation of applicable water quality standards, (2) found that the river in question was already degraded in water quality and that effluent from the sewage treatment plant could be expected to contribute to the river's ongoing deterioration even though it would not detectably affect water quality, and (3) determined that the EPA's decision was arbitrary and capricious because the EPA had misinterpreted Oklahoma water quality standards and failed to consider the important and

131

relevant fact of the river's degraded status (908 F2d 595).

On certiorari, the United States Supreme Court reversed. In an opinion by STEVENS, J., expressing the unanimous view of the court, it was held that the EPA's decision to issue the NPDES permit was authorized by the Clean Water Act, as (1) the Act did not prohibit any discharge of effluent that would reach waters already in violation of existing water quality standards; (2) the CJO's interpretation of the Oklahoma water quality standards was reasonable and consistent with the purposes and principles of the Act, and the EPA's reasonable, consistently held interpretation of the Oklahoma standards was entitled to substantial deference since the standards had been incorporated into EPA regulations, and thus had a federal character at least insofar as they affected the issuance of a permit in another state; (3) the ALJ's findings that the sewage plant discharge would not lead to a detectable change in four primary measures of water quality under the Oklahoma standards were supported by substantial evidence; and (4) although it might arguably be wise to prohibit any discharge into the river in question, it was not arbitrary for the EPA to conclude, given perceived benefits to the river and in Arkansas, that allowing the discharge would be even wiser, and such policy decisions were properly made by the EPA rather than by the courts.

COUNSEL

Lawrence G. Wallace argued the cause for petitioner Environmental Protection Agency in No. 90-1266.

Edward W. Warren argued the cause for petitioners Arkansas, et al., in No. 90-1262.

Robert A. Butkin argued the cause for respondents in both cases.

MYRA JO COLLINS, Petitioner

v

CITY OF HARKER HEIGHTS, TEXAS

503 US —, 117 L Ed 2d 261, 112 S Ct 1061

Argued November 5, 1991.
Decided February 26, 1992.

Decision: 42 USCS § 1983 held not to provide remedy for municipal employee's death, because failure to train or warn about known workplace hazards does not violate Fourteenth Amendment's due process clause.

SUMMARY

An employee of the sanitation department of a Texas city died of asphyxia after entering a manhole to unstop a sewer line. The employee's widow brought suit against the city under 42 USCS § 1983, which suit alleged that (1) the employee had a right, under the due process clause of the Federal Constitution's Fourteenth Amendment, to be free from unreasonable risks of harm to his body, mind, and emotions and to be protected from the city's supposed custom and policy of deliberate indifference toward the safety of its employees, and (2) the city had violated that right by following a custom and policy of not training its employees about the dangers of working in sewer lines and manholes, not providing safety equipment at job sites, and not providing safety warnings. The United States District Court for the Western District of Texas dismissed the complaint on the ground that a constitutional violation had not been alleged. The United

States Court of Appeals for the Fifth Circuit, affirming, (1) did not reach the question whether the city had violated the employee's constitutional rights, but (2) denied recovery on the ground that there had been no abuse of government power, which the Court of Appeals had found to be a necessary element of a § 1983 action (916 F2d 284).

On certiorari, the United States Supreme Court affirmed. In an opinion by STEVENS, J., expressing the unanimous view of the court, it was held that no remedy for the employee's death was provided under 42 USCS § 1983, because (1) the due process clause did not impose an independent federal obligation upon municipalities to provide certain minimal levels of safety and security in the workplace, since (a) the text of the clause, being phrased as a limitation on a state's power to act rather than as a guarantee of certain minimal levels of safety and security, did not support the view that a governmental employer's duty to provide its employees with a safe working environment was a substantive component of the clause, and (b) historically, the guarantee of due process had been applied to deliberate decisions of government officials to deprive a person of life, liberty, or property; and (2) the city's alleged failure to train or warn its employees was not arbitrary, or conscience-shocking, in a constitutional sense, since (a) the due process clause did not purport to supplant traditional state tort law in laying down rules of conduct to regulate liability for injuries that attended living together in society, (b) this principle applied with special force to claims asserted against public employees, because state law, rather than the Federal Constitution, generally governed the substance of the employment relationship, and (c) the due process clause was not a

135

guarantee against incorrect or ill-advised personnel decisions, as it was presumed that the administration of government programs was based on a rational decisionmaking process, and decisions concerning such matters as the training of sewer-maintenance employees must be made by locally elected representatives, rather than by federal judges interpreting the basic charter of government for the entire country.

COUNSEL

Sanford Jay Rosen argued the cause for petitioner.

Lucas A. Powe, Jr. argued the cause for respondent.

DONALD J. WILLY, Petitioner

v

COASTAL CORPORATION et al.

503 US —, 117 L Ed 2d 280, 112 S Ct 1076

Argued December 3, 1991.
Decided March 3, 1992.

Decision: Federal District Court held authorized to impose sanctions pursuant to Rule 11 of Federal Rules of Civil Procedure, even though court is later determined to lack subject matter jurisdiction.

SUMMARY

After a terminated employee, alleging that his firing violated provisions of various federal and state environmental statutes, sued his former employer in a Texas state court, the employer removed the case to the United States District Court for the Southern District of Texas. The District Court (1) rejected the employee's contention that it lacked subject matter jurisdiction, and (2) dismissed the case for failure to state a claim. Prior to the dismissal, the employee's attorney had filed a 1,200-page, unindexed, unnumbered pile of materials and had pleaded carelessly; based on this conduct, which was unrelated to the employee's effort to convince the District Court that it lacked subject matter jurisdiction, the District Court imposed—pursuant to Rule 11 of the Federal Rules of Civil Procedure, which authorizes the imposition of sanctions, including an order to pay the other party's reasonable attorney's fees, against a party, or the party's attorney, who signs a paper, filed in a District Court, that is not well grounded in fact—sanctions in the form of an award of attorney's fees against the employee and his attorney. Concluding that the District Court had lacked subject matter jurisdiction because the complaint raised no claims arising under federal law, the United States Court of Appeals for the Fifth Circuit reversed the District Court judgment as to dismissal, instructed that the case be remanded to state court, upheld the imposition of Rule 11 sanctions, and remanded to the District Court for recalculation of the amount of the attorney's fees award (855 F2d 1160). After the District Court imposed sanctions in a recalculated amount, the Court of Appeals, rejecting the employee's contention that in the absence of subject matter jurisdiction the District Court lacked federal constitutional authority to impose Rule 11 sanctions, affirmed the District Court award (915 F2d 965).

On certiorari, the United States Supreme Court affirmed. In an opinion by REHNQUIST, Ch. J., expressing the unanimous view of the court, it was held that the District Court had authority to impose the Rule 11 sanctions, because (1) the expansive language of Federal Civil Procedure Rule 1—which provides that the Rules govern procedures in Federal District Courts in all suits of a civil nature—and Rule 81(c)—which provides that the Rules apply to civil actions removed to the District Courts from the state courts and govern procedure after removal—indicate a clear intent to have the Rules, including Rule 11, apply to all District Court civil proceedings; and (2) imposition of the sanctions was permissible under the Federal Constitution's Article III —which limited the subject matter jurisdiction of federal courts to certain cases or controversies— since (a) Congress, acting pursuant to its authority

under the Constitution's Article I, § 8, cl 18 to make
all laws necessary and proper to the establishment
of the lower federal courts, could enact laws regulating the conduct of those courts and the means by
which their judgments were enforced, (b) the employee had effectively conceded both Congress' general power to regulate the courts and its specific
power to authorize the imposition of sanctions, (c) a
final determination of lack of subject matter jurisdiction of a case in a Federal District Court does not
automatically wipe out all proceedings had in the
District Court when it operated under the misappre-
hension that it had jurisdiction, (d) concern for the
maintenance of orderly procedure justified not up-
setting the sanction order, (e) the order, which was
collateral to the merits of the case, did not raise the
issue of the court's adjudicating the merits of a case
or controversy over which it lacked jurisdiction, and
(f) the interest in having rules of procedure obeyed
did not disappear upon a subsequent determination
that the court lacked subject matter jurisdiction.

COUNSEL

Michael A. Maness argued the cause for petitioner.
Michael L. Beatty argued the cause for respondents.

JOHN J. McCARTHY, Petitioner

v

LARRY MADIGAN et al.

503 US —, 117 L Ed 2d 291, 112 S Ct 1081

Argued December 9, 1991.

Decided March 4, 1992.

Decision: Federal prisoner held not required to exhaust Federal Bureau of Prisons' internal grievance procedure before initiating Bivens action solely for money damages.

SUMMARY

Regulations promulgated by the Federal Bureau of Prisons (28 CFR §§ 542.10-542.16) establish an internal grievance procedure which permitted prisoners to seek formal review of complaints relating to any aspect of their imprisonment, but do not provide for any kind of hearing or for the granting of any particular type of relief. Under the regulations, (1) prisoners must file a formal written complaint within 15 calendar days of the date on which the basis for the complaint occurred, although extensions "shall" be allowed if a valid reason for delay is demonstrated (§ 542.13(b)); (2) the warden must respond to a complaint within 15 days (§ 542.14); (3) prisoners not satisfied with the warden's response have 20 days to appeal to the Bureau's Regional Director (§ 542.15), who has 30 days to respond (§ 542.14); and (4) prisoners who are still not satisfied have 30 days to appeal to the Bureau's General Counsel (§ 542.15), who has 30 days to respond (§ 542.14). A prisoner in a federal
140

penitentiary filed a pro se Bivens complaint in the United States District Court for the District of Kansas against four prison employees—the hospital administrator, two psychologists, and a physician—which complaint (1) alleged that the employees had violated the prisoner's rights under the Federal Constitution's Eighth Amendment by their deliberate indifference to his medical and psychiatric problems, and (2) specifically stated that the prisoner sought money damages only. The District Court dismissed the complaint on the ground that the prisoner had failed to exhaust prison administrative remedies. On appeal, the United States Court of Appeals for the Tenth Circuit, affirming, ruled that exhaustion of the Bureau's grievance procedures was required before the prisoner could bring such a Bivens action, even though the procedures could not result in an award of money damages, because the exhaustion rule was not keyed to the type of relief sought but to the need for preliminary fact-finding to determine whether there was a possible Bivens cause of action (914 F2d 1411).

On certiorari, the United States Supreme Court reversed. In an opinion by BLACKMUN, J., joined by WHITE, STEVENS, O'CONNOR, KENNEDY, and SOUTER, JJ., it was held that a federal prisoner need not resort to the Bureau's internal grievance procedure before initiating a Bivens action solely for money damages, because (1) Congress has not meaningfully addressed the appropriateness of requiring exhaustion in this context; (2) the grievance procedure regulations heavily burden the individual interests of the petitioning inmate by (a) imposing short, successive filing deadlines that create a high risk of forfeiture of a claim for failure to comply, and (b) not authorizing an award of monetary damages; and

(3) the interests of the Bureau do not weigh heavily in favor of exhaustion in view of the remedial scheme and particular claim presented, since, while the Bureau has a substantial interest in encouraging internal resolution of grievances and preventing the undermining of its authority by unnecessary resort of prisoners to the federal courts, (a) the Bureau's alleged failure to render medical care in the case at hand implicates only tangentially the Bureau's authority to control and manage the federal prisons, (b) the Bureau does not bring to bear any special expertise on the type of issue presented, and (c) the grievance procedure does not substantially advance the interests of judicial economy, given that no formal factfindings are made and no formal factual record of an appropriate type is created.

REHNQUIST, Ch. J., joined by SCALIA and THOMAS, JJ., concurred in the judgment, expressing the view that a federal prisoner need not exhaust the procedures promulgated by the Bureau before bringing an action seeking monetary damages, because the grievance procedures in question do not provide for any award of monetary damages, but that the general principles of exhaustion discussed by the court do not apply without modification in the context of a Bivens claim, and the grievance procedure filing deadlines are not a proper basis for excusing exhaustion.

COUNSEL

Paul M. Smith argued the cause for petitioner.

Maureen E. Mahoney argued the cause for respondents.

DAVID DAWSON, Petitioner

v

DELAWARE

503 US —, 117 L Ed 2d 309, 112 S Ct 1093

Argued November 12, 1991.
Decided March 9, 1992.

Decision: Introduction at capital sentencing proceeding of evidence as to defendant's membership in white racist prison gang held to violate
First Amendment where evidence had no relevance to issues in proceeding.

SUMMARY

A white man who, following his escape from a
Delaware prison, had allegedly killed a white woman
and stolen her car and some money was tried and
convicted in the Superior Court in and for Kent
County, Delaware on charges including first-degree
murder. Prior to the penalty phase of the trial, the
prosecution gave notice that it intended to introduce expert testimony regarding the origin and
nature of a prison gang known as the Aryan Brotherhood, as well as the fact that the defendant had
the words "Aryan Brotherhood" tattooed on his
hand; but the defense argued that this evidence was
inflammatory and irrelevant and that its admission
would violate the defendant's rights under the Federal Constitution's First and Fourteenth Amendments. In return for the prosecution's agreement
not to call its expert witnesses, the defendant
agreed to a stipulation stating that (1) the Aryan
Brotherhood was a white racist prison gang that

143

began in California in the 1960s in response to gangs of racial minorities, and (2) separate gangs calling themselves the Aryan Brotherhood existed in many state prisons, including Delaware's. At the penalty hearing, the prosecution read the stipulation to the jury and introduced evidence regarding the defendant's tattoo and his lengthy criminal record, while the defense offered mitigating testimony from family members and noted that the defendant had earned good time credits in prison for enrolling in drug and alcohol programs. The jury (1) found, as aggravating circumstances, that the murder had been committed (a) by an escaped prisoner, (b) during the commission of a burglary, and (c) for pecuniary gain; (2) determined that the aggravating evidence outweighed the mitigating evidence; and accordingly (3) issued a binding recommendation that the defendant be sentenced to death. The Supreme Court of Delaware, affirming, (1) stated that punishing a person for expressing his views or associating with certain people was substantially different from allowing evidence of a defendant's character to be considered where that character was a relevant inquiry, and (2) concluded that, because the Aryan Brotherhood evidence properly focused the jury's attention on the defendant's character, that evidence was properly introduced during the penalty hearing (581 A2d 1078).

On certiorari, the United States Supreme Court vacated and remanded. In an opinion by REHN-QUIST, Ch. J., joined by WHITE, BLACKMUN, STEVENS, O'CONNOR, SCALIA, KENNEDY, and SOUTER, JJ., it was held that (1) the introduction of the Aryan Brotherhood evidence under the circumstances presented violated the defendant's rights under the Federal Constitution's First Amendment, because the evidence proved nothing more than the defendant's abstract beliefs and had no relevance to the issues being decided in the capital sentencing proceeding, given that (a) the stipulation said nothing about the beliefs of the Aryan Brotherhood "chapter" at the state prison in question, while inviting the jury to infer that those beliefs were identical to those of the California chapter, (b) even if the chapter to which the defendant allegedly belonged was racist, those beliefs had no apparent relevance to the case at hand, since both the defendant and his victim were white and elements of racial hatred were therefore not involved in the killing, (c) since the prosecution did not prove that the Aryan Brotherhood had committed or endorsed any unlawful or violent acts, the evidence was not relevant to help prove any aggravating circumstances, and (d) the evidence was not relevant to rebut any mitigating evidence of good character offered by the defendant, since the evidence could not be viewed as relevant "bad" character evidence in its own right; and (2) the question whether the wrongful admission of the evidence was harmless error was not before the Supreme Court and would be left open for consideration on remand.

BLACKMUN, J., concurred, expressing the view that the opinion of the court did not require application of harmless-error review on remand.

THOMAS, J., dissented, expressing the view that (1) evidence that the Aryan Brotherhood was a prison gang and that the defendant was a member was relevant in the capital sentencing proceeding because such evidence supported an inference that the defendant engaged in unlawful activity while in prison, as jurors may be assumed to know the nature of a prison gang; and (2) the description of the Aryan Brotherhood as a racist gang tended to rebut the defendant's evidence of good character.

COUNSEL

Bernard J. O'Donnell argued the cause for petitioner.

Richard E. Fairbanks, Jr. argued the cause for respondent.

———————

GENERAL MOTORS CORPORATION, et al.,
Petitioners

v

EVERT ROMEIN et al.

503 US —, 117 L Ed 2d 328, 112 S Ct 1105

Argued December 10, 1991.
Decided March 9, 1992.

Decision: State-mandated payment of workers' compensation benefits withheld under "benefit coordination" statute held not to violate contract clause or due process clause of Federal Constitution.

SUMMARY

A Michigan statute containing a "benefit coordination" provision that allowed employers to decrease workers' compensation benefits to disabled employees who were eligible to receive wage-loss compensation from other employer-funded sources became effective on March 31, 1982, but did not specify whether the provision was to be applied to workers who had been injured before that date. To nullify a Michigan Supreme Court decision holding that the provision applied to such workers, the state legislature passed into law in 1987 a statute that required employers to pay to disabled employees the workers' compensation benefits that had been withheld in reliance on the coordination statute. Two employers, who had been ordered to pay nearly $25 million that they had withheld based on such reliance, challenged the 1987 statute, alleging that it was unfairly retroactive and violated the

Federal Constitution's contract clause (Art I, § 10, cl
1)—which prohibits a state from passing any law
impairing the obligation of contracts—and the due
process clause of the Federal Constitution's Fourteenth Amendment. The Michigan Supreme Court
upheld the statute on the grounds that (1) the
employers had no vested rights in coordination for
contract clause purposes, and (2) the statute's retroactive provision furthered a rational legislative purpose (436 Mich 515, 462 NW2d 555).

On certiorari, the United States Supreme Court
affirmed. In an opinion by O'CONNOR, J., expressing
the unanimous view of the court, it was held that
the 1987 statute (1) did not violate the contract
clause by allegedly substantially impairing the obligation of employment contracts that were entered
into after collective bargaining between the employers and employees, because (a) there was no contractual agreement regarding the specific workers'
compensation terms allegedly at issue, since the
contracts, which made no express mention of workers' compensation benefits and were formed before
the coordination statute was enacted, did not contain an implied term consisting of a promise to pay
the amount of workers' compensation required by
law for each payment period, which obligation was
completed by making payments for any disability
period, (b) the employers' alleged right to rely on
past payment periods as closed was not a contractual term incorporated by law into employment
contracts, regardless of the assent, express or implied, of the parties, (c) the 1987 statute did not
change the legal enforceability of the contracts, and
(d) reading every workplace regulation into the
private contractual arrangements of employers and
employees would prevent the contract clause from

enabling individuals to order their personal and business affairs according to their particular needs and interests, would severely limit the ability of state legislatures to amend their regulatory legislation, and, taken to an extreme, would render the contract clause entirely dependent on state law; and (2) did not, as a result of the 1987 statute's retroactive payment provision, violate the due process clause, because the retroactive payment provision was a rational means of meeting the legitimate legislative purpose of correcting the state court decision, where the payment provision (a) preserved the delicate legislative compromise that had been struck with respect to workers' compensation benefit rates by the coordination statute and another earlier state statute, and (b) equalized the payments made by employers who had gambled on the state court decision with the payments made by employers who had not gambled on the decision.

COUNSEL

Kenneth S. Geller argued the cause for petitioners.

Theodore Sachs argued the cause for respondents.

JOSEPH WILLIAMS, Petitioner

v

UNITED STATES

503 US —, 117 L Ed 2d 341, 112 S Ct 1112

Argued November 6, 1991.
Decided March 9, 1992.

Decision: Reviewing court held authorized, in appropriate circumstances, to affirm sentence in which Federal District Court's departure from Sentencing Guidelines' range is based on valid and invalid factors.

SUMMARY

As authorized by the Sentencing Reform Act of 1984 (18 USCS §§ 3551 et seq., 28 USCS §§ 991-998), the United States Sentencing Commission has formulated Sentencing Guidelines (18 USCS Appx Ch 1-7) establishing sentencing ranges for different categories of federal offenses and defendants. Under 18 USCS § 3553(b), the Act permits Federal District Courts to depart from a presumptive sentencing range prescribed by the Guidelines only when the court finds an aggravating or mitigating circumstance not adequately taken into consideration by the Sentencing Commission in formulating the Guidelines. With respect to a sentence that is being reviewed on appeal, the Act requires in certain circumstances—(1) under 18 USCS § 3742(f)(1), if the sentence was imposed in violation of law or as a result of an incorrect application of the Guidelines, and (2) under 18 USCS § 3742(f)(2), if the sentence is an unreasonable departure from the applicable

sentencing range—that a case be remanded for
resentencing. An accused was convicted, in the
United States District Court for the Western District
of Wisconsin, of violating a federal statute prohibiting a convicted felon from possessing a firearm.
Although the accused's applicable sentencing range,
based on his criminal history category and offense
level, was 18 to 24 months in prison, the District
Court imposed 27 months' imprisonment on the
grounds that the accused's criminal history category
was inadequate because it did not include two convictions that were too old to be counted in the
Guidelines' criminal history calculation, and because
it did not reflect several prior arrests. The United
States Court of Appeals for the Seventh Circuit
agreed with the District Court that the outdated
convictions were reliable information indicating
more extensive criminal conduct than was reflected
in the accused's criminal history category, but the
Court of Appeals, considering the Guidelines' prohibition against basing a sentence departure on a
prior arrest record alone, determined that the District Court's reliance on the accused's prior arrests
not resulting in prosecution was invalid because the
District Court had not adequately explained the
factual basis for its use of those arrests as a ground
for departure. Concluding that the accused's sentence was reasonable in light of the outdated convictions, the Court of Appeals affirmed the sentence
(910 F2d 1574).

On certiorari, the United States Supreme Court
vacated and remanded. In an opinion by O'CONNOR,
J., joined by REHNQUIST, Ch. J., and BLACKMUN,
STEVENS, SCALIA, SOUTER, and THOMAS, JJ., it was
held that (1) a Court of Appeals may affirm a
District Court sentence that is outside the applicable

Guidelines range—if the party defending the sentence avoids a remand under 18 USCS § 3742(f)(1) by persuading the Court of Appeals that the District Court would have imposed the same sentence absent the erroneous factor, and if the Court of Appeals is satisfied that the sentencing departure is reasonable under 18 USCS § 3742(f)(2)—because (a) a sentence can be reasonable even if some of the reasons give by a District Court to justify a departure from the presumptive Guidelines range are invalid, provided that the remaining reasons are sufficient to justify the magnitude of the departure, (b) the Act does not alter a Court of Appeals' traditional deference to a District Court's exercise of its sentencing discretion, where the selection of the appropriate sentence from within the Guidelines range, as well as the decision to depart from the Guidelines range, are left solely to the sentencing court, and where, except to the extent specifically directed by statute, it is not the role of an appellate court to substitute its judgment for that of the sentencing court as to a sentence's appropriateness, and (c) Congress' amendment of the Act in 1986 to delete certain provisions that authorized an appellate court to correct a sentence determined to have been imposed as a result of an incorrect application of the Guidelines confirmed the view that it is the prerogative of a District Court to determine in the first instance the sentence that should be imposed under the Guidelines; but (2) whether the accused's sentence was imposed as a result of the District Court's erroneous consideration of the prior arrest record would have to be determined on remand, where the Supreme Court was unable to ascertain from the opinion of the Court of Appeals whether it (a) concluded that the District Court would have

152

imposed the same sentence even without relying on the prior arrest record, or, instead (b) affirmed the sentence simply on the basis that it was reasonable under § 3742(f)(2).

WHITE, J., joined by KENNEDY, J., dissented, expressing the view that the Court of Appeals judgment should be affirmed, because (1) rather than probing the mind of the sentencing judge and trying to determine what portion of a departure from the Sentencing Guidelines' range the judge assigned to the different grounds for departure, an appellate court must assess for itself whether valid reasons stated by the District Court justify the magnitude of departure; and (2) this the Court of Appeals did without error, where it determined that, despite the District Court's error concerning the accused's prior arrest record, (a) the District Court correctly had determined that his criminality was not reflected properly in the criminal history category, and (b) the relevant evidence justified the 3-month upward departure in the sentence.

COUNSEL

Kenneth H. Hanson argued the cause for petitioner.

Amy L. Wax argued the cause for respondent.

JAMES R. STRINGER, Petitioner

v

LEE ROY BLACK, Commissioner, Mississippi
Department of Corrections, et al.

503 US —, 117 L Ed 2d 367, 112 S Ct 1130

Argued December 9, 1991.
Decided March 9, 1992.

Decision: Rule of decisions holding aggravating
circumstances unconstitutionally vague in capital sentencing proceeding held retroactively
available to support federal habeas corpus relief.

SUMMARY

A man accused of planning the armed robbery of
a home, which plan included killing the occupants
of the home, and of participating in the robbery, in
the course of which the occupants were in fact shot
to death by another robber, was indicted for capital
murder and was tried and convicted in the Circuit
Court of the First Judicial District of Hinds County,
Mississippi. In the sentencing phase of the trial, the
circuit court instructed the jury on statutory aggravating factors, including the factor that the murder
was "especially heinous, atrocious, or cruel," as to
which factor the court followed the statutory language for the most part and offered no further
definition. The jury found that three statutory aggravating factors were present in the case, including
the "especially heinous, atrocious, or cruel" factor,
and the accused was sentenced to death. The Supreme Court of Mississippi affirmed the conviction

and sentence (454 So 2d 468), and the United States Supreme Court, in 1985, denied certiorari. After unsuccessfully seeking state postconviction relief, the accused filed a federal habeas corpus petition in the United States District Court for the Southern District of Mississippi, which petition contended in part that the "heinous, atrocious, or cruel" aggravating factor was so vague as to render the sentence arbitrary in violation of the cruel and unusual punishment clause of the Federal Constitution's Eighth Amendment. The District Court, in denying the petition, found the vagueness claim to be (1) procedurally barred, and (2) without merit (675 F Supp 356). In 1988, the United States Court of Appeals for the Fifth Circuit affirmed on the merits, as it held that there was no constitutional infirmity in the jury's consideration of the "heinous, atrocious, or cruel" aggravating factor because the two other aggravating factors were unchallenged (862 F2d 1108). The United States Supreme Court (494 US 1074, 108 L Ed 2d 831, 110 S Ct 1800) vacated and remanded for reconsideration in the light of Clemons v Mississippi (1990) 494 US 738, 108 L Ed 2d 725, 110 S Ct 1441. On remand, the Court of Appeals reinstated its previous judgment, as it held that the accused was not entitled to rely on Clemons or the related case of Maynard v Cartwright (1988) 486 US 356, 100 L Ed 2d 372, 108 S Ct 1853—which decisions had treated "heinous, atrocious, or cruel" statutory aggravating circumstances as unconstitutionally vague—because those decisions had announced a new rule after the accused's sentence became final (909 F2d 111).

On certiorari, the United States Supreme Court reversed and remanded. In an opinion by KENNEDY, J., joined by REHNQUIST, Ch. J., and WHITE, BLACK-

155

MUN, STEVENS, and O'CONNOR, JJ., it was held that the accused was entitled to rely on the decisions in Maynard v Cartwright and Clemons v Mississippi, as (1) the Maynard decision, which invalidated a death sentence because of the vagueness of a similarly phrased statutory aggravating circumstance, was controlled by Godfrey v Georgia (1980) 446 US 420, 64 L Ed 2d 398, 100 S Ct 1759, and did not announce a "new rule"; (2) although there were differences in the use of aggravating factors under the Mississippi and Georgia capital sentencing systems, in that the Mississippi system required that aggravating factors be weighed against mitigating evidence while the Georgia system did not, the fact that Mississippi was a "weighing" state only gave emphasis to the requirement that aggravating factors be defined with some degree of precision; (3) at the time the petitioner's sentence became final, United States Supreme Court precedents did not permit state appellate courts to apply a rule of automatic affirmance to any death sentence supported by multiple aggravating factors when one of those factors was invalid; (4) the Clemons decision did not announce a "new rule" in applying the requirement of precise definition of aggravating factors to the Mississippi capital sentencing system; and (5) the view expressed by the Court of Appeals, prior to the Clemons decision, that the Godfrey decision did not apply to Mississippi, was relevant to but not dispositive of the new-rule inquiry, had not been adopted by the Supreme Court of Mississippi, and was erroneous.

SOUTER, J., joined by SCALIA and THOMAS, JJ., dissented, expressing the view that precedent at the time the accused's conviction and sentence became final, and prior to the United States Supreme

Court's decision in Maynard v Cartwright, did not dictate the rule that weighing a vague aggravating circumstance necessarily violated the Eighth Amendment even when there was a finding of at least one other, unobjectionable aggravating circumstance.

COUNSEL

Kenneth J. Rose argued the cause for petitioner.
Marvin L. White, Jr. argued the cause for respondents.

———————

CONNECTICUT NATIONAL BANK, Petitioner

v

THOMAS M. GERMAIN, Trustee for the Estate of O'SULLIVAN'S FUEL OIL CO., INC.

503 US —, 117 L Ed 2d 391, 112 S Ct 1146

Argued January 21, 1992.
Decided March 9, 1992.

Decision: Federal Court of Appeals held to have jurisdiction under 28 USCS § 1292 to review interlocutory order by Federal District Court sitting as appellate court in bankruptcy.

SUMMARY

The trustee for a company that was undergoing bankruptcy proceedings in the United States Bankruptcy Court for the District of Connecticut filed suit in a Connecticut state court against a bank that was the successor in interest to one of the company's creditors, which suit sought to hold the bank liable for various torts and breaches of contract. The bank removed the suit to the United States District Court for the District of Connecticut, which referred the suit to the Bankruptcy Court. The trustee then filed a demand for a jury trial, and the Bankruptcy Court denied the bank's motion to strike the demand (103 BR 388). The District Court affirmed (112 BR 57). The bank filed a petition for leave to appeal with the United States Court of Appeals for the Second Circuit; but the Court of Appeals dismissed the petition for lack of jurisdiction, as it ruled that, with respect to cases in which Federal District Courts sit as appellate courts in bankruptcy, 28 USCS § 158(d)—which gives the Federal Courts of Appeals jurisdiction over appeals from all final decisions of the District Courts in such cases—precludes by negative implication any interlocutory review under 28 USCS § 1292, which gives the Courts of Appeals jurisdiction over certain interlocutory orders of the District Courts (926 F2d 197).

On certiorari, the United States Supreme Court reversed and remanded. In an opinion by THOMAS, J., joined by REHNQUIST, Ch. J., and SCALIA, KENNEDY, and SOUTER, JJ., it was held that a Federal Court of Appeals has jurisdiction under § 1292 to review interlocutory orders issued by a Federal District Court sitting as an appellate court in a bankruptcy case or proceeding, so long as a party to the case or proceeding meets the conditions imposed by § 1292, because (1) 28 USCS § 1291 confers jurisdiction on the Courts of Appeals over final decisions of the District Courts acting in any capacity, and § 158(d) applies to appeals from not only all final decisions by District Courts when they act as bankruptcy appellate courts, but also all final decisions by bankruptcy appellate panels which may be established, so that (a) each section confers jurisdiction over cases which the other section does not reach, (b) giving effect to both §§ 1291 and 158(d) therefore would not render either section wholly superfluous, and (c) it is unnecessary to read § 158(d) as precluding Courts of Appeals, by negative implication, from exercising jurisdiction under § 1291 over appeals from decisions by District Courts sitting as appellate courts in bankruptcy; (2) there is no reason to infer from either § 158(d) or § 1292 that Congress meant to limit appellate review of interlocutory orders in bankruptcy proceedings, as (a) § 1292 provides for Court of Appeals review of interlocutory District Court orders without limiting this to cases where District Courts sit as trial courts in bankruptcy rather than as appellate courts in bankruptcy, and (b) § 158(d) is silent as to review of interlocutory orders; and (3) although it is contended that legislative history points to a different result, judicial inquiry into the applicability of § 1292 begins and ends with what § 1292 says and what § 158(d) does not say.

STEVENS, J., concurred in the judgment, expressing agreement with the court's textual analysis, and expressing the view that legislative history supports the bank's interpretation of § 158(d).

O'CONNOR, J., joined by WHITE and BLACKMUN, JJ., concurred in the judgment, expressing the view that (1) the construction of the statutes as allowing Federal Courts of Appeals to review interlocutory appeals in bankruptcy cases renders § 158(d) largely superfluous; but (2) it is more likely that Congress inadvertently created a redundancy than that Congress intended to withdraw appellate jurisdiction over interlocutory bankruptcy appeals by the roundabout method of reconferring jurisdiction over appeals from final bankruptcy orders.

COUNSEL

Janet C. Hall argued the cause for petitioner.

Thomas M. Germain argued the cause for respondent.

ROBERT G. HOLMES, Jr., Petitioner

v

SECURITIES INVESTOR PROTECTION
CORPORATION et al.

503 US —, 117 L Ed 2d 532, 112 S Ct 1311

Argued November 13, 1991.
Decided March 24, 1992.

Decision: Securities Investor Protection Corp. held
unable to maintain RICO suit under 18 USCS
§ 1964(c) against party to scheme that allegedly
disabled broker-dealers from meeting obligations to customers.

SUMMARY

The Securities Investor Protection Corporation
(SIPC) brought suit in the United States District
Court for the Central District of California against a
person who was alleged to be one of several conspirators in a stock manipulation scheme that disabled two broker-dealers from meeting obligations
to customers. It was alleged that the scheme had
triggered SIPC's authority, pursuant to a provision
of the Securities Investor Protection Act (SIPA) (15
USCS § 78fff-3(b)(2)), to advance funds to the broker-dealers' trustees in order to reimburse the customers. SIPC claimed that the alleged conspirators
had violated § 10(b) of the Securities Exchange Act
of 1934 (15 USCS § 78j(b)), the Securities and
Exchange Commission's Rule 10b-5 (17 CFR
§ 240.10b-5), and various provisions of the Racketeer Influenced and Corrupt Organizations Act
(RICO) (18 USCS §§ 1961-1968), and that SIPC

161

was thus entitled to recover treble damages under a provision of RICO (18 USCS § 1964(c)). The District Court, entering summary judgment for the defendant on the RICO claims, held that (1) SIPC did not meet the purchaser-seller requirements for standing to assert RICO claims that were predicated on § 10(b) and Rule 10b-5, given that SIPC was not a purchaser or seller of securities, and (2) SIPC had not shown that the defendant's alleged acts were the proximate cause of SIPC's losses. On appeal, the United States Court of Appeals for the Ninth Circuit reversed and remanded on the grounds that (1) the RICO cause of action under § 1964(c) does not impose a purchaser-seller requirement for standing, and (2) the District Court had erred in finding no proximate cause (908 F2d 1461).

On certiorari, the United States Supreme Court reversed and remanded. In an opinion by SOUTER, J., joined by REHNQUIST, Ch. J., and BLACKMUN, KENNEDY, and THOMAS, JJ., and joined in part (except for holding 3 below) by WHITE, STEVENS, and O'CONNOR, JJ., it was held that (1) SIPC could not recover damages under 18 USCS § 1964(c) on the theory that SIPC was subrogated to the rights of those customers who did not purchase manipulated securities, given that the alleged conspirators' conduct did not proximately cause the nonpurchasing customers' injury; (2) a provision of SIPA (15 USCS § 78eee(d)), under which SIPC is deemed to be a party in interest as to all matters arising in a liquidation proceeding and is deemed to have intervened with respect to all such matters, did not—either alone or with 18 USCS § 1964(c)—give SIPC a right to sue to recover the funds advanced to the trustees pursuant to 15 USCS § 78fff-3(b)(2), given that § 78eee(d) says nothing about the conditions necessary for SIPC's recovery as a plaintiff; and (3) under the circumstances, it was inopportune to resolve the issue whether every RICO plaintiff who sues under § 1964(c) and claims securities fraud as a predicate offense must have purchased or sold a security.

O'CONNOR, J., joined by WHITE and STEVENS, JJ., concurring in part and concurring in the judgment, expressed the view that (1) the civil RICO provisions have a proximate cause element; but (2) the court should have considered the standing question before deciding whether SIPC was proximately injured by the defendant; and (3) a plaintiff need not be a purchaser or a seller to assert RICO claims predicated on securities fraud, given that the relevant predicate offense is § 32 of the 1934 Act (15 USCS § 78ff(a)), a criminal provision as to which the purchaser-seller standing requirement is of no import.

SCALIA, J., concurring in the judgment, expressed the view that (1) the purchaser-seller limitation applicable to private actions under Rule 10b-5 does not apply in civil RICO cases alleging Rule 10b-5 violations as predicate acts, given that the action under 18 USCS § 1964 is congressionally created, unlike the action under Rule 10b-5, which action was created by the court itself; and (2) a proximate cause requirement applied to SIPC's action, and this requirement was not met.

COUNSEL

Jack I. Samet argued the cause for petitioner.

G. Robert Blakely argued the cause for respondents.

UNITED STATES, Petitioner

v

R. L. C.

503 US —, 117 L Ed 2d 559, 112 S Ct 1329

Argued December 10, 1991.
Decided March 24, 1992.

Decision: Juvenile Delinquency Act provision limiting detention to maximum term authorized for one convicted as adult held to refer to maximum sentence authorized under United States Sentencing Guidelines.

SUMMARY

A juvenile was charged with causing the death of a child by driving a stolen car in a reckless manner while intoxicated. Because the juvenile was a member of an Indian band and the accident occurred on an Indian reservation, proceedings were instituted in a Federal District Court, which proceedings resulted in a determination that the juvenile had committed an act of juvenile delinquency under 18 USCS § 5031 by acts that would have constituted the crime of involuntary manslaughter under 18 USCS §§ 1112(a) and 1153 if committed by an adult. Applying a provision of the Juvenile Delinquency Act (18 USCS § 5037(c)(1)(B)) which required the length of official detention in certain circumstances to be limited to "the maximum term of imprisonment that would be authorized if the juvenile had been tried and convicted as an adult," the District Court committed the juvenile to official detention for 3 years, that being the maximum

164

sentence for involuntary manslaughter under 18 USCS § 1112(b). The United States Court of Appeals for the Eighth Circuit, however, vacated the juvenile's sentence and remanded for resentencing, as the court held that (1) the cap imposed by § 5037(c)(1)(B) was the sentence a court could have imposed on a similarly situated adult after applying the United States Sentencing Guidelines (18 USCS Appx Ch 1-7); (2) because the juvenile in the case at hand had the lowest possible criminal history level, the Guidelines would yield a sentencing range of 15 to 21 months for a similarly situated adult; and therefore (3) the maximum period of detention to which the juvenile could be sentenced was 21 months (915 F2d 320).

On certiorari, the United States Supreme Court affirmed. In an opinion by SOUTER, J., joined in pertinent part by REHNQUIST, Ch. J., and WHITE, STEVENS, SCALIA, KENNEDY, and THOMAS, JJ., it was held that the limitation imposed by § 5037(c)(1)(B), though ambiguously phrased, referred to the maximum sentence that could be imposed if a juvenile were being sentenced after application of the United States Sentencing Guidelines, and not only to the maximum term of imprisonment provided for by the statute defining the offense. Also, SOUTER, J., joined by REHNQUIST, Ch. J., and WHITE and STEVENS, JJ., expressed the view that (1) the textual evolution and legislative history of § 5037 supported the conclusion that the section was better understood as requiring a focused inquiry into the maximum sentence that would be available under the Guidelines in the circumstances of the particular juvenile, rather than an abstract consideration of the penalty permitted in punishment of the adult offense; and (2) application of the rule of lenity was unnecessary

165

in the case at hand, since the rule had always been reserved for those situations in which a reasonable doubt persisted about a statute's intended scope even after resort to the language and structure, legislative history, and motivating policies of the statute.

SCALIA, J., joined by KENNEDY and THOMAS, JJ., concurred in part and concurred in the judgment, expressing the view that (1) when a criminal statute is ambiguous, the rule of lenity prescribes the result, namely, that the more lenient interpretation must prevail; and (2) it is not consistent with the rule of lenity to construe a textually ambiguous penal statute against a criminal defendant on the basis of legislative history.

THOMAS, J., concurred in part and concurred in the judgment, expressing the view that the rule of lenity is not triggered merely because a statute appears textually ambiguous on its face, but operates only if ambiguity remains at the end of the process of applying judicially established principles of statutory construction.

O'CONNOR, J., joined by BLACKMUN, J., dissented, expressing the view that (1) Congress, in enacting the Sentencing Reform Act of 1984 (18 USCS §§ 3551 et seq., 28 USCS §§ 991-998), which authorized establishment of the United States Sentencing Guidelines, had intended to leave settled practice in juvenile sentencing undisturbed; and (2) the cumbersome process of determining a comparable Guideline maximum threatened to dominate the juvenile sentencing hearing at the expense of considerations more relevant to juveniles.

COUNSEL

Paul J. Larkin, Jr. argued the cause for petitioner.
Katherian D. Roe argued the cause for respondent.

NATIONWIDE MUTUAL INSURANCE
COMPANY, et al., Petitioners

v

ROBERT T. DARDEN

503 US —, 117 L Ed 2d 581, 112 S Ct 1344

Argued January 21, 1992.
Decided March 24, 1992.

Decision: ERISA provision (29 USCS § 1002(6))
defining "employee" as "any individual employed by an employer," held to incorporate
traditional agency-law criteria for identifying
master-servant relationships.

SUMMARY

Under 29 USCS § 1132(a), a participant in an
employee benefit plan is allowed to bring an action
to enforce the substantive provisions of the Employee Retirement Income Security Act of 1974
(ERISA) (29 USCS §§ 1001 et seq.). A "participant"
is defined in 29 USCS § 1002(7) as any employee or
former employee who is or may become eligible to
receive a benefit from an employee benefit plan,"
and an "employee" is defined in § 3(6) of ERISA
(29 USCS § 1002(6)) as "any individual employed
by an employer." Contracts between an insurer and
an insurance agent provided that (1) the agent, who
operated an insurance agency, would sell only the
insurer's policies, (2) the insurer would enroll the
agent in the insurer's retirement plan for agents,
and (3) the agent would forfeit his entitlement to
plan benefits if, within a year of termination of the
parties' contractual relationship, and within 25 miles

168

of the agent's prior business location, he sold insurance for the insurer's competitors. One month after the contractual relationship was terminated, the agent began to sell insurance for the insurer's competitors. After the insurer contended that the agent's new business activities disqualified him from receiving plan benefits, the agent sued for the benefits under § 1132(a) and claimed that the benefits were nonforfeitable because they had already vested under the terms of ERISA. Applying common-law agency principles, the United States District Court for the Eastern District of North Carolina granted summary judgment to the insurer on the ground that the agent had been an independent contractor rather than an employee of the insurer. Reversing and remanding, the United States Court of Appeals for the Fourth Circuit held that common-law agency principles were inapplicable and that an ERISA plaintiff could qualify as an employee by showing that he or she (1) had a reasonable expectation of receiving pension benefits, (2) relied on this expectation, and (3) lacked the economic power to contract out of benefit plan forfeiture provisions (796 F2d 701). On remand, the District Court applied the Court of Appeals' standard and held that the agent had been an employee of the insurer (717 F Supp 388). The Court of Appeals affirmed (922 F2d 203).

On certiorari, the United States Supreme Court reversed and remanded. In an opinion by SOUTER, J., expressing the unanimous view of the court, it was held that the term "employee" in § 1002(6)) incorporates traditional agency-law criteria for identifying master-servant relationships, because (1) the nominal definition in § 1002(6) is completely circular and explains nothing, (2) no other ERISA provision gives specific guidance on the term's meaning or suggests that construing it to incorporate traditional agency-law principles would thwart the congressional design or lead to absurd results, (3) application of traditional agency-law criteria generally turns on factual variables within an employer's knowledge, thus permitting categorical judgments about the "employee" status of ERISA claimants with similar job descriptions, and (4) agency-law principles comport with recent Supreme Court precedents and with the common understanding, reflected in those precedents, of the difference between an employee and an independent contractor.

COUNSEL

George R. Ragsdale argued the cause for petitioners.

Christopher J. Wright argued the cause for the United States as amicus curiae.

Marion G. Follin, III argued the cause for respondent.

———————

UNITED STATES, Petitioner

v

RICHARD WILSON

503 US —, 117 L Ed 2d 593, 112 S Ct 1351

Argued January 15, 1992.
Decided March 24, 1992.

Decision: Federal sentencing credit under 18 USCS
§ 3585(b) for certain presentence time served
held required to be computed by Attorney
General after convicted federal defendant has
begun to serve sentence.

SUMMARY

Under 18 USCS § 3585(b), a defendant convicted
of a federal crime has a right to receive credit for
time spent in official detention before the defendant's sentence begins, as a result of the offense for
which the sentence was imposed, or as a result of
any other charge for which the defendant was arrested after the commission of the offense for which
the sentence was imposed, that has not been credited against another sentence. Former 18 USCS
§ 3568 expressly required the United States Attorney General to award the credit, but § 3585(b),
which recodifies the former § 3568, is written in the
passive voice, and does not mention the Attorney
General. An accused who had allegedly committed
several crimes in Tennessee was arrested by Tennessee authorities and held in state custody pending
the outcome of federal and state prosecutions. The
accused eventually pleaded guilty to various federal
and state charges. On November 29, 1989, the

United States District Court for the Middle District of Tennessee, in sentencing the accused to a federal term of imprisonment, denied the accused's request for credit for time served during presentence state custody. On December 12, 1989, a Tennessee trial court, in sentencing the accused to a state term of imprisonment, granted the accused such credit. Later that day, Tennessee authorities transferred the accused to federal custody, and he began serving his federal sentence. However, on appeal of the District Court's refusal to grant credit for the time spent in presentence state custody, the United States Court of Appeals for the Sixth Circuit—in ruling that the accused had a right to such credit and that the District Court should have awarded the credit to the accused—expressed the view that (1) § 3585(b)'s radical departure from the language of the former § 3568 expressed a congressional intent to rescind the Attorney General's authority to award credit; and (2) a District Court has the initial authority and duty to apply the mandate of § 3585(b) at the time that the court imposes sentence for a federal offense (916 F2d 1115).

On certiorari, the United States Supreme Court reversed. In an opinion by THOMAS, J. joined by REHNQUIST, Ch. J., and BLACKMUN, O'CONNOR, SCALIA, KENNEDY, and SOUTER, JJ., it was held that under § 3585(b), the appropriate credit for certain presentence time spent in official detention is to be computed by the United States Attorney General after a federal criminal defendant has begun to serve his or her sentence, rather than by a Federal District Court at the time of sentencing, because (1) Congress, by using in § 3585(b) the verbs "was imposed" and "has spent" in the past and present perfect tenses, has indicated that computation must

172

occur after a defendant begins his or her sentence; (2) given that federal defendants do not always begin to serve their sentences immediately, a District Court could only speculate about the amount of time spent in presentence detention by such defendants; (3) the phrase "has not been credited" confirms this interpretation, for, if a defendant is being separately sentenced by a federal and a state court, the credit should not arbitrarily depend on the timing or order of the sentencing by the two courts; (4) since § 3585(b) provides a right to a credit which a District Court cannot determine at the time of sentencing, the Attorney General has no choice but to make the determination, for 18 USCS § 3621(a) gives the Attorney General, through the Bureau of Prisons, the responsibility of administering sentences; (5) Congress' conversion of active phrasing in former § 3568 into passive phrasing in § 3585(b) is a rather slim ground for presuming an intention to change the Bureau's well-established procedures for determining the credit; (6) the presumption that Congress contemplated a change by amending the statute is overcome by the conclusions that (a) a District Court cannot perform the necessary calculations at the time of sentencing, and (b) the Attorney General, in implementing a sentence, cannot avoid computing the credit; and (7) this interpretation does not render the revision which produced § 3585(b) meaningless, as § 3585(b) still alters former § 3568 in other ways.

STEVENS, J., joined by WHITE, J., dissenting, expressed the view that (1) the Supreme Court's rigid interpretation of § 3585(b), a remedial statute, was not supported by the text, legislative history, or underlying policies of § 3585(b); and (2) although sometimes all issues relating to a credit determination under § 3585(b) would not be ripe for decision at the time of sentencing, a District Court ought to have authority to make an initial credit determination in appropriate cases.

COUNSEL

Amy L. Wax argued the cause for petitioner.
Henry A. Martin argued the cause for respondent.

SUE SUTER, et al., Petitioners

v

ARTIST M. et al.

503 US —, 118 L Ed 2d 1, 112 S Ct 1360

Argued December 2, 1991.
Decided March 25, 1992.

Decision: Provision of Adoption Assistance and
Child Welfare Act of 1980 (42 USCS § 671(a)
(15)) held not enforceable in private action
under 42 USCS § 1983 or in suit directly under
Act.

SUMMARY

Under a provision of the Adoption Assistance and
Child Welfare Act of 1980 (42 USCS § 671(a)), a
state is eligible for reimbursement by the Federal
Government for certain expenses incurred in administering foster care and adoption services, if the
state submits a plan for approval by the Secretary of
Health and Human Services. Pursuant to § 671(a)
(3), such a plan must provide that the plan shall be
"in effect" in all of the state's political subdivisions
and be mandatory upon them; § 671(a)(15) requires
that the plan provide that "reasonable efforts" will
be made to prevent removal of children from their
homes and to facilitate reunification of families
where removal has occurred. Children who were
beneficiaries of the Act filed a class action in the
United States District Court for the Northern District of Illinois against officials of Illinois' department of children and family services, in which action
it was alleged that the officials violated § 671(a)(15),

in that the department failed promptly to assign caseworkers to children placed in the department's custody and promptly to reassign cases when caseworkers were on leave from the department. The District Court, denying a motion to dismiss, held that the Act contained an implied cause of action and that suit could also be brought to enforce the Act under 42 USCS § 1983 (726 F Supp 690). The District Court subsequently entered an injunction setting requirements as to the assignment of caseworkers. The United States Court of Appeals for the Seventh Circuit affirmed on appeal (917 F2d 980).

On certiorari, the United States Supreme Court reversed. In an opinion by REHNQUIST, Ch. J., joined by WHITE, O'CONNOR, SCALIA, KENNEDY, SOUTER, and THOMAS, JJ., it was held that (1) § 671(a)(15) does not confer on its beneficiaries a private right of action under § 1983 to obtain enforcement of the "reasonable efforts" clause, given that (a) although the Act is mandatory in its terms, the requirement of § 671(a) goes only so far as to insure that the state have a plan approved by the Secretary which contains certain features, (b) although § 671(a)(3) provides that the plan must be in effect in all political subdivisions of the state, the phrase "in effect" is not intended to otherwise modify the word "plan," (c) no statutory guidance is found as to how a state's "reasonable efforts" are to be measured, and a state's compliance with this directive is, within broad limits, left up to the state, (d) other sections of the Act provide enforcement mechanisms, other than remedies under § 1983, for the reasonable efforts clause, (e) the language of other sections of the Act shows that Congress knew how to impose precise requirements on the states, aside from the submission of a plan to be approved by the Secretary, when Congress intended to do so, (f) the regulations promulgated by the Secretary to enforce the Act do not evidence a view that § 671(a) places any requirement for state receipt of federal funds other than the submission of a plan to be approved by the Secretary, and (g) to the extent that legislative history may be relevant, an examination leads to the conclusion that Congress—although concerned that the required reasonable efforts be made by the states—indicated that the Act left a great deal of discretion to the states; and (2) § 617(a)(15) does not create an implied right of action such that private individuals could bring suit directly under the Act to enforce the "reasonable efforts" clause, given that Congress did not intend to create such a remedy.

BLACKMUN, J., joined by STEVENS, J., dissenting, expressed the view that the beneficiaries of the Act had a cause of action under § 1983, and that the Court of Appeals' judgment should have been affirmed.

COUNSEL

Christina M. Tchen argued the cause for petitioners.

John G. Roberts, Jr. argued the cause for the United States, as amicus curiae, supporting petitioners.

Michael Dsida argued the cause for respondents.

UNITED STATES, Petitioner

v

FRANK DENNIS FELIX

503 US —, 118 L Ed 2d 25, 112 S Ct 1377

Argued January 14, 1992.

Decided March 25, 1992.

Decision: Double jeopardy held not to bar federal conspiracy prosecution where some overt acts were based on substantive offenses for which defendant was previously convicted.

SUMMARY

An individual who allegedly had manufactured methamphetamine at a facility in Oklahoma, until the facility was raided and shut down by federal agents, was subsequently arrested in Missouri, where he had taken delivery of chemicals and equipment used in methamphetamine production. The individual was charged and tried in the United States District Court for the Western District of Missouri on charges of attempt to manufacture methamphetamine. In the course of the trial the prosecution, in order to establish criminal intent, introduced evidence of the individual's previous drug manufacturing activities in Oklahoma, and the District Court instructed the jury that this evidence was admissible only to show the individual's state of mind with respect to the materials he had attempted to purchase in Missouri. The individual was convicted, and his conviction and sentence were affirmed by the United States Court of Appeals for the Eighth Circuit. The individual was subsequently indicted in the United States District Court for the Eastern District of Oklahoma on charges including (1) conspiracy to manufacture, possess, and distribute methamphetamine, which charge was supported by various overt acts including two based on conduct that had been the subject of the Missouri prosecution; (2) manufacture and possession of methamphetamine and related chemicals in Oklahoma; and (3) maintaining a methamphetamine manufacturing lab in Oklahoma. The individual was convicted, but the United States Court of Appeals for the Tenth Circuit reversed as to the above charges on the ground that they were barred by the double jeopardy clause of the Federal Constitution's Fifth Amendment, as the court (1) cited Grady v Corbin (1990) 495 US 508, 109 L Ed 2d 548, 110 S Ct 2084, to the effect that double jeopardy bars a subsequent prosecution where the government, to establish an essential element of an offense charged in that prosecution, will prove conduct that constitutes an offense for which the defendant has already been prosecuted; (2) observed, with regard to the Oklahoma conspiracy charge, that the prosecution in both trials had proved that the individual had learned to make and had manufactured methamphetamine in Oklahoma and had sought to purchase more materials in Missouri; and (3) noted, with regard to the substantive Oklahoma charges, that the direct evidence supporting those charges—namely, the individual's purchase of materials and manufacture of methamphetamine in Oklahoma—had been introduced in the Missouri trial to show intent (926 F2d 1522).

On certiorari, the United States Supreme Court reversed. In an opinion by REHNQUIST, Ch. J., joined by WHITE, O'CONNOR, SCALIA, KENNEDY, SOUTER, and THOMAS, JJ., as to holding 1 below, and expressing the unanimous view of the court as to holding 2 below, it was held that (1) prosecution of a defendant for conspiracy, where certain of the overt acts relied on by the government are based on substantive offenses for which the defendant has been previously convicted, does not violate the double jeopardy clause, because a substantive crime and a conspiracy to commit that crime are not the same offense for double jeopardy purposes—a rule which antedated, and was not questioned in, Grady v Corbin; and (2) the double jeopardy clause did not bar the prosecution of the individual on the substantive counts of the Oklahoma indictment, because (a) the actual crimes charged in each case were different in both time and place, with no common conduct linking the alleged offenses, and thus none of the offenses prosecuted in the Oklahoma case was in any sense the same offense as that for which the defendant was prosecuted in Missouri, and (b) the fact that the government offers in evidence in one prosecution acts of misconduct that are ultimately charged as criminal offenses in a second prosecution does not result in a bar to the second prosecution under the double jeopardy clause, as the introduction of relevant evidence of particular misconduct in a case under Rule 404(b) of the Federal Rules of Evidence is not the same thing as prosecution for that conduct.

STEVENS, J., joined by BLACKMUN, J., concurred in part and concurred in the judgment, expressing the view that the double jeopardy clause did not bar prosecution of the individual for the conspiracy charge under the rule of Grady v Corbin, because the overt acts at issue did not meaningfully establish an essential element of the conspiracy, since there is no overt act requirement in the federal drug conspiracy statute and the overt acts did not establish an agreement between the individual and his alleged coconspirators.

COUNSEL

William C. Bryson argued the cause for petitioner.

Scott M. Anderson argued the cause for respondent.

———

WILLIAM BARNHILL, Petitioner

v

ELLIOT JOHNSON, Trustee

503 US —, 118 L Ed 2d 39, 112 S Ct 1386

Argued January 14, 1992.
Decided March 25, 1992.

Decision: Transfer of check, for purposes of determining whether transfer is voidable under 11 USCS § 547(b)(4)(A) as occurring within 90 days of bankruptcy filing, held to occur on date drawee bank honors check.

SUMMARY

A group of debtors made a payment on a bona fide debt by delivering a check to a creditor on November 18, 1985, which check was dated November 19 and was honored by the drawee bank on November 20. On February 18, 1986, the debtors filed petitions for reorganization under Chapter 11 of the Bankruptcy Code (11 USCS §§ 1101-1174), which petitions were consolidated into a single bankruptcy proceeding. The trustee for the bankruptcy estate filed an adversary proceeding against the creditor in the United States Bankruptcy Court for the District of New Mexico, which proceeding claimed that the check payment was avoidable under 11 USCS § 547(b)(4)(A) as a "transfer" made within 90 days before the date of the filing of the bankruptcy petition, as the trustee asserted that the "transfer" occurred for purposes of § 547(b) on the date the check was honored by the drawee bank, which date, as the parties agreed, was the 90th day

182

before the bankruptcy filing. The Bankruptcy Court held that the transfer occurred on the date the check was delivered to the creditor, and accordingly dismissed the trustee's claim (97 BR 69). The United States District Court for the District of New Mexico affirmed (111 BR 337). However, the United States Court of Appeals for the Tenth Circuit, holding that a payment by check is deemed to have occurred for purposes of § 547(b) when the check is honored by the drawee bank, reversed the judgment of the District Court and remanded the case for further proceedings (931 F2d 689).

On certiorari, the United States Supreme Court affirmed. In an opinion by REHNQUIST, Ch. J., joined by WHITE, O'CONNOR, SCALIA, KENNEDY, SOUTER, and THOMAS, JJ., it was held that, in determining whether a transfer occurred within the 90-day preference period of § 547(b)(4)(A), a transfer by check is deemed to occur on the date the drawee bank honors the check, because (1) there is no unconditional transfer of the debtor's interest in property prior to the date the check is honored; (2) only when the debtor has directed the drawee bank to honor the check, and the bank has done so, has the debtor implemented a "mode, direct or indirect . . . of disposing of property or an interest in property" within the definition of a transfer in 11 USCS § 101(54); (3) having received the check gives the creditor at most a chose in action against the debtor, which cannot fairly be characterized as even a "conditional" right to property or an interest in property under § 101(54); (4) the date-of-honor rule is consistent with 11 USCS § 547(e)(2)(A)—which provides that a transfer occurs at the time the transfer takes effect between the transferor and the transferee—as the transfer of funds cannot be said

183

to take effect until the moment of honor, particularly where the transferor retains the ability to stop payment on the check until the very last; and (5) no support for a different rule is provided by statements by members of Congress that payment is considered to be made when the check is delivered for purposes of the preferential transfer avoidance exceptions of 11 USCS §§ 547(c)(1) and 547(c)(2).

STEVENS, J., joined by BLACKMUN, J., dissented, expressing the view that a "transfer" of property occurs for purposes of § 547(b) on the date a check is delivered to the transferee, provided that the check is honored within 10 days.

COUNSEL

William J. Arland, III argued the cause for petitioner.

Nancy S. Cusack argued the cause for respondent.

NATIONAL RAILROAD PASSENGER
CORPORATION, et al., Petitioners

v

BOSTON & MAINE CORPORATION et al.
(No. 90-1419)

INTERSTATE COMMERCE COMMISSION and
UNITED STATES, Petitioners

v

BOSTON & MAINE CORPORATION et al.
(No. 90-1769)

503 US —, 118 L Ed 2d 52, 112 S Ct 1394

Argued January 13, 1992.
Decided March 25, 1992.

Decision: Interstate Commerce Commission held to
have authority, under 45 USCS § 562(d)(1), to
require conveyance of track from railroad to
Amtrak for purpose of reconveying track to
second railroad.

SUMMARY

The National Railroad Passenger Corporation
(Amtrak), a private, for-profit corporation created by
the Rail Passenger Service Act of 1970 (45 USCS
§§ 501 et seq.), operates passenger trains, generally
on existing tracks owned and used by freight railroads, through means including "trackage rights"
agreements. In addition, under 45 USCS § 562(d)
(1), if a railroad and Amtrak are unable to agree
upon terms for the sale to Amtrak of railroad

185

property "required" for intercity rail passenger service, Amtrak may apply to the Interstate Commerce Commission (ICC) for an order establishing Amtrak's need for the property and requiring the conveyance of the property from the railroad to Amtrak on reasonable terms and conditions, including just compensation. Pursuant to § 562(d)(1), Amtrak's need for the property is deemed to be established, unless the ICC finds that (1) conveyance of the property to Amtrak would significantly impair the railroad's ability to carry out its obligations as a common carrier; and (2) Amtrak's obligation to provide rail passenger service can adequately be met by the acquisition of alternative property. When Amtrak became dissatisfied with a railroad's maintenance of a 48.8-mile segment of track used by an Amtrak passenger service, Amtrak reached a preliminary agreement with a second railroad which owned other parts of the same line, to the effect that (1) Amtrak would acquire the segment in question, reconvey the segment to the second railroad, and provide some funds for upgrading and rehabilitation; while (2) the second railroad would provide the balance of the upgrade funds, maintain the track, and grant trackage rights to Amtrak and the first railroad. Amtrak then made a purchase offer to the first railroad, but when Amtrak interpreted a response as a rejection, Amtrak instituted ICC proceedings. Eventually, the ICC—in issuing a final decision which ordered the segment's conveyance to Amtrak, with just compensation to the first railroad of more than $2.3 million—expressed the view, in the ICC's first decided case involving condemnation powers under § 562(d), that (1) Amtrak had met the statutory conditions for the institution of proceedings; and (2) the first railroad had established neither of the two statutory criteria to rebut the statutory presumption of need. On petition for review, the United States Court of Appeals for the District of Columbia Circuit—in granting the petition and in ordering a remand for further proceedings—expressed the view that § 562(d) did not permit Amtrak to condemn railroad property which Amtrak intended to convey to another railroad, for no deference was due to the ICC's contrary interpretation, as § 562(d) was unambiguous in light of its language and history (286 App DC 1, 911 F2d 743). While rehearing was pending, Congress in 1990, in specific response to the Court of Appeals' decision, added to § 562(d)(1) a provision to the effect that Amtrak may subsequently convey title or other interest in acquired property to a third party, if the reconveyance is found by the ICC to further the purposes of the statute (PL 101-641, § 9(a)); this amendment was made applicable to all pending cases (PL 101-641, § 9(b)). The Court of Appeals, however, in denying rehearing, expressed the view that, while the 1990 addition made it clear that Amtrak was authorized to reconvey property subsequent to a condemnation that was otherwise valid under § 562(d), the addition did not change the § 562(d) limitation that the property be "required" in the first place (288 App DC 196, 925 F2d 427).

On certiorari, the United States Supreme Court reversed the judgment of the Court of Appeals and remanded the case for further proceedings. In an opinion by KENNEDY, J., joined by REHNQUIST, Ch. J., and STEVENS, O'CONNOR, SCALIA, and SOUTER, JJ., it was held that (1) for purposes of § 562(d)(1), deference would be given to the ICC's interpretation of the term "required" for intercity rail passenger service to mean useful or appropriate,

187

rather than indispensable or necessary, because (a) § 562(d)(1) was ambiguous in some respects, (b) the ICC's interpretation was reasonable, (c) the ICC's interpretation was consistent with Congress' 1990 addition to § 562(d)(1), for, while the addition did not modify the specific language at issue, the addition confirmed the ICC's view, and (d) the fact that the ICC's decision had not in so many words articulated the ICC's interpretation of "required" did not mean that deference might not be given to that interpretation, since the only reasonable reading of the ICC's decision, and the only plausible explanation of the issues that the ICC addressed after considering the factual submissions by all of the parties, was that the ICC decision had been based on that interpretation; and (2) under the ICC's interpretation of the term "required," the ICC did not exceed its authority in ordering the first railroad to convey the segment to Amtrak, for the purpose of reconveying the segment to the second railroad, in connection with the agreement between Amtrak and the second railroad, because (a) the ICC's view that such use was sufficient to satisfy the "required" command was a reasonable interpretation and application of the statute, and (b) the ICC was not required to make specific findings regarding Amtrak's actual need for the condemnation.

WHITE, J., joined by BLACKMUN and THOMAS, JJ., dissenting, expressed the view that, as the 1990 addition to § 562(d)(1) made clear, § 562(d) did not unambiguously prohibit transactions such as the sale and leaseback agreement in question between Amtrak and the second railroad, but (1) the ICC's definition of what was "required" for intercity rail passenger service (a) was not addressed in the ICC proceedings or in the ICC's argument to the Court

188

of Appeals, (b) debuted in the ICC's briefs before the Supreme Court, and (c) thus, was a post hoc rationalization not entitled to deference; (2) the Supreme Court's conclusion, based upon the ICC's presumed interpretation, that the ICC was not obligated to make specific findings as to whether property was required for service magnified the ICC's mistake; and (3) because the ICC had failed to provide a clear, authoritative construction, the case ought to be returned to the ICC.

COUNSEL

John G. Roberts, Jr. argued the cause for petitioners.

Irwin Goldbloom argued the cause for respondents.

F. DALE ROBERTSON, Chief, United States Forest
Service, et al., Petitioners

v

SEATTLE AUDUBON SOCIETY et al.

503 US —, 118 L Ed 2d 73, 112 S Ct 1407

Argued December 2, 1992.
Decided March 25, 1992.

Decision: Provision that statute meets requirements
of earlier statutes on which specified pending
cases involving logging and endangered spotted
owl are based, held not to violate Federal Constitution's Article III.

SUMMARY

Old-growth forests in the Pacific Northwest are
home to the northern spotted owl, which is on the
Federal Government's endangered species list. In
accordance with environmentalists' position that
harvesting timber in these forests would kill the
owls, two separate suits—one concerning national
forests in Oregon and Washington that were managed by the United States Forest Service, and the
other concerning forests in Oregon that were managed by the federal Bureau of Land Management
(BLM)—alleging the violation of a combined total of
five different federal statutes were filed by environmental groups challenging proposed timber harvesting. In the Forest Service case, the United States
District Court for the Western District of Washington preliminarily enjoined certain proposed timber
sales; while in the BLM case, the United States
District Court for the District of Oregon twice dis-

missed the action, and the United States Court of
Appeals for the Ninth Circuit twice enjoined some
of the challenged harvesting pending appeal (884
F2d 1233; 866 F2d 302). In response to this ongoing litigation, Congress enacted § 318 of the Department of the Interior and Related Agencies Appropriations Act, 1990 (103 Stat 745), which required some harvesting in the forests managed by
the Forest Service and the BLM, but prohibited
harvesting altogether in certain areas of the forests.
In § 318(b)(6)(A), it was stated that "Congress
hereby determines and directs that" management of
the forests according to §§ 318(b)(3) and 318(b)(5)
was adequate consideration to meet the statutory
requirements that were the basis for the two cases
initiated by the environmental groups, which cases
were identified in § 318(b)(6)(A) by name and caption number. After both District Courts held that
§ 318(b)(6)(A) did not violate the Federal Constitution's Article III by purporting to direct the results
in the two pending cases, the United States Court of
Appeals for the Ninth Circuit (1) consolidated the
ensuing appeals; (2) held that § 318(b)(6)(A) was
unconstitutional on the ground that, in enacting
§ 318(b)(6)(A), Congress had directed particular decisions in the cases without amending or repealing
the statutes underlying the litigation; and (3) reversed the District Court judgments (914 F2d 1311).

On certiorari, the United States Supreme Court
reversed and remanded. In an opinion by THOMAS,
J., expressing the unanimous view of the court, it
was held that § 318(b)(6)(A) did not violate Article
III, because (1) § 318(b)(6)(A) compelled changes in
law, not findings or results under old law, by replac-

ing the legal standards of the provisions of the five statutes underlying the original claims with the standards set forth in §§ 318(b)(3) and 318(b)(5), since § 318(b)(6)(A)'s operation modified the five old provisions, where (a) before § 318(b)(6)(A) was enacted, the original claims would have failed only if the challenged harvesting violated none of the old provisions, while (b) under § 318(b)(6)(A), the claims would fail if the harvesting violated neither of the two new provisions; (2) nothing in § 318(b)(6)(A) purported to direct any particular findings of fact or applications of law to fact; (3) the inclusion in § 318(b)(6)(A) of the preface "Congress . . . directs that" did not undermine the conclusion that Congress was directing, to federal agencies and to courts, a change in law rather than specific results, since a statutory directive, even without such a preface, binds both the executive officials who administer the statute and the judges who apply it in particular cases; (4) the fact that § 318(b)(6)(A) deemed compliance with new requirements to meet old requirements did not indicate that § 318(b)(6)(A) did not modify the old requirements, where Congress' enactment of an entirely separate statute deeming compliance with that statute to meet earlier statutory requirements was a modification of the earlier requirements through operation of the canon that specific statutory provisions qualify general ones; and (5) § 318(b)(6)(A)'s explicit reference to the pending cases served only to identify the five statutory requirements that were the bases for the cases, where § 318(b)(6)(A) affected the adjudication of the cases to the extent of effectively modifying the provisions at issue in the cases.

192

COUNSEL

Kenneth W. Starr argued the cause for petitioners.

Todd D. True argued the cause for respondents.

UNITED STATES DEPARTMENT OF
COMMERCE, et al., Appellants

v

MONTANA et al.

503 US —, 118 L Ed 2d 87, 112 S Ct 1415

Argued March 4, 1992.
Decided March 31, 1992.

Decision: Apportionment of members of Congress
among several states according to method of
equal proportions under 2 USCS § 2a held not
to violate Article I, § 2 of Federal Constitution.

SUMMARY

Article I, § 2 of the Federal Constitution requires
that seats in the United States House of Representatives be apportioned among the several states "according to their respective Numbers"—that is, according to the population of each state. After trying
various methods of allocating seats, Congress in
1941 enacted a statute (codified at 2 USCS § 2a)
which provided that after each decennial census the
"method of equal proportions" would be used to
determine the number of Representatives to which
each state was entitled. Under the 1990 census,
application of the method of equal proportions
required, among other results, that the state of
Montana, which previously had two seats in the
House, would form a single congressional district,
while the state of Washington, which previously had
eight seats, would gain a ninth. Various plaintiffs
including Montana officials filed suit against federal
defendants in the United States District Court for

the District of Montana, which suit (1) included
assertions that apportionment according to the
method of equal proportions under § 2a violated
Article I, § 2 because the method did not achieve
the greatest possible equality in the number of
individuals per representative, and (2) offered evidence that apportionment by the alternative
"method of the harmonic mean"—under which
Montana would have two seats and Washington
eight, while other states would have the same number of seats as under the method of equal proportions—would result in lower absolute differences
from ideal district size. A three-judge District Court
granted Montana's motion for summary judgment
as to the above claim, as the court ruled that (1) the
principle of equal representation for equal numbers
of people, previously applied by the United States
Supreme Court to the apportionment of congressional seats within states, should also be applied to the
apportionment of seats among the states; (2) under
that standard, the only population variances among
congressional districts that were acceptable were
those that were unavoidable despite a good-faith
effort to achieve absolute equality, or for which
justification was shown; (3) the population variance
between Montana's single district and the ideal
district could not be justified under that standard;
and (4) Congress' decision to adopt the method of
equal proportions in 1941 was not entitled to deference, because (a) the decision was made without the
benefit of the Supreme Court's subsequent jurisprudence adopting the "one-person, one-vote" rule,
and (b) the method had been followed automatically
in subsequent reapportionments without reconsideration in the light of changing circumstances (775 F
Supp 1358).

On direct appeal, the Supreme Court reversed. In an opinion by STEVENS, J., expressing the unanimous view of the court, it was held that (1) the constitutionality of Congress' selection among alternative methods of apportionment was not barred from judicial review under the political question doctrine; and (2) Congress acted within its constitutional authority in enacting the statutory reapportionment procedure in 1941 and in applying the method of equal proportions after the 1990 census, because, although the requirement that Representatives be apportioned among the states "according to their respective Numbers" might be found to embody the same principle of equality applied in the context of intrastate redistricting, it was not clear that the facts of the case at hand established a violation of the one-person, one-vote standard, since (a) apportionment of Representatives among the states is constrained by the constitutional requirements that each state shall have at least one Representative and that district boundaries may not cross state lines, which requirements make it virtually impossible to have districts with the same population in any pair of states, (b) apportionment by the method of harmonic mean, though decreasing the absolute differences from ideal district size, would increase the relative differences, (c) Congress' apparently good-faith choice of a method of apportionment commanded far more deference than a state districting decision that could be reviewed under a relatively rigid mathematical standard, and (d) the automatic application of the method of equal proportions under § 2a was not unconstitutional, as, assuming that a set formula is otherwise constitutional, the use of a procedure that is administered efficiently and that avoids partisan controversy supports, rather than undermines, the legitimacy of congressional action.

COUNSEL

Kenneth W. Starr argued the cause for appellants.
Marc Racicot argued the cause for appellees.

———————

ROBERT R. FREEMAN, et al., Petitioners

v

WILLIE EUGENE PITTS et al.

503 US —, 118 L Ed 2d 108, 112 S Ct 1430

Argued October 7, 1991.
Decided March 31, 1992.

Decision: Federal court in ongoing school desegregation case held to have discretion to order incremental withdrawal of supervision over Georgia school district.

SUMMARY

In Green v County School Board (1968) 391 US 430, 20 L Ed 2d 716, 88 S Ct 1689, the United States Supreme Court held that (1) the time for "deliberate speed" in eliminating de jure school segregation had run out; (2) the obligation of schools once segregated by law was to come forward with a plan that promised to work realistically "now"; and (3) student assignments, faculty, staff, transportation, extracurricular activities, and physical facilities had to be free from racial discrimination. Shortly thereafter, black schoolchildren and their parents instituted a class action in the United States District Court for the Northern District of Georgia for the desegregation of a Georgia county school system which had once been segregated by law. The school system voluntarily began working with the Federal Government to devise a comprehensive desegregation plan, and the District Court in June 1969 entered a consent order approving the proposed plan. For the next 17 years, judicial intervention into the affairs of the school system was limited and infrequent, but demographic changes occurred, including (1) an increase in the overall proportion of black students from 5.6 percent to 47 percent, and (2) a shift in residential patterns, so that the population of the northern half of the county became predominantly white, and the southern half became predominantly black. In 1986, school officials, seeking a declaration that the school system had satisfied its duty and had achieved unitary status, filed a motion for final dismissal. Although evidence of racial imbalance was presented —such as evidence that during the 1986-1987 school year, 50 percent of the black students attended schools that were more than 90 percent black—the District Court's eventual findings included statements to the effect that (1) the county's population changes had not been caused by the school system's policies, but rather by independent factors; (2) throughout the period of supervision, the court had been impressed by the school system's successes and dedication to providing a quality education for all students; (3) the system had traveled the often long road to unitary status almost to its end; and (4) the system was a unitary system with respect to student assignments, transportation, physical facilities, and extracurricular activities, but vestiges of the dual system remained in the areas of teacher and principal assignments, resource allocation, and quality of education. Accordingly, the District Court ruled that it would order no further relief as to the unitary areas, but that the school system had to address the problems in the other areas. On appeal, the United States Court of Appeals for the Eleventh Circuit—in affirming in part, reversing in part, and ordering a remand—expressed the view that (1) the District Court had correctly concluded that the school system had not yet achieved unitary status, but had erred by considering the Green factors as separate categories; (2) a school system achieves unitary status only after it has satisfied all the Green factors at the same time for a number of years; (3) because the school system in question had not satisfied this test, the system could not shirk its constitutional duties by pointing to demographic shifts; and (4) the system's officials, who bore the responsibility for the racial imbalance, would have to take actions that might be awkward, inconvenient, or even bizarre in order to correct that imbalance, such as pairing and clustering of schools, drastic gerrymandering of school zones, grade reorganization, and busing (887 F2d 1438).

On certiorari, the Supreme Court reversed the judgment of the Court of Appeals, remanded the case to the Court of Appeals for further proceedings, and ordered each party to bear its own costs. In an opinion by KENNEDY, J., joined by REHNQUIST, Ch. J., and WHITE, SCALIA, and SOUTER, JJ., it was held that (1) a federal court in a school desegregation case has the authority and discretion to order an incremental or partial withdrawal of the court's supervision and control with respect to discrete categories in which a school district has achieved compliance with a court-ordered desegregation plan, before full compliance has been achieved in every area of school operations; (2) among the factors which may inform the court's sound discretion in ordering partial withdrawal are (a) whether there has been full and satisfactory compliance with the court's desegregation decree in those aspects of the system where supervision is to be withdrawn, (b) whether retention of judicial control is necessary or practicable to achieve compliance with the decree in other facets of the school system, and (c) whether the affected school district has demonstrated, to the public and to the parents and students of the once disfavored race, the district's good-faith commitment to the whole of the court's decree and to those provisions of the law and the Federal Constitution that were the predicate for judicial intervention in the first instance; (3) the District Court did not, as a matter of law, lack discretion to permit the school system to regain control over student assignments, transportation, physical facilities, and extracurricular activities, while retaining court supervision over the areas of faculty and administrative assignments and the quality of education, where full compliance had not been demonstrated, for there was no requirement that until there was full compliance, heroic measures had to be taken to insure racial balance in student assignments systemwide in the late phases of carrying out a decree, when the imbalance was attributable to independent demographic forces, rather than to the prior de jure segregation system or to a later violation by the school system; and (4) on remand, the Court of Appeals was to determine what issues were open for the Court of Appeals' further consideration in light of the parties' arguments and the principles set forth by the Supreme Court, and thereupon was to order further proceedings as necessary, or order an appropriate remand to the District Court.

SCALIA, J., concurring, expressed the view that (1) while the Supreme Court's decision would be of great assistance to the citizens of the county in question, the decision would have little effect upon the many other school districts that were still being supervised by federal judges, since the decision turned upon the relatively rare circumstance of a finding that no portion of the current racial imbalance was a remnant of prior de jure discrimination; and (2) while the Supreme Court must continue to prohibit, without qualification, all racial discrimination in schools, and to afford remedies that eliminate not only the discrimination but also its identified consequences, the court was close to the time in which the it must (a) acknowledge that it has become absurd to assume that constitutional violations dating from 24 years ago or earlier continue to have an appreciable effect on the current operations of schools, (b) lay aside the extraordinary and increasingly counterfactual presumption of Green v County School Board, and (c) revert to the ordinary principles of the nation's law, democratic heritage, and educational tradition, that (i) plaintiffs alleging equal protection violations must prove intent and causation and not merely the existence of racial disparity, (ii) public schooling, even in the South, should be controlled by locally elected authorities acting in conjunction with parents, and (iii) it is desirable to permit pupils to attend schools nearest their homes.

SOUTER, J., concurring, expressed the view that his understanding of the inquiry required by a Federal District Court applying the principles set out by the Supreme Court was that (1) the list of specific factors in Green v County School Board ought not to be treated as exclusive; (2) although demographic changes influencing the composition of a school's student population might well have no causal link to prior de jure segregation, judicial control of student assignments might still be necessary to remedy persisting vestiges of the unconstitutional dual system, such as remaining imbalance in

faculty assignments; and (3) additional causal relationships between or among unconstitutional acts of
school segregation and various Green-type factors
might occur, such as where (a) the dual school
system was itself a cause of the demographic shifts,
or (b) after a District Court has relinquished supervision of a remedied aspect of the school system,
future imbalance in that remedied Green-type factor
would be caused by remaining vestiges of the dual
system in the unremedied factors.

BLACKMUN, J., joined by STEVENS and O'CONNOR,
JJ., concurring in the judgment, expressed the view
that (1) it was error in the case at hand for both (a)
the District Court, ignoring the fact that the majority of black students in the county in question had
never attended a school that was not disproportion-
ately black, to relinquish control over student assignments, upon a finding that the school system
had achieved unitary status in that aspect, and (b)
the Court of Appeals to order the school system to
take extraordinary measures to correct all manifesta-
tions of that racial imbalance; (2) whether the District Court in the case at hand had to order the
school system to balance student assignments depended on whether (a) the current imbalance was
traceable to school policy, and (b) such an order
was necessary to fashion an effective remedy; (3)
whether a District Court must order changes in
student assignments generally depends on whether
(a) it is necessary or practicable to achieve compliance in other aspects of the school system, and (b) a
school district's conduct was a contributing cause of
the racially identifiable schools; and (4) the Court of
Appeals ought to review the District Court's finding
that the school system had met its burden of prov-

ing that the racially identifiable schools were in no way the result of past segregation.

THOMAS, J., did not participate.

COUNSEL

Rex E. Lee argued the cause for petitioners.

Solicitor General Kenneth W. Starr argued the cause for the United States, as amicus curiae, by special leave of court.

Christopher A. Hansen argued the cause for respondents.

———

JOHN K. YEE, et al., Petitioners

v

CITY OF ESCONDIDO, CALIFORNIA

503 US —, 118 L Ed 2d 153, 112 S Ct 1522

Argued January 22, 1992.
Decided April 1, 1992.

Decision: Mobile home rent control ordinance,
viewed in context of California statute restricting termination of mobile home park tenancy,
held not to constitute physical "taking" under
Fifth Amendment.

SUMMARY

California's mobile home residency law (MRL) (1)
limited the bases on which a mobile home park
owner could terminate a mobile home owner's
rental of space in the park; (2) generally prohibited
park owners from requiring the removal of a mobile
home when it was sold; (3) prohibited park owners
from charging transfer fees for such sales; and (4)
prohibited park owners from disapproving of a
purchaser who was able to pay the rent. Following
enactment of the MRL, a California city enacted a
mobile home rent control ordinance which set back
existing rents to the level of 2 years earlier and
required park owners to obtain the approval of the
city council for any rent increases. The owners of
two mobile home parks in the city filed suit against
the city in the Superior Court of San Diego County,
California, which suit (1) contended that the combined effect of the rent control ordinance and the
MRL amounted to a "taking" of property by perma-

nent physical occupation, for which just compensation was required under the Federal Constitution's Fifth Amendment, because the state law generally required park owners to accept the purchaser of a mobile home as a new tenant, and, as a result, existing tenants had been able to monetize the value of living in a rent-controlled jurisdiction by raising the price of used mobile homes, transferring to the tenants a discrete interest in land—the right to occupy the land indefinitely at sub-market rent—which amounted to a right of physical occupation; and (2) sought damages and declaratory and injunctive relief. The Superior Court sustained the city's demurrer and dismissed the park owners' complaint; and the California Court of Appeal, Fourth District, affirmed (224 Cal App 3d 1349, 274 Cal Rptr 551). After the Supreme Court of California denied discretionary review, the park owners petitioned the United States Supreme Court for certiorari, which the Supreme Court granted only as to the question whether the Court of Appeal had erred in disagreeing with decisions of two Federal Courts of Appeals, which decisions had held that similar mobile home rent control ordinances effected physical takings of property for purposes of the Fifth Amendment.

On certiorari, the United States Supreme Court affirmed. In an opinion by O'CONNOR, J., joined by REHNQUIST, Ch. J., and WHITE, STEVENS, SCALIA, KENNEDY, and THOMAS, JJ., it was held that (1) the rent control ordinance, even when considered in conjunction with the MRL, did not authorize a per se "taking" of the park owners' property by compelled physical occupation, because (a) the park owners had voluntarily rented their land to mobile home owners and were not compelled to continue doing so, (b) the ordinance and MRL, on their face, merely regulated the park owners' use of their property by regulating the relationship between landlord and tenant, (c) the alleged transfer of wealth from park owners to incumbent mobile home owners did not in itself convert regulation into physical invasion, and (d) neither the claim that the ordinance differed from apartment rent control—in that the ordinance benefited incumbent mobile home owners but not future owners, who would be forced to purchase the homes at a premium—nor the claim that the ordinance prevented park owners from choosing their tenants by threatening to raise rents for potential tenants they disfavored, had anything to do with whether the ordinance caused a physical taking; (2) the Supreme Court would not consider a claim that the ordinance constituted a denial of substantive due process, because (a) the park owners did not include a due process claim in their complaint nor raise such a claim before the state appellate court, and (b) the state courts did not address the claim; and (3) even though a facial challenge to the ordinance as a regulatory "taking," which challenge alleged that the ordinance did not substantially advance a legitimate state interest no matter how the ordinance was applied, was ripe for review regardless of the fact that the park owners had not sought rent increases under the ordinance, that challenge would not be reviewed by the Supreme Court, because (a) the regulatory taking claim was not fairly included within the sole takings question presented by the park owners' petition for certiorari, (b) Rule 14.1(a) of the Supreme Court Rules therefore created a heavy presumption against the Supreme Court's consideration of the regulatory taking claim, and (c) the park owners had not overcome that presumption.

BLACKMUN, J., concurred in the judgment, expressing the view that (1) the rent control ordinance was not a physical "taking" of property; (2) the substantive due process and regulatory takings claims were not properly raised before the Supreme Court; and (3) because the regulatory takings claim was not properly raised, it was unnecessary to decide whether the claim was ripe or which arguments would be relevant to such a claim.

SOUTER, J., concurred in the judgment, joining in the court's opinion except for its references to the relevance and significance of the petitioners' allegations to a claim of regulatory taking.

COUNSEL

Robert J. Jagiello argued the cause for petitioners.
Carter G. Phillips argued the cause for respondent.

––––––––––––

KEITH JACOBSON, Petitioner

v

UNITED STATES

503 US —, 118 L Ed 2d 174, 112 S Ct 1535

Argued November 6, 1991.
Decided April 6, 1992.

Decision: Government held to have failed, as matter
of law, to establish that individual was predisposed to illegally receive mailing of sexually
explicit depictions of children and hence was
not entrapped.

SUMMARY

At a time when receipt of such magazines was
legal under both federal and Nebraska law, a Nebraska farmer ordered and received from a bookstore two magazines containing photographs of
nude preteen and teenage boys. After Congress
passed the Child Protection Act of 1984 (18 USCS
§§ 2251 et seq.)—which, in 18 USCS § 2252(a)(2)
(A), criminalized the receipt through the mails of
sexually explicit depictions of children—postal in-
spectors found the farmer's name on the bookstore
mailing list, and, as a result, the Postal Service
sought to explore the farmer's willingness to place a
mail order that would violate § 2252(a)(2)(A), by
mailing him letters from three fictitious organizations—which letters discussed (1) protection and
promotion of sexual freedom and freedom of
choice, and (2) funding of lobbying efforts by cata-
log sales—and from a bogus pen pal who stated an
interest in materials depicting the sexual activities of

young men. The farmer responded to the letters by
answering questionnaires and expressing interest in
the organizations' goals. Twenty-six months after
the Postal Service had commenced sending the mail,
the Customs Service, using the name of a fictitious
organization, mailed the farmer an advertisement
for photographs of young boys engaging in sex, in
response to which advertisement the farmer placed
an order that was never filled. The Postal Service,
posing as yet another fictitious organization that
sold sexually explicit materials, then mailed the
farmer a letter that called concerns about pornography hysterical nonsense and decried international
censorship. After the farmer ordered and received
from this fictitious organization, through the mail, a
pornographic magazine depicting young boys engaged in various sexual activities, the farmer was
arrested. A search of his home revealed the magazines bought from the bookstore and the materials
sent by the government during its investigation, but
revealed no other materials indicating that the
farmer collected or was actively interested in child
pornography. At the farmer's trial in the United
States District Court for the District of Nebraska on
charges of violating § 2252(a)(2)(A), the jury was
instructed on the farmer's entrapment defense and
the farmer was convicted. Concluding that the
farmer was not entrapped as a matter of law, the
United States Court of Appeals for the Eighth Circuit affirmed (916 F2d 467).

On certiorari, the United States Supreme Court
reversed. In an opinion by WHITE, J., joined by
BLACKMUN, STEVENS, SOUTER, and THOMAS, JJ., it
was held that the government, which did not dispute that it had induced the farmer to violate
§ 2252(a)(2)(A), had failed, as a matter of law, to

adduce evidence to support the jury verdict that the farmer was predisposed, prior to and independent of the acts of the government and beyond a reasonable doubt, to violate § 2252(a)(2)(A)(5), since (1) the fact that the farmer legally ordered and received the two magazines from the bookstore did little to further the government's burden of proving predisposition, particularly where the farmer presented unchallenged testimony that he did not know until the magazines arrived that they would depict minors; (2) the prosecution's evidence gathered during the investigation also failed to carry the government's burden, where (a) the farmer's responses to the many communications prior to the criminal act were at most indicative of certain personal inclinations, and did not support an inference that the farmer would violate § 2252(a)(2)(A), and (b) the strong arguable inference was that, by waiving the banner of individual rights and disparaging the legitimacy and constitutionality of efforts to restrict the availability of sexually explicit materials, the government not only excited the farmer's interest in sexually explicit materials banned by law, but also exerted substantial pressure on him to obtain and read such materials as part of a fight against censorship and the infringement of individual rights; and (3) Congress had not intended that the detection and enforcement processes of § 2252(a)(2)(A) should include instigation by government officials of an act on the part of persons otherwise innocent in order to lure them to its commission and to punish them.

O'CONNOR, J., joined by REHNQUIST, Ch. J., and KENNEDY, J., and joined by SCALIA, J., as to point 1 below, dissented, expressing the view that (1) it was reasonable for the jury to infer that the farmer was

predisposed beyond a reasonable doubt to violate
§ 2252(a)(2)(A), even if other inferences from the
evidence also were possible, and (2) although the
fact that the farmer's purchase of the two magazines
from the bookstore was legal may have had some
relevance to the question of predisposition, it was
not dispositive.

COUNSEL

George H. Moyer, Jr. argued the cause for petitioner.

Paul J. Larkin, Jr. argued the cause for respondent.

———————

JOE MARIO TREVINO, Petitioner

v

TEXAS

503 US —, 118 L Ed 2d 193, 112 S Ct 1547

Decided April 6, 1992.

Decision: Accused's objection under equal protection clause to state's race-based use of peremptory challenges prior to Supreme Court's decision in Batson v Kentucky held preserved for review by Supreme Court.

SUMMARY

In 1984, before jury selection in an accused's trial in a Texas state court for murder and rape, the accused, who was Hispanic, filed a motion to prohibit the use of peremptory challenges based merely on the fact of race. The accused alleged that (1) the state historically had used its peremptory challenges to strike prospective black jurors and other minorities who were otherwise qualified; and (2) by so doing, the state had deprived the accused of (a) due process and a fair trial, and (b) a jury representing a fair cross section of the community, in violation of the Federal Constitution's Sixth Amendment. Although the accused requested a hearing, the trial court delayed ruling on the motion. During voir dire, the trial court denied the accused's renewed motion after the prosecution used its peremptory challenges to excuse the only three black members of the venire, notwithstanding the argument of counsel for the accused that (1) five members of the United States Supreme Court had expressed the

213

view that Swain v Alabama (1965) 380 US 202, 13 L
Ed 2d 759, 85 S Ct 824—which required a showing
of racial exclusion from juries in "case after case" in
order to establish a violation of the equal protection
clause of the Federal Constitution's Fourteenth
Amendment—ought to be re-examined; and (2) the
Texas courts should anticipate the Supreme Court's
modification of the burden of proof required under
Swain v Alabama. After an all-white jury returned a
verdict of guilty and the trial court sentenced the
accused to death, the individual appealed to the
Court of Criminal Appeals of Texas. In a brief filed
prior to the Supreme Court's decision in Batson v
Kentucky (1986) 476 US 79, 90 L Ed 2d 69, 106 S
Ct 1712—which held that, where a defendant makes
a prima facie showing that the state has exercised its
peremptory challenges to exclude members of the
defendant's racial group from the jury, the state
bears the burden of coming forward with a race-
neutral justification—the accused (1) included an
argument caption which made an express reference
to the Fourteenth Amendment; (2) contended that
the state's race-based use of challenges violated the
accused's rights to due process and to an impartial
jury fairly drawn from a representative cross section
of the community, in violation of the Sixth and
Fourteenth Amendments as well as state constitutional provisions; (3) asserted that he was renewing
the objections pressed at trial; and (4) acknowledged the rule of Swain v Alabama, but noted that
the question would be reconsidered by the Supreme
Court in Batson v Kentucky. The Court of Criminal
Appeals, affirming the accused's conviction and sentence, expressed the view that (1) the Sixth Amendment did not prohibit the use of peremptory challenges to exclude potential jurors based on race;
214

and (2) the arguments made by the accused did not amount to reliance on the equal protection clause (815 SW2d 592).

Granting leave to proceed in forma pauperis and granting certiorari, the United States Supreme Court reversed and remanded. In a per curiam opinion expressing the unanimous view of the court, it was held that (1) under the circumstances, the accused had preserved, both in trial court and before the Court of Criminal Appeals, an equal protection objection to the state's race-based use of peremptory challenges prior to the Supreme Court's decision in Batson v Kentucky; and (2) although the excluded jurors were not members of the same protected class as the accused, there was legal support for the accused's claim that the prosecution's use of peremptory challenges to exclude such jurors violated the equal protection clause.

———————

UNITED STATES, Plaintiff

v

STATE OF ALASKA

503 US —, 118 L Ed 2d 222, 112 S Ct 1606

Argued February 24, 1992.
Decided April 21, 1992.

Decision: Secretary of Army held authorized under § 10 of Rivers and Harbors Appropriation Act (33 USCS § 403) to condition approval of port construction on Alaska's disclaimer of federal-state boundary change.

SUMMARY

Under § 10 of the Rivers and Harbors Appropriation Act of 1899 (RHA) (33 USCS § 403), it is unlawful to build any structures in any water of the United States except on plans authorized by the United States Secretary of the Army. A Department of the Army regulation (33 CFR § 320.4(f)) provides that (1) applications for structures or works affecting coastal waters will be reviewed to determine whether the coast line or base line might be altered; (2) if it is determined that such a change might occur, coordination with the Attorney General and the Solicitor of the Department of the Interior is required before final action is taken; and (3) the Solicitor's comments are to be requested concerning the effects of the proposed work on the outer continental rights of the United States. Another regulation (33 CFR § 320.4(a)(1)) requires the Secretary to determine whether issuance of a construction permit would affect the public interest. The city

216

of Nome, Alaska, applied to the Department of the
Army's Alaska District Corps of Engineers, pursuant
to § 10 of the RHA and § 404 of the Clean Water
Act (33 USCS § 1344), for a federal permit to build
port facilities extending into Norton Sound. The
Solicitor of the Department of the Interior issued an
opinion stating that the Nome project would cause
an accretion to Alaska's coastline, and that this
change would affect federal offshore mineral leasing
because the federal-state boundary was measured
from the coastline. On the Solicitor's recommendation, the Corps of Engineers advised the state of
Alaska that the permit would not be issued until a
waiver or quitclaim deed was issued to preserve the
coastline and the federal-state boundary. An Alaska
state agency submitted a conditional disclaimer of
rights to additional submerged lands that could be
claimed by the state under the Submerged Lands
Act (SLA) (43 USCS §§ 1301 et seq.) as a result of
the port construction, and the Secretary, through
the Corps of Engineers, issued the permit. Subsequently, the Department of the Interior proposed a
lease sale for minerals in Norton Sound. Alaska,
alleging that the proposal involved submerged lands
subject to the Nome project disclaimer, announced
the state's intention to file suit challenging the
Corps of Engineers' authority to require a waiver of
the state's rights to submerged lands. The United
States filed a bill of complaint against Alaska in the
United States Supreme Court, and the Supreme
Court granted leave to commence the action. The
United States and Alaska both filed motions for
summary judgment.

The Supreme Court granted the United States'
motion for summary judgment and denied Alaska's
motion for summary judgment. In an opinion by

WHITE, J., expressing the unanimous view of the court, it was held that (1) the Secretary acted within his discretion, under § 10 of the RHA, in conditioning approval of the Nome port construction on a disclaimer by Alaska of a change in the federal-state boundary; (2) the Secretary's authority, in considering whether to issue a § 10 construction permit, is not confined solely to considerations of navigation; (3) 33 CFR § 320.4(f), in authorizing the Secretary to consider a project's consequences on the federal-state boundary, does not conflict with a provision of the SLA (43 USCS § 1312) which provides that a coastal state's boundary extends 3 miles from the state's coastline; (4) the Secretary is not barred from considering, as part of the public interest review process under § 10 of the RHA, whether the construction would change federal-state boundaries, merely because such consideration may, in certain circumstances, permit the Secretary effectively to establish one boundary for international purposes, pursuant to the Convention on the Territorial Sea and the Contiguous Zone (15 UST 1607, TIAS No. 5639), and a different boundary for domestic purposes, pursuant to the SLA; and (5) the Corps of Engineers did not act in an arbitrary or capricious manner in the case at hand.

COUNSEL

Jeffrey P. Minear argued the cause for plaintiff.
John G. Gissberg argued the cause for defendant.

_____

KEYTON E. BARKER and PAULINE BARKER,
et al., Petitioners

v

KANSAS et al.

503 US —, 118 L Ed 2d 243, 112 S Ct 1619

Argued March 3, 1992.
Decided April 21, 1992.

Decision: Kansas' income tax on military retirement
benefits, but not on state and local government
retirement benefits, held inconsistent with 4
USCS § 111 prohibition against discriminatory
taxes.

SUMMARY

It is provided in 4 USCS § 111 that the United
States consents to state taxation of the pay or
compensation for personal service of a United
States officer or employee, if the taxation does not
discriminate against the officer or employee because
of the source of the pay or compensation. In Davis v
Michigan Dept. of Treasury (1989) 489 US 803, 103
L Ed 2d 891, 109 S Ct 1500, the United States
Supreme Court held that (1) the retention of immunity in § 111 was coextensive with the prohibition
against discriminatory taxes embodied in the federal
constitutional doctrine of intergovernmental tax immunity; and (2) under these principles, a Michigan
income tax law was invalid, where the law imposed
taxes on benefits received on federal civil service
retirees, but not on benefits received by state and
local government retirees. Kansas' income tax taxed
the benefits received from the United States by

military retirees, but did not tax the benefits received by retired state and local government employees. After the Davis decision, two class actions by military-retiree taxpayers—and, where applicable, their joint-taxpayer spouses—were filed in a Kansas district court against the state, the state department of revenue, and various state officials. The actions were consolidated. The taxpayers, who sought declaratory and injunctive relief, as well as tax refunds, included allegations that Kansas' income tax discriminated against them in favor of state and local government retirees, in violation of § 111 and the principles of intergovernmental tax immunity. The district court, however, granted summary judgment against the taxpayers. On appeal, the Supreme Court of Kansas, in affirming, expressed the view that Kansas' income tax did not violate § 111 and the principles of intergovernmental tax immunity, because of significant differences between military retirees and state and local government retirees, such as the difference that military retirement benefits constituted reduced pay for current services, rather than deferred compensation for past services (249 Kan 186, 815 P2d 46).

On certiorari, the United States Supreme Court reversed the judgment of the Kansas Supreme Court and remanded the case for further proceedings. In an opinion by WHITE, J., expressing the unanimous view of the court, it was held that under the principles of Davis v Michigan Dept. of Treasury, Kansas' income tax on benefits received from the United States by military retirees, but not on benefits received by retired state and local government employees, was inconsistent with § 111, because, for purposes of § 111, military retirement benefits were to be considered deferred pay for past services, and in this respect, military retirement benefits were not significantly different from the benefits paid to Kansas state and local government retirees, in light of (1) the manner in which these benefits were calculated, (2) prior United States Supreme Court decisions concerning military retirement, (3) congressional intent as expressed in other provisions treating military retirement pay, and (4) Kansas' income tax treatment of federal retirement benefits.

STEVENS, J., joined by THOMAS, J., concurring, expressed the view that, while the case at hand was controlled by Davis v Michigan Dept. of Treasury, (1) the Davis decision had seriously misapplied the doctrine of intergovernmental tax immunity; and (2) such misapplication was subject to review and correction by Congress.

COUNSEL

Kevin M. Fowler argued the cause for petitioners.

John F. Manning argued the cause for the United States, as amicus curiae, by special leave of the court.

James A.D. Bartle argued the cause for respondents.

UNITED STATES DEPARTMENT OF ENERGY,
Petitioner

v

OHIO et al. (No. 90-1341)

OHIO, et al., Petitioners

v

UNITED STATES DEPARTMENT OF ENERGY
(No. 90-1517)

503 US —, 118 L Ed 2d 255, 112 S Ct 1627

Argued December 3, 1991.
Decided April 21, 1992.

Decision: Federal sovereign immunity held not waived as to state-imposed punitive fines under Clean Water Act (33 USCS §§ 1251 et seq.) and Resource Conservation and Recovery Act (42 USCS §§ 6901 et seq.).

SUMMARY

The Clean Water Act (CWA) (33 USCS §§ 1251 et seq.), which prohibits the discharge of pollutants into navigable waters without a permit, and the Resource Conservation and Recovery Act of 1976 (RCRA) (42 USCS §§ 6901 et seq.), which imposes a permit program regulating the disposal of hazardous waste, give the United States Environmental Protection Agency (EPA) primary authority to issue such permits, but allow the EPA to authorize a state to supplant the federal permit program with a state program under certain circumstances. The extent to

222

which federally operated facilities are subject to the requirements of the CWA and the RCRA is governed by 33 USCS § 1323(a) and 42 USCS § 6961, respectively, and actions by private citizens, including states, to enforce the CWA and the RCRA against persons who violate those statutes are authorized by 33 USCS § 1365(a) and 42 USCS § 6972(a), respectively. In an action brought in the United States District Court for the Southern District of Ohio against the United States Department of Energy (DOE) concerning pollution from a uranium-processing plant operated in Ohio by the DOE, the State of Ohio sought state and federal civil penalties for alleged past violations of the CWA and the RCRA and of state laws enacted to supplant those statutes. The DOE conceded that the CWA and RCRA render federal agencies liable for coercive fines—that is, fines imposed to induce compliance with injunctions or other judicial orders designed to modify behavior prospectively—but asserted sovereign immunity from punitive fines—that is, fines imposed to punish past violations of the CWA and RCRA or state laws supplanting them. The District Court, however, held that both statutes, in both their federal-facilities and citizen-suit sections, waived federal sovereign immunity from punitive fines (689 F Supp 760). On appeal, the United States Court of Appeals for the Sixth Circuit, in affirming in part without considering the CWA's federal-facilities section, held that Congress had waived immunity from punitive fines in the CWA's federal-facilities section and the RCRA's citizen-suit section, but not in the RCRA's federal-facilities section (904 F2d 1058).

On certiorari, the United States Supreme Court reversed the judgment of the Court of Appeals and

remanded the case for further proceedings. In an opinion by SOUTER, J., expressing the unanimous opinion of the court as to holding 3 below, and joined by REHNQUIST, Ch. J., and O'CONNOR, SCALIA, KENNEDY, and THOMAS, JJ., as to holdings 1 and 2 below, it was held that Congress had not waived federal sovereign immunity from liability for civil fines for past violations of the CWA or the RCRA, or of state law supplanting the federal regulation, in (1) § 1365(a) or § 6972(a), because (a) the inclusion in CWA and RCRA of the United States as a "person" covered by those statutes must go no further than to the clauses subjecting the United States to suit, since the inference can be only that a special definition not described in the CWA or RCRA as being for purposes of the section or subchapter in which the special definition occurs was intended to have the more limited application to the special definition's own clause or sentence alone, and (b) this textual analysis passes the test of giving effect to all the language of the citizen-suit sections; (2) § 1323(a)—which subjects the United States to CWA liability for civil penalties arising under federal law—because (a) § 1323(a)'s use of the term "sanction" carries no necessary implication that a reference to punitive fines is intended, (b) the fact that the text of § 1323(a) speaks of sanctions in the context of enforcing process as distinct from substantive requirements is a good reason to infer that § 1323(a) uses "sanction" in its coercive sense, to the exclusion of punitive fines, and (c) fines authorized under an EPA-approved state permit program do not arise under federal law; or (3) § 6961—which subjects the Federal Government to all state requirements with respect to the RCRA— because (a) "all . . . requirements" can reasonably
224

be interpreted as including substantive standards and the means for implementing those standards, but excluding punitive measures, (b) § 6961 makes no mention of any mechanism for penalizing past violations, and (c) the drafters' only specific reference to an enforcement mechanism describes "sanction" as a coercive means of injunction enforcement.

WHITE, J., joined by BLACKMUN and STEVENS, JJ., concurring in part and dissenting in part, (1) agreed that § 6961 does not effect an unambiguous waiver of federal sovereign immunity from punitive civil penalties under the RCRA; but (2) expressed the view that (a) §§ 1323(a) and 1365(a) unambiguously waive federal sovereign immunity from punitive civil penalties under the CWA, and (b) § 6972(a) unambiguously waives federal sovereign immunity from punitive civil penalties under the RCRA.

COUNSEL

James A. Feldman argued the cause for petitioner and cross/respondent.

Jack A. Van Kley argued the cause for respondents and cross/petitioners.

ROBERT J. TAYLOR, Trustee, Petitioner

v

FREELAND & KRONZ, WENDELL G. FREELAND
and RICHARD F. KRONZ

503 US —, 118 L Ed 2d 280, 112 S Ct 1644

Argued March 2, 1992.
Decided April 21, 1992.

Decision: Bankruptcy trustee held barred, after expiration of 30-day period, from contesting validity of exemption claimed by debtor under 11
USCS § 522(*l*), despite lack of colorable basis
for claim.

SUMMARY

A debtor filed a complaint against her employer
for alleged race and sex discrimination, and a local
government agency found the employer liable but
did not calculate damages. After the agency's decision had been reversed by a state trial court and
reinstated by an intermediate state appellate court,
and while the employer's appeal to the state's highest court was pending, the debtor filed a petition for
liquidation under Chapter 7 of the Bankruptcy Code
(11 USCS §§ 701-766). On a schedule filed pursuant
to § 522(*l*) of the Code (11 USCS § 522(*l*)), the
debtor claimed as exempt property the money that
she expected to win in her discrimination lawsuit.
The debtor's bankruptcy trustee, though considering the potential proceeds of the lawsuit to be
property of the bankruptcy estate, did not believe
that the lawsuit had any value, and decided not to
object to the exemption. However, the employer,

after losing the appeal, settled the case by agreeing to pay the debtor approximately $110,000, partly by means of a check for $71,516.25 which the debtor signed over to her attorneys. The trustee then filed a complaint against the attorneys in the United States Bankruptcy Court for the Western District of Pennsylvania, which complaint sought to recover $67,349, the alleged value of the estate's interest in the lawsuit at the time that the bankruptcy petition was filed. In ordering the attorneys to return $23,483.75 plus interest to the bankruptcy estate, the Bankruptcy Court ruled that although the trustee had failed to object to the debtor's claimed exemption within 30 days as required by Rule 4003(b) of the Bankruptcy Rules, (1) there must be a statutory basis for a claimed exemption before the failure of a party in interest to object has any legal effect, and (2) the debtor had no statutory basis for claiming the proceeds of the lawsuit as exempt (105 BR 288). The United States District Court for the Western District of Pennsylvania affirmed (118 BR 272); but the United States Court of Appeals for the Third Circuit reversed, as it held that § 522(*l*)— which expressly states that unless a party in interest objects, the property claimed as exempt is exempt— must be interpreted literally (938 F2d 420).

On certiorari, the United States Supreme Court affirmed. In an opinion by THOMAS, J., joined by REHNQUIST, Ch. J., and WHITE, BLACKMUN, O'CONNOR, SCALIA, KENNEDY, and SOUTER, JJ., it was held that the trustee's failure to timely object to the debtor's claimed exemption prevented him from challenging the validity of the exemption regardless of whether the debtor had a colorable statutory basis for claiming the exemption, because (1) although deadlines may lead to unwelcome results, they prompt parties to act and produce finality; (2) if the trustee did not know the value of the lawsuit, he could have sought a hearing on the issue or asked the Bankruptcy Court for an extension of time to object, and he did neither; and (3) to the extent that existing penalties for improper conduct in bankruptcy proceedings did not limit bad-faith claims of exemptions by debtors, Congress may enact new provisions to prevent so-called "exemption by declaration," but the Supreme Court had no authority to limit the application of § 522(*l*) to exemptions claimed in good faith.

STEVENS, J., dissented, expressing the view that (1) the doctrine of equitable tolling applies to the limitations period in Rule 4003(b); and (2) the filing of a frivolous claim for an exemption is tantamount to fraud for purposes of deciding when the period begins to run.

COUNSEL

Timothy B. Dyk argued the cause for petitioner.

Phillip S. Simon argued the cause for respondents.

———————

JAMES GOMEZ and DANIEL VASQUEZ,
Petitioners

v

UNITED STATES DISTRICT COURT for the
NORTHERN DISTRICT of CALIFORNIA, et al.

503 US —, 118 L Ed 2d 293, 112 S Ct 1652

Decided April 21, 1992.

Decision: Application to vacate stay of accused's
execution by cyanide gas in California granted
by Supreme Court, where accused had not
challenged method of execution in prior habeas
corpus petitions.

SUMMARY

An accused who had been convicted of murder
and sentenced to death in California, and who later
had unsuccessfully filed numerous state and federal
habeas corpus petitions, filed an action, under 42
USCS § 1983, in the United States District Court for
the Northern District of California, in which action
the accused sought to stay his execution on the
ground that his execution by cyanide gas would
constitute cruel and unusual punishment, which is
prohibited by the Federal Constitution's Eighth
Amendment. The accused had not raised such a
claim in his prior habeas corpus petitions. The
District Court granted a stay of execution, and the
United States Court of Appeals for the Ninth Circuit
entered orders staying the execution.

On application to vacate the stay of execution, the
United States Supreme Court vacated the stay. In a
per curiam opinion expressing the view of REHN-

QUIST, Ch. J., and WHITE, O'CONNOR, SCALIA, KEN-
NEDY, SOUTER, and THOMAS, JJ., it was held that (1)
the accused had made no convincing showing of
cause for his failure to raise the claim in his prior
habeas corpus petitions; and (2) even if the accused's claim was not barred on the ground that it
was a successive claim for relief, the Supreme Court
would not consider the claim—whether it was
framed as a habeas corpus petition or as an action
under 42 USCS § 1983—on its merits, where (a) the
claim could have been brought more than a decade
earlier, and (b) there was no good reason for the
accused's abusive delay in bringing the claim, which
delay was compounded by last-minute attempts to
manipulate the judicial process.

STEVENS, J., joined by BLACKMUN, J., dissenting,
expressed the view that the application to vacate the
stay should be denied, because (1) the accused's
claim that his execution by exposure to cyanide gas
would constitute cruel and unusual punishment had
merit, in light of (a) all that was known about the
extreme and unnecessary pain inflicted by execution
by cyanide gas, and (b) the availability of more
humane and less violent methods of execution; (2)
California should have revisited its 55-year-old statute requiring execution by cyanide gas, since (a)
three members of the Supreme Court had indicated
in 1983 that execution by exposure to cyanide gas
raised sufficiently serious questions under the
Eighth Amendment to merit review by writ of certiorari, and (b) thereafer, four of the seven states
which had authorized execution by exposure to
cyanide gas abandoned such method; and (3) if
execution by cyanide gas was unconstitutional, California lacked the power to impose such punishment,
and the accused's delay in raising his claim—even if

unjustified—could not endow California with the
authority to violate the Constitution.

———————

J. C. KEENEY, Superintendent, Oregon State
Penitentiary, Petitioner

v

JOSE TAMAYO-REYES

504 US —, 118 L Ed 2d 318, 112 S Ct 1715

Argued January 15, 1992.
Decided May 4, 1992.

Decision: Federal habeas corpus petitioner, seeking
evidentiary hearing on claim that material facts
were not adequately developed in state proceedings, held generally required to show (1)
cause for failure to develop facts, and (2) prejudice resulting from such failure.

SUMMARY

In 1984, a Cuban immigrant with little education
and almost no knowledge of English was charged
with murder. After the accused was provided with a
defense attorney and an interpreter, an Oregon
judge held a plea hearing, and accepted the accused's plea of nolo contendere to first-degree manslaughter. Two years later, the accused brought a
collateral attack on the plea in a postconviction
proceeding in the Circuit Court for Marion County,
Oregon. In his petition, the accused alleged that his
plea had not been knowing and intelligent, and
therefore was invalid, because the interpreter had
not translated accurately and completely for him the
mens rea element of manslaughter. The Oregon
Circuit Court, dismissing the petition after a hearing, found that the accused had been properly
served by his interpreter and that the interpreter

had correctly, fully, and accurately translated the communications between the accused and his attorney. The Oregon Court of Appeals affirmed, and the Oregon Supreme Court denied review. Thereafter, the accused filed a habeas corpus petition in the United States District Court for the District of Oregon. The accused, seeking a federal evidentiary hearing on whether his plea of nolo contendere was unconstitutional, alleged that the material facts concerning the interpreter's translation were not adequately developed at the state postconviction hearing. The District Court, however, ruled that no evidentiary hearing was required, since the accused's failure to develop the material facts relevant to his federal claim was attributable to inexcusable neglect. On appeal, the United States Court of Appeals for the Ninth Circuit, reversing in pertinent part, expressed the view that (1) the material facts had not been adequately developed in the accused's state postconviction proceedings due to the negligent failure of the accused's counsel; and (2) since the accused had not deliberately bypassed the orderly procedure of the state courts, the accused was entitled to a federal evidentiary hearing on the question whether the mens rea element of manslaughter had been properly explained to him (926 F2d 1492).

On certiorari, the United States Supreme Court reversed the judgment of the Court of Appeals and remanded the case to the District Court for further proceedings. In an opinion by WHITE, J., joined by REHNQUIST, Ch. J., and SCALIA, SOUTER, and THOMAS, JJ., it was held that (1) if a federal habeas corpus petitioner challenges a state court conviction on the ground that the state courts committed constitutional error, then the petitioner, in order to be entitled to an evidentiary hearing on a claim that material facts were not adequately developed in the earlier state court proceedings, must show either (a) cause for the petitioner's failure to develop the facts, and actual prejudice resulting from such failure, or (b) that a fundamental miscarriage of justice would result from failure to hold a federal evidentiary hearing; (2) the decision of the Supreme Court in Townsend v Sain (1963) 372 US 293, 9 L Ed 2d 770, 83 S Ct 745, insofar as such decision held that the deliberate bypass standard was applicable in determining whether a federal habeas corpus petitioner was entitled to an evidentiary hearing on a claim that material facts were not adequately developed in state court proceedings, would be overruled by the Supreme Court; and (3) it was incorrect to assert that Congress, in adopting 28 USCS § 2254(d), a federal habeas corpus provision, after the Townsend v Sain decision, assumed the continuing validity of all aspects of the Townsend v Sain decision, including the Townsend v Sain requirement of an evidentiary hearing in all cases involving the petitioner's failure to develop material facts in state court proceedings where there was not a deliberate bypass of such proceedings by the petitioner.

O'CONNOR, J., joined by BLACKMUN, STEVENS, and KENNEDY, JJ., dissenting, expressed the view that (1) the balance of state and federal interests regarding whether a federal court should consider a claim raised in a petition for habeas corpus review cannot be lifted and transposed to the different question whether, once the court has decided to consider the claim, the court should hold an evidentiary hearing; (2) the enactment of § 2254(d) by Congress 3 years after the Supreme Court's decision in Townsend v Sain presumed the continuing validity of that case, including the portion of the decision that recognized a deliberate bypass exception to a federal habeas corpus petitioner's right to a hearing where the material facts were not adequately developed in state court proceedings; (3) if the assertion of the accused in the case at hand that he had pleaded nolo contendere to a crime that he did not understand was true, his conviction had been unconstitutionally obtained and he was entitled to a writ of habeas corpus; and (4) given that the accused's claim was properly before the Federal District Court in his first federal petition for a writ of habeas corpus, the accused's right to prove his claim at a hearing ought not to be cut off.

KENNEDY, J., dissenting, joined the opinion of O'CONNOR, J., and also expressed the view that (1) the ambit of the Supreme Court's holding in the case at hand was confined to those few cases in which the factual record developed in state court proceedings was inadequate to resolve the legal question; (2) the concept of factual inadequacy comprehended only those petitions with respect to which there was a realistic possibility that an evidentiary hearing would make a difference in the outcome; and (3) with respect to federal habeas corpus petitions which presented questions which federal courts were bound to decide in order to protect constitutional rights, steps should not be taken which diminished the likelihood that federal courts would base their legal decision on an accurate statement of the facts.

COUNSEL

Jack L. Landau argued the cause for petitioner.
Steven T. Wax argued the cause for respondent.

GEORGE F. DENTON, Director of Corrections of
California, et al., Petitioners

v

MIKE HERNANDEZ

504 US —, 118 L Ed 2d 340, 112 S Ct 1728

Argued February 24, 1992.
Decided May 4, 1992.

Decision: Dismissal of in forma pauperis action as
factually frivolous under 28 USCS § 1915(d)
held (1) appropriate where alleged facts are
irrational or incredible, and (2) reviewable for
abuse of discretion.

SUMMARY

Under 28 USCS § 1915(d), a federal court is
allowed to dismiss an in forma pauperis action if the
court is satisfied that the action is frivolous. A
California state prison inmate, proceeding pro se
against various prison officials, filed, in forma pauperis, five civil rights actions alleging that the inmate was drugged and homosexually raped a total
of 28 times by inmates and officials at different
prisons. A Federal District Court, however, finding
the inmate's factual allegations to be "wholly fanci-
ful," adopted a magistrate's recommendation that
the actions be dismissed as frivolous. The inmate
appealed the dismissals of three of the five actions.
Reviewing the dismissals de novo, the United States
Court of Appeals for the Ninth Circuit, reversing
and remanding, held that the actions could not be
dismissed as frivolous because it was impossible to
236

take judicial notice that none of the alleged rapes had occurred (861 F2d 1421). The United States Supreme Court, on certiorari, vacated the judgement of the Court of Appeals and remanded the case to the Court of Appeals for reconsideration in light of the Supreme Court's intervening decision in Neitzke v Williams (1989) 490 US 319, 104 L Ed 2d 338, 109 S Ct 1827, which held that a complaint is frivolous under § 1915(d) when the complaint lacks an arguable basis in either law or fact (493 US 801, 107 L Ed 2d 7, 110 S Ct 37). On remand, the Court of Appeals adhered to its earlier judgment and to its earlier position concerning judicial notice (929 F2d 1374).

On certiorari, the Supreme Court vacated and remanded. In an opinion by O'CONNOR, J., joined by REHNQUIST, Ch. J., and WHITE, SCALIA, KENNEDY, SOUTER, and THOMAS, JJ., it was held that (1) under § 1915(d), a dismissal based on a finding of factual frivolousness is appropriate when the facts alleged by the plaintiff rise to the level of the irrational or the wholly incredible, regardless of whether there are judicially noticeable facts available to contradict the facts alleged, where (a) the initial assessment of an in forma pauperis plaintiff's factual allegations must be weighted in favor of the plaintiff, and (b) a complaint may not be dismissed under § 1915(d) simply because a court finds the plaintiff's allegations unlikely; (2) a dismissal of an in forma pauperis action as factually frivolous under § 1915(d) is properly reviewed, on appeal, for an abuse of discretion, because a frivolousness determination under § 1915(d) is discretionary; and (3) thus, the Court of Appeals erred in the case at hand in reviewing de novo the dismissals of the inmate's actions.

237

STEVENS, J., joined by BLACKMUN, J., dissented, expressing the view that the judgment of the Court of Appeals ought to be affirmed, because the decision of the Court of Appeals was entirely consistent with the standard concerning dismissal under § 1915(d) announced by the Supreme Court.

COUNSEL

James Ching argued the cause for petitioners.

Richard W. Nichols argued the cause for respondent.

———————

UNITED STATES, Petitioner

v

JOHN H. WILLIAMS, Jr.

504 US —, 118 L Ed 2d 352, 112 S Ct 1735

Argued January 22, 1992.
Decided May 4, 1992.

Decision: United States Court of Appeals held to exceed its authority by imposing rule under which prosecutor must present to grand jury substantial exculpatory evidence in prosecutor's possession.

SUMMARY

An Oklahoma investor was indicted by a federal grand jury for allegedly defrauding a bank in violation of 18 USCS § 1014. After arraignment, a United States District Court granted the investor's motion for disclosure of all exculpatory portions of the grand jury transcripts. Upon reviewing this material, the investor demanded that the District Court dismiss the indictment on the ground that the prosecution had failed to fulfill its obligation, under a rule established in a prior decision of the United States Court of Appeals for the Tenth Circuit, to present substantial exculpatory evidence to the grand jury. The District Court ultimately ordered the indictment dismissed without prejudice, on the ground that the withheld evidence rendered gravely suspect the grand jury's decision to indict. The Court of Appeals for the Tenth Circuit, affirming on appeal, (1) expressed adherence to the rule of the prior decision regarding the disclosure of substantial exculpatory evidence; (2) held that the District Court's determination that substantial exculpatory evidence had been withheld from the grand jury was not clearly erroneous; (3) held that the District Court's finding that the failure to present such evidence rendered the indictment suspect was not clearly erroneous; and (4) held that it was not an abuse of discretion for the District Court to grant the motion to dismiss the indictment (899 F2d 898).

On certiorari, the United States Supreme Court reversed and remanded. In an opinion by SCALIA, J., joined by REHNQUIST, Ch. J., and WHITE, KENNEDY, and SOUTER, JJ., it was held that (1) the petition for certiorari should not be dismissed as improvidently granted on the ground that the question presented —whether an indictment may be dismissed because the government failed to present substantial exculpatory evidence to the grand jury—was never raised below; and (2) the Court of Appeals exceeded its authority by imposing a rule under which the prosecutor must present to the grand jury substantial exculpatory evidence in the prosecutor's possession, since (a) the federal courts have no authority to prescribe such a duty pursuant to the courts' inherent supervisory authority over their own proceedings, and (b) such a rule could not be justified as a means of assuring the right, under the Federal Constitution's Fifth Amendment, to the judgment of an independent and informed grand jury, given that (i) the rule would neither preserve nor enhance the traditional functioning of the grand jury that the Fifth Amendment demands, but rather would alter the grand jury's historic role by transforming the grand jury from an accusatory body to an adjudicatory body, (ii) the grand jury has no obligation to consider all substantial exculpatory evidence, (iii) it would run counter to the history of the grand jury institution to permit an indictment to be challenged on the ground that there was incompetent or inadequate evidence before the grand jury, and (iv) it would make little sense for a court to abstain from reviewing the evidentiary support for the grand jury's judgment while scrutinizing the sufficiency of the prosecutor's presentation.

STEVENS, J., joined by BLACKMUN and O'CONNOR, JJ., and joined in part (as to holding 2 below) by THOMAS, J., dissenting, expressed the view that (1) the writ of certiorari should have been dismissed as improvidently granted, given that (a) the contention at issue was not advanced in either the District Court or the Court of Appeals but was raised in a different case, and (b) granting certiorari under such circumstances appeared to favor the Federal Government over the ordinary litigant; and (2) a prosecutor conducting a grand jury inquiry must, before seeking an indictment against a subject of the investigation, present or otherwise disclose to the grand jury substantial evidence which directly negates the guilt of such a person, where the prosecutor is personally aware of such evidence.

COUNSEL

Solicitor General Kenneth W. Starr argued the cause for petitioner.

James C. Lang argued the cause for respondent.

TERRY FOUCHA, Petitioner

v

LOUISIANA

504 US —, 118 L Ed 2d 437, 112 S Ct 1780

Argued November 4, 1991.
Decided May 18, 1992.

Decision: Louisiana statute, permitting indefinite detention of insanity acquittees who are not mentally ill but who do not prove they would not be dangerous, held to violate Fourteenth Amendment's due process clause.

SUMMARY

A criminal defendant was found by a Louisiana trial court to have been insane at the time of the offense, and accordingly the court ruled that he was not guilty by reason of insanity. The person was committed to a psychiatric facility until such time as doctors recommended that he be released, and until further order of the court. When the superintendent of the facility and a three-member panel at the facility recommended that the person be conditionally discharged, the trial judge appointed a commission of two doctors, who reported that the person was in remission from mental illness, but that he had an antisocial personality, and that this condition was not a mental disease but was untreatable. One of the doctors testified that the person had been involved in several altercations at the facility and that the doctor would not feel comfortable in certifying that the person would not be a danger to himself or to other people. After it was stipulated that the other doctor would have given essentially the same testimony, the court ruled that the person was dangerous to himself and to others and ordered him returned to the facility. The Court of Appeals of Louisiana refused supervisory writs. The Supreme Court of Louisiana, affirming, held that (1) neither the due process clause nor the equal protection clause of the Federal Constitution's Fourteenth Amendment was violated by a Louisiana statutory provision under which an insanity acquittee who has been committed to a mental hospital, but whose release from the hospital has been recommended by a hospital review panel, may be returned to the hospital after a court hearing, regardless of whether the acquittee is then mentally ill, if the acquittee fails to prove that the acquittee is not dangerous; and (2) the person had not carried the burden of proving that he was not dangerous (563 So 2d 1138).

On certiorari, the United States Supreme Court reversed. In that portion of the opinion by WHITE, J., joined by BLACKMUN, STEVENS, O'CONNOR, and SOUTER, JJ., which constituted the opinion of the court, it was held that (1) the Louisiana statute, insofar as it permitted the indefinite detention of insanity acquittees who were not mentally ill but who did not prove that they would not be dangerous, violated the due process clause; and (2) under the circumstances, the state was not entitled to perpetuate the confinement of the person in question solely on the basis of his antisocial personality, given that (a) even if such continued confinement were constitutionally permissible, keeping the person against his will in a mental institution was improper absent a determination in civil commitment proceedings of a current mental illness and dangerousness, (b) if the person could no longer be held as an insanity acquittee in a mental hospital, he was entitled to constitutionally adequate procedures to establish the grounds for his confinement, (c) the state had no punitive interest in imprisoning the person for the purposes of deterrence and retribution, and (d) the state had not explained why, if the person had committed criminal acts while at the psychiatric facility, the state's interest would not be vindicated by other permissible ways of dealing with patterns of criminal conduct. Also, WHITE, J., joined by BLACKMUN, STEVENS, and SOUTER, JJ., expressed the view that the Louisiana statute discriminated against the person in violation of the equal protection clause.

O'CONNOR, J., concurring in part and concurring in the judgment, (1) agreed that Louisiana could not, consistent with the due process clause, indefinitely confine the person in a mental facility on the ground that the person, although not mentally ill, might be dangerous to himself or to others if released; and (2) expressed the view that (a) it might be permissible for Louisiana to confine an insanity acquittee who had regained sanity if, unlike the situation in the case at hand, the nature and duration of detention were tailored to reflect pressing public safety concerns related to the acquittee's continuing dangerousness, (b) the court's holding placed no new restriction on the states' freedom to determine whether and to what extent mental illness should excuse criminal behavior, and (c) it was unnecessary for the court to reach equal protection issues on the facts presented.

KENNEDY, J., joined by REHNQUIST, Ch. J., dissenting, expressed the view that (1) the conditions for incarceration imposed by Louisiana were in accord with legitimate and traditional state interests, vindicated after full and fair procedures; and (2) the majority impermissibly conflated the standards for civil and criminal commitment.

THOMAS, J., joined by REHNQUIST, Ch. J., and SCALIA, J., dissenting, expressed the view that nothing in the Constitution, the Supreme Court's precedents, or society's traditions authorized the court to invalidate the Louisiana scheme either (1) on the ground that the scheme provided for the continued confinement of insanity acquittees who, although still dangerous, have recovered their sanity, or (2) on the ground that the scheme provided for the indefinite confinement of sane insanity acquittees in a mental facility.

COUNSEL

James P. Manasseh argued the cause for petitioner.

Pamela S. Moran argued the cause for respondent.

DAVID RIGGINS, Petitioner

v

NEVADA

504 US —, 118 L Ed 2d 479, 112 S Ct 1810

Argued January 15, 1992.

Decided May 18, 1992.

Decision: Nevada court's judgment upholding conviction reversed and remanded, where defendant claimed that forced administration of antipsychotic drug during trial violated rights under Sixth and Fourteenth Amendments.

SUMMARY

After being taken into custody on a homicide charge, a defendant complained to a psychiatrist about hearing voices in his head and having trouble sleeping. The psychiatrist prescribed an antipsychotic drug, with which the defendant had been successfully treated in the past, and an antiepileptic drug. Following a determination by the District Court of Clark County, Nevada, that the defendant was competent to stand trial, the defense moved for an order suspending administration of both drugs until the end of the defendant's trial, on the grounds that (1) continued administration of these drugs infringed on his freedom; (2) the effect on his demeanor and mental state during trial would deny him due process; and (3) because he intended to offer an insanity defense at trial, he had a right to show jurors his true mental state. The District Court held an evidentiary hearing at which one psychiatrist testified that taking the defendant off the medication would not render him incompetent to stand trial or noticeably alter his behavior; another psychiatrist concurred as to competence and stated that the effects of the antipsychotic drug would not be noticeable to jurors if medication continued; a third psychiatrist expressed the view that the antipsychotic drug made the defendant calmer and more relaxed, that an excessive dose would cause drowsiness, and that the defendant's behavior if taken off the drug was unpredictable; and a fourth psychiatrist maintained that the defendant was incompetent to stand trial, and would likely regress into manifest psychosis and become very difficult to manage if taken off the antipsychotic drug. The District Court denied the motion to terminate medication in a one-page order which gave no indication of the court's rationale. At the close of a trial in which the defendant presented expert testimony about the effect of the antipsychotic drug on his demeanor, the jury found the defendant guilty of murder and robbery and sentenced him to death. In affirming the conviction and sentence, the Supreme Court of Nevada held that (1) the expert testimony at trial was sufficient to inform the jury of the effects of the antipsychotic drug on the defendant's demeanor and testimony; and (2) thus, while the defendant's demeanor was relevant to his insanity defense, the denial of his motion to terminate medication was neither an abuse of discretion nor a violation of the defendant's trial rights (808 P2d 535).

On certiorari, the United States Supreme Court reversed and remanded. In an opinion by O'CONNOR, J., joined by REHNQUIST, Ch. J., and WHITE, BLACKMUN, STEVENS, and SOUTER, JJ., it was held that reversal was required because the state courts had failed to make findings sufficient to justify the

247

forced administration of the drug to the defendant during his trial—given that the trial court had made no determination concerning the need for the drug or its medical appropriateness and had made no findings about reasonable alternatives—and this error may have violated the defendant's rights under the Federal Constitution's Sixth and Fourteenth Amendments, including his right to a full and fair trial and his due process liberty interest in freedom from unwanted antipsychotic drugs, since (1) it was possible that potential drug side effects testified to by experts at the hearing on the defendant's motion impacted not only his outward appearance, but also the content of his testimony on direct or cross-examination, his ability to follow the proceedings, or the substance of his communication with counsel; (2) efforts to prove or disprove actual prejudice from the record before the Supreme Court would be futile, and guesses whether the outcome of the trial might have been different if the motion had been granted would be purely speculative; (3) even though the defendant was allowed at trial to present expert testimony about the effect of the drug on his demeanor, an unacceptable risk of trial prejudice remained; and (4) as the record contained no finding that might support a conclusion that administration of antipsychotic medication was necessary to accomplish an essential state policy, there was no basis for saying that the substantial probability of trial prejudice in the case at hand was justified.

KENNEDY, J., concurred in the judgment, expressing the view that (1) absent an extraordinary showing by the state, the due process clause prohibits prosecuting officials from administering involuntary doses of antipsychotic medicines for purposes of rendering an accused competent for trial in most cases; and (2) it is doubtful that such a showing can be made given the present understanding of the properties of these drugs.

THOMAS, J., joined in part (except as to point 3 below) by SCALIA, J., dissented, expressing the view that (1) the defendant's inability to introduce evidence of his mental condition by appearing at trial in an unmedicated state did not render his trial fundamentally unfair; (2) it could not be concluded that the defendant had had less than a full and fair trial merely because of the possibility that the antipsychotic drug had side effects, where the defendant had no claim of legal incompetence and had failed to allege specific facts to support a claim that he could not participate effectively in his defense; (3) the defendant could not complain about a deprivation of his liberty interest in avoiding unwanted medication, because (a) the record contained no finding of fact with respect to his claim that the medication was involuntary, (b) he did not raise this claim below, and (c) the Supreme Court had granted certiorari to determine whether forced medication during trial violated the right to a full and fair trial, not whether the state courts had made the necessary findings to support forced medication; and (4) the precedent establishing such a liberty interest involved a civil action for damages and injunctive relief, and ought not to be expanded to include the remedy of reversing a criminal conviction.

COUNSEL

Mace J. Yampolsky argued the cause for petitioner.

James Tufteland argued the cause for respondent.

HOWARD WYATT, Petitioner

v

BILL COLE and JOHN ROBBINS, II

504 US —, 118 L Ed 2d 504, 112 S Ct 1827

Argued January 14, 1992.

Decided May 18, 1992.

Decision: Private defendants who invoke state replevin, garnishment, and attachment statutes that are later declared unconstitutional, held not entitled to qualified immunity from suit under 42 USCS § 1983.

SUMMARY

After two partners in a cattle business were unable to reach an agreement dissolving the partnership, one partner, with the assistance of an attorney, filed against the other partner in a Mississippi state court a complaint under the Mississippi replevin statute, which gave a judge no discretion to deny a writ of replevin. Pursuant to the complaint and the required bond posted by the first partner, the state court ordered a county sheriff to seize certain personal property from the second partner. Following a postseizure hearing, the state court dismissed the first partner's complaint and ordered the property returned to the second partner. When the first partner refused to comply with the order, the second partner brought, under 42 USCS § 1983 in the United States District Court for the Southern District of Mississippi, a civil rights suit challenging the replevin statute's federal constitutionality, seeking injunctive relief, and seeking damages from the first partner and his attorney and from the sheriff and deputies involved in the seizure. The District Court held that the replevin statute's failure to afford judges discretion to deny writs of replevin violated due process rights (710 F Supp 180); and the District Court (1) dismissed the suit against the government officials on the ground that they were entitled to qualified immunity from a § 1983 suit, and (2) held that the first partner and his attorney were entitled to qualified immunity concerning conduct arising prior to the replevin statute's invalidation. The United States Court of Appeals for the Fifth Circuit affirmed the District Court's grant of qualified immunity to the first partner and his attorney (928 F2d 718).

On certiorari, the United States Supreme Court reversed and remanded. In an opinion by O'CON-NOR, J., joined by WHITE, BLACKMUN, STEVENS, SCALIA, and KENNEDY, it was held that private defendants who invoke state replevin, garnishment, and attachment statutes that are later declared to be federally unconstitutional, are not entitled to qualified immunity from a suit under § 1983 for invoking the state statutes, since (1) § 1983 creates a species of tort liability that on its face admits of no immunities, and (2) even if there were sufficient common-law support to conclude that private defendants in § 1983 suits should be entitled to a defense based on good faith or probable cause, private defendants still would not be entitled to the qualified immunity from § 1983 suits which the Supreme Court had accorded government officials, where the special policy concerns mandating qualified immunity for government officials—the necessity to preserve the officials' ability to serve the public good or to insure that talented candidates are not deterred by the

251

threat of damage suits from entering public office—
are not applicable to private parties, as the public
interest will not be unduly impaired if private individuals are required to proceed to trial to resolve
their legal disputes.

KENNEDY, J., joined by SCALIA, J., concurred in the
court's opinion, expressing the view that on remand, it ought to be open (1) to the first partner, at
least in theory, to argue that the second partner's
bad faith eliminated any reliance on the replevin
statute, and (2) to the first partner to show good
faith, even if some construction of a reasonable
person in the first partner's position would have
acted in a different way.

REHNQUIST, Ch. J., joined by SOUTER and THOMAS,
JJ., dissenting, expressed the view that (1) a defendant similarly situated to the first partner and his
attorney would have enjoyed an immunity at common law at the time § 1983 was adopted, and (2)
important public policy concerns suggest the need
for an immunity for the first partner and his attorney, where the historic purpose of § 1983 is directed to the acts of state officials rather than private parties.

COUNSEL

Jim Waide argued the cause for petitioner.
Joseph P. McNamara argued the cause for respondents.

HAROLD RAY WADE, Petitioner

v

UNITED STATES

504 US —, 118 L Ed 2d 524, 112 S Ct 1840

Argued March 23, 1992.
Decided May 18, 1992.

Decision: Federal Government's refusal to request lesser sentence so as to reflect accused's substantial assistance in prosecuting another person held subject to review for constitutional violations, but particular accused held to have raised no claim to such review.

SUMMARY

With respect to the sentencing of a convicted federal criminal defendant, (1) 18 USCS § 3553(e) empowers a Federal District Court, upon motion of the government, to impose a sentence below a statutory minimum to reflect the defendant's substantial assistance to the government in the investigation or prosecution of another person who has committed an offense; and (2) § 5K1.1 of the Federal Sentencing Guidelines permits a District Court to depart from the Guidelines if the government files a motion stating that the defendant has provided substantial assistance in the investigation and prosecution of another person who has committed an offense. An accused pleaded guilty to four federal, drug-related counts which, according to a presentence report, made the accused subject to a 10-year mandatory minimum sentence under one statute and Guidelines provision, plus a 5-year sentence

253

under another statute and Guidelines provision. Although the accused had given law enforcement officials information that led them to arrest another drug dealer, and although the accused's counsel urged a Federal District Court to impose a sentence below the 10-year minimum to reward the accused for his assistance to the government, the District Court (1) noted that the government had filed no motion as contemplated in §§ 3553(e) and 5K1.1; (2) ruled that without such a motion, the court had no power to go below a mandatory minimum; and (3) sentenced the accused to 180 months in prison. On appeal, the United States Court of Appeals for the Fourth Circuit, in affirming the District Court's judgment, expressed the view that (1) absent a motion by the government, a District Court has no authority to depart downward from a mandatory minimum sentence on the ground of the defendant's substantial assistance; and (2) a District Court is not authorized to inquire into the government's motives for filing no such motion (936 F2d 169).

On certiorari, the United States Supreme Court affirmed. In an opinion by SOUTER, J., expressing the unanimous view of the court, it was held that (1) in both §§ 3553(e) and 5K1.1, the condition limiting a court's sentencing authority gives the government a power, not a duty, to file a motion when a defendant has substantially assisted; and (2) even though a prosecutor's discretion to refuse to file such a motion is subject to constitutional limitations that District Courts can enforce—so that a court has the authority to review such a refusal and to grant a remedy if the court finds that the refusal was based on an unconstitutional motive such as the defendant's race or religion, or was not rationally related to any legitimate government end—the accused in

the case at hand was entitled to no relief, because
the accused raised no claim to such review, where
(a) the accused had never alleged, or claimed to
have evidence tending to show, that the government
refused to file such a motion for suspect reasons
such as the accused's race or religion, (b) the record
showed no support for the accused's contention of
frustration in trying to plead an adequate claim, and
(c) the accused's claim as presented to the District
Court failed to rise to the level warranting judicial
inquiry.

COUNSEL

J. Matthew Martin argued the cause for petitioner.
Robert A. Long, Jr. argued the cause for respondent.

ROGER KEITH COLEMAN, Petitioner

v

CHARLES E. THOMPSON, Warden, et al.

504 US —, 119 L Ed 2d 1, 112 S Ct 1845

Decided May 20, 1992.

Decision: Application for stay of execution denied where Federal District Court found that alleged exculpatory evidence produced by defense did not amount to colorable claim of innocence.

SUMMARY

After an accused had been convicted, in a Virginia trial court, of rape and capital murder and had been sentenced to death, the accused unsuccessfully pursued direct appeals, a state habeas corpus petition, and a federal habeas corpus petition, as to the last of which the lower federal courts held, and the United States Supreme Court affirmed (501 US ——, 115 L Ed 2d 640, 111 S Ct 2546), that certain claims which had been raised in the state habeas corpus proceedings were barred by procedural default. In the twelfth round of judicial review, 11 years after the beginning of the case, the accused presented alleged exculpatory evidence to a Federal District Court, which, however, found that the evidence did not even amount to a colorable claim of innocence.

On application for stay of execution—which application was presented to REHNQUIST, Ch. J., and by him referred to the full United States Supreme Court—the Supreme Court denied the application. In a per curiam opinion expressing the view of

REHNQUIST, Ch. J., and WHITE, O'CONNOR, SCALIA, KENNEDY, and THOMAS, JJ., it was held that the Supreme Court (1) was not well-positioned to second guess the District Court's factual conclusion, and (2) had no basis for concluding that the accused had produced substantial evidence that he might be innocent.

STEVENS, J., concurred in the denial of a stay and would have denied the petition for writ of certiorari.

BLACKMUN, J., dissented, expressing the view that the accused had produced substantial evidence that he might be innocent of the crime for which he was sentenced to die, and that he should not be executed without a hearing at which his evidence could be fully presented.

SOUTER, J., would have granted the application for stay of execution.

———————

CHARLES W. BURSON, Attorney General and
Reporter for Tennessee, Petitioner

v

MARY REBECCA FREEMAN

504 US —, 119 L Ed 2d 5, 112 S Ct 1846

Argued October 8, 1992.
Decided May 26, 1992.

Decision: Tennessee statute prohibiting solicitation
of votes and display or distribution of campaign
literature within 100 feet of entrance to polling
place held not to violate First and Fourteenth
Amendments.

SUMMARY

A city council candidate's campaign treasurer
brought an action in the Davidson County, Tennessee, Chancery Court, which action sought a declaratory judgment that a state statute prohibiting the
solicitation of votes and the display or distribution
of campaign literature within 100 feet of the entrance to a polling place violated, among other
provisions, the Federal Constitution's First and
Fourteenth Amendments. The chancellor, in dismissing the suit, determined that (1) the statute was
a content neutral and reasonable time, place, and
manner restriction; (2) the 100-foot boundary
served a compelling state interest in protecting
voters from interference, harassment, and intimidation during the voting process; and (3) there was an
alternative channel for the treasurer to exercise her
free speech rights outside the 100-foot boundary.
The Supreme Court of Tennessee, however, re-

119 L Ed 2d 5

versed, as it held that the statute violated the First Amendment, because (1) the statute was a content-based restriction on speech, in that the statute regulated a specific subject matter and a certain category of speakers; (2) such a content-based statute could not be upheld unless (a) the burden placed on free speech rights was justified by a compelling state interest, and (b) the means chosen bore a substantial relation to that interest and were the least intrusive means of achieving the goal; (3) the state had shown a compelling interest in banning such speech within the polling place itself, but not in regulating the premises around the polling place, so that the statute was not narrowly tailored; (4) other state statutes prohibiting voter intimidation or interference with elections provided a less restrictive alternative; and (5) a showing of a compelling interest in preventing congestion and disruption at the entrances to polling places might justify a shorter campaign-free radius (802 SW2d 210).

On certiorari, the United States Supreme Court reversed and remanded. Although unable to agree on an opinion, five members of the court agreed that the Tennessee statute prohibiting the solicitation of votes and the display or distribution of campaign literature within 100 feet of the entrance to a polling place did not violate the First and Fourteenth Amendments.

BLACKMUN, J., announced the judgment of the court and, in an opinion joined by REHNQUIST, Ch. J., and WHITE and KENNEDY, JJ., expressed the view that (1) the 100-foot campaign-free zone was a facially content-based restriction on political speech in a public forum, and as such had to be subjected to exacting scrutiny under either a free speech theory or an equal protection theory, so that the state was required to show that the statute was necessary to serve a compelling state interest and was narrowly drawn to achieve that end; (2) some such restricted zone was necessary in order to serve the compelling state interest in preventing voter intimidation and election fraud, as (a) there was a widespread and time-tested consensus among the states and other democracies in favor of a secret ballot, secured in part by a restricted zone around the voting compartments, (b) laws against voter intimidation and interference were not sufficient, and (c) the failure to regulate all speech within the restricted zone did not render the statute fatally underinclusive; and (3) while governmental regulation of vote solicitation could, at some measurable distance from the polls, become an impermissible burden on First Amendment rights, the 100-foot boundary was on the constitutional side of the line, as (a) a state was not required to prove empirically that an election regulation was perfectly tailored to secured a compelling interest, but could act with foresight, provided that the regulation was reasonable and did not significantly impinge on constitutionally protected rights, and (b) the minor geographic limitation prescribed by the statute in question did not constitute such a significant impingement.

KENNEDY, J., concurred, expressing the view that (1) neither a general content-based proscription of speech nor a content-based proscription of speech in a public forum could be justified unless the speech fell within one of a limited set of well-defined categories; (2) there was a narrow area in which the First Amendment permitted freedom of expression to yield, to the extent necessary, for the accommodation of another constitutional right; and

(3) such principle could be applied in the case at hand without danger that the general rule banning content restrictions would be engulfed by the analysis, for the statute in question protected the integrity of the polling place where citizens exercised the fundamental right to vote, and the state was not using this justification to suppress legitimate expression.

SCALIA, J., concurred in the judgment, expressing the view that (1) because restrictions on speech around polling places were a venerable part of American tradition, the Tennessee statute in question did not restrict speech in a traditional public forum, and the exacting scrutiny which the plurality purported to apply was therefore inappropriate; and (2) the statute, though a content-based restriction on speech, was constitutional because it was a reasonable, viewpoint-neutral regulation of a nonpublic forum.

STEVENS, J., joined by O'CONNOR and SOUTER, JJ., dissented, expressing the view that (1) the state was required to show that its regulation was necessary to serve a compelling state interest and was narrowly drawn to achieve that end, because the speech and conduct prohibited was classic political expression; and (2) the state had not made the required showing, as (a) of the two different functions of statutes creating campaign-free zones, protecting orderly access to the polls was a compelling state interest, but preventing last-minute campaigning was not, (b) the size of the campaign-free zone created by some state laws—30,000 square feet under the statute in question—was far greater than necessary to maintain order and indicated that censorship of election day campaigning was the animating force behind these restrictions, (c) the statute in question also selectively prohibited speech based on content and furthered no asserted state interest in doing so, and (d) the "exacting" scrutiny applied by the plurality improperly allowed a restriction's long history to substitute for present necessity, lightened the state's burden of proof in showing that a restriction on speech was narrowly tailored, and shifted the burden of proving the necessity of content discrimination from the state to the plaintiff.

THOMAS, J., did not participate.

COUNSEL

Charles W. Burson, pro se, argued the cause for petitioner.

John E. Herbison argued the cause for respondent.

UNITED STATES, Petitioner

v

THERESE A. BURKE, CYNTHIA R. CENTER, and
LINDA G. GIBBS

504 US —, 119 L Ed 2d 34, 112 S Ct 1867

Argued January 21, 1992.
Decided May 26, 1992.

Decision: Backpay received in settlement of claims
under Title VII of Civil Rights Act of 1964 held
not excludible from gross income under
§ 104(a)(2) of Internal Revenue Code as damages for personal injuries.

SUMMARY

As part of the settlement of an action brought
under Title VII of the Civil Rights Act of 1964 (42
USCS §§ 2000e et seq.) in the United States District
Court for the Eastern District of Tennessee, certain
female employees of the Tennessee Valley Authority
(TVA)—which employees allegedly had been the
victims of sex discrimination with respect to salary
rates—received backpay, from which federal income
taxes were withheld. After the Internal Revenue
Service (IRS) disallowed the employees' claims for
refunds of the taxes, the employees brought in the
District Court a refund action alleging that the
backpay awards should be excluded from their gross
incomes under § 104(a)(2) of the Internal Revenue
Code (26 USCS § 104(a)(2)) as "damages received
(whether by suit or agreement and whether as lump
sums or periodic payments) on account of personal
injuries or sickness." The District Court ruled that

263

because the employees had received, rather than compensatory or other damages, only backpay that was due to the employees as a result of the TVA's discriminatory underpayments, the settlement proceeds could not be excluded from gross income as damages received on account of personal injuries (53 CCH EPD ¶ 39863, 90-1 USTC ¶ 50203). The United States Court of Appeals for the Sixth Circuit, in reversing, held that the backpay awards pursuant to Title VII were excludible from gross income under § 104(a)(2), because the TVA's unlawful sex discrimination constituted a personal, tort-like injury to the employees (929 F2d 1119, 55 BNA FEP Cas 632, 56 CCH EPD ¶ 40680, 91-1 USTC ¶ 50175, 67 AFTR 2d 91-749).

On certiorari, the United States Supreme Court reversed. In an opinion by BLACKMUN, J., joined by REHNQUIST, Ch. J., and WHITE, STEVENS, and KENNEDY, JJ., it was held that the backpay payments received in settlement of claims under Title VII, prior to its amendment in 1991, were not excludible from gross income under § 104(a)(2), because (1) in order to come within the § 104(a)(2) income exclusion, the employees had to show that Title VII redresses a tort-like personal injury, since the IRS regulation codified at 26 CFR § 1.104-1(c) provides that the term "damages received (whether by suit or agreement)" means an amount received through prosecution of a suit based upon tort or tort-type rights, or through a settlement agreement entered into in lieu of such prosecution; (2) consideration of the remedies available under Title VII was critical, as the concept of tort is inextricably bound up with remedies; and (3) Title VII did not redress tort-like personal injuries within the meaning of §§ 104(a)(2) and 1.104-1(c), since (a) the fact that employment

264

discrimination causes harm to individuals does not automatically imply that there exists a tort-like "personal injury" for purposes of federal income tax law, and (b) notwithstanding a common-law tradition of broad tort damages, and notwithstanding the existence of federal antidiscrimination statutes offering similarly broad remedies, nothing in Title VII's remedial scheme—which consisted of injunctive relief and the payment of wages that were properly due and, if paid in the ordinary course, would be fully taxable—purported to recompense a plaintiff for any of the other traditional harms associated with personal injury.

SCALIA, J., concurring in the judgment, expressed the view that the employees in question did not receive their backpay payments "on account of personal injuries" within the meaning of § 104(a)(2) because the employees' injuries were not to the employees' physical or mental health.

SOUTER, J., concurring in the judgment, expressed the view that (1) an accession to wealth is not to be excluded from income unless some provision of the Internal Revenue Code clearly so entails, and (2) in the case at hand, there was no such clear application of § 104(a)(2) as interpreted by § 1.104-1(c).

O'CONNOR, J., joined by THOMAS, J., dissenting, expressed the view that (1) the purposes and operation of Title VII are closely analogous to those of tort law, and (2) this similarity ought to determine the excludability of recoveries for personal injury under § 104(a)(2).

COUNSEL

Jeffrey P. Minear argued the cause for petitioner.
Joseph E. Finley argued the cause for respondents.

———————

JOHN H. EVANS, Jr., Petitioner

v

UNITED STATES

504 US —, 119 L Ed 2d 57, 112 S Ct 1881

Argued December 9, 1991.

Decided May 26, 1992.

Decision: Affirmative act of inducement by public official, such as demand, held not to be necessary element of Hobbs Act offense of extortion "under color of official right" (18 USCS § 1951(b)(2)).

SUMMARY

In the Hobbs Act (18 USCS § 1951), which imposes criminal penalties for such acts as extortion affecting commerce, extortion is defined as "the obtaining of property from another, without his consent, induced by wrongful use of actual or threatened force, violence, or fear, or under color of official right" (18 USCS § 1951(b)(2)). As part of an investigation into allegations of public corruption in the Atlanta area as to matters including property rezoning, a federal agent (1) posed as a real estate developer; (2) sought the assistance of a Georgia county commissioner in a supposed effort to rezone a tract of land; and (3) eventually handed the commissioner $8,000 in the form of a $1,000 check payable to the commissioner's campaign and $7,000 in cash. The commissioner was later convicted in a Federal District Court on two federal charges, including a charge of extortion in violation of the Hobbs Act, after a trial in which the court's instruc-

267

tion to the jury as to extortion included a statement to the effect that if a public official demanded or accepted money in exchange for a specific requested exercise of his or her official power, such a demand or acceptance constituted a violation of the Hobbs Act, regardless of whether the payment was made in the form of a campaign contribution. On appeal, the United States Court of Appeals for the Eleventh Circuit, in upholding the two convictions, expressed the view that—even though the trial court's extortion instruction had not required the jury to find that the commissioner had demanded or requested the money or that he had conditioned the performance of any official act upon the money's receipt— passive acceptance of a benefit by a public official was sufficient to form the basis of a Hobbs Act violation if the official knew that he was being offered the payment in exchange for a specific, requested exercise of his official power (910 F2d 790).

On certiorari, the United States Supreme Court affirmed. In an opinion by STEVENS, J., joined by WHITE, BLACKMUN, and SOUTER, JJ., joined in part (as to holdings 1-3 below) by O'CONNOR, J., and joined in part (as to holding 4 below) by KENNEDY, J., it was held that (1) an affirmative act of inducement by a public official, such as a demand, is not a necessary element of the offense of extortion "under color of official right" prohibited by the Hobbs Act, because the lack of such a requirement is consistent with the common-law definition of extortion which Congress intended to adopt in the Hobbs Act; (2) in a Hobbs Act prosecution for extortion under color of official right, the government need show only that a public official has obtained a payment to which the official is not entitled, knowing that the payment was made in return for official acts; (3) the jury instruction in the case at hand (a) satisfied the quid pro quo requirement for conviction, and (b) did not need to include a statement that an affirmative step was an element of the offense; and (4) common-law extortion was not limited to wrongful takings under a false pretense of official right.

O'CONNOR, J., concurring in part and concurring in the judgment, expressed the view that (1) the court correctly decided that an act of inducement was not an element of the offense of extortion under color of official right; but (2) the issue whether common-law extortion was limited to wrongful takings under a false pretense of official right was not fairly included in the question on which the court had granted certiorari, and sound prudential reasons suggested that the court ought not to address that issue.

KENNEDY, J., concurring in part and concurring in the judgment, expressed the view that (1) the court's holding 2 above required a quid pro quo as an element of the government's case in a prosecution under § 1951; (2) the court's opinion could be interpreted in a way that was consistent with such a requirement; and (3) in the case at hand, the prosecution had established a quid pro quo that embodied the necessary elements of a Hobbs Act violation, and the jury instruction on the extortion charge had complied with the quid pro quo requirement.

THOMAS, J., joined by REHNQUIST, Ch.J., and SCALIA, J., dissenting, expressed the view that (1) although the court correctly presumed that Congress knew the meaning of common-law extortion when Congress enacted the Hobbs Act, the court misapprehended that meaning and misconstrued the statute, where the common-law meaning was that the offense of extortion involved not merely a wrongful taking by a public official, but a wrongful taking under a false pretense of official right; (2) the court's extension of a reasonable, but textually and historically artificial, quid pro quo limitation from the context of campaign contributions to all cases of official extortion was both unexplained and inexplicable, except insofar as the limitation might serve to rescue the court's definition of extortion from substantial overbreadth; (3) the court disregarded well-established principles of construction by choosing not only the harshest interpretation of a criminal statute, but also the interpretation that maximized federal criminal jurisdiction over state and local officials; and (4) the court's opinion, by breaching the boundaries on criminal conduct set by the legislature, created a potential for prosecutorial abuse.

COUNSEL

C. Michael Abbott argued the cause for petitioner.

William C. Bryson argued the cause for respondent.

———

QUILL CORPORATION, Petitioner

v

NORTH DAKOTA, by and Through its Tax
Commissioner, HEIDI HEITKAMP

504 US —, 119 L Ed 2d 91, 112 S Ct 1904

Argued January 22, 1992.
Decided May 26, 1992.

Decision: Federal Constitution's commerce clause
(Art I, § 8, cl 3), but not due process clause of
Fourteenth Amendment, held to bar enforcement of North Dakota use tax against out-of-
state mail-order house.

SUMMARY

North Dakota imposed a use tax on property
purchased for storage, use, or consumption within
the state. Under the tax statute, every retailer maintaining a place of business in the state was required
to collect the tax from the consumer and remit the
tax to the state. The term "retailer maintaining a
place of business in this state" was defined in a
1987 statutory provision to include every person
who engaged in regular or systematic solicitation of
a consumer market in the state. State regulations
defined "regular or systematic solicitation" to mean
three or more advertisements within a 12-month
period. A mail-order house incorporated in Delaware, with offices and warehouses in three other
states, had no offices or warehouses in North Dakota and no employees who worked or resided in
North Dakota. However, the mail-order house made
annual sales of almost $1,000,000 to about 3,000

customers in North Dakota. This business was solicited through catalogs and flyers that were sent into North Dakota by mail. The mail-order house delivered all merchandise to its North Dakota customers by mail or common carrier from out-of-state locations. Because the mail-order house refused to collect the use tax from its North Dakota customers, North Dakota filed an action in a North Dakota district court to require the mail-order house to pay taxes, as well as interest and penalties, on all such sales made after July 1, 1987. The mail-order house alleged that the use tax statute, as applied to the mail-order house, violated the Federal Constitution's commerce clause (Art I, § 8, cl 3) and the due process clause of the Federal Constitution's Fourteenth Amendment. The district court, ruling in favor of the mail-order house, found that North Dakota had failed to establish a sufficient nexus between the mail-order house and the state. The Supreme Court of North Dakota, reversing on appeal, held that (1) neither the commerce clause nor the due process clause required a physical-presence nexus with the state as a prerequisite to the legitimate exercise of state power over an out-of-state retailer; and (2) the mail-order house's economic presence in North Dakota depended on services and benefits provided by the state—such as creating an economic climate that fostered demand for the mail-order house's products, maintaining a legal infrastructure which protected that market, and disposing of the 24 tons of solid waste generated annually by the mail-order house's mailings—and therefore generated a constitutionally sufficient nexus to justify imposition of the duty to collect the use tax (470 NW2d 203).

272

On certiorari, the United States Supreme Court reversed and remanded. In an opinion by STEVENS, J., expressing the unanimous view of the court as to holding 1 below, and joined by REHNQUIST, Ch. J., and BLACKMUN, O'CONNOR, and SOUTER, JJ., as to holdings 2 and 3 below, it was held that (1) the due process clause did not bar enforcement of the use tax against the mail-order house, given that (a) the mail-order house had purposefully directed its activities at North Dakota residents, (b) the magnitude of such contacts was more than sufficient for due process purposes, and (c) the use tax was related to the benefits that the mail-order house received from access to the state; but (2) a vendor whose only connection with customers in a taxing state is by common carrier or the United States mail is free from state-imposed duties to collect sales and use taxes, because such a vendor lacks the substantial nexus with the taxing state required by the commerce clause; and (3) because Congress is free to disagree with the Supreme Court's evaluation of the burdens that use taxes impose on interstate commerce, Congress remained free to decide whether, when, and to what extent the states may burden interstate mail-order concerns with a duty to collect use taxes.

SCALIA, J., joined by KENNEDY and THOMAS, JJ., concurring in part and concurring in the judgment, expressed the view that (1) for purposes of the due process clause, a state's jurisdiction to tax, or to compel collection of taxes as agent for the state, may properly be asserted on the basis of contacts with the state through the mail; and (2) a previous Supreme Court decision, holding that the commerce clause prohibits a state from imposing the duty of use-tax collection on a seller whose only connection with the state is through common carrier or the mail, should be adhered to on the basis of stare decisis.

WHITE, concurring in part and dissenting in part, expressed the view that neither the due process clause nor the commerce clause restricts a state's power to impose use-tax collection responsibilities on out-of-state mail-order businesses that do not have a physical presence in the state.

COUNSEL

John E. Gaggini argued the cause for petitioner.

Nicholas J. Spaeth argued the cause for respondent.

CHEMICAL WASTE MANAGEMENT, INC.,
Petitioner

v

GUY HUNT, Governor of Alabama, et al.

504 US —, 119 L Ed 2d 121, 112 S Ct 2009

Argued April 21, 1992.
Decided June 1, 1992.

Decision: Disposal fee imposed by Alabama on hazardous waste generated out of state, but not on waste generated in state, held to violate Federal Constitution's commerce clause (Art I, § 8, cl 3).

SUMMARY

Alabama enacted a statute imposing (1) on the operator of each in-state site for the disposal of hazardous waste, a base fee of $26.50 per ton for all hazardous waste disposed of at the site, and (2) an "additional fee" of $72.00 per ton for waste generated outside of Alabama and disposed of at such an in-state site. The operator of an Alabama commercial landfill facility for hazardous waste disposal, alleging that the additional fee violated various provisions including the Federal Constitution's commerce clause (Art I, § 8, cl 3), filed against defendants including the Governor of Alabama a state-court suit seeking declaratory relief and an injunction against enforcement of the state statute. The trial court, finding the only basis for the additional fee to be the origin of the waste, held that the additional fee violated the commerce clause. On appeal, the Alabama Supreme Court, reversing in pertinent part, held that the additional fee advanced legitimate local purposes that could not be adequately served by reasonable nondiscriminatory alternatives (584 So 2d 1367, 33 Envt Rep Cas 1433, 22 ELR 20171).

On certiorari, the United States Supreme Court reversed and remanded. In an opinion by WHITE, joined by BLACKMUN, STEVENS, O'CONNOR, SCALIA, KENNEDY, SOUTER, and THOMAS, JJ., it was held that the additional fee violated the commerce clause, because (1) no state may attempt to isolate itself from a problem common to the several states by raising barriers to the free flow of interstate trade; (2) the additional fee facially discriminated against hazardous waste generated outside of the state; (3) the statute overall plainly discouraged the full operation of the landfill facility in question; (4) such burdensome state taxes imposed on interstate commerce alone were typically struck down without further inquiry once they were found to discriminate against out-of-state commerce; (5) the only basis for the additional fee was the origin of the waste; (6) whatever the fee's ultimate purpose, that purpose could not be accomplished by discriminating against articles of commerce coming from outside the state unless there was some reason, apart from the origin of the articles, to treat them differently; and (7) the state had not shown that the discrimination was demonstrably justified by a valid factor unrelated to economic protectionism, since (a) less discriminatory alternatives were available to alleviate the state's concern with the volume of waste, and (b) the state's concerns with environmental conservation, the health and safety of the state's citizens, and the state's possible future financial and environmental risks did not vary with such waste's point of origin in a way allowing foreign, but not local, waste to be burdened.

REHNQUIST, Ch. J., dissented, expressing the view that states (1) need not ban all waste disposal as a precondition to protecting themselves from hazardous or noxious materials brought across the states' borders, and (2) may take actions legitimately directed at the preservation of the states' natural resources, even if those actions incidentally work to disadvantage some out-of-state waste generators.

COUNSEL

Andrew J. Pincus argued the cause for petitioner.

Edwin S. Kneedler argued the cause for the United States, as amicus curiae, by special leave of the court.

Bert S. Nettles argued the cause for respondents.

_____

FORT GRATIOT SANITARY LANDFILL, INC.,
Petitioner

v

MICHIGAN DEPARTMENT OF NATURAL
RESOURCES et al.

504 US —, 119 L Ed 2d 139, 112 S Ct 2019

Argued March 30, 1992.
Decided June 1, 1992.

Decision: Michigan statute barring private landfill
owner from accepting solid waste originating
outside county in which landfill was located
held to violate Federal Constitution's commerce
clause (Art I, § 8, cl 3).

SUMMARY

Provisions of a Michigan solid waste management
statute prohibited any person from accepting for
disposal any solid waste that was not generated in
the county in which the disposal area was located,
unless acceptance of such waste was explicitly authorized in that county's approved solid waste management plan. A private sanitary landfill owner, whose
application to county authorities for permission to
accept a certain amount of out-of-state waste was
denied on the ground that the county's management
plan did not authorize acceptance of any out-of-
county waste, filed an action in the United States
District Court for the Eastern District of Michigan
against state and county officials, and sought (1) a
declaratory judgment that the waste-import restrictions violated the Federal Constitution's commerce
clause (Art I, § 8, cl 3), and (2) an injunction

barring enforcement of the restrictions. The District Court, however, denied the owner's motion for summary judgment, as the court expressed the view that (1) the provisions did not discriminate against interstate commerce on their face, because their restrictions applied to waste from other Michigan counties as well as to waste from out of state; (2) there was no discrimination in practical effect, because counties were given discretion to accept out-of-state waste; and (3) the incidental effect of the provisions on interstate commerce was not clearly excessive in relation to the public health and environmental benefits derived by the state (732 F Supp 761). The District Court subsequently dismissed the complaint. On appeal, the United States Court of Appeals for the Sixth Circuit agreed with the District Court's analysis, and affirmed the decision that no constitutional violation had occurred (931 F2d 413).

On certiorari, the United States Supreme Court reversed. In an opinion by STEVENS, J., joined by WHITE, O'CONNOR, SCALIA, KENNEDY, SOUTER, and THOMAS, JJ., it was held that the Michigan statute's waste-import restrictions violated the commerce clause as applied to nonhazardous wastes and to privately owned and operated landfills—where the state had not identified any reason, apart from origin, why solid waste coming from outside a county should be treated differently from solid waste coming from within the county—because the provisions in question were not distinguishable from another state's restrictions, which had been held invalid in a prior Supreme Court decision, either (1) on the ground that the Michigan restrictions treated waste from counties within the state no differently than waste from other states, as a state may not avoid the strictures of the commerce clause by curtailing the movement of articles of commerce through subdivisions of the state rather than through the state itself; (2) on the ground that some Michigan counties did accept out-of-state waste; or (3) on the ground that the Michigan statute constituted a comprehensive health and safety regulation rather than economic protectionism of the state's limited landfill capacity, as the state had not met its burden of proving that the waste-import-restriction provisions furthered health and safety concerns that could not be adequately served by nondiscriminatory alternatives.

REHNQUIST, Ch. J., joined by BLACKMUN, J., dissented, expressing the view that (1) Supreme Court precedents did not foreclose the possibility that a state statute attacked on commerce clause grounds could be defended by pointing to the statute's effects on intrastate commerce; (2) the waste-import restrictions in question were part of a comprehensive approach to the disposal of solid wastes generated within the state, and thus were different from the simple outright ban invalidated in the prior decision; and (3) the case ought to be remanded for further proceedings to give the state an opportunity to show that the restrictions were directed to legitimate local concerns rather than to improper economic protectionism.

COUNSEL

Harold B. Finn, III argued the cause for petitioner.

Thomas L. Casey argued the cause for respondents.

DAN MORALES, Attorney General of Texas,
Petitioner

v

TRANS WORLD AIRLINES, INC. et al.

504 US —, 119 L Ed 2d 157, 112 S Ct 2031

Argued March 3, 1992.
Decided June 1, 1992.

Decision: Enforcement, through state consumer-
protection laws, of restrictions on advertising of
airline fares held pre-empted by provision of
Airline Deregulation Act of 1978 (49 USCS
Appx § 1305(a)(1)).

SUMMARY

A provision of the Airline Deregulation Act of
1978 (49 USCS Appx § 1305(a)(1)) prohibits states
from enforcing any law "relating to rates, routes, or
services" of any air carrier. In 1987, the National
Association of Attorneys General (NAAG) adopted a
set of guidelines that contained detailed standards
which governed, among other things, the content
and format of airline advertising. The guidelines
directed to fare advertising established requirements
with respect to print, broadcast, and billboard advertisements of fares; fare availability; inclusion of
taxes and surcharges in fares; disclosure of round-
trip fares; and the use of the word "sale" or similar
terms. After the guidelines were adopted, the Attorney General of Texas, and several other NAAG
members, sent to the major airlines a memorandum,
in which it was stated that the practice of not
disclosing all fare surcharges was a violation of the

members' respective state laws on deceptive advertising and trade practices. Several months later,
after the Texas Attorney General's office sent to
several airlines letters which served as formal no-
tices of intent to sue—pursuant to Texas statutes
prohibiting deceptive trade practices, under which
civil penalties and consumer treble-damage actions
were available for multiple violations—the airlines
filed suit against the Texas Attorney General in the
United States District Court for the Western District
of Texas. The airlines, seeking a declaratory judgment and injunctive relief from any action by Texas
in conjunction with the NAAG guidelines, claimed
that state regulation of fare advertisements was pre-
empted by § 1305(a)(1). The District Court granted
the airlines' motion for a preliminary injunction
(712 F Supp 99), and the United States Court of
Appeals for the Fifth Circuit, affirming, expressed
the view that § 1305(a)(1) expressly pre-empted
state deceptive advertising laws as applied to airline
fare advertising (897 F2d 773). Subsequently, the
District Court permanently enjoined Texas from
taking any enforcement action which would restrict
any aspect of the airlines' fare advertising or operations relating to rates, routes, or services, and the
Court of Appeals affirmed (949 F2d 141).

On certiorari, the United States Supreme Court
affirmed in part and reversed in part. In an opinion
by SCALIA, J., joined by WHITE, O'CONNOR, KEN-
NEDY, and THOMAS, JJ., it was held that (1) the
enforcement of the fare advertising guidelines
through a state's general consumer-protection laws
was pre-empted by § 1305(a)(1), because (a) the
ordinary meaning of the words "relating to" in
§ 1305(a)(1)—like the similarly worded pre-emption
provision of the Employee Retirement Income Secu-

rity Act of 1974 (ERISA) (29 USCS § 1144(a))—
required that state enforcement actions having a
connection with or reference to airline rates, routes,
or services be pre-empted, (b) the guidelines on fare
advertising each bore a reference to air fares, and
collectively established binding requirements as to
how tickets might be marketed if they were to be
sold at given prices, and (c) the obligations imposed
by the guidelines on fare advertising, by severely
burdening the airlines' ability to place substantial
restrictions on the availability of lower priced seats
and to advertise the lower fares, had a significant
impact upon the airlines' ability to market their
product, and hence a significant impact upon the
fares they charged; but (2) although the District
Court could award injunctive relief under the circumstances, the injunction had to be vacated insofar
as it restrained the operation of state laws with
respect to matters other than the airlines' fare advertising, since the Texas Attorney General had
threatened to enforce only the obligations described
in the NAAG guidelines regarding fare advertising.

STEVENS, J., joined by REHNQUIST, Ch. J., and
Blackmun, J., dissenting, expressed the view that (1)
the determination that § 1305(a)(1) pre-empted
state regulation of deceptive advertising, insofar as
such determination was made by giving § 1305(a)(1)
a broad reading similar to ERISA's pre-emption
provision—which contained similar, but by no
means identical, language—(a) disregarded established canons of statutory construction, and (b) gave
§ 1305(a)(1) a construction that was neither compelled by its text nor supported by its legislative
history; and (2) even if state regulation of deceptive
advertising could "relat[e] to rates" within the
meaning of § 1305(a)(1) if such regulation had a

significant impact upon rates, the airlines had not proved that compliance with the NAAG guidelines on fare advertising would have a significant effect on their ability to market their product and, therefore, on their rates.

SOUTER, J., did not participate.

COUNSEL

Stephan Gardner argued the cause for petitioner.

Keith A. Jones argued the cause for respondents.

Stephen L. Nightingale argued the cause for the United States, as amicus curiae, by special leave of the court.

———————

ALAN B. BURDICK, Petitioner

v

MORRIS TAKUSHI, Director of Elections of
Hawaii, et al.

504 US —, 119 L Ed 2d 245, 112 S Ct 2059

Argued March 24, 1992.
Decided June 8, 1992.

Decision: Hawaii's prohibition on write-in voting
held not to violate rights of state's voters under
Federal Constitution's First and Fourteenth
Amendments.

SUMMARY

Hawaii election law requires a candidate to participate in a new-party, established-party, or nonparti-
san primary election in order to obtain a position
on the general election ballot. The primaries are
open—that is, all registered voters may choose in
which primary to vote. The law provides that a
candidate may appear on a primary ballot by filing
nominating papers, containing a specified number
of voter signatures, 60 days before the primary. A
registered voter in Hawaii who notified state officials
that he wished to cast write-in votes was advised by
the officials that the law did not provide for write-in
voting and that any write-in votes would be ignored.
The voter filed suit against the officials in the
United States District Court for the District of Hawaii, which ruled that the failure to provide for
write-in voting constituted a violation of the voter's
rights of freedom of expression and association
under the Federal Constitution's First Amendment.

285

On appeal, the United States Court of Appeals for the Ninth Circuit vacated the judgment and directed the District Court to abstain from reaching the federal constitutional issue until state courts had determined whether Hawaii's election laws permitted write-in voting (846 F2d 587). On remand, the District Court certified questions to the Supreme Court of Hawaii, which held that the state laws barred write-in voting (70 Haw 498, 776 P2d 824). The District Court then granted the voter's renewed motion for summary judgment and injunctive relief (737 F Supp 582). The Court of Appeals, in reversing on appeal, expressed the view that although the prohibition on write-in voting placed some restrictions on the voter's rights of expression and association under the Constitution's First and Fourteenth Amendments, that burden was justified in light of (1) the ease of access to Hawaii's ballots, (2) the alternatives available to the voter for expressing political beliefs, (3) the state's broad powers to regulate elections, and (4) the state's interests in fostering political stability, an informed electorate, and the integrity of the election process (937 F2d 415).

On certiorari, the United States Supreme Court affirmed. In an opinion by WHITE, J., joined by REHNQUIST, Ch. J., and O'CONNOR, SCALIA, SOUTER, and THOMAS, JJ., it was held that, for purposes of the First and Fourteenth Amendments, Hawaii's prohibition on write-in voting, and the requirement that a candidate participate in the open primary in order to obtain a position on the general election ballot, did not unconstitutionally limit access to the ballot by party or independent candidates, and did not unreasonably interfere with the right of voters

286

to associate and have candidates of their choice placed on the ballot, since (1) any burden on voters' freedom of choice and association was a very limited one, given that (a) the state provided for easy access to the ballot, and (b) there was nothing content based about a flat ban on all forms of write-in ballots; (2) the prohibition on write-in voting promoted the state's legitimate interests in (a) guarding against party raiding in the primary election, (b) avoiding the possibility of unrestrained factionalism at the general election, and (c) averting sore-loser candidacies in the general election; and (3) such state interests outweighed a voter's limited interest in waiting until the eleventh hour to choose a candidate.

KENNEDY, J., joined by BLACKMUN and STEVENS, JJ., dissenting, expressed the view that, while the voter's right to freedom of expression was not at stake in the case at hand, (1) the ban on write-in voting deprived some Hawaii voters of any substantial voice in selecting candidates for the entire range of offices at issue in a particular election, (2) the interests proffered by the state were not advanced to any significant degree by the ban, and (3) thus, the ban was unconstitutional.

COUNSEL

Arthur N. Eisenberg argued the cause for petitioner.

Steven S. Michaels argued the cause for respondents.

———

EASTMAN KODAK COMPANY, Petitioner

v

IMAGE TECHNICAL SERVICES, INC., et al.

504 US —, 119 L Ed 2d 265, 112 S Ct 2072

Argued December 10, 1992.
Decided June 8, 1992.

Decision: Photocopier manufacturer held not entitled to summary judgment dismissing federal
antitrust claims as to (1) tying arrangement
between parts and service, and (2) monopolization of sale of service.

SUMMARY

A company which manufactured and sold photo-
copiers and micrographic equipment also sold service and noncompatible replacement parts for such
equipment. In the early 1980's, a number of independent service organizations (ISOs) began servic-
ing the company's equipment. In 1985 and 1986,
the company allegedly adopted a policy under which
the company supposedly (1) sold parts only to
buyers of the company's equipment who either used
the company's service or repaired their own equipment; and (2) limited access to other sources of
parts by the ISOs by forbidding entities which
manufactured parts for the company to sell such
parts to anyone other than the company, pressuring
other entities not to sell the company's parts to the
ISOs, and taking steps to restrict the availability of
used equipment. In 1987, the ISOs filed an action in
the United States District Court for the Northern
District of California against the company. The
288

ISOs, proffering evidence that the company controlled nearly 100 percent of the parts market and 80 to 95 percent of the service market, alleged that the company had unlawfully (1) tied the sale of service for the company's equipment to the sale of parts, in violation of § 1 of the Sherman Act (15 USCS § 1); and (2) monopolized and attempted to monopolize the sale of service for the company's equipment, in violation of § 2 of the Sherman Act (15 USCS § 2). The company moved for summary judgment on both claims, and the District Court granted the company's motion. On appeal, the United States Court of Appeals for the Ninth Circuit, reversing, expressed the view that (1) the ISOs had presented sufficient evidence, for summary judgment purposes, to disprove the company's contention that its parts policy was justified; (2) with respect to the § 1 claim, (a) there were disputed issues of fact whether service and parts were distinct markets, and whether a tying arrangement existed, and (b) the ISOs had presented evidence from which a trier of fact could conclude that the company had sufficient economic power in the parts market to restrain competition in the service market; and (3) with respect to the § 2 claim, sufficient evidence existed to support a finding that the company's implementation of its parts policy involved a specific intent to monopolize (903 F2d 612).

On certiorari, the United States Supreme Court affirmed. In an opinion by BLACKMUN, J., joined by REHNQUIST, Ch. J., and WHITE, STEVENS, KENNEDY, and SOUTER, JJ., it was held that the company had not met the requirements of Rule 56(c) of the Federal Rules of Civil Procedure with respect to the company's motion for summary judgment as to either Sherman Act claim, because (1) as to the § 1 claim, (a) the company did not dispute that its arrangement affected a substantial volume of interstate commerce in the parts market, (b) a reasonable trier of fact could find that the company's service and parts were two distinct products, (c) evidence of the company's policy on parts sales, along with allegations by the ISOs that the company's control over the parts market had excluded competition and boosted service prices, were sufficient to entitle the ISOs to a trial on their claim that the company had power in the parts market to force unwanted purchases of the company's service, and (d) notwithstanding the existence of competition in the equipment market, the company had failed to meet its burden of demonstrating that the inference of market power in the service and parts markets was unreasonable; and (2) as to the § 2 claim, (a) the ISOs' evidence with respect to the company's control of the parts and service markets—which evidence indicated the company's possession of monopoly power—was sufficient to survive summary judgment, (b) the relevant market from the perspective of an owner of the company's equipment was composed of only those companies that serviced such equipment, and (c) none of the company's asserted business justifications for its exclusionary action was sufficient to entitle the company to a judgment as a matter of law.

SCALIA, J., joined by O'CONNOR and THOMAS, JJ., dissenting, expressed the view that (1) neither logic nor experience suggested, let alone compelled, application of the per se prohibition against tying arrangements under § 1, and the monopolization doctrine under § 2, to a seller's behavior in its single-brand aftermarkets, where—as it had to be assumed in the case at hand—the seller was without power at the interbrand level; (2) although the aftermarket tie alleged in the case at hand could have instead been evaluated under the rule of reason, the case's disposition did not require such examination, where the ISOs apparently had waived their rule-of-reason claim in the District Court, and, accordingly, the Court of Appeals' judgment on the § 1 claim ought to have been reversed outright; and (3) an antitrust defendant which lacked the relevant market power sufficient to permit invocation of the per se prohibition against tying under § 1 all the more lacked the monopoly power that warranted heightened scrutiny under § 2 of such defendant's allegedly exclusionary behavior.

COUNSEL

Donn P. Pickett argued the cause for petitioner.
James F. Rill argued the cause for respondents.

UNITED STATES, Petitioner

v

THOMPSON/CENTER ARMS COMPANY

504 US —, 119 L Ed 2d 308, 112 S Ct 2102

Argued January 13, 1992.
Decided June 8, 1992.

Decision: Tax payment for "making" firearm held not required, under provision of National Firearms Act (26 USCS § 5821), where pistol and kit allowing conversion of pistol into firearm are packaged as unit.

SUMMARY

Under the National Firearms Act (NFA) (26 USCS §§ 5801 et seq), one provision (26 USCS § 5821) levies a tax of $200 per firearm made upon anyone "making" a "firearm," which term is defined in 26 USCS § 5845(a)(3) to include short-barreled rifles— that is, rifles with barrels less than 16 inches long— and to exclude pistols and long-barreled rifles—that is, rifles with barrels 16 inches or more in length. The manufacturer of a type of pistol, and of a kit that could be used to convert such pistols within a few minutes into rifles with either a 21-inch barrel or a 10-inch barrel, was advised by the Bureau of Alcohol, Tobacco, and Firearms that, when the conversion kit was possessed or distributed with the pistol, the unit consisting of the pistol and the kit constituted a firearm subject to the NFA. The manufacturer responded by (1) paying the $200 tax imposed for making a single firearm, (2) applying for permission under 26 USCS § 5822 to package the
292

pistol and conversion kit as a unit, and (3) filing a refund claim. After more than 6 months had elapsed without a response to the refund claim, the manufacturer brought a suit against the United States in the United States Claims Court and alleged that the unit was not a firearm within the meaning of the NFA because the manufacturer had not assembled a short-barreled rifle from the unit's components The Claims Court, concluding that the unit was a firearm, entered summary judgment for the government (19 Cl Ct 725). The United States Court of Appeals for the Federal Circuit, reversing, held that a short-barreled rifle must be assembled in order to be "made" within the meaning of the NFA (924 F2d 1041).

On certiorari, the United States Supreme Court affirmed. Although unable to agree on an opinion, five members of the court agreed that the language of the NFA could not be construed to require the manufacturer to pay, with respect to the pistol and the conversion kit packaged as a unit, the tax imposed under § 5821, because (1) the NFA is ambiguous as to the NFA's applicability to such a unit, and (2) it was proper to apply the rule of lenity to resolve the ambiguity in the manufacturer's favor.

SOUTER, J., announced the judgment of the court and, in an opinion joined by REHNQUIST, Ch. J., and O'CONNOR, J., expressed the view that (1) under the NFA, the aggregation of a set of parts that could be used to make nothing but a short-barreled rifle must fall within the definition of "making," in § 5821, because (a) "make" is defined in 26 USCS § 5845(i) for purposes of the NFA to include not only "putting together," but also "manufacturing . . . or otherwise producing a firearm," (b) if a firearm were made only at the moment it was put together, the

293

additional language in § 5845(i) would be redundant, so that Congress must have understood "making" to cover more than final assembly and some disassembled aggregation of parts had to be included under the NFA, and (c) the narrowest combination of parts that might be so included is a set of parts that could be used to make nothing but a short-barreled rifle; (2) application of the ordinary rules of statutory construction left an ambiguity as to whether the mere possibility of the unit comprised of the pistol and conversion kit being used to assemble an NFA-regulated firearm was enough to place the unit within the scope of "making" such a regulated firearm, because neither the statute's language or structure, nor its purpose or history provide any definitive guidance on this issue; and (3) it was proper to apply the rule of lenity and resolve the ambiguity in favor of the manufacturer, because the NFA, although it is a tax statute that was being construed in a civil setting, has criminal applications that carry no additional requirement of willfulness.

SCALIA, J., joined by THOMAS, J., concurring in the court's judgment, (1) agreed with the plurality that application of the NFA to the pistol and conversion kit was sufficiently ambiguous to trigger the rule of lenity, leading to the conclusion that the kit was not covered by the NFA; but (2) expressed the view that the ambiguity pertained to (a) the fundamental issue whether the making of an NFA-regulated firearm includes the manufacture, without assembly, of component parts because the NFA's definition of the particular firearm—which definition in the case at hand was § 5845(a)(3)'s description of a rifle with a barrel less than 16 inches long—does not so indicate, and (b) whether the conversion kit's short-

barreled combination, even when assembled, was
intended to be fired from the shoulder, which intent
is required under the definition of "rifle" in
§ 5845(c).

WHITE, J., joined by BLACKMUN, STEVENS, and
KENNEDY, JJ., dissenting, (1) agreed with the plurality that under the NFA, "making" a firearm includes
a dissembled aggregation of parts where the assemblage of such parts result in a firearm, but (2)
expressed the view that, when a weapon comes
within the scope of the definition of a "firearm"
under the NFA, the fact that the weapon may also
have a form that is not regulated under the NFA
provides no basis for failing to comply with the
requirements of the NFA.

STEVENS, J., dissenting, (1) agreed that under the
NFA, the manufacturer had made a firearm even
though the manufacturer had not assembled the
firearm's constituent parts, but (2) expressed the
view that the government should prevail in the case
at hand even if the NFA were ambiguous, because
the rule of lenity should not be applied in favor of
the manufacturer as though this were a criminal
prosecution, but rather the case should be treated
as a civil case testing the Federal Government's
interpretation of an important regulatory statute.

COUNSEL

James A. Feldman argued the cause for petitioner.
Stephen P. Halbrook argued the cause for respondent.

DENNIS SOCHOR, Petitioner

v

FLORIDA

504 US —, 119 L Ed 2d 326, 112 S Ct 2114

Argued March 2, 1992.
Decided June 8, 1992.

Decision: Florida trial judge's improper weighing in capital sentencing hearing of aggravating factor not supported by evidence, in violation of Eighth Amendment, held not cured by state appellate review.

SUMMARY

A man accused of attempting to rape a woman, and of strangling her to death when her resistance angered him, was convicted in a Florida trial court of first-degree murder and kidnapping. At a capital sentencing hearing, aggravating and mitigating evidence was presented, and the jury was instructed that it could consider statutory or nonstatutory mitigating circumstances and weigh them against any aggravating circumstances, which might include (1) that the crime was "especially wicked, evil, atrocious or cruel" (the "heinousness factor"); or (2) that the crime was committed "in a cold, calculated and premeditated manner, without any pretense of moral or legal justification" (the "coldness factor"). The jury recommended the death penalty, but, in accordance with Florida law, did not report specific findings as to aggravating or mitigating circumstances. The trial judge adopted the jury's recommendation after finding (1) four aggravating circumstances, including the two described above, and (2) no mitigating circumstances. The Supreme Court of Florida, in affirming the accused's convictions and death sentence, (1) declined to reverse on the accused's claim that the heinousness factor was unconstitutionally vague, on the grounds that this claim (a) had been waived for failure to object, and (b) lacked merit in any event; (2) rejected the accused's claim of insufficient evidence to support the heinousness factor; and (3) found that the evidence did not support the coldness factor, but affirmed the death sentence nevertheless, as the court expressed the view that (a) the trial court had carefully weighed the aggravating circumstances against the lack of mitigating circumstances, (b) even without the coldness factor, there remained three aggravating circumstances to be weighed against no mitigating circumstances, (c) striking one aggravating circumstance when there were no mitigating circumstances did not necessarily require resentencing, and (d) under the circumstances of the case, and in comparison with other death cases, the accused's death sentence was "proportionate" to his crime (580 So 2d 595).

On certiorari, the United States Supreme Court vacated and remanded. In an opinion by SOUTER, J., joined in part (as to holdings 1 and 2 below) by REHNQUIST, Ch. J., and WHITE, O'CONNOR, SCALIA, KENNEDY, and THOMAS, JJ., joined in part (as to holding 3 below) by REHNQUIST, Ch. J., and WHITE, O'CONNOR, KENNEDY, and THOMAS, JJ., joined in part (as to holding 4 below) by REHNQUIST, Ch. J., and WHITE, BLACKMUN, STEVENS, O'CONNOR, KENNEDY, and THOMAS, JJ., and joined in part (as to holding 5 below) by BLACKMUN, STEVENS, O'CONNOR, and KENNEDY, JJ., it was held that (1) the

297

United States Supreme Court did not have jurisdiction to review the accused's claim that the trial judge's instruction on the "heinousness factor" was unconstitutional, because the Florida Supreme Court's rejection of the claim was based on the alternative state ground that the claim was not preserved for appeal due to the accused's failure to object at trial; (2) the trial judge's weighing of the "heinousness factor" did not violate the Federal Constitution's Eighth Amendment, because (a) the Florida Supreme Court had consistently held that heinousness was properly found if a defendant strangled a conscious victim, and (b) the trial judge had to be presumed to have been familiar with this body of case law; (3) it could not be known whether the jury below actually relied on the "coldness factor," so as to violate the Eighth Amendment, because it would not be presumed that the jury erroneously considered a theory that was unsupported by the evidence; (4) the trial judge's weighing of the "coldness factor" violated the Eighth Amendment, given the Florida Supreme Court's finding that the factor was unsupported by the evidence; and (5) the accused's death sentence therefore could not stand on the existing record of appellate review, as the error could not be taken as cured by the Florida Supreme Court's consideration of the case, because that court did not explain or even declare a belief that the trial judge's error was harmless beyond a reasonable doubt.

O'CONNOR, J., concurred, expressing the view that the mere addition of the words "harmless error" to the Florida Supreme Court's opinion would not have sufficed to satisfy the Eighth Amendment.

REHNQUIST, Ch. J., joined by WHITE and THOMAS, JJ., concurred in part and dissented in part, expressing the view that the Florida Supreme Court cured the trial judge's error in weighing the "coldness factor," by finding the error harmless.

STEVENS, J., joined by BLACKMUN, J., concurred in part and dissented in part, expressing the view that (1) the trial judge's instruction on the "heinousness factor" was unconstitutionally vague; (2) the accused's failure to object to the instruction at trial did not deprive the Florida Supreme Court or the United States Supreme Court of the power to correct the obvious constitutional error; (3) erroneous jury instructions at the penalty phase of a Florida capital case are not necessarily harmless, despite the claim that the jury's role is purely advisory, because under Florida law, the jury's recommendations must be given great weight and are usually followed in practice; and (4) the Florida Supreme Court, on remand, therefore ought to conduct harmless error analysis with regard to the heinousness instruction.

SCALIA, J., concurred in part and dissented in part, expressing the view that (1) the Eighth Amendment does not require any consideration of mitigating evidence; (2) the weighing of aggravating and mitigating circumstances in the case at hand was therefore not constitutionally required; and (3) any error in the weighing process therefore raised no federal question.

COUNSEL

Gary Caldwell argued the cause for petitioner.
Carolyn M. Snurkowski argued the cause for respondent.

MANUEL LUJAN, Jr., Secretary of the Interior,
Petitioner

v

DEFENDERS OF WILDLIFE et al.

504 US —, 119 L Ed 2d 351, 112 S Ct 2130

Argued December 3, 1991.
Decided June 12, 1992.

Decision: Environmental groups held to lack standing to challenge regulation interpreting § 7(a)
(2) of Endangered Species Act (16 USCS
§ 1536(a)(2)) not to apply to actions taken in
foreign nations.

SUMMARY

Section 7(a)(2) of the Endangered Species Act
(ESA) (16 USCS § 1536(a)(2)) requires each federal
agency to consult with the United States Secretary
of the Interior to insure that any action authorized,
funded, or carried out by such agency is not likely
to jeopardize the continued existence of any endangered or threatened species. In 1978, the Fish and
Wildlife Service and the National Marine Fisheries
Service, on behalf of the Secretary of the Interior
and the Secretary of Commerce respectively, promulgated a joint regulation stating that the obligations imposed by § 7(a)(2) extended to actions taken
in foreign nations. However, a revised joint regulation (50 CFR § 402.01), promulgated in 1986, reinterpreted § 7(a)(2) to require consultation only for
actions taken in the United States or on the high
seas. Organizations dedicated to wildlife conservation and other environmental causes filed an action

SUMMARIES 119 L Ed 2d 351

against the Secretary of the Interior in the United States District Court for the District of Minnesota to seek (1) a declaratory judgment that the regulation was in error as to the geographical scope of § 7(a) (2), and (2) an injunction requiring the Secretary to promulgate a new regulation restoring the initial interpretation. The District Court granted the Secretary's motion to dismiss for lack of standing (658 F Supp 43). On appeal, the United States Court of Appeals reversed and remanded (851 F2d 1035). On remand, the District Court (1) denied a motion by the Secretary for summary judgment on the standing issue, (2) granted the organizations' motion for summary judgment on the merits, and (3) ordered the Secretary to publish a revised regulation (707 F Supp 1082). The Court of Appeals, affirming, said that the organizations' standing was supported by (1) an affidavit, filed by a member of one of the organizations, stating that the member had traveled to Egypt to observe the habitat of the endangered Nile crocodile and intended to do so again, and that she would suffer harm as a result of the role of the United States in overseeing and developing water projects in Egypt; (2) another member's affidavit, which stated that (a) the member had traveled to Sri Lanka to observe the habitat of endangered species such as the Asian elephant and the leopard, (b) a development project funded by a United States agency might severely shorten the future of these species, and (c) this threat harmed the member because she intended to return to Sri Lanka in the future in an attempt to see these species; and (3) a showing that the organizations had suffered a "procedural injury" based on the Secretary's failure to follow the consultation procedure required by § 7(a)(2) (911 F2d 117).

On certiorari, the United States Supreme Court reversed and remanded. In that portion of an opinion by SCALIA, J., joined by REHNQUIST, Ch. J., and WHITE, KENNEDY, SOUTER, and THOMAS, JJ., which comprised the opinion of the court, it was held that the organizations could not validly assert standing based on (1) the organization members' affidavits, which did not support a finding of actual or imminent injury; (2) an "ecosystem nexus" theory, under which any person who uses any part of a contiguous ecosystem adversely affected by a funded activity would have standing to challenge that activity even if the activity was located a great distance away; (3) an "animal nexus" approach, whereby anyone who has an interest in studying or seeing endangered animals anywhere on the globe would have standing to challenge a federal decision that threatens such animals; (4) a "vocational nexus" approach, under which anyone with a professional interest in such animals would have standing to sue; or (5) on the theory that the citizen-suit provision of the ESA (16 USCS § 1540(g)) creates in all persons a procedural right to consultation under § 7(a)(2), so that anyone can file suit in federal court to challenge the Secretary's failure to follow the assertedly correct consultative procedure, notwithstanding an inability to allege any discrete injury flowing from that failure. In addition, SCALIA, J., joined by REHNQUIST, Ch. J., and WHITE and THOMAS, JJ., expressed the view that the organizations had failed to show that any relief that the District Court could have provided would have redressed the organizations' alleged injury.

KENNEDY, J., joined by SOUTER, J., concurring in part and concurring in the judgment, expressed the view that (1) the organizations had failed to demonstrate that they had sustained an injury that would support standing, but (2) in different circumstances, a nexus theory similar to the theories proffered by the organizations in the case at hand might support a claim to standing.

STEVENS, J., concurring in the judgment, expressed the view that (1) reversal of the Court of Appeals' judgment was proper, because the consultation requirement in § 7(a)(2) does not apply to activities in foreign countries; but (2) the organizations had standing, because (a) the threatened injury to their interest in protecting the environment and studying endangered species was imminent, and (b) the injury was redressable in the litigation at hand.

BLACKMUN, J., joined by O'CONNOR, J., dissenting, expressed the view that (1) the organizations raised genuine issues of fact, both as to injury and as to redressability, that were sufficient to survive a motion for summary judgment on standing; (2) environmental plaintiffs who allege "ecosystem nexus" or vocational or professional injury should not be required to show physical proximity to the alleged wrong; and (3) some classes of procedural duties are so enmeshed with the prevention of substantive, concrete harm that an individual plaintiff may be able to demonstrate a sufficient likelihood of injury solely through the breach of that procedural duty.

COUNSEL

Edwin S. Kneedler argued the cause for petitioner.

Brian B. O'Neill argued the cause for respondents.

REPUBLIC OF ARGENTINA and BANCO
CENTRAL DE LA REPUBLICA ARGENTINA,
Petitioners

v

WELTOVER, INC., et al.

504 US —, 119 L Ed 2d 394, 112 S Ct 2160

Argued April 1, 1992.
Decided June 12, 1992.

Decision: Commercial exception in Foreign Sovereign Immunities Act held to authorize Federal District Court's jurisdiction over civil suit concerning Argentina's alleged default on certain public bonds.

SUMMARY

The Foreign Sovereign Immunities Act of 1976 (FSIA) (28 USCS §§ 1602 et seq.), which generally grants foreign states and certain of their instrumentalities immunity from suit in courts of the United States, is subject to an exception, under 28 USCS § 1605(a)(2), where a foreign state is not immune from a suit based upon an act outside the territory of the United States "in connection with a commercial activity" as a foreign state elsewhere, if such act causes a "direct effect in the United States." The FSIA, in 28 USCS § 1603(d), defines commercial activity to mean either a regular course of commercial conduct or a particular commercial transaction or act, and § 1603(d) provides that the commercial character of an activity shall be determined by reference to the nature of the course of conduct of a particular transaction or act, rather than by refer-
304

ence to its purpose. The Republic of Argentina issued certain bonds as part of a plan to stabilize the Argentine currency; such bonds provided for payment in United States dollars and for payment, at the election of the creditor, in several markets including New York. When Argentina unilaterally rescheduled the bonds' maturity dates, two Panamanian corporations and a Swiss bank—all of which held bonds and had elected to receive payment in New York—brought a breach-of-contract suit against Argentina and its central bank in the United States District Court for the Southern District of New York. That court, in denying a motion to dismiss, expressed the view that subject-matter jurisdiction was proper under the FSIA's commercial exception (753 F Supp 1201). On appeal, the United States Court of Appeals for the Second Circuit, in affirming, expressed the view that the commercial exception applied, because (1) the bonds' issuance as public debt was a commercial activity; and (2) there had been a direct effect in the United States (941 F2d 145).

On certiorari, the United States Supreme Court affirmed. In an opinion by SCALIA, J., expressing the unanimous view of the court, it was held that the District Court had properly asserted jurisdiction, under the FSIA's commercial exception, over the plaintiffs' breach-of-contract claim based on Argentina's alleged default through the rescheduling of the maturity dates on the bonds, because (1) the issuance of the bonds was a "commercial activity," for (a) the bonds were in almost all respects garden-variety debt instruments, and (b) under § 1603(d), it was irrelevant why Argentina participated in the bond market in the manner of a private actor; (2) the rescheduling was taken "in connection with" that commercial activity; and (3) the rescheduling had a "direct effect in the United States," for money that was supposed to have been delivered to a New York bank for deposit had not been forthcoming.

COUNSEL

Richard J. Davis argued the cause for petitioners.

Richard W. Cutler argued the cause for respondents.

Jeffrey P. Minear argued the cause for the United States, as amicus curiae, by special leave of the court.

———————

FEDERAL TRADE COMMISSION, Petitioner

v

TICOR TITLE INSURANCE COMPANY et al.

504 US —, 119 L Ed 2d 410, 112 S Ct 2169

Argued January 13, 1992.

Decided June 12, 1992.

Decision: Supervision by states of title-search rate-setting held not sufficiently active to give title insurance companies state-action immunity from federal antitrust liability.

SUMMARY

Under the state-action doctrine established by United States Supreme Court precedents, a state law or regulatory scheme can be the basis for immunity from the federal antitrust laws if the state (1) has articulated a clear and affirmative policy to allow anticompetitive conduct, and (2) provides active supervision of anticompetitive conduct undertaken by private actors. The Federal Trade Commission (FTC) filed an administrative complaint against various title insurance companies and charged the companies with violating § 5(a)(1) of the Federal Trade Commission Act (15 USCS § 45(a)(1)) in Arizona, Connecticut, Montana, and Wisconsin, by engaging in horizontal price fixing, through privately organized rating bureaus, of their fees for title searches, examinations, and settlements. In considering the companies' defense that their rate-fixing activities were entitled to state-action immunity, an Administrative Law Judge (ALJ) found, in part, that (1) in each of the four states, the rating

307

bureau was licensed by the state and authorized to establish joint rates for its members, which rates would become effective unless the state rejected them within a specified period; and (2) although this system provided a theoretical mechanism for substantive state review, rate filings in the four states had in fact been subject to only minimal scrutiny by state regulators. The FTC conceded that the affirmative-policy test for state-action immunity had been met in all four states, and the ALJ concluded that the active-supervision test had been met in Arizona and Montana, but not in Connecticut or Wisconsin. On review, the FTC (1) held that none of the four states had conducted active supervision, so that the companies were not entitled to immunity in any of those states; and (2) found antitrust violations in those states (112 FTC 1122). However, the FTC's order was vacated by the United States Court of Appeals for the Third Circuit, which (1) held that the existence of a state regulatory program, if staffed, funded, and empowered by law, satisfies the requirement of active supervision; and (2) concluded that the companies' conduct was entitled to state-action immunity in all four states (922 F2d 1122). The Supreme Court granted certiorari to consider the questions (1) whether the Court of Appeals was correct in its statement of law and in its application of law to fact—as to which question the parties confined their briefing to the regulatory regimes of Montana and Wisconsin—and (2) whether the Court of Appeals exceeded its authority in departing from the factual findings made by the ALJ and adopted by the FTC—as to which question the parties focussed their briefing on the regulatory regimes of Arizona and Connecticut (502 US ——, 116 L Ed 2d 25, 112 S Ct 47).

On certiorari, the Supreme Court reversed the judgment of the Court of Appeals as to the first question, and remanded for further proceedings as to the second question. In an opinion by KENNEDY, J., joined by WHITE, BLACKMUN, STEVENS, SCALIA, and SOUTER, JJ., it was held that (1) both elements of the above state-action immunity test must be complied with, and not only the "clear articulation" requirement; (2) in order to satisfy the "active supervision" requirement, parties claiming state-action immunity where prices or rates are set as an initial matter by private parties, subject only to a veto if the state chooses to exercise it, must show that state officials have undertaken the necessary steps to determine the specifics of the price fixing or ratesetting scheme, and the mere potential for state supervision is not an adequate substitute for a decision by the state; (3) under this standard, there was no "active supervision" by state officials in Montana and Wisconsin, and the actions of the companies in those states were therefore not immune from antitrust liability, where (a) in both states, the applicable regulatory schemes allowed rates filed by the rating bureaus with state agencies to become effective unless they were rejected by state officials within a specified time, and (b) the potential for state supervision under this "negative option" rule was not realized in fact, as (i) rate filings in those states were at most checked for mathematical accuracy, while some were unchecked altogether, (ii) a rate filing became effective in Montana despite the failure of the rating bureau to provide additional information requested by state officials, and (iii) in Wisconsin, additional information requested by state officials was provided after a lapse of 7 years, during which time the rate filing

119 L Ed 2d 410   DECISIONS: 1991-92 TERM

remained in effect; and (4) the case would be remanded to give the Court of Appeals an opportunity to re-examine its determinations with respect to Arizona and Connecticut.

SCALIA, J., concurred, expressing the view that, while the Supreme Court's standard of "active supervision" would be a source of uncertainty and litigation, these consequences were acceptable because (1) the standard was compelled by the "active supervision" doctrine, which had not been challenged in the case at hand; and (2) the antitrust exemption for state-programmed private collusion was dubious in the first place.

REHNQUIST, Ch. J., joined by O'CONNOR and THOMAS, JJ., dissented, expressing the view that (1) the Court of Appeals followed the correct standard in applying the "active supervision" requirement; and (2) the different conclusion reached by the Court of Appeals by reviewing the facts in light of this standard did not constitute a rejection of the FTC's factual findings.

O'CONNOR, J., joined by THOMAS, J., dissented, expressing the view that (1) the practical effect of the majority's interpretation of the "active supervision" requirement would be to diminish states' regulatory flexibility by eliminating "negative option" regulatory schemes such as those of the states in question; (2) liability under the antitrust laws should not depend on how enthusiatically state officials carried out their statutory duties, a circumstance over which regulated entities had no control; and (3) the majority's opinion offered no guidance as to what level of supervision would suffice.

COUNSEL

Lawrence G. Wallace argued the cause for petitioner.

John C. Christie, Jr. argued the cause for respondents.

―――――

BURLINGTON NORTHERN RAILROAD
COMPANY, Petitioner

v

WILLIAM D. FORD and THOMAS L. JOHNSON

504 US —, 119 L Ed 2d 432, 112 S Ct 2184

Argued April 20, 1992.
Decided June 12, 1992.

Decision: Equal protection held not violated by
Montana venue rules allowing civil suit against
Montana corporation in only county of principal
place of business, but against foreign corporation in any county.

SUMMARY

A Montana statute provides that the proper place
for a civil trial is (1) a defendant's county of residence, or (2) if no defendant resides in the state,
any county designated in the plaintiff's complaint.
The position of the Supreme Court of Montana has
been that (1) a corporation, unless it is incorporated
in Montana, does not reside in the state for venue
purposes, and (2) a Montana corporation resides in
the Montana county in which the corporation has its
principal place of business. Two employees of a
railroad, which was incorporated in Delaware and
had its principal place of business in Texas, sought,
in suits against the railroad in a state trial court in
Montana, to recover under a federal statute for
alleged on-the-job injuries. In each case, the railroad moved to change venue to the county in which
the railroad claimed to have its principal place of
business in Montana. The trial court denied each
312

motion, and the railroad brought interlocutory appeals. After consolidating the cases, the Supreme Court of Montana (1) rejected the railroad's argument that the Montana venue rules discriminated in violation of the equal protection clause of the Federal Constitution's Fourteenth Amendment, and (2) affirmed the trial court judgments (819 P2d 169).

On certiorari, the United States Supreme Court affirmed. In an opinion by SOUTER, J., expressing the unanimous view of the court, it was held that, although Montana's civil venue rules combined to permit a plaintiff to sue a domestic corporation in only the one county in which the corporation had its principal place of business, but to sue a foreign corporation in any Montana county, the rules did not violate the railroad's rights under the equal protection clause, because (1) since the venue rules neither deprived the railroad of a fundamental right nor classified along suspect lines, the rules, unless they failed to rationally further legitimate state ends, did not deny equal protection to the railroad; (2) the venue rules could be understood as rationally furthering a legitimate state interest, in adjusting the disparate interests of the parties to a lawsuit in the place of trial; and (3) the railroad, having headquarters outside the state, would not have benefited from a scheme based on domicile, and therefore could not complain about the state's use of the state of incorporation as a surrogate for domicile.

COUNSEL

Betty Jo Christian argued the cause for petitioner.
Joel I. Klein argued the cause for respondents.

313

UNITED STATES, Petitioner

v

HUMBERTO ALVAREZ-MACHAIN

504 US —, 119 L Ed 2d 441, 112 S Ct 2188

Argued April 1, 1992.

Decided June 15, 1992.

Decision: Forcible abduction of Mexican citizen to United States held not to violate extradition treaty with Mexico, and thus, not to prohibit citizen's trial in Federal District Court on criminal charges.

SUMMARY

The Extradition Treaty, May 4, 1978, [1979] United States-United Mexican States (31 UST 5059, TIAS No. 9656) provides (1) in Article 22(1), that the treaty shall apply to specified offenses committed before and after the treaty entered into effect; and (2) in Article 9, that (a) neither contracting party shall be bound to deliver up its own nationals, but the executive authority of the requested party shall, if not prevented by that party's laws, have the power to deliver such nationals up, if, in the party's discretion, it is deemed proper to do so, and (b) if extradition is not granted pursuant to the prior provision, the requested party shall submit the case to the party's competent authorities for the purpose of jurisdiction, provided that the party has jurisdiction over the offense. A Mexican citizen and resident was indicted in the United States on numerous federal charges for allegedly participating in the kidnap and murder of a Drug Enforcement Adminis-
314

tration (DEA) agent and the agent's pilot. The accused was forcibly abducted from Mexico to the United States and was arrested in the United States by DEA officials. On a motion by the accused to dismiss the indictment, the United States District Court for the Central District of California (1) concluded that, although DEA agents were not personally involved in the accused's abduction, they were responsible for it; (2) ruled that the court lacked jurisdiction to try the accused, because the abduction violated the extradition treaty; (3) discharged the accused; and (4) ordered that the accused be repatriated to Mexico (745 F Supp 599). On appeal, the United States Court of Appeals for the Ninth Circuit, in affirming, expressed the view that (1) the forcible abduction of a Mexican national from Mexico by an agency of the United States without the consent or acquiescence of the Mexican Government violated the extradition treaty; and (2) with respect to the abduction of the accused, the proper remedy was the indictment's dismissal and the accused's repatriation, as (a) the requisite findings of United States involvement had been made, and (b) letters from the Mexican Government to the United States Government served as an official protest of the treaty violation (946 F2d 1466).

On certiorari, the United States Supreme Court reversed and remanded. In an opinion by REHNQUIST, Ch. J., joined by WHITE, SCALIA, KENNEDY, SOUTER, and THOMAS, JJ., it was held that, even if the accused's forcible abduction might have been "shocking" and in violation of general principles of international law, the abduction was not in violation of the 1978 extradition treaty, the accused did not thereby acquire a defense to the jurisdiction of United States courts, and the fact of the accused's forcible abduction did not therefore prohibit the accused's trial in the District Court for alleged violations of the criminal laws of the United States, because (1) in view of the general United States rule that a forcible abduction does not impair a court's jurisdiction to try a person for a crime, the language of the treaty, in the context of the history of negotiation and practice under the treaty, did not support the proposition that the treaty prohibited abductions outside of the treaty's terms; and (2) to infer from the treaty and its terms that the treaty contained an implied prohibition against obtaining the presence of an individual outside of the treaty's terms would go beyond established precedent and practice, with only the most general of international law principles to support such an inference.

STEVENS, J., joined by BLACKMUN and O'CONNOR, JJ., dissenting, expressed the view that (1) although the treaty contained no express promise to refrain from forcible abductions in the territory of the other nation, the treaty's manifest scope and object plainly implied a mutual undertaking to respect territorial integrity; (2) this interpretation was confirmed by a consideration of the legal context in which the treaty was negotiated; (3) with respect to such abductions, the Supreme Court's opinion failed to differentiate between (a) the conduct of private citizens, which did not violate any treaty obligation, and (b) conduct expressly authorized by the Executive Branch of the Federal Government, which constituted a violation of international law; and (4) the fact, if true, that the accused had participated in an especially brutal murder of an American law enforcement agent might explain the Executive Branch's intense interest in punishing the accused in United States courts, but such an explanation pro-

vided no justification for disregarding the rule of
law that the Supreme Court had a duty to uphold.

COUNSEL

Kenneth W. Starr argued the cause for petitioner.
Paul Hoffman argued the cause for respondent.

CAROL ANKENBRANDT, as Next Friend and
Mother of L. R. and S. R., Petitioner

v

JON A. RICHARDS and DEBRA KESLER

504 US —, 119 L Ed 2d 468, 112 S Ct 2206

Argued March 31, 1992.
Decided June 15, 1992.

Decision: Domestic relations exception to federal
courts' diversity jurisdiction held inapplicable to
woman's child-abuse tort claim against her former husband and his female companion.

SUMMARY

A woman who was a citizen of Missouri brought
suit in the United States District Court for the
Eastern District of Louisiana against her former
husband and his female companion, who were citizens of Louisiana. The complaint, which alleged that
the District Court had jurisdiction based on the
diversity of citizenship provision of 28 USCS
§ 1332, sought monetary damages for the defendants' alleged sexual and physical abuse of two
daughters of the plaintiff and her former husband.
The plaintiff asserted that a Louisiana state court
had previously entered a judgment terminating the
former husband's parental rights because of the
alleged abuse. The District Court, granting the
defendants' motion to dismiss the suit, (1) said that
the case fell into a "domestic relations" exception
to diversity jurisdiction, and (2) invoking the doctrine of Younger v Harris (1971) 401 US 37, 27 L
Ed 2d 669, 91 S Ct 746, under which a federal court

will abstain from interfering with a pending state proceeding, said that abstention was a doctrine designed to promote federal-state comity, and that abstention was required when the rendering of a decision would disrupt the establishment of a coherent state policy. The United States Court of Appeals for the Fifth Circuit affirmed (934 F2d 1262).

On certiorari, the United States Supreme Court reversed and remanded. In an opinion by WHITE, J., joined by REHNQUIST, Ch. J., and O'CONNOR, SCALIA, KENNEDY, and SOUTER, JJ., it was held that (1) a valid domestic relations exception to diversity jurisdiction exists—as a matter of construction of 28 USCS § 1332 rather than of the Federal Constitution (Art III, § 2)—which exception divests the federal courts of power to issue divorce, alimony, and child custody decrees; (2) the domestic relations exception had no place in the case at hand, given that the lawsuit in no way sought a divorce, alimony, or child custody decree; and (3) it was clearly erroneous for the District Court to abstain from exercising jurisdiction pursuant to the Younger doctrine, since (a) there was no allegation of any pending state proceedings, and (b) the plaintiff contended that state proceedings had ended prior to her filing the federal lawsuit.

BLACKMUN, J., concurring in the judgment, expressed the view that (1) the District Court had jurisdiction over the lawsuit in question, and (2) federal courts should not entertain claims for divorce, alimony, and child custody, but (3) the practice of the federal courts in refusing to hear domestic relations cases was precedent at most for continued discretionary abstention rather than mandatory limits on federal jurisdiction.

STEVENS, J., joined by THOMAS, J., concurring in the judgment, expressed the view that (1) the case at hand did not come within any domestic relations exception that might exist, and (2) consideration of whether any domestic relations cases necessarily fall outside of the jurisdiction of the federal courts—and of what, if any, principle would justify such an exception to federal jurisdiction—should have been left for another day.

COUNSEL

Richard Lynn Ducote argued the cause for petitioner.

Paul S. Weindenfeld argued the cause for respondents.

———————

DERRICK MORGAN, Petitioner

v

ILLINOIS

504 US —, 119 L Ed 2d 492, 112 S Ct 2222

Argued January 21, 1992.
Decided June 15, 1992.

Decision: Illinois trial court held to violate due
process by refusing to ask potential jurors, on
voir dire in capital case, whether they would
automatically impose death penalty if defendant
was convicted.

SUMMARY

The trial of a capital offense in Illinois is conducted in two phases, with the same jury being used
in each phase. If the defendant is convicted of first-
degree murder in the first phase, a separate sentencing hearing is held as the second phase to determine the existence of aggravating and mitigating
factors, and the defendant is sentenced to death if
the jury unanimously determines that (1) at least
one statutory aggravating factor exists, and (2) there
are no mitigating factors sufficient to preclude the
imposition of a death sentence. An Illinois trial
court, conducting voir dire in a capital case, questioned each venire—at the request of the prosecution, and over defense objections—whether any
member had moral or religious scruples that would
prevent the member from imposing the death penalty regardless of the facts. The trial court refused a
defense request to ask prospective jurors whether
they would automatically vote to impose the death

penalty if they found the defendant guilty, as the trial court found that it had asked substantially the same question in a different manner—the court having asked (1) 9 of the 12 jurors eventually impaneled whether they would follow his instructions on the law even if they disagreed, and (2) all of the jurors whether they felt that they could be fair and impartial. When impaneled, the jurors swore an oath to render a verdict according to the law and the evidence. The jury thereafter convicted the defendant of first-degree murder and sentenced him to death. In affirming the conviction and sentence on appeal, the Supreme Court of Illinois held that (1) there is no rule requiring a trial court to "life qualify" a jury to exclude all jurors who believe that the death penalty should be imposed in every murder case; and (2) the defendant's sentence was valid, given that none of the jurors actually selected either (a) expressed any views that would call his or her impartiality into question, or (b) was shown to be biased in favor of the death penalty (142 Ill 2d 410, 154 Ill Dec 534, 568 NE2d 755).

On certiorari, the United States Supreme Court reversed and remanded. In an opinion by WHITE, J., joined by BLACKMUN, STEVENS, O'CONNOR, KENNEDY, and SOUTER, JJ., it was held that the trial court's refusal to inquire into whether potential jurors would automatically vote to impose the death penalty if the defendant were convicted violated the due process clause of the Federal Constitution's Fourteenth Amendment, and that the defendant's sentence therefore could not stand, because (1) a juror who will automatically vote for the death penalty in every case will fail in good faith to consider the

322

evidence of aggravating and mitigating circumstances, and to determine whether the latter is sufficient to preclude imposition of the death penalty, as required by state statute and by the court's instructions; (2) if voir dire were not available to expose the foundation of the defendant's challenge for cause against automatic-death jurors, the defendant's right not to be tried by such jurors would be nugatory and meaningless; and (3) neither general fairness and "follow the law" questions, nor the jurors' oath, were sufficient to satisfy the defendant's right to make inquiry.

SCALIA, J., joined by REHNQUIST, Ch. J., and THOMAS, J., dissented, expressing the view that (1) an Illinois juror who would always impose the death penalty for capital murder was not "partial" for purposes of the Constitution's Sixth or Fourteenth Amendments, because the state law in question in the case at hand, and the trial court's instructions thereunder, did not preclude a juror from taking the view that a death sentence was always warranted for capital murder, but rather permitted each juror to determine whether a particular item of evidence was mitigating; (2) the Constitution's Eighth Amendment did not prohibit a juror from always advocating a death sentence at the weighing stage, but required only that a sentencer be allowed to consider mitigating evidence; and (3) even if the instructions below required jurors to be open to voting against the death penalty on the basis of allegedly mitigating circumstances, jurors who would defy this element of the instructions could be identified by general questions concerning fairness and willingness to follow the law.

COUNSEL

Allen H. Andrews, III argued the cause for petitioner.

Kenneth L. Gillis argued the cause for respondent.

JOHN R. PATTERSON, Trustee, Petitioner

v

JOSEPH B. SHUMATE, Jr.

504 US —, 119 L Ed 2d 519, 112 S Ct 2242

Argued April 20, 1992.
Decided June 15, 1992.

Decision: Interest in ERISA-qualified pension plan
held subject to transfer restriction under "applicable nonbankruptcy law," and thus excludable
from property of bankruptcy estate under 11
USCS § 541(c)(2).

SUMMARY

Under § 541(c)(2) of the Bankruptcy Code (11
USCS § 541(c)(2)), a debtor's beneficial interest in
property that is subject to a transfer restriction
enforceable under "applicable nonbankruptcy law"
is excluded from the bankruptcy estate. In order to
qualify for coverage under the Employee Retirement
Income Security Act of 1974 (ERISA) (29 USCS
§§ 1001 et seq.), an employee pension plan is required, under § 206(d)(1) of ERISA (29 USCS
§ 1056(d)(1)), to provide that benefits provided under the plan may not be assigned or alienated. In
terminating and liquidating a furniture corporation's
pension plan that contained the antialienation provision required for ERISA qualification, the trustee
with respect to the corporation's bankruptcy provided full distribution of employee interests in the
plan to every employee except the corporate president, who had filed a petition for personal bankruptcy. The trustee with respect to the president's

bankruptcy filed against the trustee for the corporation an adversary proceeding in the Bankruptcy Court for the Western District of Virginia to recover the president's interest in the plan for the benefit of the president's bankruptcy estate, and the president sought to have the United States District Court for the Western District of Virginia, which already had jurisdiction over a related proceeding, compel the trustee for the corporation to pay the president's interest in the plan directly to the president. After the bankruptcy proceeding was consolidated with the District Court action, the District Court (1) ruled that the president's interest should not be excluded from the president's bankruptcy estate under § 541(c)(2), because (a) § 541(c)(2)'s reference to "nonbankruptcy law" embraced only state law, and (b) the president's interest did not qualify under Virginia law as a spendthrift trust; and (2) ordered the trustee for the corporation to pay the president's interest to the president's bankruptcy estate (83 BR 404, 9 EBC 1819). The United States Court of Appeals for the Fourth Circuit reversed and expressed the view that under § 541(c)(2), the president's interest in the ERISA-qualified pension plan should be excluded from the president's bankruptcy estate (943 F2d 362, 21 BCD 1617, 14 EBC 2340).

On certiorari, the United States Supreme Court affirmed. In an opinion by BLACKMUN, J., expressing the unanimous view of the court, it was held that for purposes of § 541(c)(2), the president's interest in the pension plan was subject to a transfer restriction under applicable nonbankruptcy law, and thus could be excluded by the debtor from the property of the bankruptcy estate, because (1) plainly read, § 541(c)

(2) encompassed any relevant nonbankruptcy law, including federal law such as ERISA, where (a) nothing in § 541(c)(2) suggested that the phrase "applicable nonbankruptcy law" referred exclusively to state law, (b) other sections of the Bankruptcy Code (11 USCS §§ 101 et seq.) expressly restricted the scope of applicable law to "state law," and (c) interpreting "applicable nonbankruptcy law" in § 541(c)(2) as including federal law accorded with prevailing interpretations of that phrase as it appeared elsewhere in the Code; (2) the antialienation provision in the plan in question constituted an enforceable transfer restriction for purposes of § 541(c)(2); and (3) it had not been shown that Congress intended to limit the § 541(c)(2) exclusion to transfer restrictions that were enforceable under only state spendthrift trust laws.

SCALIA, J., concurred, expressing the view that in interpreting statutes, (1) attention to text and application of an agreed-upon methodology are appropriate, and (2) consistent usage of particular phrases within various provisions of the same statute is to be presumed.

COUNSEL

G. Steven Agee argued the cause for petitioner.

Kevin R. Huennekens argued the cause for respondent.

Christopher J. Wright argued the cause for the United States, as amicus curiae, by special leave of the court.

ALLIED-SIGNAL, INC., as Successor-in-Interest to
THE BENDIX CORPORATION, Petitioner

v

DIRECTOR, DIVISION OF TAXATION

504 US —, 119 L Ed 2d 533, 112 S Ct 2251

Argued March 4, 1992.
Reargued April 22, 1992.
Decided June 15, 1992.

Decision: "Unitary business principle" held to (1) govern states' federal constitutional power to tax nondomiciliary corporations' income, and (2) prevent state's taxation of gain on particular stock sale.

SUMMARY

A Delaware corporation which had its commercial domicile and corporate headquarters in Michigan, and which conducted business in all 50 states and in 22 foreign countries, was organized into four major operating groups, including an aerospace/electronics group, each of which groups was under separate management but had a chief executive officer who reported to the corporate chairman and chief executive officer. The Delaware corporation, whose primary operations in New Jersey were the development and manufacture of aerospace products, acquired, by purchases on the open market, 20.6 percent of the stock of a New Jersey corporation which had its principal offices in New York, and which produced nonferrous metals. After owning the stock for over 2 years, the Delaware corporation generated income of $211.5 million by selling the
328

stock back to the New Jersey corporation. After New
Jersey assessed the Delaware corporation for income
taxes on an apportioned amount of income that
included in the base the income from the stock sale,
the Delaware corporation sued for a refund in the
New Jersey Tax Court. The parties stipulated that
during the time the Delaware corporation owned
the stock, the two corporations were unrelated en-
terprises each of whose activities had nothing to do
with the other, and that the Delaware corporation,
although it held 2 of the 14 seats on the New Jersey
corporation's board of directors, did not exert any
control over the New Jersey corporation. The Tax
Court held that the assessment was proper (10 NJ
Tax 46), and the Superior Court of New Jersey,
Appellate Division, affirmed (237 NJ Super 328, 568
A2d 59). The Supreme Court of New Jersey (1) held
that the gain from the stock sale was, under the
Federal Constitution, properly taxable as income
earned in the Delaware corporation's unitary business, and (2) affirmed the Superior Court judgment
(125 NJ 20, 592 A2d 536).

On certiorari, with the Delaware corporation having been replaced by its successor-in-interest as a
party to the litigation, the United States Supreme
Court reversed and remanded. In an opinion by
KENNEDY, J., joined by WHITE, STEVENS, SCALIA, and
SOUTER, JJ., it was held that (1) the "unitary business principle"—which, pursuant to the requirements of the Federal Constitution's commerce
clause (Art I, § 8, cl 3) and the due process clause
of the Federal Constitution's Fourteenth Amendment, permits states to tax a corporation on an
apportionable share of the multistate business carried on by the corporation in part in the taxing state
if the business is unitary—is an appropriate device

for ascertaining whether a state, in taxing the income of a nondomiciliary corporation, has transgressed its constitutional limitations; and (2) the stipulated facts made clear that under Supreme Court precedents, New Jersey did not have the constitutional power to include in the Delaware corporation's tax base the income from the stock sale, where none of the three factors—functional integration, centralization of management, and economies of scale—focused on as indicators of a unitary business in a prior Supreme Court case were present.

O'CONNOR, J., joined by REHNQUIST, Ch. J., and BLACKMUN and THOMAS, JJ., dissenting, (1) agreed with the court that the unitary business principle should not be replaced by a rule allowing a state to tax a proportionate share of all the income generated by any corporation doing business in the state, but (2) expressed the view that (a) the sucessor-in-interest had failed to show by clear and cogent evidence that the income derived by the Delaware corporation from its investment in the New Jersey corporation was not operationally related to the Delaware corporation's aerospace business conducted in New Jersey, and (b) therefore, New Jersey ought to be able to apportion and tax that income.

COUNSEL

Andrew L. Frey argued the cause for petitioner.
Mary R. Hamill argued the cause for respondent.

STEPHANIE NORDLINGER, Petitioner

v

KENNETH HAHN, in his Capacity as Tax Assessor
for Los Angeles County, et al.

505 US —, 120 L Ed 2d 1, 112 S Ct 2326

Argued February 25, 1992.
Decided June 18, 1992.

Decision: Equal protection held not violated by
California Constitution's real property tax system which generally assesses property on value
at time of acquisition, rather than on current
value.

SUMMARY

The real property tax assessment system established by a 1978 amendment to the California Constitution generally combined a 1 percent ceiling on
real property tax rates based on assessed valuations
for the 1975-1976 tax year with a 2 percent cap on
annual increases in assessed valuations, subject to
an exception that new construction or a change in
ownership generally triggered a reassessment up to
the current appraised value. Two exemptions were
authorized from the reassessment requirement for
(1) persons aged 55 and older who exchanged
principal residences, and (2) children who acquired
property from their parents. A Los Angeles County,
California, homeowner exhausted her administrative
remedies and brought suit in the Los Angeles
County Superior Court against defendants including
the county tax assessor. The homeowner (1) sought
a tax refund and a declaration that the California

constitutional amendment's assessment system violated the equal protection clause of the Federal
Constitution's Fourteenth Amendment, and (2) alleged that after she had purchased her home in
1988, she was paying about five times more in taxes
than neighbors who had owned comparable homes
within the same residential district since 1975. The
Superior Court, however, sustained a demurrer and
dismissed the complaint without leave to amend. On
appeal, the Court of Appeal of California, Second
Appellate District, in affirming, expressed the view
that the assessment system survived equal protection review, because the system was supported by at
least two rational bases, in that the system (1)
prevented property taxes from reflecting unduly
inflated and unforeseen current values; and (2)
allowed property owners to estimate future liability
with substantial certainty (225 Cal App 3d 1259,
275 Cal Rptr 684). The Supreme Court of California denied review.

On certiorari, the United States Supreme Court
affirmed. In an opinion by BLACKMUN, J., joined by
REHNQUIST, Ch. J., and WHITE, O'CONNOR, SCALIA,
KENNEDY, and SOUTER, JJ., and joined in part by
THOMAS, J., it was held that, because the homeowner lacked standing to assert the federal constitutional right to travel as a basis for heightened equal
protection scrutiny of the California assessment system, the appropriate standard of equal protection
review was whether the system's difference in treatment between newer and older owners rationally
furthered a legitimate state interest, and that under
such standard, the system did not violate the equal
protection clause, where (1) the California amendment was enacted to achieve the benefits of, and
essentially embodied, an "acquisition value" system

—under which the assessment of real property was related to the value of the property at the time of acquisition—rather than a system of assessing property at its current value, (2) the California system, which did not discriminate between newer and older owners with respect to either the tax rate or the annual rate of adjustment in assessments, treated newer owners differently with respect to only the basis on which the newer owners' property was initially assessed, (3) there were at least two rational or reasonable considerations that justified denying a new owner the benefits of older owners' lower assessments, as the state (a) had a legitimate interest in local neighborhood preservation, continuity, and stability, and could therefore legitimately decide to structure the tax system to discourage rapid turnovers in ownership, and (b) could legitimately conclude that a new owner did not have the same reliance interest warranting protection against higher taxes as did an existing owner, and (4) the two narrow exemptions from the reassessment requirement also rationally furthered legitimate state interests.

THOMAS, J., concurring in part and concurring in the judgment, expressed the view that, while the California assessment system was constitutional pursuant to a rational-basis review under the equal protection clause, (1) a prior decision which the court purported to distinguish—Allegheny Pittsburgh Coal Co. v County Com. of Webster County (1989) 488 US 336, 102 L Ed 2d 688, 109 S Ct 633 —could not be distinguished, and (2) there was no benefit, and much risk, in refusing to confront directly the Allegheny Pittsburgh decision, as the court's attempt to distinguish that decision left the court's equal protection jurisprudence in disarray.

STEVENS, J., dissenting, expressed the view that the California assessment system violated the equal protection clause, because the severe inequalities created by the system were arbitrary and unreasonable and did not rationally further a legitimate state interest.

COUNSEL

Carlyle W. Hall, Jr. argued the cause for petitioner.

Rex E. Lee argued the cause for respondents.

GEORGIA, Petitioner

v

THOMAS McCOLLUM, WILLIAM JOSEPH
McCOLLUM, and ELLA HAMPTON McCOLLUM

505 US —, 120 L Ed 2d 33, 112 S Ct 2348

Argued February 26, 1992.
Decided June 18, 1992.

Decision: Fourteenth Amendment's equal protection clause held to prohibit Georgia criminal
defendants from engaging in purposeful racial
discrimination in exercise of peremptory challenges of potential jurors.

SUMMARY

The United States Supreme Court successively
held (1) in Batson v Kentucky (1986) 476 US 79, 90
L Ed 2d 69, 106 S Ct 1712, that, under the equal
protection clause of the Federal Constitution's Fourteenth Amendment, a state criminal defendant could
establish a prima facie case of a prosecutor's purposeful racial discrimination in the selection of jurors based solely on the prosecutor's exercise, at the
defendant's trial, of peremptory challenges to exclude members of the defendant's own race; and (2)
in Edmonson v Leesville Concrete Co. (1991, US)
114 L Ed 2d 660, 111 S Ct 2077, a federal civil
case, that racial discrimination in a private civil
litigant's exercise of peremptory challenges constituted state action which violated the equal protection component of the due process clause of the
Constitution's Fifth Amendment. A Georgia grand
jury indicted several white criminal defendants on

335

charges of assault and battery against two alleged victims who were African-Americans. Before jury selection began, the prosecution moved to prohibit the defendants from exercising peremptory challenges in a racially discriminatory manner. The trial judge, however, in denying the motion, expressed the view that neither Georgia law nor federal law prohibited criminal defendants from exercising peremptory strikes in a racially discriminatory manner. On immediate appeal, the Supreme Court of Georgia, in affirming, (1) distinguished Edmonson v Leesville Concrete Co. as involving a civil action; and (2) declined, in view of what the court called the long history of jury trials as an essential element of the protection of human rights, to diminish the free exercise of peremptory strikes by criminal defendants (261 Ga 473, 405 SE2d 688). A motion for reconsideration was denied.

On certiorari, the United States Supreme Court reversed and remanded. In an opinion by BLACKMUN, J., joined by REHNQUIST, Ch. J., and WHITE, STEVENS, KENNEDY, and SOUTER, JJ., it was held that the Fourteenth Amendment's equal protection clause prohibits a state criminal defendant from engaging in purposeful racial discrimination in the exercise of peremptory challenges to exclude potential jurors, because (1) such an action inflicts harm on the dignity of persons and the integrity of courts; (2) such an action constitutes state action for equal protection purposes, as (a) the claimed constitutional deprivation results from the exercise of a right or privilege having its source in state authority, (b) a defendant charged with such discrimination can be described as a state actor, and (c) the adversarial relationship between a defendant and the prosecution does not negate the governmental character of the action; (3) a prosecutor—that is, the state—has third-party standing to raise such an equal protection claim on behalf of the excluded jurors; and (4) the interests served by prohibiting such an exercise of peremptory challenges are not required to give way to the constitutional rights of a defendant, including the defendant's rights, under the Constitution's Sixth Amendment, to the effective assistance of counsel and to trial by an impartial jury.

REHNQUIST, Ch. J., concurring, expressed the view that while he continued to believe that Edmonson v Leesville Concrete Co., supra—in which he had dissented—had been wrongly decided, so long as the Edmonson decision remained the law, that decision controlled the disposition of the case at hand on the issue of state action under the Fourteenth Amendment.

THOMAS, J., concurring in the judgment, expressed the view that (1) while, as a matter of first impression, he might have shared the dissent's view that a criminal defendant's use of peremptory strikes could not violate the Fourteenth Amendment —as not involving state action—Edmonson v Leesville Concrete Co., supra, which the defendants in the case at hand had not challenged, governed and required the opposite conclusion; and (2) while the Supreme Court's decision protected jurors, the decision took the court (a) further from its prior premise that securing representation of a criminal defendant's race on the jury might help to overcome racial bias and provide the defendant with a better chance of having a fair trial, and (b) down a slope of peremptory-challenge inquiry that had no clear stopping point.

O'Connor, J., dissenting, expressed the view that (1) the Supreme Court, in a result which was not compelled by the court's prior precedents, had reached the "remarkable" conclusion that criminal defendants being prosecuted by the state acted on behalf of their adversary when such defendants exercised peremptory challenges during jury selection; and (2) while it was frustrating that the Constitution did not give federal judges the reach to wipe all marks of racism from every courtroom in the land, such limitations were the necessary and intended consequence of the Fourteenth Amendment's state action requirement.

Scalia, J., dissenting, expressed the view that (1) while the Supreme Court's decision followed logically from Edmonson v Leesville Concrete Co., supra, that case had been wrongly decided; (2) a criminal defendant, in the process of defending against the state, ought not to be held to be acting on behalf of the state; and (3) the court, in the interest of promoting the supposedly greater good of race relations in society as a whole, abused the Constitution to destroy the ages-old right of criminal defendants to exercise peremptory challenges as such defendants wished, to secure a jury that they considered fair.

COUNSEL

Harrison W. Kohler argued the cause for petitioner.

Michael R. Dreeben argued the cause for the United States, as amicus curiae, by special leave of the court.

Robert H. Revell, Jr. argued the cause for respondents.

———————

KRAFT GENERAL FOODS, INC., Petitioner

v

IOWA DEPARTMENT OF REVENUE AND
FINANCE

505 US —, 120 L Ed 2d 59, 112 S Ct 2365

Argued April 22, 1992.
Decided June 18, 1992.

Decision: Iowa business tax statute's treatment of
corporation's dividends received from foreign
subsidiary held to violate Federal Constitution's
foreign commerce clause.

SUMMARY

An Iowa statute which imposed a business tax on
corporations doing business in Iowa followed the
federal income tax scheme for the calculation of a
corporation's taxable income, insofar as the Iowa
statute allowed a deduction for dividends which a
corporation received from its domestic subsidiaries,
but not for those received from its foreign subsidiaries. However, while the federal scheme allowed a
parent corporation a credit for taxes paid to a
foreign country on the earnings underlying dividends received from a foreign subsidiary, the Iowa
statute did not allow a credit for taxes paid to a
foreign country. Notwithstanding these provisions, a
corporation which was subject to the Iowa tax de-
ducted foreign subsidiary dividends in computing its
taxable income on its Iowa tax return. The Iowa
Department of Revenue and Finance assessed a
deficiency. Following the denial of the corporation's
340

administrative protest, the corporation challenged the assessment in the Iowa state courts. Noting that the corporation had failed to demonstrate that Iowa businesses received a commercial advantage over foreign commerce due to Iowa's taxing scheme, the Supreme Court of Iowa (465 NW2d 664) rejected the corporation's claim that the disparate treatment of domestic and foreign subsidiary dividends violated the Federal Constitution's foreign commerce clause (Art I, § 8, cl 3).

On certiorari, the United States Supreme Court reversed and remanded. In an opinion by STEVENS, J., joined by WHITE, O'CONNOR, SCALIA, KENNEDY, SOUTER, and THOMAS, JJ., it was held that the Iowa statute (1) facially discriminated against foreign commerce, and (2) therefore violated the Federal Constitution's foreign commerce clause.

REHNQUIST, Ch. J., joined by BLACKMUN, J., dissenting, expressed the view that, since the record was largely devoid of any evidence to suggest that Iowa's taxing scheme systematically worked to discourage foreign commerce to the advantage of its domestic counterpart, the statute did not facially discriminate in violation of the commerce clause.

COUNSEL

Jerome B. Libin argued the cause for petitioner.
Marcia Mason argued the cause for respondent.
Kent L. Jones argued the cause for the United States, as amicus curiae, by special leave of the court.

341

MARY GADE, Director, Illinois Environmental
Protection Agency, Petitioner

v

NATIONAL SOLID WASTES MANAGEMENT
ASSOCIATION

505 US —, 120 L Ed 2d 73, 112 S Ct 2374

Argued March 23, 1992.
Decided June 18, 1992.

Decision: Illinois licensing statutes held pre-empted
by OSH Act (29 USCS §§ 651 et seq.) to extent
that statutes establish occupational safety and
health standards for training of hazardous waste
workers.

SUMMARY

In 1986, the Occupational Safety and Health
Administration (OSHA)—pursuant to authority delegated by the United States Secretary of Labor—
promulgated interim regulations (later made final)
which specified detailed training requirements for
employees engaged in hazardous waste operations.
In 1988, while OSHA's interim regulations were in
effect, the state of Illinois—without receiving the
approval of the Secretary of Labor for a state plan
for the development and enforcement of an occupational safety and health standard—enacted two acts
which required the licensing of (1) hazardous waste
equipment operators, and (2) laborers working at
hazardous waste cleanup sites. The Illinois licensing
acts imposed certain initial and continuing requirements as to license applicants in both categories.
Shortly before the Illinois licensing acts were to go
342

into effect, a hazardous waste trade association brought an action in Federal District Court against the director of the Illinois Environmental Protection Agency (IEPA). The association sought to enjoin the IEPA from enforcing the Illinois licensing acts on the ground that such acts were pre-empted by the Occupational Safety and Health Act (OSH Act) (29 USCS §§ 651 et seq.) and the interim regulations promulgated thereunder by OSHA. The District Court ruled that, because the Illinois licensing acts protected public safety in addition to promoting job safety, such acts were not pre-empted. On appeal, the United States Court of Appeals for the Seventh Circuit (1) vacated the District Court's judgment, expressing the view that the OSH Act pre-empted all state laws that constitute, in a clear and substantial way, regulation of worker health and safety, unless the Secretary of Labor—upon a state's submission of a pre-emption plan under § 18(b) of the OSH Act (29 USCS § 667(b))—has approved the state law explicitly; and (2) remanded the case to the District Court without considering which provisions of the Illinois licensing acts were pre-empted by the OSH Act (918 F2d 671).

On certiorari, the United States Supreme Court affirmed. O'CONNOR, J., announced the judgment of the court, and in a part of her opinion which constituted the opinion of the court and which was joined by REHNQUIST, Ch. J., and WHITE, SCALIA, and KENNEDY, JJ., it was held that (1) a state law that directly, substantially, and specifically regulated occupational safety and health—even if such law was a dual-impact law that addressed public safety as well as occupational safety concerns—was an "occupational safety and health standard" within the meaning of the OSH Act, which under § 18(b) pre-empted all state occupational safety and health standards relating to any occupational safety or health issue with respect to which a federal standard had been promulgated; and (2) the Illinois licensing acts were pre-empted by the OSH Act to the extent that such acts established occupational safety and health standards for training those who work with hazardous wastes. Also, O'CONNOR, J., joined by REHNQUIST, Ch. J., and WHITE and SCALIA, JJ., expressed the view that (1) nonapproved state regulation of occupational safety and health issues for which a federal standard was in effect was pre-empted impliedly, as in conflict with the full purposes and objectives of the OSH Act; and (2) the negative implications of the text of § 18(b) did not address expressly the issue of federal pre-emption of state law.

KENNEDY, J., concurring in part and concurring in the judgment, (1) agreed that the OSH Act preempted all state occupational safety and health standards relating to any occupational safety or health issue with respect to which a federal standard has been promulgated; but (2) expressed the view that such result was mandated by the express terms of § 18(b), rather than by principles of conflict preemption.

SOUTER, J., joined by BLACKMUN, STEVENS, and THOMAS, JJ., dissenting, expressed the view that (1) federal pre-emption of state law can be found only where there is a clear congressional purpose to supplant exercises of the states' traditional police powers; (2) the text of the OSH Act failed to support the conclusion that § 18 of the OSH Act (29 USCS § 667)—the provisions of which deal with state standards and plans—pre-empted state regula-

tion of any occupational safety or health issue as to
which there was a federal standard; and (3) the
enforcement of the Illinois licensing acts was not
prohibited by the Federal Constitution's supremacy
clause (Art VI, cl 2) as long as compliance with
federally promulgated standards did not render obe-
dience to Illinois' regulations impossible.

COUNSEL

John A. Simon argued the cause for petitioner.
Donald T. Bliss argued the cause for respondent.

FORSYTH COUNTY, GEORGIA, Petitioner

v

THE NATIONALIST MOVEMENT

505 US —, 120 L Ed 2d 101, 112 S Ct 2395

Argued March 31, 1992.
Decided June 19, 1992.

Decision: County ordinance empowering administrator to adjust public-speech permit fee based
on amount of hostility likely to be created by
speech's content held to violate First Amendment.

SUMMARY

Forsyth County, Georgia, enacted an ordinance
that (1) required permits for parades, assemblies,
demonstrations, and other private uses of public
property, (2) required every permit applicant to pay
a fee of not more than $1,000 for each day on
which such activities were to take place, and (3)
empowered the county administrator to adjust the
fee's amount to meet the expense incident to the
ordinance's administration and to the maintenance
of public order in connection with the licensed
activity. As implemented and construed by the
county, the ordinance did not require the administrator to rely on any objective factors or to provide
any explanation in deciding how much to charge. A
private organization proposed to conduct a rally on
a Saturday afternoon on courthouse steps in the
county in opposition to the federal Martin Luther
King, Jr. holiday. The county imposed a $100 fee
for the rally. The organization, which did not pay

the fee or hold the rally, instituted an action against the county in the United States District Court for the Northern District of Georgia, in which action the court was requested to enjoin the county from interfering with the organization's plans. The District Court, denying such injunctive relief, (1) found that the determination of the organization's fee was based solely on the content-neutral criteria of the actual costs incurred investigating and processing the application, and (2) held that the ordinance, as applied in the case at hand, was not unconstitutional. A panel of the United States Court of Appeals for the Eleventh Circuit, reversing, held that the ordinance violated the Federal Constitution's First Amendment in that the fee of up to $1,000 a day was more than nominal and thus exceeded the constitutional threshold (913 F2d 885). The Court of Appeals subsequently voted to vacate the panel's opinion and to rehear the case en banc (921 F2d 1125), but the Court of Appeals ultimately reinstated the panel opinion (934 F2d 1482).

On certiorari, the United States Court of Appeals affirmed. In an opinion by BLACKMUN, J., joined by STEVENS, O'CONNOR, KENNEDY, and SOUTER, JJ., it was held that (1) the ordinance, as implemented and construed by the county, violated the free speech guarantees of the Constitution's First and Fourteenth Amendments because (a) there were no narrowly drawn, reasonable, and definite standards guiding the hand of the county administrator, so that nothing in the ordinance or its application prevented the administrator from encouraging some views and discouraging others through the arbitrary application of fees, and (b) the fee assessed would depend on the administrator's measure of the amount of hostility likely to be created by the speech based on the speech's content, given that the administrator, in order to assess accurately the cost of security for parade participants, would necessarily examine the content of the message that was conveyed, estimate the response of others to that content, and judge the number of police necessary to meet that response; and (2) given such constitutional violations, neither the $1,000 cap on the fee charged, nor even some lower nominal cap, could save the ordinance for First Amendment purposes.

REHNQUIST, Ch. J., joined by WHITE, SCALIA, and THOMAS, JJ., dissenting, expressed the view that (1) the Constitution does not limit a parade license fee to a nominal amount; (2) there were no factual findings in the case at hand as to the scope or administration of the ordinance; and accordingly (3) the case should have been remanded for consideration of these issues.

COUNSEL

Robert S. Stubbs, III argued the cause for petitioner.

Richard Barrett argued the cause for respondent.

———————

NEW YORK, Petitioner

v

UNITED STATES et al. (No. 91-543)

———

COUNTY OF ALLEGANY, NEW YORK, Petitioner

v

UNITED STATES et al. (No. 91-558)

———

COUNTY OF CORTLAND, NEW YORK, Petitioner

v

UNITED STATES et al. (No. 91-563)

505 US —, 120 L Ed 2d 120, 112 S Ct 2408

Argued March 30, 1992.
Decided June 19, 1992.

Decision: State "take title" provision of Low-Level Radioactive Waste Policy Amendments Act of 1985 (42 USCS § 2021e(d)(2)(C)) held to violate Tenth Amendment, but to be severable from remainder of Act.

SUMMARY

The Low-Level Radioactive Waste Policy Amendments Act of 1985 (42 USCS §§ 2021b et seq.) embodied a compromise whereby "sited" states—that is, states having low-level radioactive waste disposal sites—agreed to extend by 7 years the period in which they would accept waste from "unsited" states, while the unsited states agreed to end

349

their reliance on the sited states by 1992. The Act required each state to be responsible for providing, either individually or in cooperation with other states, for the disposal of wastes generated within its borders, and three types of incentives were provided to encourage state compliance: (1) under the "monetary incentives" provisions of 42 USCS §§ 2021e(d) (1), 2021e(d)(2)(A), 2021e(d)(2)(B), sited states were authorized to collect a surcharge for accepting waste during the 7 year extension, and a portion of those surcharges would go into an escrow account held by the United States Secretary of Energy and would be paid out to states which met a series of deadlines in complying with their obligations under the Act; (2) under the "access incentives" provisions of 42 USCS § 2021e(e)(2), states failing to comply with the statutory deadlines could be charged multiple surcharges by sited states for a certain period and then denied access altogether; and (3) under the "take title" provision of 42 USCS § 2021e(d)(2) (C), each state that fails to provide for the disposal of internally generated waste by a specific date must, upon request of the waste's generator or owner, take title to the waste, be obligated to take possession of the waste, and become liable for all damages incurred by the generator or owner as a consequence of the state's failure to take possession promptly. The state of New York and two of its counties, seeking a declaratory judgment that the Act violated the Federal Constitution's Tenth Amendment and the Constitution's guarantee clause (Art IV, § 4, guaranteeing to the states a republican form of government), filed suit against the United States in the United States District Court for the Northern District of New York. The District Court dismissed the complaint (757 F Supp 10), and the

United States Court of Appeals for the Second Circuit affirmed (942 F2d 114).

On certiorari, the United States Supreme Court affirmed in part and reversed in part. In an opinion by O'CONNOR, J., expressing the unanimous view of the court in part (as to points 1 and 2 below) and joined in part (as to points 3-5 below) by REHNQUIST, Ch. J., and SCALIA, KENNEDY, SOUTER, and THOMAS, JJ., it was held that (1) the "monetary incentive" provisions were not inconsistent with the Tenth Amendment, because (a) the surcharge authorization was a proper exercise of Congress' authority under the Constitution's commerce clause (Art I, § 8, cl 3) to authorize states to burden interstate commerce, (b) the Secretary's collection of a portion of the surcharges was no more than a federal tax on interstate commerce, and (c) the distribution of the escrow fund was a proper conditional exercise of Congress' authority under the Constitution's spending clause (Art I, § 8, cl 1); (2) the "access incentive" provisions of the Act did not violate the Tenth Amendment, but rather represented a conditional exercise of Congress' commerce power along the lines of those previously held by the Supreme Court to be within Congress' authority; (3) the "take title" provision was unconstitutional, either as lying outside Congress' enumerated powers or as violating the Tenth Amendment, because (a) an instruction to state governments to take title to waste, standing alone, would be beyond the authority of Congress, (b) a direct order to regulate, standing alone, would also be invalid, and therefore (c) Congress lacked the power to offer the states a choice between the two; (4) neither the "monetary incentive" provisions nor the "access incentive" provisions violated the guarantee

351

clause, because (a) the provisions offered the states a legitimate choice rather than issuing an unavoidable command, so that the states retained the ability to set their legislative agendas and state government officials remained accountable to the local electorate, and (b) the twin threats that a state might lose out on a share of federal spending or that generators of radioactive waste might lose out-of-state disposal outlets did not pose any realistic threat of altering the form or method of functioning of state government; and (5) the invalid "take title" provision could be severed without doing violence to the rest of the Act, which therefore could remain in force, because the Act contained other incentives to encourage the states to attain local or regional self-sufficiency in the disposal of radioactive waste.

WHITE, J., joined by BLACKMUN and STEVENS, JJ., concurred in part and dissented in part, joining the court's opinion as to points 1 and 2 above, but expressing the view that (1) the Act represented a hard-fought agreement among the states—including New York—as refereed by Congress, rather than federal direction of state action; (2) New York should be estopped from asserting the unconstitutionality of the "take title" provision, which sought to insure that the state, after deriving substantial advantages from the Act, either live up to its bargain by establishing an in-state waste facility or assume liability for its failure to act; (3) such an incursion on state sovereignty can be deemed ratified by the consent of state officials; and (4) there was no precedential support for the general proposition that Congress cannot directly compel states to enact and enforce federal regulatory programs.

STEVENS, J., concurred in part and dissented in part, expressing the view that the Constitution does not prohibit Congress from simply commanding state governments to implement congressional legislation.

COUNSEL

Peter H. Schiff argued the cause for petitioners.

Lawrence G. Wallace argued the cause for federal respondents.

William B. Collins argued the cause for state respondents.

———————

WISCONSIN DEPARTMENT OF REVENUE,
Petitioner

v

WILLIAM WRIGLEY, JR., CO.

505 US —, 120 L Ed 2d 174, 112 S Ct 2447

Argued January 22, 1992.
Decided June 19, 1992.

Decision: State held not prohibited, under 15 USCS
§ 381(a), from imposing tax on gum manufacturer's income, where manufacturer's in-state
activities include replacement, supply, and storage of gum.

SUMMARY

A chewing gum manufacturer based in Chicago,
Illinois, sold gum through a nationwide marketing
system. The manufacturer's midwestern district included a Milwaukee region covering most of Wisconsin and parts of other states. Within Wisconsin,
the manufacturer did not (1) own or lease real
property, (2) operate any manufacturing, training,
or warehouse facility, or (3) have a telephone listing
or bank account. However, the manufacturer did
conduct business activities within Wisconsin which
included (1) the replacement of retailers' stale gum
by sales representatives, from stock in the sales
representatives' possession, at no cost to retailers;
(2) the supplying of gum through "agency stock
checks," for which retailers were to be billed later
by a wholesaler for the quantity supplied; (3) the
storage of gum, display racks, and promotional
literature; (4) the rental of space for storage of such
354

materials; (5) the regional manager's recruitment, training, and evaluation of employees, which activities were conducted either in the basement of the manager's home or at a hotel or motel; and (6) the regional manager's intervention in credit disputes, which involved contacting the Chicago office in situations involving important accounts. In 1980, the Wisconsin Department of Revenue issued a franchise tax assessment against the manufacturer, based upon a percentage of the manufacturer's apportionable income during 6 preceding years. The manufacturer objected to the assessment and contended that, since its activities in Wisconsin were limited to the "solicitation of orders" within the meaning of 15 USCS § 381(a)—which generally prohibited a state from taxing income derived within the state from interstate commerce where the only business activities within the state consisted of "solicitation of orders" for tangible goods—the manufacturer was immune from Wisconsin franchise taxes. The Wisconsin Tax Appeals Commission upheld the imposition of the tax against the manufacturer. The Wisconsin Circuit Court for Dane County, Wisconsin, reversed on the merits (CCH Wis Tax Rptr ¶ 203-000); the Wisconsin Court of Appeals reversed the Circuit Court's decision (153 Wis 2d 559, 451 NW2d 444); and the Supreme Court of Wisconsin in turn reversed the Court of Appeals' decision, which result disallowed the imposition of the tax (160 Wis 2d 53, 465 NW2d 800).

On certiorari, the United States Supreme Court reversed and remanded. In an opinion by SCALIA, J., joined by WHITE, STEVENS, SOUTER, and THOMAS, JJ., and joined by O'CONNOR, J., as to holdings 1 and 2 below, it was held that (1) the term "solicitation of orders" in § 381(a) generally included those activities which are entirely ancillary to requests for purchases—that is, those that serve no independent business function apart from their connection to the soliciting of orders—except that the maintenance of an office within the state is beyond the "solicitation of orders" even if engaged in exclusively to facilitate requests for purchases, but the term "solicitation of orders" excluded those activities that a company would have reason to engage in anyway, but chooses to allocate to its in-state sales force; (2) the determination whether in-state activity other than the solicitation of orders was sufficiently de minimis to avoid loss of the tax immunity conferred by § 381(a) depended upon whether such activity established a nontrivial additional connection with the taxing state; and (3) the taxation prohibition contained in § 381(a) was inapplicable in light of the manufacturer's activities within Wisconsin in replacing stale gum, supplying gum through "agency stock checks," storing gum, display racks, and promotional literature, and renting space for such storage, because such activities could not reasonably be viewed as requests for orders covered by § 381(a), were not ancillary to requesting orders, and when taken together, were not de minimis.

O'CONNOR, J., concurring in part and concurring in the judgment, expressed the view that (1) the replacement of stale gum by the manufacturer's sales representatives did not serve an independent business function; but (2) the storage of gum and the use of agency stock checks were not ancillary to solicitation and were not de minimis, and thus the manufacturer's income was subject to taxation by Wisconsin.

KENNEDY, J., joined by REHNQUIST, Ch. J., and BLACKMUN, J., dissenting, expressed the view that

(1) § 381(a) exempted business activities performed in connection with solicitation if reasonable buyers would consider such activities to be a part of the solicitation itself, and not a significant and independent service or component of value; (2) under such rule, the manufacturer's business activities in Wisconsin were the solicitation of orders within the meaning of § 381(a); and (3) the replacement of stale gum and the supplying of gum through agency stock checks were not activities that could be said to have provided their own component of significant value, but rather were activities conducted in the course of solicitation as to which the legal effect should be the same.

COUNSEL

F. Thomas Creeron, III argued the cause for petitioner.

E. Barrett Prettyman, Jr. argued the cause for respondent.

AMERICAN NATIONAL RED CROSS, Petitioner

v

S. G. and A. E.

505 US —, 120 L Ed 2d 201, 112 S Ct 2465

Argued March 3, 1992.
Decided June 19, 1992.

Decision: Original federal court jurisdiction over all cases to which American National Red Cross is party held conferred by "sue and be sued" provision (36 USCS § 2) of Red Cross' federal corporate charter.

SUMMARY

The "sue and be sued" provision (36 USCS § 2) of the federal corporate charter of the American National Red Cross—as amended in 1947 by the addition of the words "State or Federal"—authorizes the Red Cross to "sue and be sued in courts of law and equity, State or Federal, within the jurisdiction of the United States." A husband and wife, who claimed that the wife had contracted Acquired Immune Deficiency Syndrome (AIDS) from a transfusion of contaminated blood supplied by the Red Cross, brought a state-law tort action against the Red Cross in the Superior Court of Merrimack County, New Hampshire. The Red Cross, however, invoked 28 USCS § 1441 to remove the suit to the United States District Court for the District of New Hampshire, and alleged federal jurisdiction on grounds including a claim that the Red Cross' "sue and be sued" provision conferred original federal jurisdiction over suits involving the Red Cross. The

District Court, in denying a motion to remand the case to state court, expressed the view that the "sue and be sued" provision conferred original federal jurisdiction. On interlocutory appeal, the United States Court of Appeals for the First Circuit, in reversing, expressed the view that the "sue and be sued" provision did not confer original federal jurisdiction (938 F2d 1494).

On certiorari, the United States Supreme Court reversed and remanded. In an opinion by SOUTER, J., joined by WHITE, BLACKMUN, STEVENS, and THOMAS, JJ., it was held that (1) the Supreme Court's prior cases supported a general rule that a "sue and be sued" provision in a corporation's congressional charter may be read to confer original federal court jurisdiction over all cases to which the corporation is a party if, but only if, the provision specifically mentions the federal courts; (2) thus, the Red Cross' "sue and be sued" provision extended beyond a grant of general corporate capacity to sue, and conferred original jurisdiction on federal courts over all cases to which the Red Cross was a party, where the 1947 amendment had resulted in a "sue and be sued" provision which was in all relevant respects identical to one on which the Supreme Court had based a holding of federal jurisdiction just 5 years prior to the amendment; and (3) the Red Cross was thereby authorized to remove from state to federal court any state-law action which the Red Cross was defending.

SCALIA, J., joined by REHNQUIST, Ch. J., and O'CONNOR and KENNEDY, JJ., dissenting, expressed the view that (1) the Supreme Court's prior cases as to the jurisdictional implications of the "sued and be sued" provisions of federally chartered corporations were best understood as applications of conventional rules of statutory construction; (2) the natural reading of the Red Cross' "sue and be sued" provision was that the provision conferred upon the Red Cross the capacity to sue and be sued in state and federal courts, but did not confer jurisdiction upon any court, state or federal; and (3) the adoption of such a natural reading would still allow the 1947 amendment to have the effect of eliminating any ambiguity as to whether the Red Cross could sue and be sued in state courts.

COUNSEL

Roy T. Englert, Jr. argued the cause for petitioner.

Ronald J. Mann argued the cause for the United States, as amicus curiae, by special leave of the court.

J. Gilbert Upton argued the cause for respondents.

ELLIS B. WRIGHT, JR., Warden and MARY SUE
TERRY, Attorney General of Virginia, Petitioners

v

FRANK ROBERT WEST, JR.

505 US —, 120 L Ed 2d 225, 112 S Ct 2482

Argued March 24, 1992.
Decided June 19, 1992.

Decision: Evidence held (1) sufficient to support
state court grand larceny conviction, and thus
(2) to require denial of federal habeas corpus
relief based on insufficiency of evidence.

SUMMARY

An accused was tried in a Virginia state court on a
charge of grand larceny after police, during a lawful
search of the accused's home, discovered several
items that had been stolen from another home 2 to
4 weeks earlier. Testifying on his own behalf at trial,
the accused admitted to a prior felony conviction,
denied having taken anything from the home from
which the items were stolen, and explained that he
had bought and sold much merchandise at flea
markets. On cross-examination, the accused testified
that he had purchased some of the stolen items
from a particular individual, but with respect to any
alleged transactions between the accused and this
individual, the accused did not make clear the number of transactions, their locations, or whether they
occurred at flea markets. Moreover, the accused
testified that he did not remember how he had
acquired certain of the stolen items. The trial court
instructed the jury that (1) Virginia law permitted an

inference that a person who failed to explain, or falsely explained, the person's possession of recently stolen property was the thief, and (2) the inference did not compromise the jury's constitutional obligation to acquit the accused unless the jury found that the state had established every element of grand larceny beyond a reasonable doubt. After the accused was found guilty and sentenced to 10 years in prison, he petitioned for an appeal, contending that the evidence was insufficient to support a finding of guilt beyond a reasonable doubt. The Supreme Court of Virginia, finding the petition to be without merit, refused the petition. Several years later, when the accused—claiming that the original trial record contained insufficient evidence to support the conviction, and that an affidavit that tended to support the accused's trial testimony constituted new evidence entitling the accused to a new trial—filed in the Supreme Court of Virginia a petition for a writ of habeas corpus, the court again denied relief. The accused then filed a petition for a writ of habeas corpus in the United States District Court for the Eastern District of Virginia. Rejecting both claims that had been rejected by the Supreme Court of Virginia, the District Court denied relief. The United States Court of Appeals for the Fourth Circuit reversed on the ground that the standard of Jackson v Virginia (1979) 443 US 307, 61 L Ed 2d 560, 99 S Ct 2781—which was decided before the accused's conviction became final on direct review, and which held that, under the due process clause of the Federal Constitution's Fourteenth Amendment, evidence is sufficient to support a state court conviction if, after viewing the evidence in the light most favorable to the prosecution, any rational trier of fact could have found the essential elements of the crime beyond a reasonable doubt—had not been met (931 F2d 262).

On certiorari, the United States Supreme Court reversed and remanded. Although unable to agree on an opinion, the members of the court unanimously agreed that the accused's request for a federal writ of habeas corpus based on the insufficiency of evidence to support the accused's conviction should be denied.

THOMAS, J., announced the judgment of the court and, in an opinion joined by REHNQUIST, Ch. J., and SCALIA, J., expressed the view that the evidence was sufficient, under the due process clause, to support the accused's conviction, and that, therefore, his request for a federal writ of habeas corpus based on insufficiency of evidence should be denied, because, regardless of whether the appropriate standard of review—for a federal court considering a habeas corpus petition involving a state court conviction and mixed constitutional questions of fact and law— was a de novo standard or a deferential standard, the trial record contained more than enough evidence to support the accused's conviction, since (1) Jackson v Virginia emphasized repeatedly the deference owed to the trier of fact and, correspondingly, the sharply limited nature of constitutional sufficiency review; (2) the case against the accused was strong, given the facts that (a) the stolen items were recovered from his home 2 to 4 weeks after they were stolen, and (b) his trial testimony failed to specify how he had acquired the items and was contradictory, vague, uncorroborated, and seemingly evasive; and (3) as the trier of fact, the jury was entitled (a) to disbelieve the accused's uncorroborated and confused testimony, (b) to discount his credibility on account of his prior felony conviction, (c) to take into account his demeanor when testifying, and (d) if the jury disbelieved the accused, to consider whatever the jury concluded to be perjured testimony as affirmative evidence of guilt.

WHITE, J., concurred in the judgment, expressing the view that under the standard of Jackson v Virginia, (1) there was sufficient evidence to support the accused's conviction, and thus (2) denial of the accused's requested writ of habeas corpus was required.

O'CONNOR, J., joined by BLACKMUN and STEVENS, JJ., concurred in the judgment, expressing the view that (1) the evidence sufficiently supported the accused's conviction, and (2) the court did not need to determine the appropriate standard of review in order to resolve the case at hand.

KENNEDY, J., concurred in the judgment, expressing the view that (1) the evidence in the case at hand was sufficient to convince a rational factfinder of guilt beyond a reasonable doubt; (2) Teague v Lane (1989) 489 US 288, 103 L Ed 2d 334, 109 S Ct 1060—in which case an accused who requested federal habeas corpus relief concerning a state court conviction was denied relief, and under the standard of which case, a habeas corpus petitioner generally cannot benefit from the announcement of a new rule of criminal procedure after the petitioner's conviction becomes final on direct appeal—should not be interpreted as calling into question the settled principle that mixed questions of fact and law were subject to plenary review on federal habeas corpus; and (3) it was not necessary for the court to consider whether the claim in the case at hand was barred by Teague v Lane.

SOUTER, J., concurred in the judgment, expressing the view that while he could not disagree with the majority that sufficient evidence supported the accused's conviction, the court should not have reached such issue, because (1) in the federal courts, the accused sought the benefit of a "new rule," and thus (2) the accused's claim was barred by Teague v Lane.

COUNSEL

Donald R. Curry argued the cause for petitioners.

Maureen E. Mahoney argued the cause for the United States, as amicus curiae, by special leave of the court.

Steven H. Goldblatt argued the cause for respondent.

UNITED STATES, Petitioner

v

ANTHONY SALERNO et al.

505 US —, 120 L Ed 2d 255, 112 S Ct 2503

Argued April 20, 1992.
Decided June 19, 1992.

Decision: Showing of "similar motive" to develop testimony held necessary, under Federal Evidence Rule 804(b)(1), for admission of grand jury testimony of witness invoking Fifth Amendment privilege.

SUMMARY

In testimony given before a federal grand jury in the Southern District of New York under a grant of immunity, two owners of a concrete construction company stated that neither they nor their company had participated in a so-called "Club" of six concrete companies to whom large construction contracts in Manhattan purportedly had been allocated during the 1980's by a criminal organization, in exchange for a share of the proceeds. The grand jury subsequently indicted several defendants on numerous counts of racketeering and fraud, based on the criminal organization's alleged activities in rigging bids on construction projects by use of the organization's influence over labor unions and its control over concrete supply. At a jury trial in the United States District Court for the Southern District of New York, the government attempted to show that the construction company owned by the grand jury witnesses belonged to the "Club." The two owners were subpoenaed by the defense to testify at trial, but both invoked their privilege against self-incrimination under the Federal Constitution's Fifth Amendment and refused to testify. The defense moved that the grand jury testimony of the two owners be admitted into evidence under Rule 804(b)(1) of the Federal Rules of Evidence, which provides that the hearsay rule does not exclude former testimony by an unavailable declarant if the party against whom such testimony is offered had an opportunity and "similar motive" to develop such testimony. The District Court, ruling that the government had not had a similar motive, denied the defense's motion, and the jury subsequently convicted the defendants. On appeal, the United States Court of Appeals for the Second Circuit, reversing, held that the District Court had erred in excluding the two owners' grand jury testimony, because the "similar motive" element of Rule 804(b)(1) evaporated when the government obtained immunized testimony in a grand jury proceeding from a witness who refused to testify at trial (937 F2d 797, amended on other grounds 952 F2d 623).

On certiorari, the United States Supreme Court reversed and remanded. In an opinion by THOMAS, J., joined by REHNQUIST, Ch. J., and WHITE, BLACKMUN, O'CONNOR, SCALIA, KENNEDY, and SOUTER, JJ., it was held that (1) in order for the owners' grand jury testimony to be admissible under Rule 804(b)(1), a showing of "similar motive" to develop such testimony was required, because (a) nothing in the language of Rule 804(b)(1) suggests that a court may admit former testimony absent satisfaction of each of the elements of Rule 804(b)(1), (b) in order to respect Congress' careful judgment as to what

367

hearsay evidence may come into evidence and what may not—as reflected in the 24 exceptions to the hearsay rule placed in Rule 803 of the Federal Rules of Evidence, and the 5 additional exceptions placed in Rule 804 of the Federal Rules of Evidence—the words that Congress enacted must be enforced, and (c) adversarial fairness did not prevent the prosecution's reliance on the "similar motive" requirement of Rule 804(b)(1), since there was no way to interpret the text of Rule 804(b)(1) to mean that "similar motive" sometimes did not need to be shown; and (2) the case would be remanded to the Court of Appeals for further consideration, since the Court of Appeals had declined to consider fully arguments whether the government had a similar motive to develop the two owners' grand jury testimony.

BLACKMUN, J., concurring, joined the court's opinion and expressed the view that (1) the inquiry as to whether the government had a similar motive to develop grand jury testimony was inherently a factual inquiry which depended in part on the similarity of the underlying issues and on the context of the grand jury questioning; and (2) remand for further consideration was appropriate in the case at hand because (a) the case involved factual issues which were unusual in complexity and in number, and (b) neither the District Court nor the Court of Appeals apparently engaged in the type of factual inquiry appropriate for resolution of the "similar motive" inquiry.

STEVENS, J., dissenting, expressed the view that that the judgment of the Court of Appeals should have been affirmed on the ground that the transcript of the two owners' grand jury testimony was admissible under the plain language of Rule 804(b)

(1), because the government clearly had an opportunity and a similar motive to develop such testimony by direct or cross-examination.

COUNSEL

James A. Feldman argued the cause for petitioner.
Michael E. Tigar argued the cause for respondents.

ROBERT WAYNE SAWYER, Petitioner

v

JOHN WHITLEY, Warden

505 US —, 120 L Ed 2d 269, 112 S Ct 2514

Argued February 25, 1992.

Decided June 22, 1992.

Decision: Accused held not to have satisfied "actual innocence" exception so as to allow federal habeas corpus consideration of successive and abusive claims challenging Louisiana death sentence.

SUMMARY

Unless a federal habeas corpus petitioner shows cause and prejudice, a federal court generally may not reach the merits of (1) successive claims which raise grounds identical to grounds heard or decided on the merits in a previous petition; (2) new claims, not previously raised, which constitute an abuse of the writ; or (3) procedurally defaulted claims in which the petitioner failed to follow applicable state procedural rules in raising the claims. There is, however, an exception—sometimes known as the "actual innocence" exception—that even if the cause-and-prejudice standard has not been met, a federal court may hear the merits of a successive, abusive, or procedurally defaulted claim if the failure to hear the claim would constitute a miscarriage of justice. An accused allegedly participated in the 1979 killing of a victim who was beaten, scalded with boiling water, and set afire. The accused was convicted of first-degree murder—that is, an intentional killing while in the process of committing aggravated arson—and sentenced to death in a Louisiana jury trial. The conviction and sentence were eventually upheld on direct review, which, among determinations, upheld as valid the jury's findings of two statutory aggravating factors that (1) the accused had been engaged in the commission of aggravated arson at the time of the murder; and (2) the murder had been committed in an especially cruel, atrocious, and heinous manner. The accused was unsuccessful in a state petition for postconviction relief, a federal habeas corpus petition, and a second state postconviction petition. The accused the filed a second habeas corpus petition in the United States District Court for the Eastern District or Louisiana, but that court, in denying relief, barred as successive of abusive claims to the effect the (1) the accused's right to the effective assistance of counsel had allegedly been violated through his counsel's failure to introduce at sentencing medical records from the accused's stay as a teenager in two mental health institutions; and (2) the police, in violation of due process, had failed to produce allegedly exculpatory evidence related to the accused's role in the offense (772 F Supp 297). On appeal, the United States Court of Appeals for the Fifth Circuit, in affirming, expressed the view that (1) with respect to the ineffective-assistance claim, (a) the claim was a successive claim which had been rejected on the merits in the first federal petition, and (b) the accused had not shown cause for failing to bring all evidence in support of that claim earlier; (2) with respect to the due process claim, (a) the accused's failure to assert the claim in his first federal petition constituted an abuse of the writ, and (b) the accused had not shown cause for that failure;

371

and (3) the accused had failed to show that he was actually innocent of the death penalty (945 F2d 812).

On certiorari, the United States Supreme Court affirmed. In an opinion by REHNQUIST, Ch. J., joined by WHITE, SCALIA, KENNEDY, SOUTER, and THOMAS, JJ., it was held that (1) for purposes of the "actual innocence" exception, a federal habeas corpus petitioner, in order to show "actual innocence" of a state death sentence, must show by clear and convincing evidence that but for a federal constitutional error, no reasonable juror would have found the petitioner eligible for the death penalty under the applicable state law—a standard which (a) allows a petitioner to show, in addition to innocence of the capital crime itself, that there was no aggravating circumstance or that some other condition of eligibility was not met, but (b) does not extend the permissible showing to the existence of additional mitigating evidence which bore on only the ultimate discretionary decision between the death penalty and life imprisonment—and (2) under that standard, the accused in the case at hand, with respect to his ineffective-assistance and due process claims, had failed to show by clear and convincing evidence that he was "actually innocent" of the death penalty to which he had been sentenced.

BLACKMUN, J., concurring in the judgment, expressed the view that (1) the fundamental miscarriages of justice in a capital proceeding that warranted federal habeas corpus redress ought to include more situations than those circumstances in which a petitioner could make out a claim of "actual innocence"; (2) the Supreme Court's opinion adopted an unduly cramped view of "actual innocence"; (3) the "actual innocence" standard in the opinion of STEVENS, J., and his application of that standard to the facts of the case at hand, were correct; and (4) there was a growing doubt as to whether, with each new Supreme Court decision constricting the ability of federal courts to remedy constitutional errors, the death penalty actually could be imposed fairly and in accordance with the requirements of the Federal Constitution's Eighth Amendment.

STEVENS, J., joined by BLACKMUN and O'CONNOR, JJ., concurring in the judgment, expressed the view that (1) the Supreme Court's definition of "actual innocence" in the capital sentencing context (a) departed from settled law, (b) imposed a too stringent burden of proof on a federal habeas corpus petitioner, and (c) incorrectly focused on eligibility for the death penalty, to the neglect of the central role of mitigating evidence; (2) the requirements of capital sentencing principles were best met by a "clearly erroneous" standard for actual innocence; and (3) the accused in the case at hand had failed to demonstrate that it was more likely than not that his death sentence was clearly erroneous.

COUNSEL

R. Neal Walker argued the cause for petitioner.

Dorothy A. Pendergast argued the cause for respondent.

Paul J. Larkin, Jr. argued the cause for the United States, as amicus curiae, by special leave of the court.

R. A. V., Petitioner

v

CITY OF ST. PAUL, MINNESOTA

505 US —, 120 L Ed 2d 305, 112 S Ct 2538

Argued December 4, 1991.
Decided June 22, 1992.

Decision: City ordinance, banning display of symbols—including burning cross—that arouse anger in others on basis of race, color, creed, religion, or gender, held facially invalid under First Amendment.

SUMMARY

The city of St. Paul, Minnesota, enacted an ordinance which made it a misdemeanor to place on public or private property a symbol, object, appellation, characterization, or graffiti—including a burning cross—which one knows or has reasonable grounds to know arouses anger, alarm, or resentment in others on the basis of race, color, creed, religion, or gender. A teenager who allegedly burned a cross inside the fenced yard of a black family was charged with violating this ordinance. In a Minnesota trial court, the teenager moved to dismiss the charge on the ground that the ordinance was substantially overbroad and impermissibly content-based and thus facially invalid under the Federal Constitution's First Amendment. The trial court granted this motion. On appeal, the Supreme Court of Minnesota, in reversing and remanding, said that (1) the ordinance was to be construed as reaching only conduct that amounts to "fighting words," that is, conduct that itself inflicts injury or tends to incite immediate violence; (2) the ordinance thus reached only expression that the First Amendment did not protect; and (3) so construed, the ordinance was a narrowly tailored means toward accomplishing the compelling governmental interest in protecting the community against bias-motivated threats to public safety and order (464 NW2d 507).

On certiorari, the United States Supreme Court reversed and remanded. In an opinion by SCALIA, J., joined by REHNQUIST, Ch. J., and KENNEDY, SOUTER, and THOMAS, JJ., it was held that the ordinance, even as narrowly construed by the Supreme Court of Minnesota, was facially violative of the First Amendment, because (1) the ordinance applied only to fighting words that insult or provoke violence on the basis of race, color, creed, religion, or gender; (2) displays containing abusive invective, no matter how vicious or severe, were thus permissible under the ordinance unless such displays were addressed to one of the specified disfavored topics, but those who wished to use fighting words in connection with other ideas were not covered; (3) the ordinance imposed viewpoint discrimination, in that fighting words that did not themselves invoke race, color, creed, religion, or gender would seemingly be usable in the placards of those arguing in favor of tolerance and equality, but such words could not be used by such speakers' opponents; (4) the ordinance did not fall within any exception to the First Amendment prohibition of content discrimination; and (5) although the ordinance could be said to promote a compelling state interest in insuring the basic human rights of members of groups that have historically been subjected to discrimination, the ordinance's content discrimination was not reasonably necessary to achieve such interests.

WHITE, J., joined by BLACKMUN and O'CONNOR, JJ., and joined in part (except as to point 2 below), by STEVENS, J., concurring in the judgment, expressed the view that (1) the Supreme Court of Minnesota's judgment should have been reversed on the ground that the ordinance, in reaching expressive conduct that causes only hurt feelings, offense, or resentment, criminalized expression protected by the First Amendment and thus was overbroad; (2) certain categories of speech, including "fighting words," are not protected by the First Amendment; and (3) if the ordinance had not been overbroad, it would have been a valid regulation of unprotected speech for purposes of the Constitution's Fourteenth Amendment equal protection clause.

BLACKMUN, J., concurring in the judgment, expressed the view that (1) the ordinance was invalid because it reached beyond fighting words to speech protected by the First Amendment, but (2) the majority's approach would either (a) result in a relaxation of the level of strict scrutiny applicable to content-based laws, or (b) be regarded as a manipulation of First Amendment doctrine to strike down an ordinance whose premise the majority opposed.

STEVENS, J., joined in part (as to points 1 and 2 below) by WHITE and BLACKMUN, JJ., expressed the view that (1) the ordinance was unconstitutionally overbroad; (2) the majority, in ruling that proscribable speech cannot be regulated based on subject matter, wrongly gave fighting words and obscenity the same sort of protection afforded core political speech; (3) not all content-based distinctions are equally infirm and presumptively invalid; and (4)

fighting words are not wholly unprotected by the
First Amendment.

COUNSEL

Edward J. Cleary argued the cause for petitioner.
Thomas J. Foley argued the cause for respondent.

TEOFILO MEDINA, JR., Petitioner

v

CALIFORNIA

505 US —, 120 L Ed 2d 353, 112 S Ct 2572

Argued February 25, 1992.

Decided June 22, 1992.

Decision: California statute, requiring that criminal defendant bear burden of proving incompetence to stand trial by preponderance of evidence, held not to violate due process.

SUMMARY

Under the California penal code, a person cannot be tried while mentally incompetent—that is, while unable, as a result of mental disorder or developmental disability, to understand the nature of the criminal proceedings or to assist defense counsel in a rational manner—but the defendant's competence is presumed, and the party claiming incompetence bears the burden of proving by a preponderance of the evidence that the defendant is incompetent. Counsel for a defendant who was charged with multiple offenses, including first-degree murder, moved in a California trial court for a pretrial hearing to determine the defendant's competency to stand trial. At the hearing, before a jury, conflicting expert testimony was heard concerning the defendant's mental condition, and the defendant engaged in several verbal and physical outbursts. The jury, instructed as to the presumption of competency and the defendant's burden of proof, found the defendant competent to stand trial. The defendant was

378

subsequently convicted and sentenced to death. In affirming the conviction and sentence, the Supreme Court of California rejected the defendant's claim that the code violated his right to due process by establishing a presumption of competence to stand trial and placing the burden of proof on him to establish otherwise (51 Cal 3d 870, 799 P2d 1282).

On certiorari, the United States Supreme Court affirmed. In an opinion by KENNEDY, J., joined by REHNQUIST, Ch. J., and WHITE, SCALIA, and THOMAS, JJ., it was held that the due process clause of the Federal Constitution's Fourteenth Amendment permits a state to apply a presumption that a criminal defendant is competent to stand trial, and to require that defendant to bear the burden of proving otherwise by a preponderance of the evidence, because (1) the allocation of the burden of proof to a defendant to prove incompetence does not offend a principle of justice so rooted in the traditions and conscience of the American people as to be ranked as fundamental; (2) although an impaired defendant might be limited in his or her ability to assist counsel in demonstrating incompetence, such inability can itself constitute probative evidence of incompetence, and defense counsel will often have the best-informed view of the defendant's ability to participate; (3) although psychiatry is not an exact science, placing the burden of proof on the defendant does not violate due process by requiring him or her to bear the risk of an erroneous finding of competency, as it is sufficient for the state to afford the defendant a reasonable opportunity to demonstrate incompetence to stand trial; (4) allocating the burden of proof to the prosecution would not serve to deter lawless conduct by police and prosecutors; and (5) there was no reason to disturb the California Supreme Court's conclusion that the state's presumption of competence was simply a restatement of the burden of proof.

O'CONNOR, J., joined by SOUTER, J., concurred in the judgment, expressing the view that (1) although historical pedigree can give a procedural practice a presumption of constitutionality, the presumption must be rebuttable, and some weight should be given to countervailing considerations of fairness in operation; but (2) the equities in this case did not weigh so much in the defendant's favor as to rebut the presumption of constitutionality.

BLACKMUN, J., joined by STEVENS, J., dissented, expressing the view that placing the burden of proving competence on the prosecution is necessary to protect adequately the underlying due process right of a defendant to be tried only if competent.

COUNSEL

Michael Pescetta argued the cause for petitioner.
Holly D. Wilkens argued the cause for respondent.

———

ESTATE OF FLOYD COWART, Petitioner

v

NICKLOS DRILLING COMPANY et al.

505 US —, 120 L Ed 2d 379, 112 S Ct 2589

Argued March 25, 1992.
Decided June 22, 1992.

Decision: Forfeiture provision of Longshore and Harbor Workers' Compensation Act (33 USCS § 933(g)) held to apply where worker not then receiving or awarded compensation from employer settles third-party claim.

SUMMARY

After a worker who was employed by a drilling company suffered an injury while working on an oil drilling platform which was located in an area subject to the Longshore and Harbor Workers' Compensation Act (LHWCA) (33 USCS §§ 901 et seq.), the worker (1) filed an administrative claim with the United States Department of Labor against the drilling company and its insurer under the LHWCA; and (2) filed an action in Federal District Court against the platform owner. The drilling company and its insurer paid the worker temporary disability payments for 10 months following the injury. In an informal notice which did not constitute an award, the Department of Labor notified the insurer that the worker was owed permanent disability payments in the total amount of $35,592.77, plus penalties and interest. No permanent disability payments were made to the worker by the drilling company or its insurer. Subsequently—and without the written ap-
381

proval of the drilling company and its insurer—the worker settled his action against the platform owner for $45,000, of which the worker received $29,350.60 after attorneys' fees and expenses. The worker then filed another administrative claim with the Department of Labor against the drilling company and its insurer under the LHWCA. The drilling company and its insurer denied liability on the grounds that under the terms of § 33(g)(2) of the LHWCA (33 USCS § 933(g)(2))—which specifies that forfeiture occurs if the "employee" fails to notify the employer of any settlement with, or judgment against, a third party, regardless of whether the employer or the employer's insurer has made payments or acknowledged entitlement to LHWCA benefits—the worker had forfeited LHWCA benefits by failing to obtain written approval from the drilling company and its insurer of the worker's settlement with the platform owner, which approval was required for a "person entitled to compensation" under § 33(g)(1) of the LHWCA (33 USCS § 933(g)(1)). An administrative law judge (ALJ), finding that the worker was not a "person entitled to compensation" under § 33(g)(1) because he was not receiving payments at the time of the settlement with the platform owner, ruled in favor of the worker and awarded him (1) $35,592.77, less the worker's net recovery from the platform owner of $29,350.60; and (2) interest, attorneys' fees, and future medical benefits. On appeal, the Benefits Review Board (BRB) affirmed the decision of the ALJ. On further appeal, the United States Court of Appeals for the Fifth Circuit, reversing the BRB, expressed the view that § 33(g) of the LHWCA was unambiguous in providing for forfeiture whenever a claimant under the LHWCA failed to get written approval of a third-party settlement (927 F2d 828).

On certiorari, the United States Supreme Court affirmed. In an opinion by KENNEDY, J., joined by REHNQUIST, Ch. J., and WHITE, SCALIA, SOUTER, and THOMAS, JJ., it was held that § 33(g) of the LHWCA applied to a worker whose employer, at the time of such settlement, was neither paying compensation to the worker nor was yet subject to an order to pay compensation under the LHWCA, because (1) the natural reading of § 33(g) supported the conclusion that a "person entitled to compensation" within the meaning of § 33(g)(1) need not be receiving compensation or have had an adjudication in the person's favor; (2) the language of § 33(g)(2) left little doubt that forfeiture would occur whether or not an employer had made payments or acknowledged liability; (3) Congress did not adopt the interpretation by the BRB of the phrase "person entitled to compensation" used in § 33(g)(1) as excluding workers not receiving compensation at the time of settlement, since administrative interpretation followed by congressional re-enactment could not overcome the plain language of a statute; (4) the phrase "person entitled to compensation" used in § 33(g) (1) appeared elsewhere in the LHWCA in contexts in which it could not be limited in reach to injured workers who were either already receiving compensation payments from their employer or in whose favor an award of compensation had been entered; (5) the worker's argument that the BRB's interpretation of the phrase "person entitled to compensation" was entitled to some weight was weakened by the BRB's inconsistent interpretations of the phrase; (6) the plain meaning of the phrase "person entitled to compensation" used in § 33(g)(1) could not be altered by the use of the word "employee" in § 33(g)(2); (7) no deference was due the prior contrary construction of § 33(g) by the Director of the Office of Workers' Compensation Programs within the Department of Labor; (8) such a construction of § 33(g) did not leave the notification requirements of § 33(g)(2) without meaning; and (9) such a construction comported with the purposes and structure of § 33 of the LHWCA (33 USCS § 933).

BLACKMUN, J., joined by STEVENS and O'CONNOR, JJ., dissenting, expressed the view that § 33(g) of the LHWCA was no bar to the worker's eligibility for benefits under the LHWCA, because (1) a claimant—such as the worker in the case at hand—whose employer denied LHWCA liability was not a "person entitled to compensation" for purposes of § 33(g)(1); (2) a consistently literal interpretation of § 33 would not require the worker to have obtained the employer's written approval of the settlement; (3) the Supreme Court's prior holding that the LHWCA was to be liberally construed in conformance with its purpose, and in a way which avoided harsh and incongruous results, was applicable to the case at hand; and (4) it was undisputed that the worker had satisfied the notice requirement of § 33(g)(2).

COUNSEL

Lloyd N. Frischhertz argued the cause for petitioner.

Michael R. Dreeben argued the cause for federal respondent.

H. Lee Lewis, Jr. argued the cause for private respondents.

THOMAS CIPOLLONE, Individually and as
Executor of the Estate of Rose D. Cipollone,
Petitioner

v

LIGGETT GROUP, INC. et al.

505 US —, 120 L Ed 2d 407, 112 S Ct 2608

Argued October 8, 1991.
Reargued January 13, 1992.
Decided June 24, 1992.

Decision: Federal cigarette labeling and advertising
statutes held to pre-empt some but not all state-
law damages claims with respect to cigarette
smoking.

SUMMARY

The Federal Cigarette Labeling and Advertising
Act of 1965 (the "1965 Act") (15 USCS §§ 1331-
1340, later amended)—which became effective on
January 1, 1966—(1) in § 2 (15 USCS § 1331),
recited statutory purposes of (a) adequately inform-
ing the public that cigarette smoking may be hazardous to health, and (b) protecting the national economy from the burden imposed by diverse, nonuni-
form, and confusing cigarette labeling and advertising regulations; (2) in § 4 (15 USCS § 1333), required a specific warning to appear on cigarette
packages; and (3) in § 5 (15 USCS § 1334), which
was captioned "Preemption," provided that (a) no
statement relating to smoking and health, other
than the statement required by § 4, would be required on any cigarette package, and (b) no statement relating to smoking and health would be

385

required in the advertising of any cigarettes the packages of which were labeled in conformity with the provisions of the 1965 Act. The 1965 Act was amended by its successor, the Public Health Cigarette Smoking Act of 1969 (the "1969 Act") (15 USCS §§ 1331-1340, later amended), which, among other changes, replaced the original § 5(b) with a new § 5(b) (15 USCS § 1334(b)), providing that no requirement or prohibition based on smoking and health would be imposed under "State law" with respect to the advertising and promotion of any cigarettes the packages of which were labeled in conformity with the provisions of the 1969 Act. In 1983, a husband and wife (1) filed a federal diversity action in the United States District Court for the District of New Jersey; (2) alleged that the wife, who had begun smoking in 1942, had developed lung cancer from smoking cigarettes manufactured and sold by three defendants; and (3) asserted numerous claims under New Jersey law, including claims to the effect that the defendants had (a) breached express warranties in their advertising, (b) failed to warn consumers about the hazards of smoking, (c) fraudulently misrepresented those hazards, and (d) conspired to deprive the public of information about smoking. The District Court, determining that the 1965 and 1969 Acts did not pre-empt state common-law actions, granted a motion to strike a preemption defense (593 F Supp 1146). On interlocutory appeal, the United States Court of Appeals for the Third Circuit, in reversing, relied on the statement of purpose in § 1331, and concluded—without identifying which specific claims in the case were pre-empted—that state-law damages actions relating to smoking and health were pre-empted, where such actions challenged (1) the inadequacy of the warning on cigarette packages, or (2) the propriety of a party's actions with respect to the advertising and promotion of cigarettes (789 F2d 181). The United States Supreme Court denied certiorari (479 US 1043, 93 L Ed 2d 857, 107 S Ct 907). The case returned to the District Court, which ruled that the failure to warn, express warranty, fraudulent misrepresentation, and conspiracy claims were barred to the extent that those claims relied on post-1965 advertising, promotional, and public relations activities (649 F Supp 664). After a lengthy trial, the jury awarded $400,000 in damages, basically through rejecting the fraudulent misrepresentation and conspiracy claims, but accepting the failure to warn and express warranty claims for pre-1966 conduct. On cross appeals, the Court of Appeals, while ordering a remand for a new trial on other grounds, affirmed the District Court's pre-emption rulings (893 F2d 541).

On certiorari, the Supreme Court affirmed in part, reversed in part, and remanded the case for further proceedings. Although there was a majority opinion for only part of the reasoning underlying the results, it was held that (1) the 1965 Act did not pre-empt state-law damages claims against cigarette manufacturers and sellers; (2) § 5(b) of the 1969 Act pre-empted state-law damages claims against cigarette manufacturers and sellers, where such claims were based on theories of (a) failure to provide a warning sufficient to make a product reasonably safe, suitable, and fit for its intended use, to the extent that a claim required a showing that the manufacturers' and sellers' post-1969 advertising or promotions ought to have included additional, or more clearly stated, warnings of the health consequences of cigarette smoking, and (b) fraudulent

387

misrepresentation, to the extent that this theory was based upon allegations that the manufacturers and sellers, through their advertising, neutralized the effect of federally mandated warning labels, in alleged violation of a state-law prohibition against statements in advertising and promotional materials that tended to minimize the health hazards associated with smoking; and (3) the 1969 Act did not pre-empt state-law damages claims against cigarette manufacturers and sellers, to the extent that such claims were viable under state law, where such claims were based upon theories of (a) failure to provide a warning sufficient to make a product reasonably safe, suitable, and fit for its intended use, to the extent that a claim relied on the manufacturers' and sellers' testing or research practices or other actions unrelated to advertising or promotion, (b) breach of an express warranty that goods conformed to an affirmation of fact or promise relating to the goods, even if the evidence of the alleged warranty consisted largely of statements made in the manufacturers' and sellers' advertising, (c) intentional fraud and misrepresentation by alleged concealment of material facts, insofar as this theory relied on a state-law duty to disclose such facts through channels of communication other than advertising or promotion, (d) intentional fraud and misrepresentation by allegedly false statements of material facts in advertising and promotions, or (e) an alleged conspiracy among the manufacturers and sellers to misrepresent or conceal material facts concerning the health hazards of smoking.

In that portion of the opinion of STEVENS, J., joined by REHNQUIST, Ch. J., and WHITE, BLACKMUN, O'CONNOR, KENNEDY, and SOUTER, JJ., which constituted the opinion of the court, it was held that (1) the pre-emptive scope of the 1965 and 1969 Acts was governed entirely by the express language of the pre-emption provision in § 5 of each statute, because when Congress has considered the issue of pre-emption and has included in the enacted legislation a provision explicitly addressing this issue, and when that provision provides a reliable indicium of congressional intent with respect to state authority, there is no need to infer congressional intent to pre-empt state laws from the substantive provisions of the legislation; and (2) § 5 of the 1965 Act only pre-empted state and federal rule making bodies from mandating particular cautionary statements on cigarette labels or in cigarette advertisements, and did not pre-empt state-law damages actions against cigarette manufacturers and sellers, where (a) § 5 on its face merely prohibited such rule making, and (b) the appropriateness of such a narrow reading was reinforced by a presumption that Congress did not intend to pre-empt state police power regulations. Also, the balance of the opinion of STEVENS, J., joined by REHNQUIST, Ch. J., and WHITE and O'CONNOR, JJ., expressed the view that (1) under § 5(b) of the 1969 Act, the court was required fairly but narrowly, and in light of the strong presumption against pre-emption, to look to each damages claim in order to determine whether that claim was in fact pre-empted, through an inquiry as to whether the legal duty which was the predicate of the claim constituted a forbidden requirement or prohibition; and (2) pursuant to such an inquiry, § 5(b) of the 1969 Act pre-empted or did not pre-empt the particular claims at issue as specified in the preceding paragraph.

BLACKMUN, J., joined by KENNEDY and SOUTER, JJ., concurring in part, concurring in the judgment in part, and dissenting in part, expressed the view that (1) neither the 1965 Act nor the 1969 Act provided the kind of unambiguous evidence of congressional intent necessary to displace state common-law damages claims; and (2) with respect to the 1969 Act, there was no principled basis for many of the asserted distinctions in the opinion of STEVENS, J., among the common-law claims at issue.

SCALIA, J., joined by THOMAS, J., concurring in the judgment in part and dissenting in part, expressed the view that (1) while the Supreme Court's doctrine that an express federal pre-emption provision eliminated implied pre-emption might be correct as to the pre-emption of an entire field, the court's doctrine worked mischief with regard to the implied pre-emption of state regulation which (a) actually conflicts with federal law, or (b) stands as an obstacle to the accomplishment and execution of Congress' purposes; (2) the court's doctrine that express pre-emption provisions had to be construed narrowly, in light of a presumption against the pre-emption of state police power regulations, announced an extraordinary and unprecedented principle of federal statutory construction; (3) the proper rule of construction for an express pre-emption provision was that the provision's language ought to be given its ordinary meaning; and (4) under that rule, (a) the 1965 Act pre-empted the failure to warn claims at issue, and (b) the 1969 Act pre-empted all of the claims at issue.

COUNSEL

Marc Z. Edell argued the cause for petitioner.

H. Bartow Farr, III argued the cause for respondents.

CITY OF BURLINGTON, Petitioner

v

ERNEST DAGUE, SR. et al.

505 US —, 120 L Ed 2d 449, 112 S Ct 2638

Argued April 21, 1992.
Decided June 24, 1992.

Decision: Enhancement of attorneys' fees above "lodestar," to reflect contingent fee agreement, held not permitted in awards under environmental fee-shifting statutes (33 USCS § 1365(d), 42 USCS § 6972(e)).

SUMMARY

Under both § 7002(e) of the Solid Waste Disposal Act (SWDA) (42 USCS § 6972(e)) and § 505(d) of the Federal Water Pollution Control Act, also known as the Clean Water Act (CWA) (33 USCS § 1365(d))—as well as under certain other federal statutes—a court is authorized to award "reasonable" attorneys' fees to a prevailing or substantially prevailing party. In an action brought in the United States District Court for the District of Vermont by a landowner whose attorneys had been retained on a contingent fee basis, it was held that (1) the defendant municipality had violated provisions of the SWDA and the CWA; and (2) the landowner was a substantially prevailing party (732 F Supp 458). Subsequently, in calculating the attorneys' fees award under the SWDA and the CWA, the District Court (1) determined that the figures advanced by the landowner for his attorneys' hourly rates and for the number of hours which the attorneys expended

392

were reasonable, producing a "lodestar" attorneys' fee of $198,027.50; and (2) granted the landowner's request for a contingency enhancement and enhanced the lodestar amount by 25 percent, or $49,506.87, upon its finding that (a) the landowner's risk of not prevailing was substantial, and (b) absent opportunity for enhancement, the landowner would have faced substantial difficulty in obtaining counsel of reasonable skill and competence in the "complicated field of law" involved. On appeal, the United States Court of Appeals for the Second Circuit affirmed in all respects (935 F2d 1343).

On certiorari, the United States Supreme Court reversed the Court of Appeals' judgment insofar as such judgment affirmed the 25-percent enhancement of the lodestar. In an opinion by SCALIA, J., joined by REHNQUIST, Ch. J., and WHITE, KENNEDY, SOUTER, and THOMAS, JJ., it was held that, in determining an award of reasonable attorneys' fees to a prevailing or substantially prevailing party under § 7002(e) of the SWDA or § 505(d) of the CWA, a court could not enhance the fee award above the lodestar amount in order to reflect the fact that the party's attorneys were retained on a contingent fee basis, because (1) the difficulty of establishing the merits of a claim was ordinarily reflected in the lodestar; (2) the relative merits of a claim—although not reflected in the lodestar—should play no part in the calculation of the award; (3) an alternative approach—which would base the availability of contingency enhancements on the difference in market treatment of contingent fee cases as a class, rather than on an assessment of the riskiness of any particular case—was unworkable; (4) there was no other basis fairly derivable from § 7002(e) of the SWDA, § 505(d) of the CWA, and other federal statutes

with similar language, by which contingency enhancement could be restricted to fewer than all
contingent fee cases; and (5) there was no contingency enhancement whatever that was compatible
with § 7002(e) of the SWDA and § 505(d) of the
CWA.

BLACKMUN, J., joined by STEVENS, J., dissenting,
expressed the view that the contingency-enhanced
attorneys' fees awarded in the case at hand were
reasonable, because (1) a "reasonable" fee was to
be a fully compensatory fee which was calculated on
the basis of rates and practices prevailing in the
relevant market; (2) it was a fact of the market that
an attorney who was paid only when the client
prevailed would tend to charge a higher fee than an
attorney who was paid regardless of outcome, and
relevant professional standards long had recognized
that such practice was reasonable; and (3) the Supreme Court's decision to the contrary (a) violated
principles which had been applied consistently in
prior cases, and (b) seriously weakened the enforcement of many civil rights and environmental statutes
for which Congress had authorized fee awards.

O'CONNOR, J., dissenting, expressed the view that
(1) a contingency enhancement of an attorneys' fees
award should be based on the difference in market
treatment of contingent fee cases as a class, rather
than on an assessment of the riskiness of any particular case; and (2) the judgment affirming the 25-
percent contingency enhancement of the attorneys'
fees award in the case at hand should have been
remanded for a market-based assessment of a suitable contingency enhancement.

COUNSEL

Michael B. Clapp argued the cause for petitioner.

Richard H. Seamon argued the cause for the United States, as amicus curiae, by special leave of court.

Barry L. Goldstein argued the cause for respondents.

ROBERT E. LEE, Individually and as Principal of
Nathan Bishop Middle School, et al., Petitioners

v

DANIEL WEISMAN, Personally and as Next Friend
of Deborah Weisman

505 US —, 120 L Ed 2d 467, 112 S Ct 2649

Argued November 6, 1991.
Decided June 24, 1992.

Decision: Inclusion of invocation and benediction
by member of clergy at public secondary school
graduation held forbidden by First Amendment's establishment of religion clause.

SUMMARY

The city of Providence, Rhode Island had a policy
of permitting its public high school and middle
school principals to invite members of the clergy to
offer invocation and benediction prayers as part of
the schools' formal graduation ceremonies. Pursuant
to this policy, the principal of a middle school
invited a rabbi to offer such prayers. The principal
gave the rabbi a pamphlet entitled "Guidelines for
Civic Occasions," which recommended that public
prayers at nonsectarian civic ceremonies be composed with inclusiveness and sensitivity. Also, the
principal advised the rabbi that the invocation and
benediction should be nonsectarian. Four days before the ceremony, the father of a graduating student sought a temporary restraining order in the
United States District Court for the District of
Rhode Island to prohibit school officials from including an invocation or benediction in the cere-

mony. The court denied the motion for lack of adequate time to consider it. Nothwithstanding that the school district did not require attendance at graduation as a condition for receipt of a diploma, the student and her family attended the graduation, where the prayers were recited. The father subsequently filed an amended complaint seeking a permanent injunction to bar various officials of the city's public schools from inviting the clergy to deliver such prayers at future graduations. The District Court granted the injunction on the ground that the school officials' actions endorsed religion and thus violated the establishment of religion clause of the Federal Constitution's First Amendment (728 F Supp 68). The United States Court of Appeals for the First Circuit affirmed (908 F2d 1090).

On certiorari, the United States Supreme Court affirmed. In an opinion by KENNEDY, J., joined by BLACKMUN, STEVENS, O'CONNOR, and SOUTER, JJ., it was held that (1) the inclusion of an invocation and benediction by a member of the clergy at a public secondary school graduation is forbidden by the establishment of religion clause where (a) state officials direct the performance of such a formal religious exercise, and (b) the state, in every practical sense, compels attendance and participation in the exercise; (2) a state may not, consistent with the establishment of religion clause, place students who object to such an exercise in the dilemma of participating in the exercise or protesting against it; and (3) the invocation and benediction in question were not rendered valid by the facts that (a) attendance at the graduation was voluntary in a legal sense, (b) the prayers were brief, (c) there was a good-faith attempt to make the prayers acceptable to most persons, and (d) for many persons, an occasion of such significance would lack meaning without such a religious exercise.

BLACKMUN, J., joined by STEVENS and O'CONNOR, JJ., concurring, expressed the view that, although proof of government coercion is sufficient to prove a violation of the establishment of religion clause, the clause prohibits government endorsement or sponsorship of religion and the government's active involvement in religion, regardless of whether citizens are coerced to conform.

SOUTER, J., joined by STEVENS and O'CONNOR, JJ., concurring, expressed the view that (1) the establishment of religion clause bars a state from sponsoring generically Theistic prayers where the state could not sponsor sectarian ones, (2) government sponsorship of prayer at a graduation ceremony is most reasonably understood as an unconstitutional official endorsement of religion, and in the case at hand, of Theistic religion, and (3) a showing of coercion is not necessary to a successful establishment clause claim.

SCALIA, J., joined by REHNQUIST, Ch. J., and WHITE and THOMAS, JJ., dissenting, expressed the view that (1) the establishment of religion clause should not have been interpreted so as to invalidate a longstanding American tradition of nonsectarian prayer at public school graduations, (2) graduation invocations and benedictions involve no psychological coercion of students to participate in religious exercises, (3) the only coercion that is forbidden by the establishment of religion clause is that which is backed by a threat of penalty, and (4) the middle school principal did not direct or control the content of the prayers in question, and thus there was no pervasive government involvement with religious activity.

COUNSEL

Charles J. Cooper argued the cause for petitioners.

Kenneth W. Starr argued the cause for the United States, as amicus curiae, in support of petitioners.

Sandra A. Blanding argued the cause for respondent.

———————

MARC GILBERT DOGGETT, Petitioner

v

UNITED STATES

505 US —, 120 L Ed 2d 520, 112 S Ct 2686

Argued October 9, 1991.
Reargued February 24, 1992.
Decided June 24, 1992.

Decision: Federal Government's negligent 8½-year delay between indictment and arrest held to violate accused's Sixth Amendment right to speedy trial despite lack of showing of actual prejudice.

SUMMARY

In February 1980, an individual was indicted on federal drug charges. Police officers acting under orders from a Drug Enforcement Administration agent went to the individual's home to arrest him 25 days later, but were told that he had left for Colombia 4 days before. Later, the agent discovered that the individual was under arrest in Panama, and secured a promise from local authorities that the individual would be expelled to the United States when the Panamanian proceedings ran their course. Instead, the individual was released in July 1982 and allowed to go to Colombia—a fact which the agent did not discover until 1985, and even then made no effort to follow up on. The individual re-entered the United States in September 1982, and thereafter lived openly under his own name and stayed within the law. In September 1988, the United States Marshal's Service discovered the individual's whereabouts through a credit check on thousands of people subject to outstanding arrest warrants, and he was arrested. The individual moved to dismiss the indictment, on the ground that the government's failure to prosecute him earlier violated his right to a speedy trial under the Federal Constitution's Sixth Amendment. A federal magistrate found that the delay between indictment and arrest was long enough to be presumptively prejudicial, and that the individual could not be faulted for any delay in asserting his right because there was no evidence that he had known of the indictment prior to his arrest; but the magistrate recommended that the motion be denied because the individual had made no affirmative showing that the delay had prejudiced him. After the United States District Court for the Middle District of Florida followed the magistrate's recommendation, the individual entered a conditional guilty plea reserving the right to appeal his ensuing conviction on the speedy trial claim. The United States Court of Appeals for the Eleventh Circuit, affirming the conviction, ruled that (1) the individual could prevail on the speedy trial claim only by (a) proving actual prejudice, or (b) establishing that three factors—the length of the delay, the reason for the delay, and his assertion of the right—weighed heavily in his favor; (2) no actual prejudice had been shown; and (3) since the government's delay had been due to negligence rather than bad faith, the three factors did not weigh so heavily against the government as to make proof of prejudice unnecessary (906 F2d 573).

On certiorari, the United States Supreme Court reversed and remanded. In an opinion by SOUTER, J., joined by WHITE, BLACKMUN, STEVENS, and KENNEDY, JJ., it was held that the 8½-year delay between the individual's indictment and arrest violated his right to a speedy trial, because (1) the extraordinary length of the delay was sufficient to trigger the speedy trial inquiry; (2) nothing in the record fatally contradicted the District Court's finding that the Federal Government was negligent in seeking the individual; (3) the individual was not to be taxed for invoking his speedy trial right only after his arrest, given that he denied being aware of his indictment prior to his arrest and that the prosecution had stipulated that it had no information to the contrary; and (4) it was reversible error, under the circumstances presented, for the Court of Appeals to hold that the individual's speedy trial claim had to fail due to the individual's failure to show actual prejudice, as the government's egregious persistence in failing to prosecute the individual was sufficient to warrant relief even without a showing of particularized trial prejudice.

O'CONNOR, J., dissented, expressing the view that a possibility of prejudice is not sufficient to support a claim that speedy trial rights have been violated.

THOMAS, J., joined by REHNQUIST, Ch. J., and SCALIA, J., dissented, expressing the view that the Sixth Amendment's speedy trial guarantee (1) was designed to prevent undue and oppressive incarceration and the anxiety and concern accompanying public accusation, neither of which was implicated in the case at hand, and (2) did not provide independent protection against either prejudice to an accused's defense or the disruption of the accused's life years after the alleged crime.

COUNSEL

William J. Sheppard argued and reargued the cause for petitioner.

Robert S. Mueller, III argued the cause for respondent.

William C. Bryson reargued the cause for respondent.

———————

INTERNATIONAL SOCIETY FOR KRISHNA
CONSCIOUSNESS, INC., and BRIAN
RUMBAUGH, Petitioners

v

WALTER LEE, Superintendent of Port Authority
Police

505 US —, 120 L Ed 2d 541, 112 S Ct 2701

Argued March 25, 1992.
Decided June 26, 1992.

Decision: Regulation prohibiting repetitive solicitation of money within airport terminals operated by public authority held reasonable and thus not violative of First Amendment.

SUMMARY

The Port Authority of New York and New Jersey operated airport terminals that were generally accessible to the public and that contained various commercial establishments such as restaurants, snack stands, bars, newsstands, and stores of various types. The Port Authority adopted a regulation forbidding, among other things, the repetitive solicitation of money within such terminals. However, such solicitation was permitted by the Port Authority in the sidewalk areas outside the terminals. A religious corporation, whose members wished to perform within the terminals a ritual involving the public solicitation of funds, brought suit against the Port Authority's police superintendent in the United States District Court for the Southern District of New York and sought declaratory and injunctive relief under 42 USCS § 1983 on the ground that the

404

regulation allegedly deprived the corporation of rights guaranteed under the Federal Constitution's First Amendment. The District Court, granting the corporation summary judgment, held that (1) under the "traditional public forum" doctrine, the terminals were akin to public streets, (2) thus, the Port Authority's regulation could be sustained only if the regulation was narrowly tailored to support a compelling state interest, and (3) the blanket prohibition on soliciting had not been shown to constitute such narrow tailoring (721 F Supp 572). The United States Court of Appeals for the Second Circuit, reversing in pertinent part on appeal, (1) declined to hold that the terminals were public forums for purposes of the First Amendment's free speech guarantee, and (2) expressed the view that the solicitation regulation was indistinguishable from one upheld in United States v Kokinda (1990) 497 US 720, 111 L Ed 2d 571, 110 S Ct 3115, involving in-person solicitations of money on a sidewalk that ran between a freestanding post office and a parking lot (925 F2d 576).

On certiorari, the United States Supreme Court affirmed. In an opinion by REHNQUIST, Ch. J., joined by WHITE, O'CONNOR, SCALIA, and THOMAS, JJ., it was held that (1) for purposes of the First Amendment's free speech guarantee, an airport terminal operated by a public authority is a nonpublic forum, given that (a) airport terminals have not immemorially been held in the public trust and used for purposes of expressive activity, (b) only in recent years has it become a common practice for various religious and nonprofit organizations to use commercial airports as a forum for the solicitation of funds, (c) such terminals in general have not been intentionally opened by their operators to such

405

activity, and (d) although many airports have expanded their function beyond merely contributing to efficient air travel, such terminals do not have as a principal purpose the promotion of free exchange of ideas; and (2) the solicitation regulation was reasonable, and thus did not violate the free speech guarantee, given that (a) such solicitation may have an especially disruptive effect in an airport terminal, (b) face-to-face solicitation presents risks of duress that are an appropriate target of regulation, (c) the access of those who would solicit the general public was quite complete, as the sidewalk area was frequented by an overwhelming percentage of airport users, and (d) the public authority could reasonably worry that even incremental effects flowing from solicitation activity within the terminals would prove to be a threat to the state's interest in crowd control.

O'CONNOR, J., concurring, expressed the view that (1) a publicly owned airport is not a public forum, (2) the proper standard of review was whether the regulation was reasonably related to maintaining the multipurpose environment that the Port Authority had deliberately created, and (3) under such a standard, the regulation was reasonable, in that face-to-face solicitation was incompatible with the airport's functioning in a way that other, permitted activities were not.

KENNEDY, J., joined in part (as to points 1 and 2 below) by BLACKMUN, STEVENS, and SOUTER, JJ., concurring in the judgment, expressed the view that (1) public forum status should be accorded to any property if the objective, physical characteristics of the property and the actual public access and uses which have been permitted by the government indicate that expressive activity would be appropriate and compatible with those uses; (2) under that standard, the airport corridors and shopping areas outside of the passenger security zones were public forums; and (3) the rule disallowing in-person solicitation of money for immediate payment was a narrow and valid regulation of the time, place, and manner of protected speech, or else was a valid regulation of the nonspeech element of expressive conduct.

SOUTER, J., joined by BLACKMUN and STEVENS, JJ., dissenting, expressed the view that (1) any piece of property that is suitable in its physical character for discourse ought to be classified as a public forum, where expressive activity is compatible with the use to which such property has actually been put; (2) unleased public areas at airports like the airports at issue ought to be deemed public forums; and (3) the solicitation regulation violated the First Amendment by failing to satisfy the requirements of (a) narrow tailoring to further a significant state interest, and (b) availability of ample alternative channels for communication.

COUNSEL

Barry A. Fisher argued the cause for petitioners.
Arthur P. Berg argued the cause for respondent.

UNITED STATES, Petitioner

v

KIRK FORDICE, Governor of Mississippi, et al.
(No. 90-1205)

———

JAKE AYERS, et al., Petitioners

v

KIRK FORDICE, Governor of Mississippi, et al.
(No. 90-6588)

505 US —, 120 L Ed 2d 575, 112 S Ct 2727

Argued November 13, 1991.
Decided June 26, 1992.

Decision: Several aspects of Mississippi's public
university system held suspect for purposes of
determining whether state had complied with its
duty to desegregate.

SUMMARY

Even after "dual" public school systems—that is,
systems which were racially segregated by law—had
been held to violate the equal protection clause of
the Federal Constitution's Fourteenth Amendment,
Mississippi's dual public university system, composed of five historically white and three historically
black institutions, remained largely segregated. In
1963, the state's three "flagship" historically white
universities enacted a policy requiring all entrants to
achieve a minimum score of 15 on a particular
college admissions test, at a time when the average
score was 18 for whites and 7 for blacks. In 1975,

private plaintiffs filed a suit—in which the United States intervened as plaintiff—in the United States District Court for the Northern District of Mississippi and alleged that state officials had failed to satisfy their obligations, under provisions including the Fourteenth Amendment and Title VI of the Civil Rights Act of 1964 (42 USCS § 2000d), to dismantle Mississippi's dual system of higher education. The parties attempted to achieve a consensual resolution through voluntary dismantlement. In 1981, the state assigned its universities three categories of missions: (1) "comprehensive"—the three flagship universities—with the greatest resources and program offerings; (2) "urban"—the sole urban university, historically black—with a more limited mission geared toward the urban setting; and (3) "regional"—the remaining four universities, two historically white and two historically black—with primarily an undergraduate role. By the mid-1980's, the student bodies of the state's universities were still predominantly white or black according to whether the universities were historically white or black, but the District Court ruled that the case ought to be dismissed, as the court expressed the view that (1) in the higher education context, the state's affirmative duty to desegregate did not contemplate either the restriction of choice or the achievement of any degree of racial balance; (2) while student enrollment and faculty and staff hiring patterns had to be examined, greater emphasis ought to be placed on current state higher education policies and practices in order to insure that they (a) were racially neutral, (b) had been developed and implemented in good faith, and (c) did not substantially contribute to the continued racial identifiability of the individual institutions; and (3) the current actions of Mississippi officials demonstrated that they were fulfilling their duty (674 F Supp 1523). On appeal, a panel of the United States Court of Appeals for the Fifth Circuit ordered a reversal and remand, on the ground that Mississippi had not complied with its duty to eliminate all of the vestiges of segregation, root and branch, in the public university system (893 F2d 732). On rehearing en banc, however, the Court of Appeals affirmed the District Court's decision and expressed the view that Mississippi had discharged its duty to dismantle its dual system of higher education, because the record made it clear that (1) the state had adopted and implemented race-neutral policies for operating its universities, and (2) all students had real freedom of choice to attend the university that the students wished (914 F2d 676).

On certiorari, the United States Supreme Court vacated and remanded. In an opinion by WHITE, J., joined by REHNQUIST, Ch. J., and BLACKMUN, STEVENS, O'CONNOR, KENNEDY, SOUTER, and THOMAS, JJ., it was held that (1) even though public elementary and secondary school desegregation remedies such as pupil assignments, busing, attendance quotas, and zoning are unavailable in the context of a public university system in which persons may freely choose whether to pursue an advanced education and which of several universities to attend, the adoption and implementation of race-neutral admissions policies do not alone suffice to demonstrate that the state has completely abandoned a prior dual university system, for purposes of determining whether the state has met its affirmative duty, under the equal protection clause and under Title VI, to dismantle that dual system; (2) thus, even after a state has established a racially neutral admissions

410

policy not animated by a discriminatory purpose, if policies traceable to the prior dual system are still in force and have discriminatory effects, then those policies must be reformed to the extent practicable and consistent with sound educational practices; (3) if the Court of Appeals had applied the correct legal standard, then it would have been apparent from the undisturbed factual findings of the District Court that there were at least several surviving Mississippi dual system aspects which were suspect, and which the state had to justify or eliminate, with respect to admissions standards, program duplication, institutional mission assignments, and continued operation of all eight universities; and (4) while the Supreme Court would not order Mississippi to upgrade its three historically black universities solely so that they might be publicly financed, exclusively black enclaves by private choice, the question whether such an increase in funding was necessary to achieve full dismantlement under the Supreme Court's standards was a different question that had to be addressed on remand.

O'CONNOR, J., concurring, emphasized that (1) it was Mississippi's burden to prove that the state had undone its prior segregation, and (2) the circumstances were narrow in which a state might maintain a policy or practice that was traceable to de jure segregation and had segregative effects.

THOMAS, J., concurring, emphasized that (1) the Supreme Court's standard as to whether a state has satisfied its obligation to dismantle a dual system of higher education was far different from the standard adopted to govern the grade school context, and (2) because the court's higher education standard did not compel the elimination of all observed racial

411

imbalance, that standard portended neither the destruction of historically black colleges nor the severing of those institutions from their distinctive histories and traditions.

SCALIA, J., concurring in the judgment in part and dissenting in part, expressed the view that (1) while the Constitution compelled Mississippi to remove all discriminatory barriers to its state-funded universities, the effectively unsustainable burden that the Supreme Court imposed (a) had no proper application in the context of higher education, (b) provided no genuine guidance to states and lower courts, and (c) was as likely to subvert as to promote the interests of those citizens on whose behalf the case at hand was brought; (2) the proper higher education standard ought to be discontinuation of discriminatory practices and adoption of a neutral admissions policy; (3) pursuant to that standard and pursuant to the lower courts' finding as to the discriminatory origin of the test requirements for admission, the District Court ought to have required Mississippi to prove that the continued use of those requirements did not have a racially exclusionary purpose and effect; and (4) while the Constitution did not require Mississippi to remedy funding disparities between its historically black and historically white institutions, that did not mean that the Constitution prohibited such equal funding.

COUNSEL

Alvin O. Chambliss, Jr. argued the cause for private petitioners.

Kenneth W. Starr argued the cause for federal petitioner.

William F. Goodman, Jr. argued the cause for respondents.

————————

TWO PESOS, INC., Petitioner

v

TACO CABANA, INC.

505 US —, 120 L Ed 2d 615, 112 S Ct 2753

Argued April 21, 1992.
Decided June 26, 1992.

Decision: Inherently distinctive trade dress held protectable from infringement, under federal trademark law (15 USCS § 1125(a)), without proof of secondary meaning.

SUMMARY

A fast-food Mexican restaurant chain, alleging that a second chain which had opened restaurants with a very similar motif had thereby infringed the first chain's trade dress in violation of § 43(a) of the Trademark Act of 1946 (Lanham Act) (15 USCS § 1125(a)) (later amended)—which provided that any person who used, in connection with any goods or services, any false description or representation was liable to any person damaged by such use— brought an action against the second chain in the United States District Court for the Southern District of Texas. The District Court instructed the jury that trade dress—that is, the total image and appearance of a business—was protected under § 43(a) if it either was inherently distinctive or had acquired a secondary meaning—that is, a unique association with a specific source. The jury found that the first chain's trade dress was inherently distinctive but had not acquired a secondary meaning, and the District Court entered a judgment for the first chain.

In affirming, the United States Court of Appeals for the Fifth Circuit (1) ruled that the District Court's instructions had adequately stated the applicable law, and that the evidence supported the jury's findings, and (2) rejected the second chain's argument that a finding of no secondary meaning contradicted a finding of inherent distinctiveness (932 F2d 1113, 19 USPQ2d 1253).

On certiorari, the United States Supreme Court affirmed. In an opinion by WHITE, J., joined by REHNQUIST, Ch. J., and BLACKMUN, O'CONNOR, SCALIA, KENNEDY, and SOUTER, JJ., it was held that the trade dress of a business may be protected under § 43(a), based on a finding of inherent distinctiveness, without proof that the trade dress has secondary meaning, because (1) recovery for trademark infringement under § 43(a) was generally available without proof of a secondary meaning; (2) there was no persuasive reason to apply different principles to trade dress, since (a) the protections of trademarks and trade dress under § 43(a) served the same statutory purpose of preventing deception and unfair competition, (b) there was no textual basis in § 43(a) for different treatment, and (c) requiring a secondary meaning for inherently distinctive trade dress would undermine the purposes of the Lanham Act (15 USCS §§ 1051 et seq.) and could have anticompetitive effects; and (3) there was no basis in § 43(a) to support the suggestion that the requirement of a secondary meaning for a trade dress came into being after some unspecified time.

SCALIA, J., concurring, expressed the view that (1) THOMAS, J., was correct in stating that the language of § 43(a) and its common-law derivation were broad enough to embrace inherently distinctive

415

trade dress; but (2) this analysis was complementary to, rather than inconsistent with, the opinion of the court.

STEVENS, J., concurring in the judgment, expressed the view that the conclusion that a secondary meaning was not required to establish a trade dress violation under § 43(a) was supported by the principle of stare decisis, in light of (1) the general consensus among the Federal Courts of Appeals that had addressed the question, and (2) Congress' codification of that consensus.

THOMAS, J., concurring in the judgment, expressed the view that (1) it followed from the language of § 43(a) that the first user of an arbitrary package, like the first user of an arbitrary word, should be entitled to a presumption the package represented the first user without having to show that it did so in fact; and (2) this rule applied under § 43(a) without regard to the rules that applied under the sections of the Lanham Act dealing with registration.

COUNSEL

Kimball J. Corson argued the cause for petitioner.
Richard G. Taranto argued the cause for respondent.

BARBARA FRANKLIN, Secretary of Commerce, et
al., Appellants

v

MASSACHUSETTS et al.

505 US —, 120 L Ed 2d 636, 112 S Ct 2767

Argued April 21, 1992.
Decided June 26, 1992.

Decision: Allocation of overseas federal employees
to home states, for purposes of congressional
reapportionment, held not "final agency action"
reviewable under APA and not unconstitutional.

SUMMARY

With regard to the statutory process for congressional reapportionment following a decennial census, (1) 13 USCS § 141 requires that the United
States Secretary of Commerce, after taking the census, report to the President of the United States the
tabulation of total population by states; and (2) 2
USCS § 2a requires that after receiving the Secretary's report, the President transmit to Congress a
statement showing the whole number of persons in
each state as ascertained under the census, and the
number of representatives to which each state will
be entitled under apportionment by the method of
equal proportions. Although the Census Bureau—
pursuant to authority delegated by the Secretary of
Commerce—had allocated federal personnel stationed overseas to particular states, for purposes of
congressional apportionment, only in the 1900 and
1970 decennial censuses, the Secretary of Commerce announced in a July 1989 decision memoran-

417

dum that overseas federal employees would be allocated to their home states in the 1990 census. In July 1990, the Census Bureau—which used "usual residence" as a standard measure of state affiliation —decided to allocate the Defense Department's overseas employees to the states based generally on "home of record" data which the employees had provided in their personnel files, although some military personnel, for whom such data was not available, were allocated based on other criteria. As a result of the Secretary of Commerce's allocations, the relative state populations were altered enough to shift a representative from Massachusetts to the state of Washington. Massachusetts and two of its registered voters brought an action in the United States District Court for the District of Massachusetts against the President and the Secretary of Commerce, and alleged that the decision to allocate federal overseas employees and the use of "home of record" data for military personnel was (1) arbitrary and capricious and an abuse of discretion, in violation of the Administrative Procedure Act (APA) (5 USCS §§ 701 et seq.); and (2) violative of the Federal Constitution under (a) Article I, § 2, clause 3, which provides that the number of representatives per state be determined by an actual enumeration of their respective numbers, and (b) § 2 of the Fourteenth Amendment, which requires that the whole number of persons "in each state" be counted in apportioning representatives. The District Court (1) rejected the constitutional challenge, but (2) ruled that the Secretary's allocation decision was arbitrary and capricious in violation of the APA. As a remedy, the District Court ordered that (1) the Secretary eliminate the overseas federal employees from the apportionment counts; and (2) the President recalculate the number of representatives per state and transmit the new calculation to Congress (785 F Supp 230).

On direct appeal, the United States Supreme Court reversed. In an opinion by O'CONNOR, J., joined as to point 1 below by REHNQUIST, Ch. J., and WHITE, SCALIA, and THOMAS, JJ., and as to point 2 below by REHNQUIST, Ch. J., and WHITE, BLACKMUN, STEVENS, KENNEDY, SOUTER, and THOMAS, JJ., it was held that (1) there was no "final agency action" within the meaning of 5 USCS § 704 —the judicial review provision of the APA—as to either the report by the Secretary of Commerce to the President required under 13 USCS § 141, or the transmission by the President to Congress of the statement required under 2 USCS § 2a, because (a) the final action that affected the states' entitlement to a particular number of representatives was the President's statement under § 2a, and (b) the President was not an "agency" within the meaning of the APA; and (2) the allocation by the Secretary of overseas federal employees to their home states did not violate Article I, § 2, clause 3 or § 2 of the Fourteenth Amendment, because (a) the Secretary's judgment that many overseas federal employees had retained their ties to the states and could and should be counted toward their states' representation in Congress was consonant with, though not dictated by, the text and history of the Constitution, and (b) the Secretary's judgment did not hamper the underlying constitutional goal of equal representation, but—assuming that employees temporarily stationed abroad have retained their ties to their home states—actually promoted equality, particularly where it had not been demonstrated that entirely eliminating overseas employees from the state

419

counts would make representation in Congress more equal. Also, O'CONNOR, J., joined by REHNQUIST, Ch. J., and WHITE and THOMAS, JJ., expressed the view that (1) Massachusetts and its registered voters in the case at hand had standing to challenge the constitutionality of the Secretary's decision to include overseas federal employees in the state population counts, because (a) it had been shown that Massachusetts would have had an additional representative if overseas employees had not been allocated at all, and (b) such injury was likely to be redressed by declaratory relief against the Secretary alone; and (2) given its redressability determination with respect to the Secretary, the Supreme Court need not decide whether the District Court's grant of injunctive relief against the President was appropriate.

STEVENS, J., joined by BLACKMUN, KENNEDY, and SOUTER, JJ., concurring in part and concurring in the judgment, expressed the view that (1) the report prepared by the Secretary of Commerce pursuant to 13 USCS § 141 was "final agency action" subject to judicial review under 5 USCS § 704, because under 2 USCS § 2a(a), the President had a ministerial duty, but no substantive role, in the computation of the census; (2) the Secretary's taking of the census was not judicially unreviewable as "committed to agency discretion by law," within the meaning of 5 USCS § 701(a)(2); (3) the Secretary's decision to allocate overseas federal employees to states was not arbitrary or capricious such that it should have been set aside under the APA; and (4) the inclusion of overseas employees in state census totals did not violate the Constitution.

SCALIA, J., concurring in part and concurring in the judgment, expressed the view that Massachusetts and its registered voters in the case at hand (1) had no cause of action under the judicial review provisions of the APA; and (2) had no standing to assert claims challenging the Secretary's allocation methods in conducting the 1990 census, since (a) the President's role in the reapportionment process was not purely ministerial, and (b) the injuries asserted could not be remedied without ordering declaratory or injunctive relief against the President, which the federal judiciary did not have the power to do.

COUNSEL

John G. Roberts, Jr. argued the cause for appellants.

Dwight Golann argued the cause for appellees.

———————

WALTER LEE, Superintendent of Port Authority
Police, Petitioner

v

INTERNATIONAL SOCIETY FOR KRISHNA
CONSCIOUSNESS, INC., et al.

505 US —, 120 L Ed 2d 669, 112 S Ct 2709

Argued March 25, 1992.
Decided June 26, 1992.

Decision: Regulation prohibiting repetitive distribution of literature within airport terminals operated by public authority held to violate First Amendment.

SUMMARY

The Port Authority of New York and New Jersey operated airport terminals that were generally accessible to the public and that contained various commercial establishments such as restaurants, snack stands, bars, newsstands, and stores of various types. The Port Authority adopted a regulation forbidding, among other things, the repetitive sale or distribution of flyers, brochures, pamphlets, books, or any other printed or written material within such terminals. However, such activities were permitted by the Port Authority in the sidewalk areas outside the terminals. A religious corporation, whose members wished to perform within the terminals a ritual involving the public distribution of religious literature, brought suit against the Port Authority's police superintendent in the United States District Court for the Southern District of New York and sought declaratory and injunctive

422

relief under 42 USCS § 1983 on the ground that the regulation allegedly deprived the corporation of rights guaranteed under the Federal Constitution's First Amendment. The District Court, granting the corporation summary judgment, held that (1) under the "traditional public forum" doctrine, the terminals were akin to public streets, (2) thus, the Port Authority's regulation could be sustained only if the regulation was narrowly tailored to support a compelling state interest, and (3) the blanket prohibition on distribution of literature had not been shown to constitute such narrow tailoring (721 F Supp 572). The United States Court of Appeals for the Second Circuit, affirming in pertinent part on appeal, (1) declined to hold that the terminals were public forums for purposes of the First Amendment's free speech guarantee, but (2) held that the Port Authority was required to provide reasonable access to the terminals for the distribution of literature (925 F2d 576).

On certiorari, the United States Supreme Court affirmed. In a per curiam opinion expressing the view of BLACKMUN, STEVENS, O'CONNOR, KENNEDY, and SOUTER, JJ., it was held that the ban on distribution of literature was invalid under the First Amendment's free speech guarantee.

O'CONNOR, J., concurring in the judgment in an opinion appearing in International Society for Krishna Consciousness, Inc. v Lee, 120 L Ed 2d, at page 554, expressed the view that (1) a publicly owned airport is not a public forum; (2) the proper standard of review was whether the regulation was reasonably related to maintaining the multipurpose environment that the Port Authority had deliberately created; and (3) under such a standard, the regulation was not reasonable, since there was no explanation offered as to how peaceful pamphleteering alone ot in conjunction with solicitation of funds—was incompatible with that environment.

KENNEDY, J., joined in part (as to point 1 below) by BLACKMUN, STEVENS, and SOUTER, JJ., concurring in the judgment in an opinion appearing in International Society for Krishna Consciousness, Inc. v Lee, 120 L Ed 2d, at page 559, expressed the view that (1) the airport corridors and shopping areas outside of the passenger security zones were public forums; and (2) unlike the provision of the Port Authority regulation upheld in International Society for Krishna Consciousness, Inc. v Lee, supra—which provision forbade the solicitation of funds in the terminals—the flat ban on the distribution or sale of printed material violated the First Amendment, given that (a) there is a great need to give the sale of literature full First Amendment protection, (b) the government interest in regulating the sale of literature was not as powerful as in the case of solicitation of funds, (c) the sale regulation was not as narrowly drawn as the solicitation rule, in that the sale regulation did not specify the receipt of money as a critical element of a violation, and (d) the sale regulation left open fewer alternative channels of communication than did the solicitation rule.

SOUTER, J., joined by BLACKMUN and STEVENS, JJ., concurring in the judgment in an opinion appearing in International Society for Krishna Consciousness, Inc. v Lee, 120 L Ed 2d, at page 570, expressed the view that (1) the Court of Appeals' judgment was properly affirmed insofar as it struck down the distribution ban; and (2) unleased public areas at airports like the airports at issue ought to be deemed public forums.

REHNQUIST, Ch. J., joined by WHITE, SCALIA, and THOMAS, JJ., dissenting, expressed the view that the Port Authority's distribution ban, no less than the ban on the solicitation of funds, was reasonable and thus valid under the First Amendment, given that (1) the risks and burdens posed by leafletting were similar to those posed by solicitation, and (2) a differential ban, permitting distribution but forbidding solicitation, might prove overly burdensome for the Port Authority to enforce.

COUNSEL

Arthur P. Berg argued the cause for petitioner.
Barry A. Fisher argued the cause for respondents.

PLANNED PARENTHOOD OF SOUTHEASTERN
PENNSYLVANIA, et al., Petitioners

v

ROBERT P. CASEY, Governor of Pennsylvania, et
al. (No. 91-744)

———

ROBERT P. CASEY, Governor of Pennsylvania, et
al., Petitioners

v

PLANNED PARENTHOOD OF SOUTHEASTERN
PENNSYLVANIA et al. (No. 91-902)

505 US —, 120 L Ed 2d 674, 112 S Ct 2791

Argued April 22, 1992.
Decided June 29, 1992.

Decision: Pennsylvania abortion legislation held
valid, except for spousal-notice provisions, under due process clause of Federal Constitution's
Fourteenth Amendment.

SUMMARY

In 1988 and 1989, a Pennsylvania abortion statute
was amended to provide that (1) a woman seeking
an abortion is required to give her informed consent prior to the abortion procedure and to be
provided, at least 24 hours before the abortion is
performed, with certain information concerning her
decision whether to undergo an abortion, (2) a
minor seeking an abortion is required to obtain the
informed consent of one of her parents or guard-
ians, but has available a judicial bypass option if the
426

minor does not wish to or cannot obtain such consent, (3) unless certain exceptions apply, a married woman seeking an abortion is required to sign a statement indicating that she has notified her husband of her intended abortion, (4) compliance with the foregoing requirements is exempted in the event of a "medical emergency," which term is defined in another statutory provision as a pregnant woman's medical condition that on the basis of a physician's good-faith clinical judgment, necessitates an immediate abortion to avert the woman's death or to avert a serious risk of substantial and irreversible impairment of a major bodily function, and (5) facilities providing abortion services are subject to certain reporting and record-keeping requirements, which do not include the disclosure of the identities of women who have undergone abortions, but which include a requirement of reporting of a married woman's failure to provide notice to her husband of her intended abortion. Before any of these provisions took effect, five abortion clinics and one physician representing himself as well as a class of physicians who provided abortion services brought suit seeking declaratory and injunctive relief on the basis of the allegation that each provision was unconstitutional on its face. The United States District Court for the Eastern District of Pennsylvania, after entering a preliminary injunction against enforcement of the provisions, held that all the provisions were unconstitutional and entered a permanent injunction against the state's enforcement of the provisions (744 F Supp 1323). The United States Court of Appeals for the Third Circuit affirmed in part and reversed in part, upholding all the provisions except for the spousal-notice requirement (947 F2d 682).

On certiorari, the United States Supreme Court affirmed in part, reversed in part, and remanded. A majority of the members of the court joined portions of an opinion holding that (1) the statutory provision defining a medical emergency did not violate the due process clause, (2) the provision requiring spousal notice violated the due process clause, and (3) the essential holding of Roe v Wade (1973) 410 US 113, 35 L Ed 2d 147, 93 S Ct 705—which held that (a) a woman has the right to choose to have an abortion before her fetus is viable and to obtain an abortion without undue interference from a state, (b) a state has the power to restrict abortions after fetal viability, if the state law imposing such a restriction contains exceptions for pregnancies which endanger a woman's life or health, and (c) a state has legitimate interests from the outset of a pregnancy in protecting the health of the pregnant woman and the life of the fetus that may become a child—should be retained and reaffirmed. Although unable to agree on an opinion as to the other statutory provisions, (1) seven members of the court (O'CONNOR, KENNEDY, and SOUTER, JJ., REHNQUIST, Ch. J., and WHITE, SCALIA, and THOMAS, JJ.) agreed that the provisions requiring informed consent, the 24-hour waiting period, and parental consent did not violate the due process clause, (2) eight members (O'CONNOR, KENNEDY, SOUTER, and STEVENS, JJ., REHNQUIST, Ch. J., and WHITE, SCALIA, and THOMAS, JJ.) agreed that the provisions requiring record keeping and reporting, at least except for the provision requiring reporting of failure to provide spousal notice, did not violate the due process clause, and (3) five members (O'CONNOR, KENNEDY, SOUTER, STEVENS, and BLACKMUN, JJ.) agreed that the provision requiring reporting of failure to provide spousal notice violated the due process clause.

In a joint opinion by O'CONNOR, KENNEDY, and SOUTER, JJ., announcing the judgment of the court, and joined in pertinent part by STEVENS and BLACKMUN, JJ., it was held that (1) the statutory provision defining a medical emergency did not violate the due process clause, because, as construed by the Court of Appeals to include serious conditions that could lead to an illness with substantial and irreversible consequences, the definition imposed no undue burden on a woman's abortion rights; (2) the provision requiring spousal notice violated the due process clause by imposing an undue burden on a woman's abortion rights, because the notice requirement enabled a husband to wield, in effect, an unconstitutional veto over his wife's decision concerning an abortion; and (3) consideration of the fundamental constitutional questions resolved by Roe v Wade, of principles of institutional integrity, and of the rule of stare decisis required that the essential holding of Roe v Wade be retained and reaffirmed. Also, O'CONNOR, KENNEDY, and SOUTER, JJ., expressed the view that (1) the provision concerning a pregnant woman's informed consent and the 24-hour waiting period did not violate the due process clause, because the provision did not place an undue burden upon a woman's right to decide whether to terminate her pregnancy; (2) the provision requiring parental consent did not violate the due process clause, because prior Supreme Court cases have upheld a parental consent requirement, provided that there is an adequate judicial bypass procedure; (3) the record-keeping and reporting requirements, except for the provision requiring reporting of failure to provide spousal notice, did not violate the due process clause, because such requirements related to maternal health and did not pose a substantial obstacle to a woman's choice; (4) the provision requiring reporting of failure to provide spousal notice violated the due process clause by placing an undue burden on a woman's choice; and (5) the trimester framework of Roe v Wade should be rejected.

STEVENS, J., concurring in part and dissenting in part, expressed the view that (1) Roe v Wade was an integral part of a correct understanding of both the concept of liberty and the basic equality of men and women; (2) a state interested in protecting fetal life after viability could go so far as to proscribe abortion during that period, except when an abortion was necessary to preserve the life or health of the mother; (3) a state could promote its preference for normal childbirth by funding childbirth, creating and maintaining alternatives to abortion, and espousing the virtues of family, but must respect an individual's freedom to choose between childbirth and abortion; (4) the court properly determined that (a) the medical emergency provision was valid, (b) the provision requiring spousal notice was invalid, and (c) the provisions requiring record keeping and reporting were valid, except that the provision requiring reporting of failure to provide spousal notice was invalid; and (5) with respect to the statutory provision concerning informed consent, (a) the portion requiring a physician or counselor to provide a woman with a range of materials clearly designed to persuade her to choose not to undergo an abortion was unconstitutional, because the state could not inject such information into a woman's deliberations just as she was weighing such an important choice, and (b) the 24-hour waiting period was unconstitutional, where there was no evidence that the mandated delay benefited women or was necessary to enable a physician to convey any relevant information to a patient.

BLACKMUN, J., concurring in the judgment in part, and dissenting in part, expressed the view that (1) the Federal Constitution and the decisions of the Supreme Court required that a state's abortion restrictions be subjected to strict scrutiny; (2) state restrictions on abortion (a) violated a woman's right of privacy by infringing upon her right to bodily integrity and depriving her of the right to make her own decision about reproduction and family planning, and (b) implicated constitutional guarantees of gender equality; (3) the trimester framework required in Roe v Wade should not be disturbed; and (4) except for the medical emergency provision which the court properly held valid, stare decisis and application of the strict scrutiny standard necessitated the invalidation of all the challenged statutory provisions, because (a) under the guise of informed consent, the statute required the dissemination of information that was not relevant to such consent, and thus advanced no legitimate state interest, (b) the 24-hour waiting period furthered no legitimate state interest, (c) the parental consent provision was not narrowly drawn to serve the state's interest in encouraging parental involvement in a minor's abortion decision, and (d) the statute's reporting requirements were not shown either to have added to the pool of scientific knowledge concerning abortion or to have been reasonably related to the state's interest in maternal health.

REHNQUIST, Ch. J., joined by WHITE, SCALIA, and THOMAS, JJ., concurring in the judgment in part and dissenting in part, expressed the view that (1) Roe v Wade was wrongly decided and should be overruled; (2) a woman's interest in having an abortion is a form of liberty protected by the due process clause, but states may regulate abortion procedures in ways rationally related to a legitimate state interest; and (3) the challenged statutory provisions should be upheld in their entirety, because (a) the informed consent provision was rationally related to the state's interest in assuring that a woman's consent to an abortion be fully informed, and the 24-hour waiting period reasonably furthered the state's legitimate interests in maternal health and in the unborn life of the fetus, (b) the parental consent provision was consistent with the Supreme Court's previous decisions involving parental consent requirements, (c) the spousal notice provision was a rational attempt to improve truthful communication between spouses and encourage collaborative decisionmaking, (d) the court properly determined that the medical emergency provision was valid, and (e) the statute's reporting requirements rationally furthered the state's legitimate interests in medical knowledge concerning maternal health and prenatal life, in gathering statistical information concerning patients, and in assuring compliance with other provisions of the statute.

SCALIA, J., joined by REHNQUIST, Ch. J., and WHITE and THOMAS, JJ., concurring in the judgment in part and dissenting in part, expressed the view that (1) a woman's liberty to abort her unborn child is not a liberty protected by the Federal Constitution, because (a) the Constitution says nothing about abortion, and (b) the longstanding traditions of American society permitted abortion to be legally proscribed; (2) applying the rational-basis test, the state statute should be upheld in its entirety; (3) Roe v Wade was plainly wrong, and the Supreme

Court should get out of this area of the law, where it has no right to be; and (4) the undue burden standard was inherently manipulable and would prove unworkable in practice.

COUNSEL

Kathryn Kolbert argued the cause for Planned Parenthood, et al.

Ernest D. Preate, Jr. argued the cause for Robert Casey, et al.

Kenneth W. Starr argued the cause for the United States, as amicus curiae, by special leave of court.

DAVID H. LUCAS, Petitioner

v

SOUTH CAROLINA COASTAL COUNCIL

505 US —, 120 L Ed 2d 798, 112 S Ct 2886

Argued March 2, 1992.
Decided June 29, 1992.

Decision: South Carolina court held to have applied wrong standard in determining whether state beachfront management statute, by barring construction, effected "taking" of property under Fifth Amendment.

SUMMARY

Under 1977 legislation, the state of South Carolina required owners of certain "critical area" coastal-zone land to obtain a permit from a coastal council before changing the use of the land. In 1986, a developer purchased two lots on a barrier island—which lots did not then qualify as a "critical area" and were zoned for single-family residential construction—and made plans to erect such residences on the lots. In 1988, however, the state enacted a Beachfront Management Act (BMA) which established a new baseline on the island and prohibited any construction of occupable improvements seaward of a line parallel to and 20 feet landward of the baseline, thereby barring the developer's plans. The developer, filing suit against the council in the South Carolina Court of Common Pleas, did not challenge the validity of the BMA as an exercise of the state's police power, but contended that the BMA's complete extinguishment of the value of his property effected a "taking" of the property for which he was entitled to just compensation. The Court of Common Pleas found that the BMA decreed a permanent ban on construction on the developer's lots, where there had been no restrictions on such use before, and had thereby deprived the developer of any reasonable economic use of the lots, rendering the lots valueless; accordingly, the court ordered the council to pay just compensation of more than $1.2 million. While the case was pending before the Supreme Court of South Carolina, the BMA was amended to authorize the council, in certain circumstances, to issue special permits for construction of habitable structures seaward of the baseline. The Supreme Court of South Carolina, reversing the judgment of the Court of Common Pleas, held that (1) in the absence of an attack on the validity of the BMA as such, the court was bound to accept the state legislature's uncontested findings that new construction in the coastal zone threatened a public resource; and (2) when a regulation respecting the use of property is designed to prevent serious public harm, no compensation is owed regardless of the regulation's effect on the property's value (304 SC 376, 404 SE2d 895).

On certiorari, the United States Supreme Court reversed and remanded. In an opinion by SCALIA, J., joined by REHNQUIST, Ch. J., and WHITE, O'CONNOR, and THOMAS, JJ., it was held that (1) the decision below was ripe for review, even though the BMA had been amended to allow the issuance of special permits and even though Supreme Court precedents reflect an insistence on knowing the nature and extent of permitted development before adjudicating the constitutionality of regulations purporting to limit such development, because although the above considerations would preclude review had the court below rested its judgment on ripeness grounds, that court had instead disposed of the developer's claim on the merits; (2) where a state seeks to sustain a regulation that deprives land of all economically beneficial use, the state may resist an asserted right to compensation under the takings clause, on the theory that there has been no "taking," only if the logically antecedent inquiry into the nature of the owner's estate shows that the proscribed use interests were not part of the owner's title to begin with, so that the severe limitation on property use is not newly legislated or decreed, but inheres in the title itself through the restrictions that background principles of the state's law of property and nuisance already place upon land ownership; (3) the court below therefore erred in rejecting the developer's claim on the merits on the basis of the state legislature's recitation of a noxious-use justification for the BMA; and (4) the case would be remanded for a determination of the state-law question whether common-law principles would have prevented the erection of any habitable or productive improvements on the developer's land.

KENNEDY, J., concurred in the judgment, expressing the view that (1) the issues presented in the case were ready for the Supreme Court's decision; (2) although the trial court's finding that the developer's property had been rendered valueless was questionable, the Supreme Court—unlike the court below on remand—had to accept the finding as entered; (3) nuisance prevention accorded with the most common expectations of owners who faced regulation, but was not the sole source of state authority to impose severe restrictions; and (4) the court below erred by reciting the general purposes for which the BMA was enacted without a determination that those purposes were in accord with the owner's reasonable expectations, and therefore sufficient to support a severe restriction on specific parcels of property.

BLACKMUN, J., dissented, expressing the view that (1) the case was not ripe for review; (2) even if there were no jurisdictional barrier, it was unwise to decide issues based on the erroneous factual premise that regulation had rendered the subject property entirely valueless; (3) the court's decision improperly placed on state legislatures the burden of showing that their legislative judgments are correct; and (4) previous takings clause jurisprudence rested on the principle that a state has full power to prohibit an owner's use of property without compensation if such use is harmful to the public, with the determination of harmfulness resting on legislative judgment rather than on common-law nuisance principles.

STEVENS, J., dissented, expressing the view that (1) the developer was not entitled to an adjudication of the merits of his permanent takings claim under the amended BMA until he exhausted his right to apply for a special permit; (2) it was not clear whether the developer had a viable "temporary taking" claim under the preamendment BMA; (3) the doctrine of judicial restraint, under which the Supreme Court will not anticipate a question of constitutional law in advance of the necessity of deciding, properly applied to the case at hand; (4) a categorical rule that total regulatory takings must be compensated was unsupported by prior decisions, arbitrary and unsound in practice, and theoretically unjustified; and (5) the court's nuisance exception

437

unwisely froze state common law and denied legislatures their traditional power to revise the law governing the rights and uses of property.

SOUTER, J., would have dismissed the writ of certiorari in the case as improvidently granted, because the case came to the Supreme Court on an unreviewable assumption—that the BMA deprived the developer of his entire economic interest in the property at issue—that was both questionable as a conclusion of Fifth Amendment law and sufficient to frustrate the Supreme Court's ability to render certain the legal premises on which the court's holding rested.

COUNSEL

A. Camden Lewis argued the cause for petitioner.

C. C. Harness, III argued the cause for respondent.

HENRY JOSE ESPINOSA, Petitioner

v

FLORIDA

505 US —, 120 L Ed 2d 854, 112 S Ct 2926

Decided June 29, 1992.

Decision: Imposition of death sentence by Florida trial court held to violate Eighth Amendment where jury rendering advisory verdict in sentencing hearing was instructed on invalid aggravating circumstance.

SUMMARY

Under Florida law, (1) after a defendant is found guilty of a capital felony, a separate sentencing proceeding is conducted to determine whether the sentence should be life imprisonment or death; (2) at the close of the hearing, the jury is instructed to weigh aggravating and mitigating circumstances, and renders an advisory verdict as to what sentence should be imposed, which verdict does not include specific findings as to aggravating and mitigating circumstances; and (3) notwithstanding the recommendation of a majority of the jury, the trial court must then weigh the aggravating and mitigating circumstances to determine finally whether the sentence will be life or death. An individual accused of first-degree murder was convicted in a Florida trial court, and at the close of the evidence in the penalty hearing the trial judge's instructions to the jury included a statement that the jury was entitled to find as an aggravating circumstance that the murder had been "especially wicked, evil, atrocious,

439

or cruel." The jury recommended that the trial court sentence the accused to death, and the trial court—finding four aggravating circumstances including the "especially heinous, atrocious, or cruel" nature of the murder—followed that recommendation. On appeal, the accused argued that the "wicked, evil, atrocious, or cruel" instruction was vague and thus left the jury with insufficient guidance as to when to find the existence of the circumstance; but the Supreme Court of Florida, affirming the accused's conviction and sentence, cited a previous decision in which the court had held that state precedents had placed a sufficiently narrowing construction on the "heinous, atrocious, or cruel" statutory aggravating circumstance (589 So 2d 887).

Granting leave to proceed in forma pauperis and granting certiorari, the United States Supreme Court reversed and remanded. In a per curiam opinion expressing the views of BLACKMUN, STEVENS, O'CONNOR, KENNEDY, SOUTER, and THOMAS, JJ., it was held that (1) if a "weighing" state—that is, a state in which the determination whether to impose the death penalty is based on a weighing of aggravating circumstances and mitigating circumstances—decides to place capital-sentencing authority in two actors rather than one, then neither actor must be permitted to weigh invalid aggravating circumstances; and (2) the trial court below thus violated the Federal Constitution's Eighth Amendment in imposing the death sentence upon the accused, because (a) the "wicked, evil, atrocious, or cruel" instruction was unconstitutionally vague, (b) although the trial court did not directly weigh any invalid aggravating circumstance, it had to be presumed that the jury had done so and that the trial court had followed state law by giving "great weight" to the resultant recommendation, (c) the trial court thus had indirectly weighed the invalid aggravating factor, and (d) this kind of indirect weighing created the same potential for arbitrariness as the direct weighing of an invalid aggravating factor.

REHNQUIST, Ch. J., and WHITE, J., dissented and would have set the case down for oral argument.

SCALIA, J., dissented, expressing the view that (1) since the Florida courts had found several constitutionally sound aggravating factors in the accused's case, the death sentence therein comported with the "narrowing" requirement of Furman v Georgia (1972) 408 US 238, 33 L Ed 2d 346, 92 S Ct 2726, which requirement was the only special capital-sentencing procedure that the Eighth Amendment demanded; and (2) the petition for certiorari ought to be denied.

GLOSSARY OF COMMON LEGAL TERMS

Abatement
The extinguishment of a lawsuit.

Abstention doctrine
The doctrine whereby a federal court may decline to exercise, or may postpone the exercise of, its jurisdiction, where a case involves a controlling question of state law.

Action
A lawsuit.

Administrative determination
A decision by a government board, agency or official, rather than by a court.

Administrator
One appointed by a court to settle the estate of a deceased person. The feminine form is "administratrix."

Admiralty
The body of law governing maritime cases.

Affidavit
A sworn written statement.

Amicus curiae
One who, not being a party to a lawsuit, assists the court in deciding the case.

Antitrust laws
Laws prohibiting restrictions on competition.

Appealable
That which may be taken to a higher court for review.

Appellant
One who appeals to a superior court from the order of an inferior court.

Appellee
A party against whom a case is appealed from an inferior court to a superior court.

Arbitration
The submission of a dispute to a selected person —not a court—for decision.

Arraign
To call a person before a judge or commissioner to answer criminal charges made against him.

Array
The whole body of persons, summoned to attend court, from whom a jury will be selected.

Assignee
One to whom property or a right is transferred.

Assignor
The transferor of property or a right.

Bill of Rights
The first ten amendments to the United States Constitution.

Brief
A written legal argument submitted to the court deciding the case.

Calendar
A list of cases awaiting decision in a court.

Capital crime
An offense punishable by death.

Cause of action
A right to legal redress.

444

Cease-and-desist order
An order to stop doing specified acts.

Certiorari
A superior court's order to a lower court to send up the record of a case for review by the superior court.

Choice of remedies
An election of which form of legal redress to seek.

Civil
Not criminal, as a civil lawsuit.

Class action
A lawsuit on behalf of persons too numerous to participate actively therein.

Commerce clause
The provision of the United States Constitution giving Congress power to regulate commerce with foreign nations, among the states.

Common law
The body of the law apart from constitutions, treaties, statutes, ordinances, and regulations.

Contempt
An exhibition of scorn or disrespect toward a judicial or legislative body.

Continuance
A postponement of proceedings.

Copyright
The exclusive privilege of publishing literary or artistic productions.

Coram nobis
A means of challenging a court's judgment, especially in criminal cases.

Court of Appeals
See United States Court of Appeals.

Cross Appeal
An appeal filed by the person against whom an appeal is taken.

De novo
Anew or over again, such as a trial de novo.

Devise
A will provision making a gift of land.

Disputes clause
A provision in a government contract for the settlement of disputes between the contractor and the government by decision of a government board or official.

District court
See United States District Court.

Diversity case
A case decided by a federal court because the parties are citizens of different states.

Double jeopardy
Placing a person twice in jeopardy of conviction for the same offense.

Due process clause
The provision of the United States Constitution that no person shall be deprived of life, liberty, or property without due process of law.

En banc
With all the judges of the court sitting.

Equal protection
The guaranty of the United States Constitution that no person or class of persons shall be denied

the same protection of the laws that is enjoyed by other persons or classes of persons in like circumstances.

Establishment clause
The provision of the United States Constitution that Congress shall make no law respecting an establishment of religion.

Federal District Court
See District court.

Federal question jurisdiction
The jurisdiction of federal courts over cases presenting questions of federal law.

Felony
A crime punishable by death or by imprisonment in a state prison.

Forma pauperis
Without the payment of legal fees in advance.

Full faith and credit clause
The provision of the United States Constitution that full faith and credit shall be given in each state to the public acts, records, and judicial proceedings of every other state.

Habeas corpus
A judicial inquiry into the legality of the restraint of a person.

Indictment
A grand jury's accusation of crime.

Interlocutory
That which settles an intervening matter but does not decide a case.

Intestate
One who dies without leaving a valid will.

Jurisdiction of subject matter
The power to decide a certain type of case.

Just compensation clause
The provision of the United States Constitution that no private property may be taken for public use without just compensation.

Laches
Delay barring the right to special forms of relief.

Legatee
One to whom personal property is given by will.

Lessee
A tenant.

Lessor
A landlord.

Libel
Written defamation; in maritime cases, a suit in court.

Lien
A charge upon property for the payment of a debt.

Local action
A lawsuit, especially one involving rights to land, which can be brought only in the place where the wrong was committed.

Maintenance and cure
The legal duty of a seaman's employer to care for him during his illness.

Mandamus
A judicial command to perform an official duty.
448

Misdemeanor
Any crime not punishable by death or by imprisonment in a state prison.

Patent
The exclusive right of manufacture, sale, or use secured by statute to one who invents or discovers a new and useful device or process.

Per curiam
By the court as a whole.

Per se
By itself.

Plaintiff
A person who brings a lawsuit.

Plenary
Full or complete.

Police power
The power inherent in the states as sovereigns and not derived under any written constitution.

Prima facie
At first sight; with regard to evidence, that which, if unexplained or uncontradicted, is sufficient to establish a fact.

Privileges and immunities clause
The provision of the United States Constitution that no state shall make or enforce any law which abridges the privileges or immunities of citizens of the United States.

Pro hac vice
For this occasion.

Pro se
For himself; in his own behalf.

449

Proximate cause
The immediate cause of injury.

Public defender
A lawyer employed by the public to defend persons accused of crime.

Recognizance
A bail bond.

Remand
To order to be sent back.

Res judicata
The doctrine that a final judgment is binding on the parties to the lawsuit and the matter cannot be relitigated.

Respondent
The defendant in an action; with regard to appeals, the party against whom the appeal is taken.

Sanction
The penalty to be incurred by a wrongdoer.

Saving clause
A statutory provision preserving rights which would otherwise be annihilated by the statute.

Seaworthy
The reasonable fitness of a vessel to perform the service which she has undertaken to perform.

Statute of frauds
A statute rendering certain types of contracts unenforceable unless in writing.

Statute of limitations
A statute fixing a period of time within which certain types of lawsuits or criminal prosecutions must be begun.

Subpoena
Legal process to require the attendance of a witness.

Substantial federal question
A question of federal law of sufficient merit to warrant decision of the case by a federal court.

Substantive offense
An offense which is complete in itself and does not depend on the establishment of another offense.

Summary judgment
A judgment without a trial.

Supremacy clause
The provision of the United States Constitution that the Constitution, federal laws enacted pursuant thereto, and federal treaties shall be the supreme law of the land, binding the judges in every state, notwithstanding any state law to the contrary.

Surety
One who binds himself with another, called the principal, for the performance of an obligation with respect to which the principal is already bound and primarily liable.

Surrogate
The judge of a court dealing largely with wills and decedents' estates.

Tort
A wrong independent of contract; a breach of duty which the law, as distinguished from a mere contract, has imposed.

Tortfeasor
One who commits a tort; a wrongdoer.

451

Transitory action
An action which may be brought wherever the defendant may be served with process.

Trespass
An injury intentionally inflicted on the person or property of another.

Trier of fact
One who decides questions of fact.

United States Code
The official compilation of statutes enacted by Congress.

United States Court of Appeals
The intermediate level of federal courts above the United States District Courts but below the Supreme Court of the United States.

United States District Court
A federal trial court.

Unseaworthy
See Seaworthy.

USC
See United States Code.

USCS
The abbreviation for United States Code Service, Lawyers Edition, which is a publication annotating the federal laws, arranged according to the numbering of the United States Code.

Venue
The place where a case may be tried.

Writ of certiorari
See Certiorari.

Writ of error coram nobis
See Coram nobis.

TABLE OF CASES

TABLE OF CASES

TABLE OF CASES

456

TABLE OF CASES

TABLE OF CASES

TABLE OF CASES

TABLE OF CASES

INDEX

ABDUCTION AND KIDNAPPING
Extradition: forcible abduction of Mexican citizen to United States held not to violate extradition treaty with Mexico, and thus, not to prohibit citizen's trial in Federal District Court on criminal charges, 119 L Ed 2d 441

ABORTION
Pennsylvania abortion legislation held valid, except for spousal-notice provisions, under due process clause of Federal Constitution's Fourteenth Amendment, 120 L Ed 2d 674

ABSENCE OR PRESENCE
Use tax: Federal Constitution's commerce clause (Art I, § 8, cl 3), but not due process clause of Fourteenth Amendment, held to bar enforcement of North Dakota use tax against out-of-state mail-order house, 119 L Ed 2d 91

ABSTENTION DOCTRINE
Diversity jurisdiction: domestic relations exception to federal courts' diversity jurisdiction held inapplicable to woman's child-abuse tort claim against her former husband and his female companion, 119 L Ed 2d 468

ABUSE OF DISCRETION
Deportation proceedings: Attorney General's denial of alien's motion to reopen deportation proceedings held not abuse of discretion, 116 L Ed 2d 823

Forma pauperis actions: dismissal of in forma pauperis action as factually frivolous under 28 USCS § 1915(d) held (1) appropriate where alleged facts are irrational or incredible, and (2) reviewable for abuse of discretion, 118 L Ed 2d 340

ABUSE OF PERSONS
Child Abuse or Neglect (this index)
Diversity jurisdiction: domestic relations exception to federal courts' diversity jurisdiction held inapplicable to woman's child-abuse tort claim against her former husband and his female companion, 119 L Ed 2d 468

INDEX

ACCESS AND ACCESSIBILITY
Labor unions: store owner held not to have committed unfair labor practice under § 8(a)(1) of National Labor Relations Act (29 USCS § 158(a)(1)) by barring nonemployee union organizers from parking lot, 117 L Ed 2d 79

ACCRETION, ALLUVION, AND AVULSION
Boundaries: Secretary of Army held authorized under § 10 of Rivers and Harbors Appropriation Act (33 USCS § 403) to condition approval of port construction on Alaska's disclaimer of federal-state boundary change, 118 L Ed 2d 222

ACQUISITION OF PROPERTY
Railroads: Interstate Commerce Commission held to have authority, under 45 USCS § 562(d)(1), to require conveyance of track from railroad to Amtrak for purpose of reconveying track to second railroad, 118 L Ed 2d 52

ACQUISITION-VALUE TAX ASSESSMENT
Property taxes: equal protection held not violated by California Constitution's real property tax system which generally assesses property on value at time of acquisition, rather than on current value, 120 L Ed 2d 1

ACTIVE SUPERVISION DOCTRINE
Title-search ratesetting: supervision by states of title-search ratesetting held not sufficiently active to give title insurance companies state-action immunity from federal antitrust liability, 119 L Ed 2d 410

ACTUAL INNOCENCE EXCEPTION
Habeas corpus: accused held not to have satisfied actual innocence exception so as to allow federal habeas corpus consideration of successive and abusive claims challenging Louisiana death sentence, 120 L Ed 2d 269

ADMINISTRATIVE LAW
Bankruptcy: Federal District Court held not to have authority, in bankruptcy case, to enjoin Federal Reserve Board proceedings against debtor bank holding company for alleged banking law violations, 116 L Ed 2d 358

Census: allocation of overseas federal employees to home states, for purposes of congressional reapportionment, held (1) not final agency action reviewable under APA; and (2) not unconstitutional, 120 L Ed 2d 636

INDEX

ADMINISTRATIVE LAW—Cont'd

Deportation: INS rule, generally requiring that bond, on which excludible alien is released pending deportability determination, contain condition forbidding unauthorized employment, held not facially invalid, 116 L Ed 2d 546

Deportation proceedings: Equal Access to Justice Act (5 USCS § 504, 28 USCS § 2412) held not to authorize award of attorneys' fees for administrative deportation proceedings before Immigration and Naturalization Service, 116 L Ed 2d 496

Endangered Species Act: environmental groups held to lack standing to challenge regulation interpreting § 7(a)(2) of Endangered Species Act (16 USCS § 1536(a)(2)) not to apply to actions taken in foreign nations, 119 L Ed 2d 351

Freedom of Information Act: exemption 6 of FOIA held to authorize deletion of names and other identifying information from reports of interviews with Haitian nationals returned to Haiti after attempting illegal emigration, 116 L Ed 2d 526

Jones Act: maritime worker whose occupation of ship repairman was listed in Longshore and Harbor Workers' Compensation Act (33 USCS § 902(3)) held not precluded from being seaman under Jones Act (46 USCS Appx § 688), 116 L Ed 2d 405

ADOPTION ASSISTANCE AND CHILD WELFARE ACT OF 1980

Provision of Adoption Assistance and Child Welfare Act of 1980 (42 USCS § 671(a)(15)) held not enforceable in private action under 42 USCS § 1983 or in suit directly under Act, 118 L Ed 2d 1

ADOPTION OF PERSONS

Reimbursement: provision of Adoption Assistance and Child Welfare Act of 1980 (42 USCS § 671(a)(15)) held not enforceable in private action under 42 USCS § 1983 or in suit directly under Act, 118 L Ed 2d 1

AD VALOREM TAXES

Indian General Allotment Act of 1887 (25 USCS §§ 331 et seq.) held (1) to permit county ad valorem tax on fee-patented reservation land, but (2) not to allow county excise tax on sales of such land, 116 L Ed 2d 687

ADVERSARY ADJUDICATIONS
Deportation proceedings: Equal Access to Justice Act (5 USCS § 504, 28 USCS § 2412) held not to authorize award of attorneys' fees for administrative deportation proceedings before Immigration and Naturalization Service, 116 L Ed 2d 496

ADVERTISING
Airline fares: enforcement, through state consumer-protection laws, of restrictions on advertising of airline fares held preempted by provision of Airline Deregulation Act of 1978 (49 USCS Appx § 1305(a)(1)), 119 L Ed 2d 157

Cigarettes: federal cigarette labeling and advertising statutes held to preempt some but not all state-law damages claims with respect to cigarette smoking, 120 L Ed 2d 407

Labor unions: store owner held not to have committed unfair labor practice under § 8(a)(1) of National Labor Relations Act (29 USCS § 158(a)(1)) by barring nonemployee union organizers from parking lot, 117 L Ed 2d 79

AGENTS AND AGENCY
ERISA provision (29 USCS § 1002(6)) defining employee as any individual employed by an employer, held to incorporate traditional agency-law criteria for identifying master-servant relationships, 117 L Ed 2d 581

Income tax: state held not prohibited, under 15 USCS § 381(a), from imposing tax on gum manufacturer's income, where manufacturer's in-state activities include replacement, supply, and storage of gum, 120 L Ed 2d 174

AGGRAVATION OF PUNISHMENT
Mitigation or Aggravation of Punishment (this index)

AGREEMENTS
Contracts and Agreements (this index)

AID OR ASSISTANCE
Lesser sentence: Federal Government's refusal to request lesser sentence so as to reflect accused's substantial assistance in prosecuting another person held subject to review for constitutional violations, but particular accused held to have raised no claim to such review, 118 L Ed 2d 524

INDEX

AIRLINE DEREGULATION

Advertising: enforcement, through state consumer-protection laws, of restrictions on advertising of airline fares held preempted by provision of Airline Deregulation Act of 1978 (49 USCS Appx § 1305(a)(1)), 119 L Ed 2d 157

AIRPORTS

Literature distribution: regulation prohibiting repetitive distribution of literature within airport terminals operated by public authority held to violate First Amendment, 120 L Ed 2d 669

Solicitation: regulation prohibiting repetitive solicitation of money within airport terminals operated by public authority held reasonable and thus not violative of First Amendment, 120 L Ed 2d 541

ALIENS

Deportation or Exclusion of Aliens (this index)

ALLOTMENTS

Taxation: Indian General Allotment Act of 1887 (25 USCS §§ 331 et seq.) held (1) to permit county ad valorem tax on fee-patented reservation land, but (2) not to allow county excise tax on sales of such land, 116 L Ed 2d 687

ALTERATION OF BOUNDARIES

Disclaimer: Secretary of Army held authorized under § 10 of Rivers and Harbors Appropriation Act (33 USCS § 403) to condition approval of port construction on Alaska's disclaimer of federal-state boundary change, 118 L Ed 2d 222

AMBIGUITY

Certainty and Definiteness (this index)

AMENDMENT OF STATUTE OR ACT

Timber harvesting: provision that statute meets requirements of earlier statutes on which specified pending cases involving logging and endangered spotted owl are based, held not to violate Federal Constitution's Article III, 118 L Ed 2d 73

INDEX

AMTRAK

Acquisition of property: Interstate Commerce Commission held to have authority, under 45 USCS § 562(d)(1), to require conveyance of track from railroad to Amtrak for purpose of reconveying track to second railroad, 118 L Ed 2d 52

ANGER

First Amendment: city ordinance, banning display of symbols —including burning cross—that arouse anger in others on basis of race, color, creed, religion, or gender, held facially invalid under First Amendment, 120 L Ed 2d 305

ANIMALS

Endangered Species Act: environmental groups held to lack standing to challenge regulation interpreting § 7(a)(2) of Endangered Species Act (16 USCS § 1536(a)(2)) not to apply to actions taken in foreign nations, 119 L Ed 2d 351

ANTIPSYCHOTIC DRUGS

Nevada court's judgment upholding conviction reversed and remanded, where defendant claimed that forced administration of antipsychotic drug during trial violated rights under Sixth and Fourteenth Amendments, 118 L Ed 2d 479

ANTISOCIAL PERSONALITY

Mentally ill persons: Louisiana statute, permitting indefinite detention of insanity acquittees who are not mentally ill but who do not prove they would not be dangerous, held to violate Fourteenth Amendment's due process clause, 118 L Ed 2d 437

ANTITRUST LAWS
Restraints of Trade, Monopolies, and Unfair Trade Practices (this index)

APPEAL, ERROR AND REVIEW

Bankruptcy: Federal Court of Appeals held to have jurisdiction under 28 USCS § 1292 to review interlocutory order by Federal District Court sitting as appellate court in bankruptcy, 117 L Ed 2d 391

Bankruptcy: Federal District Court held not to have authority, in bankruptcy case, to enjoin Federal Reserve Board proceedings against debtor bank holding company for alleged banking law violations, 116 L Ed 2d 358

INDEX

ARMED FORCES—Cont'd

Veterans' Reemployment Rights Act: provision of Veterans' Reemployment Rights Act (38 USCS § 2024(d)) held not to limit length of military service after which member of Armed Forces retains right to civilian reemployment, 116 L Ed 2d 578

ARMY CORPS OF ENGINEERS

Boundaries: Secretary of Army held authorized under § 10 of Rivers and Harbors Appropriation Act (33 USCS § 403) to condition approval of port construction on Alaska's disclaimer of federal-state boundary change, 118 L Ed 2d 222

ARREST

Immunity: Secret Service agents held entitled to qualified immunity in lawsuit involving alleged unlawful arrest where agents had reasonable grounds to believe that arrestee had threatened President, 116 L Ed 2d 589

ARYAN BROTHERHOOD

Gang membership: introduction at capital sentencing proceeding of evidence as to defendant's membership in white racist prison gang held to violate First Amendment where evidence had no relevance to issues in proceeding, 117 L Ed 2d 309

ASSASSINATION OF PRESIDENT

Immunity: Secret Service agents held entitled to qualified immunity in lawsuit involving alleged unlawful arrest where agents had reasonable grounds to believe that arrestee had threatened President, 116 L Ed 2d 589

ASSEMBLIES

Public-speech permit fees: county ordinance empowering administrator to adjust public-speech permit fee based on amount of hostility likely to be created by speech's content held to violate First Amendment, 120 L Ed 2d 101

ASSESSMENTS
Value and Valuation (this index)

ASSIGNMENTS

Bankruptcy: trustee liquidating and distributing property as part of plan under Chapter 11 of Bankruptcy Code held required, as to income attributable to property, to file federal income tax returns and pay tax, 117 L Ed 2d 196

ASSIGNMENTS—Cont'd

ERISA: interest in ERISA-qualified pension plan held subject to transfer restriction under applicable nonbankruptcy law, and thus excludible from property of bankruptcy estate under 11 USCS § 541(c)(2), 119 L Ed 2d 519

ASSISTANCE OF COUNSEL

Attorneys at Law (this index)

ASSOCIATION, FREEDOM OF

Freedom of Association (this index)

ASYLUM

Deportation or Exclusion of Aliens (this index)

ATROCIOUS CONDUCT

Heinous, Atrocious, or Cruel Conduct (this index)

ATTACHMENT

Private defendants who invoke state replevin, garnishment, and attachment statutes that are declared unconstitutional, held not entitled to qualified immunity from suit under 42 USCS § 1983, 118 L Ed 2d 504

ATTORNEY GENERAL

Alien release bond: INS rule generally requiring that bond on which excludible alien is released, pending deportability determination, contain condition forbidding unauthorized employment held not facially invalid, 116 L Ed 2d 546

Credit for time served: federal sentencing credit under 18 USCS § 3585(b) for certain presentence time served held required to be computed by Attorney General after convicted federal defendant has begun to serve sentence, 117 L Ed 2d 593

Reopening deportation proceedings: Attorney General's denial of alien's motion to reopen deportation proceedings held not abuse of discretion, 116 L Ed 2d 823

ATTORNEYS AT LAW

Habeas corpus: federal habeas corpus petitioner, seeking evidentiary hearing on claim that material facts were not adequately developed in state proceedings, held generally required to show (1) cause for failure to develop facts, and (2) prejudice resulting from such failure, 118 L Ed 2d 318

INDEX

BANKRUPTCY—Cont'd
Taxation—Cont'd
– sovereign immunity of United States held not unequivocally waived with respect to bankruptcy trustee's claim against Internal Revenue Service for monetary relief, 117 L Ed 2d 181

Transfer of check, for purposes of determining whether transfer is voidable under 11 USCS § 547(b)(4)(A) as occurring within 90 days of bankruptcy filing, held to occur on date drawee bank honors check, 118 L Ed 2d 39

BASE LINES
Alterations: Secretary of Army held authorized under § 10 of Rivers and Harbors Appropriation Act (33 USCS § 403) to condition approval of port construction on Alaska's disclaimer of federal-state boundary change, 118 L Ed 2d 222

BATSON V KENTUCKY
Peremptory challenges: accused's objection under equal protection clause to state's race-based use of peremptory challenges prior to Supreme Court's decision in Batson v Kentucky held preserved for review by Supreme Court, 118 L Ed 2d 193

BATTERED CHILD SYNDROME
Due process: introduction of evidence to prove battered child syndrome at California murder trial for allegedly killing infant, and jury instruction as to evidence's use, held not to violate due process, 116 L Ed 2d 385

BATTERY
Judicial immunity: state judge held immune from 42 USCS § 1983 suit for money damages for alleged use of excessive force by police officers in bringing public defender into courtroom pursuant to judge's alleged order, 116 L Ed 2d 9

BEACHFRONT MANAGEMENT ACT
Eminent domain: South Carolina court held to have applied wrong standard in determining whether state beachfront management statute, by barring construction, effected taking of property under Fifth Amendment, 120 L Ed 2d 798

INDEX

BED OR BANK OF WATERS
Boundaries: Secretary of Army held authorized under § 10 of Rivers and Harbors Appropriation Act (33 USCS § 403) to condition approval of port construction on Alaska's disclaimer of federal-state boundary change, 118 L Ed 2d 222

BELIEF
Opinion or Belief (this index)

BENEDICTION PRAYERS
First Amendment: inclusion of invocation and benediction by member of clergy at public secondary school graduation held forbidden by First Amendment's establishment of religion clause, 120 L Ed 2d 467

BIRTH
Abortion: Pennsylvania abortion legislation held valid, except for spousal-notice provisions, under due process clause of Federal Constitution's Fourteenth Amendment, 120 L Ed 2d 674

BIVENS ACTIONS
Grievance procedures: federal prisoner held not required to exhaust Federal Bureau of Prisons' internal grievance procedure before initiating Bivens action solely for money damages, 117 L Ed 2d 291

Immunity: Secret Service agents held entitled to qualified immunity in lawsuit involving alleged unlawful arrest where agents had reasonable grounds to believe that arrestee had threatened President, 116 L Ed 2d 589

BONDS
Default: commercial exception in Foreign Sovereign Immunities Act held to authorize Federal District Court's jurisdiction over civil suit concerning Argentina's alleged default on certain public bonds, 119 L Ed 2d 394

Deportation: INS rule generally requiring that bond on which excludible alien is released, pending deportability determination, contain condition forbidding unauthorized employment held not facially invalid, 116 L Ed 2d 546

INDEX

BOOKS
Son of Sam laws: New York statute, requiring that criminal's income from books or other works describing crime be escrowed and made available to victims of crime, held inconsistent with Federal Constitutions's First Amendment, 116 L Ed 2d 476

BOUNDARIES
Rivers and Harbors Appropriation Act: Secretary of Army held authorized under § 10 of Rivers and Harbors Appropriation Act (33 USCS § 403) to condition approval of port construction on Alaska's disclaimer of federal-state boundary change, 118 L Ed 2d 222

BRIBERY
Hobbs Act: affirmative act of inducement by public official, such as demand, held not to be necessary element of Hobbs Act offense of extortion under color of official right (18 USCS § 1951(b)(2)), 119 L Ed 2d 57

BRIEFS
Notice of appeal: informal brief filed in Federal Court of Appeals held effective as notice of appeal under Rule 3 of Federal Rules of Appellate Procedure, if filing of brief is timely and conveys information required by Rule 3, 116 L Ed 2d 678

BROCHURES
Distribution: regulation prohibiting repetitive distribution of literature within airport terminals operated by public authority held to violate First Amendment, 120 L Ed 2d 669

BROKERS
Agents and Agency (this index)

BUILDING AND CONSTRUCTION WORK
Boundaries: Secretary of Army held authorized under § 10 of Rivers and Harbors Appropriation Act (33 USCS § 403) to condition approval of port construction on Alaska's disclaimer of federal-state boundary change, 118 L Ed 2d 222

BURDEN OF PROOF
Presumptions and Burden of Proof (this index)

INDEX

BUREAU OF ALCOHOL, TOBACCO, AND FIREARMS
Tax payment for making firearm held not required, under provision of National Firearms Act (26 USCS § 5821), where pistol and kit allowing conversion of pistol into firearm are packaged as unit, 119 L Ed 2d 308

BUSINESS AND COMMERCE
Commerce (this index)

BUSING
Desegregation: federal court in ongoing school desegregation case held to have discretion to order incremental withdrawal of supervision over Georgia school district, 118 L Ed 2d 108

BYLAWS
LMRDA claims: right to jury trial held applicable to union member's LMRDA claim; § 301(a) of LMRA held to grant federal jurisdiction over member's claim that local violated international union's constitution, 116 L Ed 2d 419

CAMPAIGNS
Extortion: affirmative act of inducement by public official, such as demand, held not to be necessary element of Hobbs Act offense of extortion under color of official right (18 USCS § 1951(b)(2)), 119 L Ed 2d 57

Solicitation of votes: Tennessee statute prohibiting solicitation of votes and display or distribution of campaign literature within 100 feet of entrance to polling place held not to violate First and Fourteenth Amendments, 119 L Ed 2d 5

CANDIDATES
Elections and Voting (this index)

CAPITAL EXPENDITURES
Income tax deductions: professional expenses incurred by target corporation in course of friendly takeover held not deductible by corporation as ordinary and necessary business expenses under § 162(a) of Internal Revenue Code (26 USCS § 162(a)), 117 L Ed 2d 226

CAPITAL OFFENSES AND PUNISHMENT
Aggravating circumstances: rule of decisions holding aggravating circumstances unconstitutionally vague in capital sentencing proceeding held retroactively available to support federal habeas corpus relief, 117 L Ed 2d 367

INDEX

CAUSE AND PREJUDICE STANDARD

Habeas corpus: federal habeas corpus petitioner, seeking evidentiary hearing on claim that material facts were not adequately developed in state proceedings, held generally required to show (1) cause for failure to develop facts, and (2) prejudice resulting from such failure, 118 L Ed 2d 318

CENSORSHIP

Cross burning: city ordinance, banning display of symbols—including burning cross—that arouse anger in others on basis of race, color, creed, religion, or gender, held facially invalid under First Amendment, 120 L Ed 2d 305

CENSUS

Allocation of overseas federal employees to home states, for purposes of congressional reapportionment, held (1) not final agency action reviewable under APA; and (2) not unconstitutional, 120 L Ed 2d 636

CERTAINTY AND DEFINITENESS

Juvenile Delinquency Act provision limiting detention to maximum term authorized for one convicted as adult held to refer to maximum sentence authorized under United States Sentencing Guidelines, 117 L Ed 2d 559

Mitigation or aggravation of punishment: imposition of death sentence by Florida trial court held to violate Eighth Amendment where jury rendering advisory verdict in sentencing hearing was instructed on invalid aggravating circumstance, 120 L Ed 2d 854

Railroads: Interstate Commerce Commission held to have authority, under 45 USCS § 562(d)(1), to require conveyance of track from railroad to Amtrak for purpose of reconveying track to second railroad, 118 L Ed 2d 52

Retroactivity: rule of decisions holding aggravating circumstances unconstitutionally vague in capital sentencing proceeding held retroactively available to support federal habeas corpus relief, 117 L Ed 2d 367

Weapons and firearms: tax payment for making firearm held not required, under provision of National Firearms Act (26 USCS § 5821), where pistol and kit allowing conversion of pistol into firearm are packaged as unit, 119 L Ed 2d 308

INDEX

CERTIORARI

Disclosure: United States Court of Appeals held to exceed its authority by imposing rule under which prosecutor must present to grand jury substantial exculpatory evidence in prosecutor's possession, 118 L Ed 2d 352

CHAPTER 7 PROCEEDINGS

Exemptions: bankruptcy trustee held barred, after expiration of 30-day period, from contesting validity of exemption claimed by debtor under 11 USCS § 522(*l*), despite lack of colorable basis for claim, 118 L Ed 2d 280

Payments on long-term debt held to qualify for ordinary course of business exception under 11 USCS § 547(c)(2) to bankruptcy trustee's power to avoid preferential transfers, 116 L Ed 2d 514

CHAPTER 11 PROCEEDINGS

Banks: Federal District Court held not to have authority, in bankruptcy case, to enjoin Federal Reserve Board proceedings against debtor bank holding company for alleged banking law violations, 116 L Ed 2d 358

CHARACTER AND REPUTATION

First Amendment: introduction at capital sentencing proceeding of evidence as to defendant's membership in white racist prison gang held to violate First Amendment where evidence had no relevance to issues in proceeding, 117 L Ed 2d 309

CHARGES

Fees and Expenses (this index)

CHARTERS

Jurisdiction: original federal court jurisdiction over all cases to which American National Red Cross is party held conferred by sue and be sued provision (36 USCS § 2) of Red Cross' federal corporate charter, 120 L Ed 2d 201

CHECKS AND DRAFTS

Bankruptcy: transfer of check, for purposes of determining whether transfer is voidable under 11 USCS § 547(b)(4)(A) as occurring within 90 days of bankruptcy filing, held to occur on date drawee bank honors check, 118 L Ed 2d 39

INDEX

CHILD ABUSE OR NEGLECT

Diversity jurisdiction: domestic relations exception to federal courts' diversity jurisdiction held inapplicable to woman's child-abuse tort claim against her former husband and his female companion, 119 L Ed 2d 468

Due process: introduction of evidence to prove battered child syndrome at California murder trial for allegedly killing infant, and jury instruction as to evidence's use, held not to violate due process, 116 L Ed 2d 385

Hearsay evidence: admission of testimony against accused under Illinois hearsay exceptions for spontaneous declarations and medical-treatment statements held not to violate Sixth Amendment's confrontation clause, 116 L Ed 2d 848

CHILD PROTECTION ACT OF 1984

Entrapment: government held to have failed, as matter of law, to establish that individual was predisposed to illegally receive mailing of sexually explicit depictions of children and hence was not entrapped, 118 L Ed 2d 174

CHILDREN AND MINORS

Abortion: Pennsylvania abortion legislation held valid, except for spousal-notice provisions, under due process clause of Federal Constitution's Fourteenth Amendment, 120 L Ed 2d 674

Child Abuse or Neglect (this index)

Child Protection Act of 1984: government held to have failed, as matter of law, to establish that individual was predisposed to illegally receive mailing of sexually explicit depictions of children and hence was not entrapped, 118 L Ed 2d 174

Entrapment: government held to have failed, as matter of law, to establish that individual was predisposed to illegally receive mailing of sexually explicit depictions of children and hence was not entrapped, 118 L Ed 2d 174

Foster care and adoption: provision of Adoption Assistance and Child Welfare Act of 1980 (42 USCS § 671(a)(15)) held not enforceable in private action under 42 USCS § 1983 or in suit directly under Act, 118 L Ed 2d 1

Juvenile Delinquency Act provision limiting detention to maximum term authorized for one convicted as adult held to refer to maximum sentence authorized under United States Sentencing Guidelines, 117 L Ed 2d 559

INDEX

CIGARETTE LABELING AND ADVERTISING ACT OF 1965

Preemption federal cigarette labeling and advertising statutes held to preempt some but not all state-law damages claims with respect to cigarette smoking, 120 L Ed 2d 407

CIRCULARS, BROCHURES, AND PAMPHLETS

Airport distribution: regulation prohibiting repetitive distribution of literature within airport terminals operated by public authority held to violate First Amendment, 120 L Ed 2d 669

CIVIL PROCEDURE RULES

Consent decree: clear showing of grievous wrong evoked by new and unforeseen conditions, held not required, under Federal Civil Procedure Rule 60(b), to modify consent decree stemming from institutional reform litigation, 116 L Ed 2d 867

Sanctions: Federal District Court held authorized to impose sanctions pursuant to Rule 11 of Federal Rules of Civil Procedure, even though court is later determined to lack subject matter jurisdiction, 117 L Ed 2d 280

Sherman Act: photocopier manufacturer held not entitled to summary judgment dismissing federal antitrust claims as to (1) tying arrangement between parts and service, and (2) monopolization of sale of service, 119 L Ed 2d 265

CIVIL RIGHTS ACT OF 1871

Replevin: private defendants who invoke state replevin, garnishment, and attachment statutes that are declared unconstitutional, held not entitled to qualified immunity from suit under 42 USCS § 1983, 118 L Ed 2d 504

CIVIL RIGHTS ACT OF 1964

Desegregation: several aspects of Mississippi's public university system held suspect for purposes of determining whether state had complied with its duty to desegregate, 120 L Ed 2d 575

Income tax: backpay received in settlement of claims under Title VII of Civil Rights Act of 1964 held not excludible from gross income under § 104(a)(2) of Internal Revenue Code as damages for personal injuries, 119 L Ed 2d 34

INDEX

CIVIL RIGHTS AND DISCRIMINATION

Business tax: Iowa business tax statute's treatment of corporation's dividends received from foreign subsidiary held to violate Federal Constitution's foreign commerce clause, 120 L Ed 2d 59

Civil Rights Act of 1871: private defendants who invoke state replevin, garnishment, and attachment statutes that are declared unconstitutional, held not entitled to qualified immunity from suit under 42 USCS § 1983, 118 L Ed 2d 504

Civil Rights Act of 1964 (this index)

Coal-fired electric utilities: Oklahoma statute requiring coal-fired electric utilities to burn mixture containing at least 10 percent Oklahoma-mined coal held to violate Federal Constitution's commerce clause (Art I, § 8, cl 3), 117 L Ed 2d 1

Cruel and unusual punishment: prisoner held able to maintain claim of cruel and unusual punishment under Federal Constitution's Eighth Amendment based on officers' excessive use of force not resulting in serious injury, 117 L Ed 2d 156

Foster care and adoption: provision of Adoption Assistance and Child Welfare Act of 1980 (42 USCS § 671(a)(15)) held not enforceable in private action under 42 USCS § 1983 or in suit directly under Act, 118 L Ed 2d 1

Immunity: state officials held subject to personal liability for damages under 42 USCS § 1983 based on official acts, where § 1983 actions were brought against officials in their individual capacities, 116 L Ed 2d 301

Income tax

– backpay received in settlement of claims under Title VII of Civil Rights Act of 1964 held not excludible from gross income under § 104(a)(2) of Internal Revenue Code as damages for personal injuries, 119 L Ed 2d 34

– Kansas' income tax on military retirement benefits, but not on state and local government retirement benefits, held inconsistent with 4 USCS § 111 prohibition against discriminatory taxes, 118 L Ed 2d 243

Lesser sentence: Federal Government's refusal to request lesser sentence so as to reflect accused's substantial assistance in prosecuting another person held subject to review for constitutional violations, but particular accused held to have raised no claim to such review, 118 L Ed 2d 524

482

INDEX

CIVIL RIGHTS REMEDIES EQUALIZATION AMENDMENT OF 1986

Sex discrimination: damages remedy held available in sex discrimination action under Title IX of Education Amendments of 1972 (20 USCS §§ 1681-1688), 117 L Ed 2d 208

CIVIL RIGHTS RESTORATION ACT OF 1987

Sex discrimination: damages remedy held available in sex discrimination action under Title IX of Education Amendments of 1972 (20 USCS §§ 1681-1688), 117 L Ed 2d 208

CIVIL SERVICE

Retirement benefits: Kansas' income tax on military retirement benefits, but not on state and local government retirement benefits, held inconsistent with 4 USCS § 111 prohibition against discriminatory taxes, 118 L Ed 2d 243

CLAIMS AGAINST GOVERNMENT

Punitive damages: Federal Tort Claims Act ban on awards of punitive damages (28 USCS § 2674) held to apply to only damages legally considered punitive under traditional common-law principles, 116 L Ed 2d 731

CLASSIFICATION

Property taxes: equal protection held not violated by California Constitution's real property tax system which generally assesses property on value at time of acquisition, rather than on current value, 120 L Ed 2d 1

CLEAN WATER ACT

Attorneys' fees: enhancement of attorneys' fees above lodestar, to reflect contingent fee agreement, held not permitted in awards under environmental fee-shifting statutes (33 USCS § 1365(d), 42 USCS § 6972(e)), 120 L Ed 2d 449

Boundaries: Secretary of Army held authorized under § 10 of Rivers and Harbors Appropriation Act (33 USCS § 403) to condition approval of port construction on Alaska's disclaimer of federal-state boundary change, 118 L Ed 2d 222

EPA's issuance of discharge permit to sewage plant, based on finding that discharges would not cause detectable violation of downstream state's water quality standards, held authorized by Clean Water Act, 117 L Ed 2d 239

CLEAN WATER ACT—Cont'd

Sovereign immunity: federal sovereign immunity held not waived as to state-imposed punitive fines under Clean Water Act (33 USCS §§ 1251 et seq.) and Resource Conservation and Recovery Act (42 USCS §§ 6901 et seq.), 118 L Ed 2d 255

CLEAR STATEMENT RULE

Federal Employers' Liability Act (45 USCS §§ 51-60) held to create cause of action, enforceable in state court, against state-owned railroad, 116 L Ed 2d 560

CLERGY

Religious freedom: inclusion of invocation and benediction by member of clergy at public secondary school graduation held forbidden by First Amendment's establishment of religion clause, 120 L Ed 2d 467

COAL-FIRED ELECTRIC UTILITIES

Commerce clause: Oklahoma statute requiring coal-fired electric utilities to burn mixture containing at least 10 percent Oklahoma-mined coal held to violate Federal Constitution's commerce clause (Art I, § 8, cl 3), 117 L Ed 2d 1

COAST OR COASTAL WATERS

Boundaries: Secretary of Army held authorized under § 10 of Rivers and Harbors Appropriation Act (33 USCS § 403) to condition approval of port construction on Alaska's disclaimer of federal-state boundary change, 118 L Ed 2d 222

Eminent domain: South Carolina court held to have applied wrong standard in determining whether state beachfront management statute, by barring construction, effected taking of property under Fifth Amendment, 120 L Ed 2d 798

COERCION OR FORCE

Duress or Coercion (this index)

COLDNESS FACTOR

Mitigation or aggravation of punishment: Florida trial judge's improper weighing in capital sentencing hearing of aggravating factor not supported by evidence, in violation of Eighth Amendment, held not cured by state appellate review, 119 L Ed 2d 326

INDEX

COLLECTIVE BARGAINING
Jury trial: right to jury trial held applicable to union member's LMRDA claim; § 301(a) of LMRA held to grant federal jurisdiction over member's claim that local violated international union's constitution, 116 L Ed 2d 419

LMRDA claims: right to jury trial held applicable to union member's LMRDA claim; § 301(a) of LMRA held to grant federal jurisdiction over member's claim that local violated international union's constitution, 116 L Ed 2d 419

Unfair labor practices: store owner held not to have committed unfair labor practice under § 8(a)(1) of National Labor Relations Act (29 USCS § 158(a)(1)) by barring nonemployee union organizers from parking lot, 117 L Ed 2d 79

Workers' compensation: state-mandated payment of workers' compensation benefits withheld under benefit coordination statute held not to violate contract clause or due process clause of Federal Constitution, 117 L Ed 2d 328

COLLEGES AND UNIVERSITIES
Schools and Education (this index)

COLORABLE CLAIM OF INNOCENCE
Stay of execution: application for stay of execution denied where Federal District Court found that alleged exculpatory evidence produced by defense did not amount to colorable claim of innocence, 119 L Ed 2d 1

COLOR OF LAW
Immunity: state officials held subject to personal liability for damages under 42 USCS § 1983 based on official acts, where § 1983 actions were brought against officials in their individual capacities, 116 L Ed 2d 301

COLOR OF RIGHT, TITLE, OR OFFICE
Extortion: affirmative act of inducement by public official, such as demand, held not to be necessary element of Hobbs Act offense of extortion under color of official right (18 USCS § 1951(b)(2)), 119 L Ed 2d 57

Replevin: private defendants who invoke state replevin, garnishment, and attachment statutes that are declared unconstitutional, held not entitled to qualified immunity from suit under 42 USCS § 1983, 118 L Ed 2d 504

COMMERCE
Commerce Clause (this index)

486

COMMERCE—Cont'd
Common Carriers (this index)

Income tax: state held not prohibited, under 15 USCS § 381(a), from imposing tax on gum manufacturer's income, where manufacturer's in-state activities include replacement, supply, and storage of gum, 120 L Ed 2d 174

Income tax deductions: professional expenses incurred by target corporation in course of friendly takeover held not deductible by corporation as ordinary and necessary business expenses under § 162(a) of Internal Revenue Code (26 USCS § 162(a)), 117 L Ed 2d 226

COMMERCE CLAUSE

Business tax: Iowa business tax statute's treatment of corporation's dividends received from foreign subsidiary held to violate Federal Constitution's foreign commerce clause, 120 L Ed 2d 59

Coal-fired electric utilities: Oklahoma statute requiring coal-fired electric utilities to burn mixture containing at least 10 percent Oklahoma-mined coal held to violate Federal Constitution's commerce clause (Art I, § 8, cl 3), 117 L Ed 2d 1

Hazardous waste disposal fees: disposal fee imposed by Alabama on hazardous waste generated out of state, but not on waste generated in state, held to violate Federal Constitution's commerce clause (Art I, § 8, cl 3), 119 L Ed 2d 121

Mail-order business: Federal Constitution's commerce clause (Art I, § 8, cl 3), but not due process clause of Fourteenth Amendment, held to bar enforcement of North Dakota use tax against out-of-state mail-order house, 119 L Ed 2d 91

Solid waste: Michigan statute barring private landfill owner from accepting solid waste originating outside county in which landfill was located held to violate Federal Constitution's commerce clause (Art I, § 8, cl 3), 119 L Ed 2d 139

Taxation: unitary business principle held to (1) govern states' federal constitutional power to tax nondomiciliary corporations' income, and (2) prevent state's taxation of gain on particular stock sale, 119 L Ed 2d 533

Waste disposal: state take title provision of Low-Level Radioactive Waste Policy Amendments Act of 1985 (42 USCS § 2021e(d)(2)(C)) held to violate Tenth Amendment, but to be severable from remainder of Act, 120 L Ed 2d 120

INDEX

COMMERCE SECRETARY

Census: allocation of overseas federal employees to home states, for purposes of congressional reapportionment, held (1) not final agency action reviewable under APA; and (2) not unconstitutional, 120 L Ed 2d 636

COMMITMENT OF PERSONS

Indefinite detention: Louisiana statute, permitting indefinite detention of insanity acquittees who are not mentally ill but who do not prove they would not be dangerous, held to violate Fourteenth Amendment's due process clause, 118 L Ed 2d 437

COMMON CARRIERS

Federal Employers' Liability Act (45 USCS §§ 51-60) held to create cause of action, enforceable in state court, against state-owned railroad, 116 L Ed 2d 560

Railroads: Interstate Commerce Commission held to have authority, under 45 USCS § 562(d)(1), to require conveyance of track from railroad to Amtrak for purpose of reconveying track to second railroad, 118 L Ed 2d 52

Use tax: Federal Constitution's commerce clause (Art I, § 8, cl 3), but not due process clause of Fourteenth Amendment, held to bar enforcement of North Dakota use tax against out-of-state mail-order house, 119 L Ed 2d 91

COMMON LAW

ERISA provision (29 USCS § 1002(6)) defining employee as any individual employed by an employer, held to incorporate traditional agency-law criteria for identifying master-servant relationships, 117 L Ed 2d 581

Hearsay evidence: admission of testimony against accused under Illinois hearsay exceptions for spontaneous declarations and medical-treatment statements held not to violate Sixth Amendment's confrontation clause, 116 L Ed 2d 848

Punitive damages: Federal Tort Claims Act ban on awards of punitive damages (28 USCS § 2674) held to apply to only damages legally considered punitive under traditional common-law principles, 116 L Ed 2d 731

COMMUNICATIONS

Labor unions: store owner held not to have committed unfair labor practice under § 8(a)(1) of National Labor Relations Act (29 USCS § 158(a)(1)) by barring nonemployee union organizers from parking lot, 117 L Ed 2d 79

INDEX

COMPELLING INTEREST TEST

Son of Sam laws: New York statute, requiring that criminal's income from books or other works describing crime be escrowed and made available to victims of crime, held inconsistent with Federal Constitutions's First Amendment, 116 L Ed 2d 476

COMPENSATION

Damages (this index)

Eminent domain: South Carolina court held to have applied wrong standard in determining whether state beachfront management statute, by barring construction, effected taking of property under Fifth Amendment, 120 L Ed 2d 798

Income Tax (this index)

Longshore and Harbor Workers' Compensation Act: forfeiture provision of Longshore and Harbor Workers' Compensation Act (33 USCS § 933(g)) held to apply where worker not then receiving or awarded compensation from employer settles third-party claim, 120 L Ed 2d 379

Lost wages: state-mandated payment of workers' compensation benefits withheld under benefit coordination statute held not to violate contract clause or due process clause of Federal Constitution, 117 L Ed 2d 328

Pensions and Retirement Benefits (this index)

Railroads: Interstate Commerce Commission held to have authority, under 45 USCS § 562(d)(1), to require conveyance of track from railroad to Amtrak for purpose of reconveying track to second railroad, 118 L Ed 2d 52

Rent control: mobile home rent control ordinance, viewed in context of California statute restricting termination of mobile home park tenancy, held not to constitute physical taking under Fifth Amendment, 118 L Ed 2d 153

Son of Sam laws: New York statute, requiring that criminal's income from books or other works describing crime be escrowed and made available to victims of crime, held inconsistent with Federal Constitutions's First Amendment, 116 L Ed 2d 476

Workers' Compensation (this index)

INDEX

COMPETENCY TO STAND TRIAL
Burden of proof: California statute, requiring that criminal defendant bear burden of proving incompetence to stand trial by preponderance of evidence, held not to violate due process, 120 L Ed 2d 353

COMPETITION
Restraints of Trade, Monopolies, and Unfair Trade Practices (this index)

COMPLAINTS
Bivens action: federal prisoner held not required to exhaust Federal Bureau of Prisons' internal grievance procedure before initiating Bivens action solely for money damages, 117 L Ed 2d 291

Disclosure: United States Court of Appeals held to exceed its authority by imposing rule under which prosecutor must present to grand jury substantial exculpatory evidence in prosecutor's possession, 118 L Ed 2d 352

COMPROMISE AND SETTLEMENT
Longshore and Harbor Workers' Compensation Act: forfeiture provision of Longshore and Harbor Workers' Compensation Act (33 USCS § 933(g)) held to apply where worker not then receiving or awarded compensation from employer settles third-party claim, 120 L Ed 2d 379

CONDEMNATION
Eminent Domain (this index)

CONDITIONAL DISCHARGE
Mentally ill persons: Louisiana statute, permitting indefinite detention of insanity acquittees who are not mentally ill but who do not prove they would not be dangerous, held to violate Fourteenth Amendment's due process clause, 118 L Ed 2d 437

CONFIDENTIALITY
Freedom of Information Act: exemption 6 of FOIA held to authorize deletion of names and other identifying information from reports of interviews with Haitian nationals returned to Haiti after attempting illegal emigration, 116 L Ed 2d 526

INDEX

CONFINEMENT
Prisons and Prisoners (this index)

CONFRONTATION OF WITNESSES
Hearsay evidence: admission of testimony against accused under Illinois hearsay exceptions for spontaneous declarations and medical-treatment statements held not to violate Sixth Amendment's confrontation clause, 116 L Ed 2d 848

CONGRESS
Apportionment of members of Congress among several states according to method of equal proportions under 2 USCS § 2a held not to violate Article I, § 2 of Federal Constitution, 118 L Ed 2d 87

Census: allocation of overseas federal employees to home states, for purposes of congressional reapportionment, held (1) not final agency action reviewable under APA; and (2) not unconstitutional, 120 L Ed 2d 636

CONSCRIPTION
Asylum: Guatemalan guerrillas' attempt to coerce Guatemalan into military service held not necessarily to constitute persecution on account of political opinion so as to make Guatemalan eligible for asylum in United States, 117 L Ed 2d 38

CONSENT
Abortion: Pennsylvania abortion legislation held valid, except for spousal-notice provisions, under due process clause of Federal Constitution's Fourteenth Amendment, 120 L Ed 2d 674

CONSENT JUDGMENT OR DECREE
Consent decree: clear showing of grievous wrong evoked by new and unforeseen conditions, held not required, under Federal Civil Procedure Rule 60(b), to modify consent decree stemming from institutional reform litigation, 116 L Ed 2d 867

CONSERVATION
Environmental Law (this index)
Wildlife Conservation (this index)

491

INDEX

CONSPIRACY

Double jeopardy held not to bar federal conspiracy prosecution where some overt acts were based on substantive offenses for which defendant was previously convicted, 118 L Ed 2d 25

Due process held not to require that general guilty verdict on federal multiple conspiracy charge be set aside if evidence is inadequate to support conviction as to one object, 116 L Ed 2d 371

Stock manipulation: Securities Investor Protection Corp. held unable to maintain RICO suit under 18 USCS § 1964(c) against party to scheme that allegedly disabled broker-dealers from meeting obligations to customers, 117 L Ed 2d 532

CONSTRUCTION AND INTERPRETATION

Abduction: forcible abduction of Mexican citizen to United States held not to violate extradition treaty with Mexico, and thus, not to prohibit citizen's trial in Federal District Court on criminal charges, 119 L Ed 2d 441

Airline fares: enforcement, through state consumer-protection laws, of restrictions on advertising of airline fares held preempted by provision of Airline Deregulation Act of 1978 (49 USCS Appx § 1305(a)(1)), 119 L Ed 2d 157

Alien release bond: INS rule generally requiring that bond on which excludible alien is released, pending deportability determination, contain condition forbidding unauthorized employment held not facially invalid, 116 L Ed 2d 546

Attorneys' fees: Equal Access to Justice Act (5 USCS § 504, 28 USCS § 2412) held not to authorize award of attorneys' fees for administrative deportation proceedings before Immigration and Naturalization Service, 116 L Ed 2d 496

Bankruptcy: debtor in bankruptcy held not entitled under 11 USCS § 506(d) to strip down creditor's lien on real property to judicially determined value of collateral, 116 L Ed 2d 903

Clean Water Act: federal sovereign immunity held not waived as to state-imposed punitive fines under Clean Water Act (33 USCS §§ 1251 et seq.) and Resource Conservation and Recovery Act (42 USCS §§ 6901 et seq.), 118 L Ed 2d 255

492

INDEX

CONSTRUCTION AND INTERPRETATION—Cont'd

Credit for time served: federal sentencing credit under 18 USCS § 3585(b) for certain presentence time served held required to be computed by Attorney General after convicted federal defendant has begun to serve sentence, 117 L Ed 2d 593

Diversity jurisdiction: domestic relations exception to federal courts' diversity jurisdiction held inapplicable to woman's child-abuse tort claim against her former husband and his female companion, 119 L Ed 2d 468

Endangered Species Act: environmental groups held to lack standing to challenge regulation interpreting § 7(a)(2) of Endangered Species Act (16 USCS § 1536(a)(2)) not to apply to actions taken in foreign nations, 119 L Ed 2d 351

ERISA: interest in ERISA-qualified pension plan held subject to transfer restriction under applicable nonbankruptcy law, and thus excludible from property of bankruptcy estate under 11 USCS § 541(c)(2), 119 L Ed 2d 519

Extortion: affirmative act of inducement by public official, such as demand, held not to be necessary element of Hobbs Act offense of extortion under color of official right (18 USCS § 1951(b)(2)), 119 L Ed 2d 57

Federal Employers' Liability Act (45 USCS §§ 51-60) held to create cause of action, enforceable in state court, against state-owned railroad, 116 L Ed 2d 560

Immunity: Secret Service agents held entitled to qualified immunity in lawsuit involving alleged unlawful arrest where agents had reasonable grounds to believe that arrestee had threatened President, 116 L Ed 2d 589

Indian General Allotment Act of 1887 (25 USCS §§ 331 et seq.) held (1) to permit county ad valorem tax on fee-patented reservation land, but (2) not to allow county excise tax on sales of such land, 116 L Ed 2d 687

Interlocutory review: Federal Court of Appeals held to have jurisdiction under 28 USCS § 1292 to review interlocutory order by Federal District Court sitting as appellate court in bankruptcy, 117 L Ed 2d 391

Internal Revenue Service: sovereign immunity of United States held not unequivocally waived with respect to bankruptcy trustee's claim against Internal Revenue Service for monetary relief, 117 L Ed 2d 181

CONSTRUCTION AND INTERPRETATION—Cont'd

Juvenile Delinquency Act provision limiting detention to maximum term authorized for one convicted as adult held to refer to maximum sentence authorized under United States Sentencing Guidelines, 117 L Ed 2d 559

Longshore and Harbor Workers' Compensation Act: forfeiture provision of Longshore and Harbor Workers' Compensation Act (33 USCS § 933(g)) held to apply where worker not then receiving or awarded compensation from employer settles third-party claim, 120 L Ed 2d 379

Public-speech permit fees: county ordinance empowering administrator to adjust public-speech permit fee based on amount of hostility likely to be created by speech's content held to violate First Amendment, 120 L Ed 2d 101

Railroads: Interstate Commerce Commission held to have authority, under 45 USCS § 562(d)(1), to require conveyance of track from railroad to Amtrak for purpose of reconveying track to second railroad, 118 L Ed 2d 52

Veterans' Reemployment Rights Act: provision of Veterans' Reemployment Rights Act (38 USCS § 2024(d)) held not to limit length of military service after which member of Armed Forces retains right to civilian reemployment, 116 L Ed 2d 578

CONSTRUCTION WORK

Boundaries: Secretary of Army held authorized under § 10 of Rivers and Harbors Appropriation Act (33 USCS § 403) to condition approval of port construction on Alaska's disclaimer of federal-state boundary change, 118 L Ed 2d 222

CONSULTATION

Endangered Species Act: environmental groups held to lack standing to challenge regulation interpreting § 7(a)(2) of Endangered Species Act (16 USCS § 1536(a)(2)) not to apply to actions taken in foreign nations, 119 L Ed 2d 351

CONSUMER PROTECTION

Airline fares: enforcement, through state consumer-protection laws, of restrictions on advertising of airline fares held preempted by provision of Airline Deregulation Act of 1978 (49 USCS Appx § 1305(a)(1)), 119 L Ed 2d 157

INDEX

CONTACTS
Use tax: Federal Constitution's commerce clause (Art I, § 8, cl 3), but not due process clause of Fourteenth Amendment, held to bar enforcement of North Dakota use tax against out-of-state mail-order house, 119 L Ed 2d 91

CONTINGENT FEES
Attorneys' fees (this index)

CONTINUING CONSENT THEORY
Appeals: Federal Government's 30-day appeal period held to have begun to run on date of Federal District Court's order denying motion to reconsider prior order suppressing evidence in pending criminal trial, 116 L Ed 2d 1

CONTRACT CLAUSE
Workers' compensation: state-mandated payment of workers' compensation benefits withheld under benefit coordination statute held not to violate contract clause or due process clause of Federal Constitution, 117 L Ed 2d 328

CONTRACTS AND AGREEMENTS
ERISA provision (29 USCS § 1002(6)) defining employee as any individual employed by an employer, held to incorporate traditional agency-law criteria for identifying master-servant relationships, 117 L Ed 2d 581

LMRDA claims: right to jury trial held applicable to union member's LMRDA claim; § 301(a) of LMRA held to grant federal jurisdiction over member's claim that local violated international union's constitution, 116 L Ed 2d 419

Son of Sam laws: New York statute, requiring that criminal's income from books or other works describing crime be escrowed and made available to victims of crime, held inconsistent with Federal Constitutions's First Amendment, 116 L Ed 2d 476

Workers' compensation: state-mandated payment of workers' compensation benefits withheld under benefit coordination statute held not to violate contract clause or due process clause of Federal Constitution, 117 L Ed 2d 328

CONTRIBUTIONS
Extortion: affirmative act of inducement by public official, such as demand, held not to be necessary element of Hobbs Act offense of extortion under color of official right (18 USCS § 1951(b)(2)), 119 L Ed 2d 57

CONTROVERSY
Coal-fired electric utilities: Oklahoma statute requiring coal-fired electric utilities to burn mixture containing at least 10 percent Oklahoma-mined coal held to violate Federal Constitution's commerce clause (Art I, § 8, cl 3), 117 L Ed 2d 1

CONVENTION ON THE TERRITORIAL SEA AND THE CONTIGUOUS ZONE
Boundaries: Secretary of Army held authorized under § 10 of Rivers and Harbors Appropriation Act (33 USCS § 403) to condition approval of port construction on Alaska's disclaimer of federal-state boundary change, 118 L Ed 2d 222

CONVERSION KITS
Weapons and firearms: tax payment for making firearm held not required, under provision of National Firearms Act (26 USCS § 5821), where pistol and kit allowing conversion of pistol into firearm are packaged as unit, 119 L Ed 2d 308

CONVEYANCE OF PROPERTY
Sale or Transfer of Property (this index)

CORPORATIONS
Bankruptcy: trustee liquidating and distributing property as part of plan under Chapter 11 of Bankruptcy Code held required, as to income attributable to property, to file federal income tax returns and pay tax, 117 L Ed 2d 196
Municipal Corporations and Other Political Subdivisions (this index)
Nondomiciliary Corporations (this index)
Red Cross: original federal court jurisdiction over all cases to which American National Red Cross is party held conferred by sue and be sued provision (36 USCS § 2) of Red Cross' federal corporate charter, 120 L Ed 2d 201
Stock and Stockholders (this index)
Takeover expenses: professional expenses incurred by target corporation in course of friendly takeover held not deductible by corporation as ordinary and necessary business expenses under § 162(a) of Internal Revenue Code (26 USCS § 162(a)), 117 L Ed 2d 226

496

INDEX

CORPORATIONS—Cont'd

Taxes: Iowa business tax statute's treatment of corporation's dividends received from foreign subsidiary held to violate Federal Constitution's foreign commerce clause, 120 L Ed 2d 59

CORRUPTION

Extortion: affirmative act of inducement by public official, such as demand, held not to be necessary element of Hobbs Act offense of extortion under color of official right (18 USCS § 1951(b)(2)), 119 L Ed 2d 57

COSTS

Fees and Expenses (this index)

COUNTIES

Preclearance: changes in decisionmaking powers of elected members of Alabama county commissions held not to be changes with respect to voting subject to preclearance requirements of § 5 of Voting Rights Act (42 USCS § 1973c), 117 L Ed 2d 51

Solid waste: Michigan statute barring private landfill owner from accepting solid waste originating outside county in which landfill was located held to violate Federal Constitution's commerce clause (Art I, § 8, cl 3), 119 L Ed 2d 139

Venue: equal protection held not violated by Montana venue rules allowing civil suit against Montana corporation in only county of principal place of business, but against foreign corporation in any county, 119 L Ed 2d 432

CREDIT FOR TIME SERVED

Federal sentencing credit under 18 USCS § 3585(b) for certain presentence time served held required to be computed by Attorney General after convicted federal defendant has begun to serve sentence, 117 L Ed 2d 593

CREDITOR

Debtor and Creditor (this index)

CREDITS

Taxation: Iowa business tax statute's treatment of corporation's dividends received from foreign subsidiary held to violate Federal Constitution's foreign commerce clause, 120 L Ed 2d 59

497

INDEX

CRIME VICTIMS BOARD
Son of Sam laws: New York statute, requiring that criminal's income from books or other works describing crime be escrowed and made available to victims of crime, held inconsistent with Federal Constitutions's First Amendment, 116 L Ed 2d 476

CRIMINAL LAW
As to particular crimes or procedures, see more specific topics

CRIMINAL RECORD
Reviewing court held authorized, in appropriate circumstances, to affirm sentence in which Federal District Court's departure from Sentencing Guidelines' range is based on valid and invalid factors, 117 L Ed 2d 341

CROSS BURNING
First amendment: city ordinance, banning display of symbols—including burning cross—that arouse anger in others on basis of race, color, creed, religion, or gender, held facially invalid under First Amendment, 120 L Ed 2d 305

CROWD CONTROL
Airport solicitations: regulation prohibiting repetitive solicitation of money within airport terminals operated by public authority held reasonable and thus not violative of First Amendment, 120 L Ed 2d 541

CRUEL AND UNUSUAL PUNISHMENT
Aggravating circumstances: rule of decisions holding aggravating circumstances unconstitutionally vague in capital sentencing proceeding held retroactively available to support federal habeas corpus relief, 117 L Ed 2d 367

Bivens action: federal prisoner held not required to exhaust Federal Bureau of Prisons' internal grievance procedure before initiating Bivens action solely for money damages, 117 L Ed 2d 291

Capital Offenses and Punishment (this index)

Excessive use of force: prisoner held able to maintain claim of cruel and unusual punishment under Federal Constitution's Eighth Amendment based on officers' excessive use of force not resulting in serious injury, 117 L Ed 2d 156

Federal Sentencing Guidelines (this index)

498

CRUEL AND UNUSUAL PUNISHMENT—Cont'd

Habeas corpus: application to vacate stay of accused's execution by cyanide gas in California granted by Supreme Court, where accused had not challenged method of execution in prior habeas corpus petitions, 118 L Ed 2d 293

Mitigation or Aggravation of Punishment (this index)

Prisons and Prisoners (this index)

CRUEL CONDUCT

Heinous, Atrocious, or Cruel Conduct (this index)

DAMAGES

Bivens action: federal prisoner held not required to exhaust Federal Bureau of Prisons' internal grievance procedure before initiating Bivens action solely for money damages, 117 L Ed 2d 291

Federal Employers' Liability Act (45 USCS §§ 51-60) held to create cause of action, enforceable in state court, against state-owned railroad, 116 L Ed 2d 560

Federal Tort Claims Act ban on awards of punitive damages (28 USCS § 2674) held to apply to only damages legally considered punitive under traditional common-law principles, 116 L Ed 2d 731

Income tax: backpay received in settlement of claims under Title VII of Civil Rights Act of 1964 held not excludible from gross income under § 104(a)(2) of Internal Revenue Code as damages for personal injuries, 119 L Ed 2d 34

Judicial immunity: state judge held immune from 42 USCS § 1983 suit for money damages for alleged use of excessive force by police officers in bringing public defender into courtroom pursuant to judge's alleged order, 116 L Ed 2d 9

LMRDA claims: right to jury trial held applicable to union member's LMRDA claim; § 301(a) of LMRA held to grant federal jurisdiction over member's claim that local violated international union's constitution, 116 L Ed 2d 419

Sex discrimination: damages remedy held available in sex discrimination action under Title IX of Education Amendments of 1972 (20 USCS §§ 1681-1688), 117 L Ed 2d 208

DATE

Time or Date (this index)

INDEX

DEATH
Capital Offenses and Punishment (this index)
Federal Tort Claims Act ban on awards of punitive damages (28 USCS § 2674) held to apply to only damages legally considered punitive under traditional common-law principles, 116 L Ed 2d 731

DEATH PENALTY TASK FORCE
Mandamus to compel Federal Court of Appeals to issue decision on second habeas corpus petition by state prisoner condemned to death, denied where state failed to object to order delaying decision, 116 L Ed 2d 669

DEBTOR AND CREDITOR
Bankruptcy (this index)
Default: commercial exception in Foreign Sovereign Immunities Act held to authorize Federal District Court's jurisdiction over civil suit concerning Argentina's alleged default on certain public bonds, 119 L Ed 2d 394
ERISA: interest in ERISA-qualified pension plan held subject to transfer restriction under applicable nonbankruptcy law, and thus excludible from property of bankruptcy estate under 11 USCS § 541(c)(2), 119 L Ed 2d 519

DECEIT
Fraud and Deceit (this index)

DECENNIAL CENSUS
Reapportionment: allocation of overseas federal employees to home states, for purposes of congressional reapportionment, held (1) not final agency action reviewable under APA; and (2) not unconstitutional, 120 L Ed 2d 636

DECEPTIVE ADVERTISING
Airline fares: enforcement, through state consumer-protection laws, of restrictions on advertising of airline fares held preempted by provision of Airline Deregulation Act of 1978 (49 USCS Appx § 1305(a)(1)), 119 L Ed 2d 157

DEDUCTIONS
Corporate takeover: professional expenses incurred by target corporation in course of friendly takeover held not deductible by corporation as ordinary and necessary business expenses under § 162(a) of Internal Revenue Code (26 USCS § 162(a)), 117 L Ed 2d 226

500

INDEX

DEDUCTIONS—Cont'd

Dividends: Iowa business tax statute's treatment of corporation's dividends received from foreign subsidiary held to violate Federal Constitution's foreign commerce clause, 120 L Ed 2d 59

DEFAULT

Bankruptcy: debtor in bankruptcy held not entitled under 11 USCS § 506(d) to strip down creditor's lien on real property to judicially determined value of collateral, 116 L Ed 2d 903

DEFINITENESS

Certainty and Definiteness (this index)

DEFINITIONS

Words and Phrases (this index)

DELAYS

Habeas corpus

– application to vacate stay of accused's execution by cyanide gas in California granted by Supreme Court, where accused had not challenged method of execution in prior habeas corpus petitions, 118 L Ed 2d 293
– mandamus to compel Federal Court of Appeals to issue decision on second habeas corpus petition by state prisoner condemned to death, denied where state failed to object to order delaying decision, 116 L Ed 2d 669

Speedy trial: Federal Government's negligent 8½-year delay between indictment and arrest held to violate accused's Sixth Amendment right to speedy trial despite lack of showing of actual prejudice, 120 L Ed 2d 520

DELIBERATE BYPASS STANDARD

Habeas corpus: federal habeas corpus petitioner, seeking evidentiary hearing on claim that material facts were not adequately developed in state proceedings, held generally required to show (1) cause for failure to develop facts, and (2) prejudice resulting from such failure, 118 L Ed 2d 318

DEMAND

Extortion: affirmative act of inducement by public official, such as demand, held not to be necessary element of Hobbs Act offense of extortion under color of official right (18 USCS § 1951(b)(2)), 119 L Ed 2d 57

501

INDEX

DE MINIMIS RULE

Income tax: state held not prohibited, under 15 USCS § 381(a), from imposing tax on gum manufacturer's income, where manufacturer's in-state activities include replacement, supply, and storage of gum, 120 L Ed 2d 174

DEMONSTRATIONS AND DEMONSTRATORS

Public-speech permit fees: county ordinance empowering administrator to adjust public-speech permit fee based on amount of hostility likely to be created by speech's content held to violate First Amendment, 120 L Ed 2d 101

DEPARTMENT OF THE INTERIOR AND RELATED AGENCIES APPROPRIATIONS ACT

Timber harvesting: provision that statute meets requirements of earlier statutes on which specified pending cases involving logging and endangered spotted owl are based, held not to violate Federal Constitution's Article III, 118 L Ed 2d 73

DEPORTATION OR EXCLUSION OF ALIENS

Asylum: Guatemalan guerrillas' attempt to coerce Guatemalan into military service held not necessarily to constitute persecution on account of political opinion so as to make Guatemalan eligible for asylum in United States, 117 L Ed 2d 38

Attorneys' fees: Equal Access to Justice Act (5 USCS § 504, 28 USCS § 2412) held not to authorize award of attorneys' fees for administrative deportation proceedings before Immigration and Naturalization Service, 116 L Ed 2d 496

Freedom of Information Act: exemption 6 of FOIA held to authorize deletion of names and other identifying information from reports of interviews with Haitian nationals returned to Haiti after attempting illegal emigration, 116 L Ed 2d 526

Release bond: INS rule generally requiring that bond on which excludible alien is released, pending deportability determination, contain condition forbidding unauthorized employment held not facially invalid, 116 L Ed 2d 546

Reopening proceedings: Attorney General's denial of alien's motion to reopen deportation proceedings held not abuse of discretion, 116 L Ed 2d 823

DEPOSITS

Son of Sam laws: New York statute, requiring that criminal's income from books or other works describing crime be escrowed and made available to victims of crime, held inconsistent with Federal Constitutions's First Amendment, 116 L Ed 2d 476

DESCRIPTION AND IDENTIFICATION

Inherently distinctive trade dress held protectable from infringement, under trademark law (15 USCS § 1125(a)), without proof of secondary meaning, 120 L Ed 2d 615

DESEGREGATION

Segregation and Desegregation (this index)

DETENTION

Mentally ill persons: Louisiana statute, permitting indefinite detention of insanity acquittees who are not mentally ill but who do not prove they would not be dangerous, held to violate Fourteenth Amendment's due process clause, 118 L Ed 2d 437

Prisons and Prisoners (this index)

DISABILITY

Workers' compensation: state-mandated payment of workers' compensation benefits withheld under benefit coordination statute held not to violate contract clause or due process clause of Federal Constitution, 117 L Ed 2d 328

DISCHARGE OR RELEASE OF PERSONS

Mentally ill persons: Louisiana statute, permitting indefinite detention of insanity acquittees who are not mentally ill but who do not prove they would not be dangerous, held to violate Fourteenth Amendment's due process clause, 118 L Ed 2d 437

DISCHARGE OR REMOVAL FROM POSITION OR OFFICE

Immunity: state officials held subject to personal liability for damages under 42 USCS § 1983 based on official acts, where § 1983 actions were brought against officials in their individual capacities, 116 L Ed 2d 301

DISCIPLINE

Cruel and unusual punishment: prisoner held able to maintain claim of cruel and unusual punishment under Federal Constitution's Eighth Amendment based on officers' excessive use of force not resulting in serious injury, 117 L Ed 2d 156

DISCLAIMER

Boundaries: Secretary of Army held authorized under § 10 of Rivers and Harbors Appropriation Act (33 USCS § 403) to condition approval of port construction on Alaska's disclaimer of federal-state boundary change, 118 L Ed 2d 222

DISCLOSURE

Airline fares: enforcement, through state consumer-protection laws, of restrictions on advertising of airline fares held preempted by provision of Airline Deregulation Act of 1978 (49 USCS Appx § 1305(a)(1)), 119 L Ed 2d 157

Freedom of Information Act: exemption 6 of FOIA held to authorize deletion of names and other identifying information from reports of interviews with Haitian nationals returned to Haiti after attempting illegal emigration, 116 L Ed 2d 526

United States Court of Appeals held to exceed its authority by imposing rule under which prosecutor must present to grand jury substantial exculpatory evidence in prosecutor's possession, 118 L Ed 2d 352

DISCONTINUANCE

Dismissal, Discontinuance, and Nonsuit (this index)

DISCRIMINATION

Civil Rights and Discrimination (this index)

DISMISSAL, DISCONTINUANCE, AND NONSUIT

Bivens action: federal prisoner held not required to exhaust Federal Bureau of Prisons' internal grievance procedure before initiating Bivens action solely for money damages, 117 L Ed 2d 291

Forma pauperis actions: dismissal of in forma pauperis action as factually frivolous under 28 USCS § 1915(d) held (1) appropriate where alleged facts are irrational or incredible, and (2) reviewable for abuse of discretion, 118 L Ed 2d 340

INDEX

DISTRICT COURTS

Sanctions: Federal District Court held authorized to impose sanctions pursuant to Rule 11 of Federal Rules of Civil Procedure, even though court is later determined to lack subject matter jurisdiction, 117 L Ed 2d 280

Sentencing guidelines. **Federal Sentencing Guidelines** (this index)

DIVERSITY OF CITIZENSHIP

Child abuse: domestic relations exception to federal courts' diversity jurisdiction held inapplicable to woman's child-abuse tort claim against her former husband and his female companion, 119 L Ed 2d 468

DIVIDENDS

Taxation: Iowa business tax statute's treatment of corporation's dividends received from foreign subsidiary held to violate Federal Constitution's foreign commerce clause, 120 L Ed 2d 59

DOMESTIC RELATIONS

Diversity jurisdiction: domestic relations exception to federal courts' diversity jurisdiction held inapplicable to woman's child-abuse tort claim against her former husband and his female companion, 119 L Ed 2d 468

DOMICILE AND RESIDENCE

Census: allocation of overseas federal employees to home states, for purposes of congressional reapportionment, held (1) not final agency action reviewable under APA; and (2) not unconstitutional, 120 L Ed 2d 636

Nondomiciliary Corporations (this index)

DOUBLE JEOPARDY

Conspiracy: double jeopardy held not to bar federal conspiracy prosecution where some overt acts were based on substantive offenses for which defendant was previously convicted, 118 L Ed 2d 25

DRAFTS

Checks and Drafts (this index)

INDEX

DRUGS AND NARCOTICS

Antipsychotic drugs: Nevada court's judgment upholding conviction reversed and remanded, where defendant claimed that forced administration of antipsychotic drug during trial violated rights under Sixth and Fourteenth Amendments, 118 L Ed 2d 479

Medical Care or Treatment (this index)

Methamphetamines: double jeopardy held not to bar federal conspiracy prosecution where some overt acts were based on substantive offenses for which defendant was previously convicted, 118 L Ed 2d 25

DUAL PUBLIC UNIVERSITY SYSTEMS

Desegregation: several aspects of Mississippi's public university system held suspect for purposes of determining whether state had complied with its duty to desegregate, 120 L Ed 2d 575

DUE PROCESS

Abortion: Pennsylvania abortion legislation held valid, except for spousal-notice provisions, under due process clause of Federal Constitution's Fourteenth Amendment, 120 L Ed 2d 674

Antipsychotic drugs: Nevada court's judgment upholding conviction reversed and remanded, where defendant claimed that forced administration of antipsychotic drug during trial violated rights under Sixth and Fourteenth Amendments, 118 L Ed 2d 479

Battered child syndrome: introduction of evidence to prove battered child syndrome at California murder trial for allegedly killing infant, and jury instruction as to evidence's use, held not to violate due process, 116 L Ed 2d 385

Death penalty: Illinois trial court held to violate due process by refusing to ask potential jurors, on voir dire in capital case, whether they would automatically impose death penalty if defendant was convicted, 119 L Ed 2d 492

Guilty verdict: due process held not to require that general guilty verdict on federal multiple conspiracy charge be set aside if evidence is inadequate to support conviction as to one object, 116 L Ed 2d 371

506

INDEX

DUE PROCESS—Cont'd

Habeas corpus: evidence held (1) sufficient to support state court grand larceny conviction, and thus (2) to require denial of federal habeas corpus relief based on insufficiency of evidence, 120 L Ed 2d 225

Incompetence: California statute, requiring that criminal defendant bear burden of proving incompetence to stand trial by preponderance of evidence, held not to violate due process, 120 L Ed 2d 353

Mail-order business: Federal Constitution's commerce clause (Art I, § 8, cl 3), but not due process clause of Fourteenth Amendment, held to bar enforcement of North Dakota use tax against out-of-state mail-order house, 119 L Ed 2d 91

Mentally ill persons: Louisiana statute, permitting indefinite detention of insanity acquittees who are not mentally ill but who do not prove they would not be dangerous, held to violate Fourteenth Amendment's due process clause, 118 L Ed 2d 437

Peremptory challenges

– accused's objection under equal protection clause to state's race-based use of peremptory challenges prior to Supreme Court's decision in Batson v Kentucky held preserved for review by Supreme Court, 118 L Ed 2d 193

– Fourteenth Amendment's equal protection clause held to prohibit Georgia criminal defendants from engaging in purposeful racial discrimination in exercise of peremptory challenges of potential jurors, 120 L Ed 2d 33

Rent control: mobile home rent control ordinance, viewed in context of California statute restricting termination of mobile home park tenancy, held not to constitute physical taking under Fifth Amendment, 118 L Ed 2d 153

Replevin: private defendants who invoke state replevin, garnishment, and attachment statutes that are declared unconstitutional, held not entitled to qualified immunity from suit under 42 USCS § 1983, 118 L Ed 2d 504

Taxation: unitary business principle held to (1) govern states' federal constitutional power to tax nondomiciliary corporations' income, and (2) prevent state's taxation of gain on particular stock sale, 119 L Ed 2d 533

INDEX

DUE PROCESS—Cont'd

Workers' compensation: state-mandated payment of workers' compensation benefits withheld under benefit coordination statute held not to violate contract clause or due process clause of Federal Constitution, 117 L Ed 2d 328

Workplace hazards: 42 USCS § 1983 held not to provide remedy for municipal employee's death, because failure to train or warn about known workplace hazards does not violate Fourteenth Amendment's due process clause, 117 L Ed 2d 261

DURESS OR COERCION

Abduction: forcible abduction of Mexican citizen to United States held not to violate extradition treaty with Mexico, and thus, not to prohibit citizen's trial in Federal District Court on criminal charges, 119 L Ed 2d 441

Airport solicitations: regulation prohibiting repetitive solicitation of money within airport terminals operated by public authority held reasonable and thus not violative of First Amendment, 120 L Ed 2d 541

Conscription: Guatemalan guerrillas' attempt to coerce Guatemalan into military service held not necessarily to constitute persecution on account of political opinion so as to make Guatemalan eligible for asylum in United States, 117 L Ed 2d 38

Cruel and unusual punishment: prisoner held able to maintain claim of cruel and unusual punishment under Federal Constitution's Eighth Amendment based on officers' excessive use of force not resulting in serious injury, 117 L Ed 2d 156

Judicial immunity: state judge held immune from 42 USCS § 1983 suit for money damages for alleged use of excessive force by police officers in bringing public defender into courtroom pursuant to judge's alleged order, 116 L Ed 2d 9

Religious freedom: inclusion of invocation and benediction by member of clergy at public secondary school graduation held forbidden by First Amendment's establishment of religion clause, 120 L Ed 2d 467

ECOSYSTEM NEXUS THEORY

Endangered Species Act: environmental groups held to lack standing to challenge regulation interpreting § 7(a)(2) of

INDEX

ECOSYSTEM NEXUS THEORY—Cont'd
Endangered Species Act (16 USCS § 1536(a)(2)) not to apply to actions taken in foreign nations, 119 L Ed 2d 351

EDUCATION
Schools and Education (this index)

EDUCATION AMENDMENTS OF 1972
Sex discrimination: damages remedy held available in sex discrimination action under Title IX of Education Amendments of 1972 (20 USCS §§ 1681-1688), 117 L Ed 2d 208

EFFLUENT STANDARDS
Discharge permits: EPA's issuance of discharge permit to sewage plant, based on finding that discharges would not cause detectable violation of downstream state's water quality standards, held authorized by Clean Water Act, 117 L Ed 2d 239

EIGHTH AMENDMENT
Cruel and Unusual Punishment (this index)

ELECTIONS AND VOTING
Apportionment of members of Congress among several states according to method of equal proportions under 2 USCS § 2a held not to violate Article I, § 2 of Federal Constitution, 118 L Ed 2d 87
Campaigns (this index)
Nominating petitions: Illinois election laws, as construed to bar new party from running county candidates for lack of 25,000 petition signatures in each electoral district, held to violate First and Fourteenth Amendments, 116 L Ed 2d 711
Preclearance: changes in decisionmaking powers of elected members of Alabama county commissions held not to be changes with respect to voting subject to preclearance requirements of § 5 of Voting Rights Act (42 USCS § 1973c), 117 L Ed 2d 51
Solicitation of votes: Tennessee statute prohibiting solicitation of votes and display or distribution of campaign literature within 100 feet of entrance to polling place held not to violate First and Fourteenth Amendments, 119 L Ed 2d 5

509

INDEX

ELECTIONS AND VOTING—Cont'd

Write-in voting: Hawaii's prohibition on write-in voting held not to violate rights of state's voters under Federal Constitution's First and Fourteenth Amendments, 119 L Ed 2d 245

ELECTRIC UTILITIES

Coal-fired electric utilities: Oklahoma statute requiring coal-fired electric utilities to burn mixture containing at least 10 percent Oklahoma-mined coal held to violate Federal Constitution's commerce clause (Art I, § 8, cl 3), 117 L Ed 2d 1

ELEVENTH AMENDMENT

Federal Employers' Liability Act (45 USCS §§ 51-60) held to create cause of action, enforceable in state court, against state-owned railroad, 116 L Ed 2d 560

State officials held subject to personal liability for damages under 42 USCS § 1983 based on official acts, where § 1983 actions were brought against officials in their individual capacities, 116 L Ed 2d 301

EMERGENCIES

Abortion: Pennsylvania abortion legislation held valid, except for spousal-notice provisions, under due process clause of Federal Constitution's Fourteenth Amendment, 120 L Ed 2d 674

EMINENT DOMAIN

Railroads: Interstate Commerce Commission held to have authority, under 45 USCS § 562(d)(1), to require conveyance of track from railroad to Amtrak for purpose of reconveying track to second railroad, 118 L Ed 2d 52

Rent control: mobile home rent control ordinance, viewed in context of California statute restricting termination of mobile home park tenancy, held not to constitute physical taking under Fifth Amendment, 118 L Ed 2d 153

South Carolina court held to have applied wrong standard in determining whether state beachfront management statute, by barring construction, effected taking of property under Fifth Amendment, 120 L Ed 2d 798

EMPLOYEE RETIREMENT INCOME SECURITY ACT OF 1974

ERISA (this index)

510

INDEX

EMPLOYEES, EMPLOYERS, AND EMPLOYMENT
Labor and Employment (this index)

EMPLOYMENT DISCRIMINATION
Civil Rights and Discrimination (this index)

ENCUMBRANCES
Liens and Encumbrances (this index)

ENDANGERED SPECIES
Standing: environmental groups held to lack standing to challenge regulation interpreting § 7(a)(2) of Endangered Species Act (16 USCS § 1536(a)(2)) not to apply to actions taken in foreign nations, 119 L Ed 2d 351

Timber harvesting: provision that statute meets requirements of earlier statutes on which specified pending cases involving logging and endangered spotted owl are based, held not to violate Federal Constitution's Article III, 118 L Ed 2d 73

ENHANCEMENT OF FEES
Attorneys' fees: enhancement of attorneys' fees above lodestar, to reflect contingent fee agreement, held not permitted in awards under environmental fee-shifting statutes (33 USCS § 1365(d), 42 USCS § 6972(e)), 120 L Ed 2d 449

ENJOYMENT OF LIFE
Federal Tort Claims Act ban on awards of punitive damages (28 USCS § 2674) held to apply to only damages legally considered punitive under traditional common-law principles, 116 L Ed 2d 731

ENJOYMENT OF PROPERTY
Eminent domain: South Carolina court held to have applied wrong standard in determining whether state beachfront management statute, by barring construction, effected taking of property under Fifth Amendment, 120 L Ed 2d 798

ENTRAPMENT
Pornography: government held to have failed, as matter of law, to establish that individual was predisposed to illegally receive mailing of sexually explicit depictions of children and hence was not entrapped, 118 L Ed 2d 174

ENVIRONMENTAL LAW

Attorneys' fees: enhancement of attorneys' fees above lodestar, to reflect contingent fee agreement, held not permitted in awards under environmental fee-shifting statutes (33 USCS § 1365(d), 42 USCS § 6972(e)), 120 L Ed 2d 449

Clean Water Act (this index)

Discharge permits: EPA's issuance of discharge permit to sewage plant, based on finding that discharges would not cause detectable violation of downstream state's water quality standards, held authorized by Clean Water Act, 117 L Ed 2d 239

Hazardous Substances (this index)

Standing: environmental groups held to lack standing to challenge regulation interpreting § 7(a)(2) of Endangered Species Act (16 USCS § 1536(a)(2)) not to apply to actions taken in foreign nations, 119 L Ed 2d 351

Timber harvesting: provision that statute meets requirements of earlier statutes on which specified pending cases involving logging and endangered spotted owl are based, held not to violate Federal Constitution's Article III, 118 L Ed 2d 73

Waste (this index)

ENVIRONMENTAL PROTECTION AGENCY

Environmental law (this index)

EQUAL ACCESS TO JUSTICE

Deportation proceedings: Equal Access to Justice Act (5 USCS § 504, 28 USCS § 2412) held not to authorize award of attorneys' fees for administrative deportation proceedings before Immigration and Naturalization Service, 116 L Ed 2d 496

Forma pauperis: leave to proceed in forma pauperis denied, under Supreme Court Rule 39.8, for individuals whose frequent in forma pauperis petitions had been rejected without recorded dissent, 116 L Ed 2d 293

EQUAL PROTECTION OF LAW

Cross burning: city ordinance, banning display of symbols— including burning cross—that arouse anger in others on basis of race, color, creed, religion, or gender, held facially invalid under First Amendment, 120 L Ed 2d 305

INDEX

EQUAL PROTECTION OF LAW—Cont'd
Desegregation
– federal court in ongoing school desegregation case held to have discretion to order incremental withdrawal of supervision over Georgia school district, 118 L Ed 2d 108
– several aspects of Mississippi's public university system held suspect for purposes of determining whether state had complied with its duty to desegregate, 120 L Ed 2d 575
Mentally ill persons: Louisiana statute, permitting indefinite detention of insanity acquittees who are not mentally ill but who do not prove they would not be dangerous, held to violate Fourteenth Amendment's due process clause, 118 L Ed 2d 437
Peremptory challenges
– accused's objection under equal protection clause to state's race-based use of peremptory challenges prior to Supreme Court's decision in Batson v Kentucky held preserved for review by Supreme Court, 118 L Ed 2d 193
– Fourteenth Amendment's equal protection clause held to prohibit Georgia criminal defendants from engaging in purposeful racial discrimination in exercise of peremptory challenges of potential jurors, 120 L Ed 2d 33
Property taxes: equal protection held not violated by California Constitution's real property tax system which generally assesses property on value at time of acquisition, rather than on current value, 120 L Ed 2d 1
Solicitation of votes: Tennessee statute prohibiting solicitation of votes and display or distribution of campaign literature within 100 feet of entrance to polling place held not to violate First and Fourteenth Amendments, 119 L Ed 2d 5
Venue: equal protection held not violated by Montana venue rules allowing civil suit against Montana corporation in only county of principal place of business, but against foreign corporation in any county, 119 L Ed 2d 432

EQUAL REPRESENTATION
Congress: apportionment of members of Congress among several states according to method of equal proportions under 2 USCS § 2a held not to violate Article I, § 2 of Federal Constitution, 118 L Ed 2d 87

513

INDEX

EQUITABLE RECOUPMENT DOCTRINE
Sovereign immunity of United States held not unequivocally waived with respect to bankruptcy trustee's claim against Internal Revenue Service for monetary relief, 117 L Ed 2d 181

EQUITABLE TOLLING DOCTRINE
Bankruptcy trustee held barred, after expiration of 30-day period, from contesting validity of exemption claimed by debtor under 11 USCS § 522(*l*), despite lack of colorable basis for claim, 118 L Ed 2d 280

ERISA
Airline fares: enforcement, through state consumer-protection laws, of restrictions on advertising of airline fares held preempted by provision of Airline Deregulation Act of 1978 (49 USCS Appx § 1305(a)(1)), 119 L Ed 2d 157

Definitions: ERISA provision (29 USCS § 1002(6)) defining employee as any individual employed by an employer, held to incorporate traditional agency-law criteria for identifying master-servant relationships, 117 L Ed 2d 581

Interest in ERISA-qualified pension plan held subject to transfer restriction under applicable nonbankruptcy law, and thus excludible from property of bankruptcy estate under 11 USCS § 541(c)(2), 119 L Ed 2d 519

ERROR
Appeal, Error, and Review (this index)

ESCROW
Son of Sam laws: New York statute, requiring that criminal's income from books or other works describing crime be escrowed and made available to victims of crime, held inconsistent with Federal Constitutions's First Amendment, 116 L Ed 2d 476

Waste disposal: state take title provision of Low-Level Radioactive Waste Policy Amendments Act of 1985 (42 USCS § 2021e(d)(2)(C)) held to violate Tenth Amendment, but to be severable from remainder of Act, 120 L Ed 2d 120

EVICTION
Rent control: mobile home rent control ordinance, viewed in context of California statute restricting termination of mobile home park tenancy, held not to constitute physical taking under Fifth Amendment, 118 L Ed 2d 153

INDEX

EVIDENCE

Competency: California statute, requiring that criminal defendant bear burden of proving incompetence to stand trial by preponderance of evidence, held not to violate due process, 120 L Ed 2d 353

Conspiracy: double jeopardy held not to bar federal conspiracy prosecution where some overt acts were based on substantive offenses for which defendant was previously convicted, 118 L Ed 2d 25

Disclosure: United States Court of Appeals held to exceed its authority by imposing rule under which prosecutor must present to grand jury substantial exculpatory evidence in prosecutor's possession, 118 L Ed 2d 352

Federal Rules of Evidence (this index)

Fifth Amendment: showing of similar motive to develop testimony held necessary, under Federal Evidence Rule 804(b)(1), for admission of grand jury testimony of witness invoking Fifth Amendment privilege, 120 L Ed 2d 255

Gang membership: introduction at capital sentencing proceeding of evidence as to defendant's membership in white racist prison gang held to violate First Amendment where evidence had no relevance to issues in proceeding, 117 L Ed 2d 309

Habeas corpus

– evidence held (1) sufficient to support state court grand larceny conviction, and thus (2) to require denial of federal habeas corpus relief based on insufficiency of evidence, 120 L Ed 2d 225

– federal habeas corpus petitioner, seeking evidentiary hearing on claim that material facts were not adequately developed in state proceedings, held generally required to show (1) cause for failure to develop facts, and (2) prejudice resulting from such failure, 118 L Ed 2d 318

Hearsay (this index)

Presumptions and Burden of Proof (this index)

Suppression: Federal Government's 30-day appeal period held to have begun to run on date of Federal District Court's order denying motion to reconsider prior order suppressing evidence in pending criminal trial, 116 L Ed 2d 1

INDEX

EXCEPTIONS, EXEMPTIONS AND EXCLUSIONS

Abortion: Pennsylvania abortion legislation held valid, except for spousal-notice provisions, under due process clause of Federal Constitution's Fourteenth Amendment, 120 L Ed 2d 674

Bankruptcy trustee held barred, after expiration of 30-day period, from contesting validity of exemption claimed by debtor under 11 USCS § 522(*l*), despite lack of colorable basis for claim, 118 L Ed 2d 280

Commercial exception in Foreign Sovereign Immunities Act held to authorize Federal District Court's jurisdiction over civil suit concerning Argentina's alleged default on certain public bonds, 119 L Ed 2d 394

Diversity jurisdiction: domestic relations exception to federal courts' diversity jurisdiction held inapplicable to woman's child-abuse tort claim against her former husband and his female companion, 119 L Ed 2d 468

ERISA: interest in ERISA-qualified pension plan held subject to transfer restriction under applicable nonbankruptcy law, and thus excludible from property of bankruptcy estate under 11 USCS § 541(c)(2), 119 L Ed 2d 519

Freedom of Information Act: exemption 6 of FOIA held to authorize deletion of names and other identifying information from reports of interviews with Haitian nationals returned to Haiti after attempting illegal emigration, 116 L Ed 2d 526

Habeas corpus: accused held not to have satisfied actual innocence exception so as to allow federal habeas corpus consideration of successive and abusive claims challenging Louisiana death sentence, 120 L Ed 2d 269

Income tax: backpay received in settlement of claims under Title VII of Civil Rights Act of 1964 held not excludible from gross income under § 104(a)(2) of Internal Revenue Code as damages for personal injuries, 119 L Ed 2d 34

Property taxes: equal protection held not violated by California Constitution's real property tax system which generally assesses property on value at time of acquisition, rather than on current value, 120 L Ed 2d 1

EXCESS AND EXCESSIVENESS

Cruel and unusual punishment: prisoner held able to maintain claim of cruel and unusual punishment under Federal

516

EXHAUSTION OF REMEDIES

Bivens action: federal prisoner held not required to exhaust Federal Bureau of Prisons' internal grievance procedure before initiating Bivens action solely for money damages, 117 L Ed 2d 291

EXPENSES

Fees and Expenses (this index)

EXPERT AND OPINION EVIDENCE

Gang membership: introduction at capital sentencing proceeding of evidence as to defendant's membership in white racist prison gang held to violate First Amendment where evidence had no relevance to issues in proceeding, 117 L Ed 2d 309

EXTORTION

Affirmative act of inducement by public official, such as demand, held not to be necessary element of Hobbs Act offense of extortion under color of official right (18 USCS § 1951(b)(2)), 119 L Ed 2d 57

EXTRADITION

Abduction: forcible abduction of Mexican citizen to United States held not to violate extradition treaty with Mexico, and thus, not to prohibit citizen's trial in Federal District Court on criminal charges, 119 L Ed 2d 441

Deportation proceedings: Attorney General's denial of alien's motion to reopen deportation proceedings held not abuse of discretion, 116 L Ed 2d 823

EXTRAJUDICIAL STATEMENTS

Hearsay evidence: admission of testimony against accused under Illinois hearsay exceptions for spontaneous declarations and medical-treatment statements held not to violate Sixth Amendment's confrontation clause, 116 L Ed 2d 848

FACULTY

Teachers and Instructors (this index)

FAIR AND IMPARTIAL TRIAL OR PROCEEDINGS

Antipsychotic drugs: Nevada court's judgment upholding conviction reversed and remanded, where defendant claimed that forced administration of antipsychotic drug during trial violated rights under Sixth and Fourteenth Amendments, 118 L Ed 2d 479

INDEX

FAIR AND IMPARTIAL TRIAL OR PROCEEDINGS —Cont'd

Death penalty: Illinois trial court held to violate due process by refusing to ask potential jurors, on voir dire in capital case, whether they would automatically impose death penalty if defendant was convicted, 119 L Ed 2d 492

Peremptory challenges: Fourteenth Amendment's equal protection clause held to prohibit Georgia criminal defendants from engaging in purposeful racial discrimination in exercise of peremptory challenges of potential jurors, 120 L Ed 2d 33

FAMILY AND RELATIVES

Diversity jurisdiction: domestic relations exception to federal courts' diversity jurisdiction held inapplicable to woman's child-abuse tort claim against her former husband and his female companion, 119 L Ed 2d 468

FEDERAL BUREAU OF PRISONS

Bivens action: federal prisoner held not required to exhaust Federal Bureau of Prisons' internal grievance procedure before initiating Bivens action solely for money damages, 117 L Ed 2d 291

FEDERAL DEPOSIT INSURANCE CORPORATION

Bankruptcy: Federal District Court held not to have authority, in bankruptcy case, to enjoin Federal Reserve Board proceedings against debtor bank holding company for alleged banking law violations, 116 L Ed 2d 358

FEDERAL EMPLOYEES COMPENSATION ACT

Jones Act: maritime worker whose occupation of ship repairman was listed in Longshore and Harbor Workers' Compensation Act (33 USCS § 902(3)) held not precluded from being seaman under Jones Act (46 USCS Appx § 688), 116 L Ed 2d 405

FEDERAL EMPLOYERS' LIABILITY ACT

Railroads: Federal Employers' Liability Act (45 USCS §§ 51-60) held to create cause of action, enforceable in state court, against state-owned railroad, 116 L Ed 2d 560

519

INDEX

FEDERAL POWER ACT

Coal-fired electric utilities: Oklahoma statute requiring coal-fired electric utilities to burn mixture containing at least 10 percent Oklahoma-mined coal held to violate Federal Constitution's commerce clause (Art I, § 8, cl 3), 117 L Ed 2d 1

FEDERAL QUESTIONS

Red Cross: original federal court jurisdiction over all cases to which American National Red Cross is party held conferred by sue and be sued provision (36 USCS § 2) of Red Cross' federal corporate charter, 120 L Ed 2d 201

FEDERAL RESERVE BANK OR SYSTEM

Bankruptcy: Federal District Court held not to have authority, in bankruptcy case, to enjoin Federal Reserve Board proceedings against debtor bank holding company for alleged banking law violations, 116 L Ed 2d 358

FEDERAL RULES OF APPELLATE PROCEDURE

Rules of Appellate Procedure (this index)

FEDERAL RULES OF CIVIL PROCEDURE

Consent decree: clear showing of grievous wrong evoked by new and unforeseen conditions, held not required, under Federal Civil Procedure Rule 60(b), to modify consent decree stemming from institutional reform litigation, 116 L Ed 2d 867

Sanctions: Federal District Court held authorized to impose sanctions pursuant to Rule 11 of Federal Rules of Civil Procedure, even though court is later determined to lack subject matter jurisdiction, 117 L Ed 2d 280

Sherman Act: photocopier manufacturer held not entitled to summary judgment dismissing federal antitrust claims as to (1) tying arrangement between parts and service, and (2) monopolization of sale of service, 119 L Ed 2d 265

FEDERAL RULES OF EVIDENCE

Conspiracy: double jeopardy held not to bar federal conspiracy prosecution where some overt acts were based on substantive offenses for which defendant was previously convicted, 118 L Ed 2d 25

INDEX

FEDERAL RULES OF EVIDENCE—Cont'd
Similar motive: showing of similar motive to develop testimony held necessary, under Federal Evidence Rule 804(b)(1), for admission of grand jury testimony of witness invoking Fifth Amendment privilege, 120 L Ed 2d 255

FEDERAL SENTENCING GUIDELINES
Juvenile Delinquency Act provision limiting detention to maximum term authorized for one convicted as adult held to refer to maximum sentence authorized under United States Sentencing Guidelines, 117 L Ed 2d 559

Lenity Rule (this index)
Lesser sentence: Federal Government's refusal to request lesser sentence so as to reflect accused's substantial assistance in prosecuting another person held subject to review for constitutional violations, but particular accused held to have raised no claim to such review, 118 L Ed 2d 524

Reviewing court held authorized, in appropriate circumstances, to affirm sentence in which Federal District Court's departure from Sentencing Guidelines' range is based on valid and invalid factors, 117 L Ed 2d 341

FEDERAL TORT CLAIMS ACT
Punitive damages: Federal Tort Claims Act ban on awards of punitive damages (28 USCS § 2674) held to apply to only damages legally considered punitive under traditional common-law principles, 116 L Ed 2d 731

FEDERAL TRADE COMMISSION ACT
Title-search ratesetting: supervision by states of title-search ratesetting held not sufficiently active to give title insurance companies state-action immunity from federal antitrust liability, 119 L Ed 2d 410

FEDERAL WATER POLLUTION CONTROL ACT
Attorneys' fees: enhancement of attorneys' fees above lodestar, to reflect contingent fee agreement, held not permitted in awards under environmental fee-shifting statutes (33 USCS § 1365(d), 42 USCS § 6972(e)), 120 L Ed 2d 449

FEE-PATENTED LANDS
Taxation: Indian General Allotment Act of 1887 (25 USCS §§ 331 et seq.) held (1) to permit county ad valorem tax on fee-patented reservation land, but (2) not to allow county excise tax on sales of such land, 116 L Ed 2d 687

INDEX

FEES AND EXPENSES

Airlines: enforcement, through state consumer-protection laws, of restrictions on advertising of airline fares held preempted by provision of Airline Deregulation Act of 1978 (49 USCS Appx § 1305(a)(1)), 119 L Ed 2d 157

Attorneys' Fees (this index)

Federal Tort Claims Act ban on awards of punitive damages (28 USCS § 2674) held to apply to only damages legally considered punitive under traditional common-law principles, 116 L Ed 2d 731

First Amendment: county ordinance empowering administrator to adjust public-speech permit fee based on amount of hostility likely to be created by speech's content held to violate First Amendment, 120 L Ed 2d 101

Foster care and adoption: provision of Adoption Assistance and Child Welfare Act of 1980 (42 USCS § 671(a)(15)) held not enforceable in private action under 42 USCS § 1983 or in suit directly under Act, 118 L Ed 2d 1

Future expenses: Federal Tort Claims Act ban on awards of punitive damages (28 USCS § 2674) held to apply to only damages legally considered punitive under traditional common-law principles, 116 L Ed 2d 731

Hazardous waste disposal

– disposal fee imposed by Alabama on hazardous waste generated out of state, but not on waste generated in state, held to violate Federal Constitution's commerce clause (Art I, § 8, cl 3), 119 L Ed 2d 121

– state take title provision of Low-Level Radioactive Waste Policy Amendments Act of 1985 (42 USCS § 2021e(d)(2)(C)) held to violate Tenth Amendment, but to be severable from remainder of Act, 120 L Ed 2d 120

Income tax deductions: professional expenses incurred by target corporation in course of friendly takeover held not deductible by corporation as ordinary and necessary business expenses under § 162(a) of Internal Revenue Code (26 USCS § 162(a)), 117 L Ed 2d 226

Title-search ratesetting: supervision by states of title-search ratesetting held not sufficiently active to give title insurance companies state-action immunity from federal antitrust liability, 119 L Ed 2d 410

522

FICA

Income tax: backpay received in settlement of claims under Title VII of Civil Rights Act of 1964 held not excludible from gross income under § 104(a)(2) of Internal Revenue Code as damages for personal injuries, 119 L Ed 2d 34

FIDUCIARIES

Trusts and Trustees (this index)

FIFTH AMENDMENT

Beachfront property: South Carolina court held to have applied wrong standard in determining whether state beachfront management statute, by barring construction, effected taking of property under Fifth Amendment, 120 L Ed 2d 798

Conspiracy

– double jeopardy held not to bar federal conspiracy prosecution where some overt acts were based on substantive offenses for which defendant was previously convicted, 118 L Ed 2d 25

– due process held not to require that general guilty verdict on federal multiple conspiracy charge be set aside if evidence is inadequate to support conviction as to one object, 116 L Ed 2d 371

Disclosure: United States Court of Appeals held to exceed its authority by imposing rule under which prosecutor must present to grand jury substantial exculpatory evidence in prosecutor's possession, 118 L Ed 2d 352

Double jeopardy held not to bar federal conspiracy prosecution where some overt acts were based on substantive offenses for which defendant was previously convicted, 118 L Ed 2d 25

Similar motive: showing of similar motive to develop testimony held necessary, under Federal Evidence Rule 804(b)(1), for admission of grand jury testimony of witness invoking Fifth Amendment privilege, 120 L Ed 2d 255

Takings Clause (this index)

FIGHTING WORDS

Cross burning: city ordinance, banning display of symbols—including burning cross—that arouse anger in others on basis of race, color, creed, religion, or gender, held facially invalid under First Amendment, 120 L Ed 2d 305

FILES AND FILING

Bankruptcy: trustee liquidating and distributing property as part of plan under Chapter 11 of Bankruptcy Code held required, as to income attributable to property, to file federal income tax returns and pay tax, 117 L Ed 2d 196

Freedom of Information Act: exemption 6 of FOIA held to authorize deletion of names and other identifying information from reports of interviews with Haitian nationals returned to Haiti after attempting illegal emigration, 116 L Ed 2d 526

Notice of appeal: informal brief filed in Federal Court of Appeals held effective as notice of appeal under Rule 3 of Federal Rules of Appellate Procedure, if filing of brief is timely and conveys information required by Rule 3, 116 L Ed 2d 678

FINALITY OR CONCLUSIVENESS

Reconsideration: Federal Government's 30-day appeal period held to have begun to run on date of Federal District Court's order denying motion to reconsider prior order suppressing evidence in pending criminal trial, 116 L Ed 2d 1

FINES, FORFEITURES, AND PENALTIES

Federal Sentencing Guidelines (this index)

Lenity Rule (this index)

Longshore and Harbor Workers' Compensation Act: forfeiture provision of Longshore and Harbor Workers' Compensation Act (33 USCS § 933(g)) held to apply where worker not then receiving or awarded compensation from employer settles third-party claim, 120 L Ed 2d 379

Pollution: federal sovereign immunity held not waived as to state-imposed punitive fines under Clean Water Act (33 USCS §§ 1251 et seq.) and Resource Conservation and Recovery Act (42 USCS §§ 6901 et seq.), 118 L Ed 2d 255

Sanctions: Federal District Court held authorized to impose sanctions pursuant to Rule 11 of Federal Rules of Civil Procedure, even though court is later determined to lack subject matter jurisdiction, 117 L Ed 2d 280

FIREARMS

Tax payment for making firearm held not required, under provision of National Firearms Act (26 USCS § 5821), where pistol and kit allowing conversion of pistol into firearm are packaged as unit, 119 L Ed 2d 308

INDEX

FIRST AMENDMENT
Freedom of Association (this index)
Freedom of Speech and Press (this index)
Gang membership: introduction at capital sentencing proceeding of evidence as to defendant's membership in white racist prison gang held to violate First Amendment where evidence had no relevance to issues in proceeding, 117 L Ed 2d 309
Nominating petitions: Illinois election laws, as construed to bar new party from running county candidates for lack of 25,000 petition signatures in each electoral district, held to violate First and Fourteenth Amendments, 116 L Ed 2d 711
Religion and Religious Societies (this index)
Solicitation of votes: Tennessee statute prohibiting solicitation of votes and display or distribution of campaign literature within 100 feet of entrance to polling place held not to violate First and Fourteenth Amendments, 119 L Ed 2d 5
Son of Sam laws: New York statute, requiring that criminal's income from books or other works describing crime be escrowed and made available to victims of crime, held inconsistent with Federal Constitutions's First Amendment, 116 L Ed 2d 476
Write-in voting: Hawaii's prohibition on write-in voting held not to violate rights of state's voters under Federal Constitution's First and Fourteenth Amendments, 119 L Ed 2d 245

FISH AND WILDLIFE SERVICE
Endangered Species Act: environmental groups held to lack standing to challenge regulation interpreting § 7(a)(2) of Endangered Species Act (16 USCS § 1536(a)(2)) not to apply to actions taken in foreign nations, 119 L Ed 2d 351

FLYERS
Distribution: regulation prohibiting repetitive distribution of literature within airport terminals operated by public authority held to violate First Amendment, 120 L Ed 2d 669

FORCE OR VIOLENCE
Duress or Coercion (this index)

FOREIGN CORPORATIONS
Nondomiciliary Corporations (this index)

INDEX

527

FOURTEENTH AMENDMENT—Cont'd

Nominating petitions: Illinois election laws, as construed to bar new party from running county candidates for lack of 25,000 petition signatures in each electoral district, held to violate First and Fourteenth Amendments, 116 L Ed 2d 711

Public-speech permit fees: county ordinance empowering administrator to adjust public-speech permit fee based on amount of hostility likely to be created by speech's content held to violate First Amendment, 120 L Ed 2d 101

Write-in voting: Hawaii's prohibition on write-in voting held not to violate rights of state's voters under Federal Constitution's First and Fourteenth Amendments, 119 L Ed 2d 245

FOURTH AMENDMENT
Search and Seizure (this index)

FRANCHISE TAX

State held not prohibited, under 15 USCS § 381(a), from imposing tax on gum manufacturer's income, where manufacturer's in-state activities include replacement, supply, and storage of gum, 120 L Ed 2d 174

FRAUD AND DECEIT

Cigarette smoking: federal cigarette labeling and advertising statutes held to preempt some but not all state-law damages claims with respect to cigarette smoking, 120 L Ed 2d 407

Stock manipulation: Securities Investor Protection Corp. held unable to maintain RICO suit under 18 USCS § 1964(c) against party to scheme that allegedly disabled broker-dealers from meeting obligations to customers, 117 L Ed 2d 532

FREEDOM OF ASSOCIATION

Gang membership: introduction at capital sentencing proceeding of evidence as to defendant's membership in white racist prison gang held to violate First Amendment where evidence had no relevance to issues in proceeding, 117 L Ed 2d 309

FREEDOM OF ASSOCIATION—Cont'd

Nominating petitions: Illinois election laws, as construed to bar new party from running county candidates for lack of 25,000 petition signatures in each electoral district, held to violate First and Fourteenth Amendments, 116 L Ed 2d 711

Write-in voting: Hawaii's prohibition on write-in voting held not to violate rights of state's voters under Federal Constitution's First and Fourteenth Amendments, 119 L Ed 2d 245

FREEDOM OF INFORMATION ACT

Exemption 6 of FOIA held to authorize deletion of names and other identifying information from reports of interviews with Haitian nationals returned to Haiti after attempting illegal emigration, 116 L Ed 2d 526

FREEDOM OF PRESS
Freedom of Speech and Press (this index)

FREEDOM OF RELIGION
Religion and Religious Societies (this index)

FREEDOM OF SPEECH AND PRESS

Airport solicitations: regulation prohibiting repetitive solicitation of money within airport terminals operated by public authority held reasonable and thus not violative of First Amendment, 120 L Ed 2d 541

Cross burning: city ordinance, banning display of symbols—including burning cross—that arouse anger in others on basis of race, color, creed, religion, or gender, held facially invalid under First Amendment, 120 L Ed 2d 305

Literature distribution: regulation prohibiting repetitive distribution of literature within airport terminals operated by public authority held to violate First Amendment, 120 L Ed 2d 669

Public-speech permit fees: county ordinance empowering administrator to adjust public-speech permit fee based on amount of hostility likely to be created by speech's content held to violate First Amendment, 120 L Ed 2d 101

Solicitation of votes: Tennessee statute prohibiting solicitation of votes and display or distribution of campaign literature within 100 feet of entrance to polling place held not to violate First and Fourteenth Amendments, 119 L Ed 2d 5

INDEX

FREEDOM OF SPEECH AND PRESS—Cont'd
Son of Sam laws: New York statute, requiring that criminal's income from books or other works describing crime be escrowed and made available to victims of crime, held inconsistent with Federal Constitutions's First Amendment, 116 L Ed 2d 476

FRINGE BENEFITS
Income tax: backpay received in settlement of claims under Title VII of Civil Rights Act of 1964 held not excludible from gross income under § 104(a)(2) of Internal Revenue Code as damages for personal injuries, 119 L Ed 2d 34

FRIVOLOUS ACTIONS
Forma pauperis: dismissal of in forma pauperis action as factually frivolous under 28 USCS § 1915(d) held (1) appropriate where alleged facts are irrational or incredible, and (2) reviewable for abuse of discretion, 118 L Ed 2d 340
Forma pauperis: leave to proceed in forma pauperis denied, under Supreme Court Rule 39.8, for individuals whose frequent in forma pauperis petitions had been rejected without recorded dissent, 116 L Ed 2d 293

FRUITS OF CRIME
Son of Sam laws: New York statute, requiring that criminal's income from books or other works describing crime be escrowed and made available to victims of crime, held inconsistent with Federal Constitutions's First Amendment, 116 L Ed 2d 476

FUNDS AND FUNDING
Airport solicitations: regulation prohibiting repetitive solicitation of money within airport terminals operated by public authority held reasonable and thus not violative of First Amendment, 120 L Ed 2d 541
Bankruptcy: transfer of check, for purposes of determining whether transfer is voidable under 11 USCS § 547(b)(4)(A) as occurring within 90 days of bankruptcy filing, held to occur on date drawee bank honors check, 118 L Ed 2d 39
Desegregation: several aspects of Mississippi's public university system held suspect for purposes of determining whether state had complied with its duty to desegregate, 120 L Ed 2d 575

FUNDS AND FUNDING—Cont'd
Preferential Transfers (this index)
Waste disposal: state take title provision of Low-Level Radioactive Waste Policy Amendments Act of 1985 (42 USCS § 2021e(d)(2)(C)) held to violate Tenth Amendment, but to be severable from remainder of Act, 120 L Ed 2d 120

FUTURE EXPENSES
Punitive damages: Federal Tort Claims Act ban on awards of punitive damages (28 USCS § 2674) held to apply to only damages legally considered punitive under traditional common-law principles, 116 L Ed 2d 731

GANGS
First Amendment: introduction at capital sentencing proceeding of evidence as to defendant's membership in white racist prison gang held to violate First Amendment where evidence had no relevance to issues in proceeding, 117 L Ed 2d 309

GARBAGE OR REFUSE
Hazardous Substances (this index)
Waste (this index)

GARNISHMENT
Private defendants who invoke state replevin, garnishment, and attachment statutes that are declared unconstitutional, held not entitled to qualified immunity from suit under 42 USCS § 1983, 118 L Ed 2d 504

GOOD FAITH
Bankruptcy trustee held barred, after expiration of 30-day period, from contesting validity of exemption claimed by debtor under 11 USCS § 522(*l*), despite lack of colorable basis for claim, 118 L Ed 2d 280
Death penalty: Illinois trial court held to violate due process by refusing to ask potential jurors, on voir dire in capital case, whether they would automatically impose death penalty if defendant was convicted, 119 L Ed 2d 492
Desegregation: federal court in ongoing school desegregation case held to have discretion to order incremental withdrawal of supervision over Georgia school district, 118 L Ed 2d 108

GOOD FAITH—Cont'd

Religious freedom: inclusion of invocation and benediction by member of clergy at public secondary school graduation held forbidden by First Amendment's establishment of religion clause, 120 L Ed 2d 467

Replevin: private defendants who invoke state replevin, garnishment, and attachment statutes that are declared unconstitutional, held not entitled to qualified immunity from suit under 42 USCS § 1983, 118 L Ed 2d 504

Speedy trial: Federal Government's negligent 8½-year delay between indictment and arrest held to violate accused's Sixth Amendment right to speedy trial despite lack of showing of actual prejudice, 120 L Ed 2d 520

GOVERNMENTAL IMMUNITY OR PRIVILEGE

Sovereign Immunity (this index)

GRADUATION CEREMONIES

Religious freedom: inclusion of invocation and benediction by member of clergy at public secondary school graduation held forbidden by First Amendment's establishment of religion clause, 120 L Ed 2d 467

GRAND JURY

Disclosure: United States Court of Appeals held to exceed its authority by imposing rule under which prosecutor must present to grand jury substantial exculpatory evidence in prosecutor's possession, 118 L Ed 2d 352

Fifth Amendment: showing of similar motive to develop testimony held necessary, under Federal Evidence Rule 804(b) (1), for admission of grand jury testimony of witness invoking Fifth Amendment privilege, 120 L Ed 2d 255

GRIEVANCE

Bivens action: federal prisoner held not required to exhaust Federal Bureau of Prisons' internal grievance procedure before initiating Bivens action solely for money damages, 117 L Ed 2d 291

GRIEVOUS WRONG STANDARD

Consent decree: clear showing of grievous wrong evoked by new and unforeseen conditions, held not required, under Federal Civil Procedure Rule 60(b), to modify consent decree stemming from institutional reform litigation, 116 L Ed 2d 867

INDEX

GROSS INCOME
Income tax (this index)

GUARANTEE CLAUSE
Waste disposal: state take title provision of Low-Level Radioactive Waste Policy Amendments Act of 1985 (42 USCS § 2021e(d)(2)(C)) held to violate Tenth Amendment, but to be severable from remainder of Act, 120 L Ed 2d 120

GUNS
Tax payment for making firearm held not required, under provision of National Firearms Act (26 USCS § 5821), where pistol and kit allowing conversion of pistol into firearm are packaged as unit, 119 L Ed 2d 308

HABEAS CORPUS
Actual innocence exception: accused held not to have satisfied actual innocence exception so as to allow federal habeas corpus consideration of successive and abusive claims challenging Louisiana death sentence, 120 L Ed 2d 269

Aggravating circumstances: rule of decisions holding aggravating circumstances unconstitutionally vague in capital sentencing proceeding held retroactively available to support federal habeas corpus relief, 117 L Ed 2d 367

Battered child syndrome: introduction of evidence to prove battered child syndrome at California murder trial for allegedly killing infant, and jury instruction as to evidence's use, held not to violate due process, 116 L Ed 2d 385

Delays: mandamus to compel Federal Court of Appeals to issue decision on second habeas corpus petition by state prisoner condemned to death, denied where state failed to object to order delaying decision, 116 L Ed 2d 669

Evidentiary hearing: federal habeas corpus petitioner, seeking evidentiary hearing on claim that material facts were not adequately developed in state proceedings, held generally required to show (1) cause for failure to develop facts, and (2) prejudice resulting from such failure, 118 L Ed 2d 318

Executions: application to vacate stay of accused's execution by cyanide gas in California granted by Supreme Court, where accused had not challenged method of execution in prior habeas corpus petitions, 118 L Ed 2d 293

533

INDEX

HABEAS CORPUS—Cont'd

Stay of execution: application for stay of execution denied where Federal District Court found that alleged exculpatory evidence produced by defense did not amount to colorable claim of innocence, 119 L Ed 2d 1

Sufficiency of evidence: evidence held (1) sufficient to support state court grand larceny conviction, and thus (2) to require denial of federal habeas corpus relief based on insufficiency of evidence, 120 L Ed 2d 225

HAITIAN NATIONALS

Freedom of Information Act: exemption 6 of FOIA held to authorize deletion of names and other identifying information from reports of interviews with Haitian nationals returned to Haiti after attempting illegal emigration, 116 L Ed 2d 526

HARASSMENT

Sexual Harassment (this index)

HARBORS

Ports and Harbors (this index)

HARMLESS ERROR

Appeal, Error, and Review (this index)

HARVESTING TIMBER

Timber Harvesting (this index)

HAZARDOUS SUBSTANCES

Attorneys' fees: enhancement of attorneys' fees above lodestar, to reflect contingent fee agreement, held not permitted in awards under environmental fee-shifting statutes (33 USCS § 1365(d), 42 USCS § 6972(e)), 120 L Ed 2d 449

Disposal fee imposed by Alabama on hazardous waste generated out of state, but not on waste generated in state, held to violate Federal Constitution's commerce clause (Art I, § 8, cl 3), 119 L Ed 2d 121

OSHA: Illinois licensing statutes held preempted by OSH Act (29 USCS §§ 651 et seq.) to extent that statutes establish occupational safety and health standards for training of hazardous waste workers, 120 L Ed 2d 73

Severability: state take title provision of Low-Level Radioactive Waste Policy Amendments Act of 1985 (42 USCS § 2021e(d)(2)(C)) held to violate Tenth Amendment, but to be severable from remainder of Act, 120 L Ed 2d 120

HAZARDOUS SUBSTANCES—Cont'd

Sovereign immunity: federal sovereign immunity held not waived as to state-imposed punitive fines under Clean Water Act (33 USCS §§ 1251 et seq.) and Resource Conservation and Recovery Act (42 USCS §§ 6901 et seq.), 118 L Ed 2d 255

HEALTH AND SAFETY

Abortion: Pennsylvania abortion legislation held valid, except for spousal-notice provisions, under due process clause of Federal Constitution's Fourteenth Amendment, 120 L Ed 2d 674

Cigarette smoking: federal cigarette labeling and advertising statutes held to preempt some but not all state-law damages claims with respect to cigarette smoking, 120 L Ed 2d 407

County landfill: Michigan statute barring private landfill owner from accepting solid waste originating outside county in which landfill was located held to violate Federal Constitution's commerce clause (Art I, § 8, cl 3), 119 L Ed 2d 139

Hazardous Substances (this index)

Medical Care or Treatment (this index)

OSHA: Illinois licensing statutes held preempted by OSH Act (29 USCS §§ 651 et seq.) to extent that statutes establish occupational safety and health standards for training of hazardous waste workers, 120 L Ed 2d 73

Workplace hazards: 42 USCS § 1983 held not to provide remedy for municipal employee's death, because failure to train or warn about known workplace hazards does not violate Fourteenth Amendment's due process clause, 117 L Ed 2d 261

HEARSAY

Confrontation of witnesses: admission of testimony against accused under Illinois hearsay exceptions for spontaneous declarations and medical-treatment statements held not to violate Sixth Amendment's confrontation clause, 116 L Ed 2d 848

Similar motive: showing of similar motive to develop testimony held necessary, under Federal Evidence Rule 804(b)(1), for admission of grand jury testimony of witness invoking Fifth Amendment privilege, 120 L Ed 2d 255

HEINOUS, ATROCIOUS, OR CRUEL CONDUCT

Cure on appeal: Florida trial judge's improper weighing in capital sentencing hearing of aggravating factor not supported by evidence, in violation of Eighth Amendment, held not cured by state appellate review, 119 L Ed 2d 326

Instructions to jury: imposition of death sentence by Florida trial court held to violate Eighth Amendment where jury rendering advisory verdict in sentencing hearing was instructed on invalid aggravating circumstance, 120 L Ed 2d 854

Retroactivity: rule of decisions holding aggravating circumstances unconstitutionally vague in capital sentencing proceeding held retroactively available to support federal habeas corpus relief, 117 L Ed 2d 367

HIGHER EDUCATION
Schools and Education (this index)

HIGH SCHOOLS
Schools and Education (this index)

HOBBS ACT

Affirmative act of inducement by public official, such as demand, held not to be necessary element of Hobbs Act offense of extortion under color of official right (18 USCS § 1951(b)(2)), 119 L Ed 2d 57

HOMICIDE

Abduction: forcible abduction of Mexican citizen to United States held not to violate extradition treaty with Mexico, and thus, not to prohibit citizen's trial in Federal District Court on criminal charges, 119 L Ed 2d 441

Aggravating circumstances: rule of decisions holding aggravating circumstances unconstitutionally vague in capital sentencing proceeding held retroactively available to support federal habeas corpus relief, 117 L Ed 2d 367

Battered child syndrome: introduction of evidence to prove battered child syndrome at California murder trial for allegedly killing infant, and jury instruction as to evidence's use, held not to violate due process, 116 L Ed 2d 385

INDEX

HUSBANDS
Spouses (this index)

IDENTIFICATION AND DESCRIPTION
Inherently distinctive trade dress held protectable from infringement, under trademark law (15 USCS § 1125(a)), without proof of secondary meaning, 120 L Ed 2d 615

IMMIGRATION AND NATIONALITY ACT
Immigration and Naturalization (this index)

IMMIGRATION AND NATURALIZATION
Asylum: Guatemalan guerrillas' attempt to coerce Guatemalan into military service held not necessarily to constitute persecution on account of political opinion so as to make Guatemalan eligible for asylum in United States, 117 L Ed 2d 38
Deportation or Exclusion of Aliens (this index)
Freedom of Information Act: exemption 6 of FOIA held to authorize deletion of names and other identifying information from reports of interviews with Haitian nationals returned to Haiti after attempting illegal emigration, 116 L Ed 2d 526

IMMUNITIES
Privileges and Immunities (this index)

IMPAIRMENT OF CONTRACT
Workers' compensation: state-mandated payment of workers' compensation benefits withheld under benefit coordination statute held not to violate contract clause or due process clause of Federal Constitution, 117 L Ed 2d 328

IMPARTIAL JURY
Jury and Jury Trial (this index)

IMPLIED ACTS AND MATTERS
Foster care and adoption: provision of Adoption Assistance and Child Welfare Act of 1980 (42 USCS § 671(a)(15)) held not enforceable in private action under 42 USCS § 1983 or in suit directly under Act, 118 L Ed 2d 1

IMPRISONMENT
Prisons and Prisoners (this index)
Sentence and Punishment (this index)

538

INCOMPETENT OR INSANE PERSONS—Cont'd

Indefinite detention: Louisiana statute, permitting indefinite detention of insanity acquittees who are not mentally ill but who do not prove they would not be dangerous, held to violate Fourteenth Amendment's due process clause, 118 L Ed 2d 437

Physical and Mental Examinations (this index)

INDECENCY, LEWDNESS, AND OBSCENITY

Entrapment: government held to have failed, as matter of law, to establish that individual was predisposed to illegally receive mailing of sexually explicit depictions of children and hence was not entrapped, 118 L Ed 2d 174

INDEPENDENT CONTRACTORS

ERISA provision (29 USCS § 1002(6)) defining employee as any individual employed by an employer, held to incorporate traditional agency-law criteria for identifying master-servant relationships, 117 L Ed 2d 581

INDIAN GENERAL ALLOTMENT ACT

Taxation: Indian General Allotment Act of 1887 (25 USCS §§ 331 et seq.) held (1) to permit county ad valorem tax on fee-patented reservation land, but (2) not to allow county excise tax on sales of such land, 116 L Ed 2d 687

INDIAN REORGANIZATION ACT

Taxation: Indian General Allotment Act of 1887 (25 USCS §§ 331 et seq.) held (1) to permit county ad valorem tax on fee-patented reservation land, but (2) not to allow county excise tax on sales of such land, 116 L Ed 2d 687

INDIANS AND INDIAN LANDS

Juvenile Delinquency Act provision limiting detention to maximum term authorized for one convicted as adult held to refer to maximum sentence authorized under United States Sentencing Guidelines, 117 L Ed 2d 559

Taxation: Indian General Allotment Act of 1887 (25 USCS §§ 331 et seq.) held (1) to permit county ad valorem tax on fee-patented reservation land, but (2) not to allow county excise tax on sales of such land, 116 L Ed 2d 687

INDEX

INDICTMENT
Disclosure: United States Court of Appeals held to exceed its authority by imposing rule under which prosecutor must present to grand jury substantial exculpatory evidence in prosecutor's possession, 118 L Ed 2d 352

INDUCEMENT
Extortion: affirmative act of inducement by public official, such as demand, held not to be necessary element of Hobbs Act offense of extortion under color of official right (18 USCS § 1951(b)(2)), 119 L Ed 2d 57

INFANTS
Children and Minors (this index)

INFORMED CONSENT
Abortion: Pennsylvania abortion legislation held valid, except for spousal-notice provisions, under due process clause of Federal Constitution's Fourteenth Amendment, 120 L Ed 2d 674

INJUNCTIONS
Airline fares: enforcement, through state consumer-protection laws, of restrictions on advertising of airline fares held preempted by provision of Airline Deregulation Act of 1978 (49 USCS Appx § 1305(a)(1)), 119 L Ed 2d 157
Bankruptcy: Federal District Court held not to have authority, in bankruptcy case, to enjoin Federal Reserve Board proceedings against debtor bank holding company for alleged banking law violations, 116 L Ed 2d 358
Desegregation: federal court in ongoing school desegregation case held to have discretion to order incremental withdrawal of supervision over Georgia school district, 118 L Ed 2d 108

INSANE PERSONS
Incompetent or Insane Persons (this index)

INSTRUCTIONS TO JURY
Battered child syndrome: introduction of evidence to prove battered child syndrome at California murder trial for allegedly killing infant, and jury instruction as to evidence's use, held not to violate due process, 116 L Ed 2d 385

INSTRUCTIONS TO JURY—Cont'd

Conspiracy: due process held not to require that general guilty verdict on federal multiple conspiracy charge be set aside if evidence is inadequate to support conviction as to one object, 116 L Ed 2d 371

Death penalty: Illinois trial court held to violate due process by refusing to ask potential jurors, on voir dire in capital case, whether they would automatically impose death penalty if defendant was convicted, 119 L Ed 2d 492

Extortion: affirmative act of inducement by public official, such as demand, held not to be necessary element of Hobbs Act offense of extortion under color of official right (18 USCS § 1951(b)(2)), 119 L Ed 2d 57

Mitigation or aggravation of punishment: Florida trial judge's improper weighing in capital sentencing hearing of aggravating factor not supported by evidence, in violation of Eighth Amendment, held not cured by state appellate review, 119 L Ed 2d 326

Mitigation or aggravation of punishment: imposition of death sentence by Florida trial court held to violate Eighth Amendment where jury rendering advisory verdict in sentencing hearing was instructed on invalid aggravating circumstance, 120 L Ed 2d 854

INSURANCE

Agents and brokers: ERISA provision (29 USCS § 1002(6)) defining employee as any individual employed by an employer, held to incorporate traditional agency-law criteria for identifying master-servant relationships, 117 L Ed 2d 581

Longshore and Harbor Workers' Compensation Act: forfeiture provision of Longshore and Harbor Workers' Compensation Act (33 USCS § 933(g)) held to apply where worker not then receiving or awarded compensation from employer settles third-party claim, 120 L Ed 2d 379

Title-search ratesetting: supervision by states of title-search ratesetting held not sufficiently active to give title insurance companies state-action immunity from federal antitrust liability, 119 L Ed 2d 410

Workers' Compensation (this index)

INTENTIONAL, WILLFUL, OR WANTON ACTS
Battered child syndrome: introduction of evidence to prove battered child syndrome at California murder trial for allegedly killing infant, and jury instruction as to evidence's use, held not to violate due process, 116 L Ed 2d 385

Cruel and unusual punishment: prisoner held able to maintain claim of cruel and unusual punishment under Federal Constitution's Eighth Amendment based on officers' excessive use of force not resulting in serious injury, 117 L Ed 2d 156

INTERCITY RAIL PASSENGER SERVICE
Acquisition of property: Interstate Commerce Commission held to have authority, under 45 USCS § 562(d)(1), to require conveyance of track from railroad to Amtrak for purpose of reconveying track to second railroad, 118 L Ed 2d 52

INTEREST IN PROPERTY
Bankruptcy: debtor in bankruptcy held not entitled under 11 USCS § 506(d) to strip down creditor's lien on real property to judicially determined value of collateral, 116 L Ed 2d 903

INTERIOR SECRETARY
Endangered Species Act: environmental groups held to lack standing to challenge regulation interpreting § 7(a)(2) of Endangered Species Act (16 USCS § 1536(a)(2)) not to apply to actions taken in foreign nations, 119 L Ed 2d 351

INTERLOCUTORY JUDGMENTS OR ORDERS
Bankruptcy: Federal Court of Appeals held to have jurisdiction under 28 USCS § 1292 to review interlocutory order by Federal District Court sitting as appellate court in bankruptcy, 117 L Ed 2d 391

INTERNAL REVENUE CODE AND SERVICE
Taxation (this index)

INTERNATIONAL LAW
Abduction: forcible abduction of Mexican citizen to United States held not to violate extradition treaty with Mexico, and thus, not to prohibit citizen's trial in Federal District Court on criminal charges, 119 L Ed 2d 441

INDEX

INVOLUNTARY MANSLAUGHTER—Cont'd

Juvenile Delinquency Act provision limiting detention to maximum term authorized for one convicted as adult held to refer to maximum sentence authorized under United States Sentencing Guidelines, 117 L Ed 2d 559

JAILS

Prisons and Prisoners (this index)

JONES ACT

Federal Employers' Liability Act (45 USCS §§ 51-60) held to create cause of action, enforceable in state court, against state-owned railroad, 116 L Ed 2d 560

Maritime worker whose occupation of ship repairman was listed in Longshore and Harbor Workers' Compensation Act (33 USCS § 902(3)) held not precluded from being seaman under Jones Act (46 USCS Appx § 688), 116 L Ed 2d 405

JUDGES

Excessive force: state judge held immune from 42 USCS § 1983 suit for money damages for alleged use of excessive force by police officers in bringing public defender into courtroom pursuant to judge's alleged order, 116 L Ed 2d 9

JUDICIAL NOTICE

Dismissal of in forma pauperis action as factually frivolous under 28 USCS § 1915(d) held (1) appropriate where alleged facts are irrational or incredible, and (2) reviewable for abuse of discretion, 118 L Ed 2d 340

JURISDICTION

Abduction: forcible abduction of Mexican citizen to United States held not to violate extradition treaty with Mexico, and thus, not to prohibit citizen's trial in Federal District Court on criminal charges, 119 L Ed 2d 441

Bankruptcy: Federal Court of Appeals held to have jurisdiction under 28 USCS § 1292 to review interlocutory order by Federal District Court sitting as appellate court in bankruptcy, 117 L Ed 2d 391

Coal-fired electric utilities: Oklahoma statute requiring coal-fired electric utilities to burn mixture containing at least 10 percent Oklahoma-mined coal held to violate Federal Constitution's commerce clause (Art I, § 8, cl 3), 117 L Ed 2d 1

INDEX

KRISHNA SOCIETY

Airport solicitations: regulation prohibiting repetitive solicitation of money within airport terminals operated by public authority held reasonable and thus not violative of First Amendment, 120 L Ed 2d 541

Literature distribution: regulation prohibiting repetitive distribution of literature within airport terminals operated by public authority held to violate First Amendment, 120 L Ed 2d 669

LABELS

Cigarette smoking: federal cigarette labeling and advertising statutes held to preempt some but not all state-law damages claims with respect to cigarette smoking, 120 L Ed 2d 407

LABOR AND EMPLOYMENT

Aliens: INS rule, generally requiring that bond, on which excludible alien is released pending deportability determination, contain condition forbidding unauthorized employment, held not facially invalid, 116 L Ed 2d 546

Collective Bargaining (this index)

Employment discrimination. **Civil Rights and Discrimination** (this index)

ERISA (this index)

Federal Employees Compensation Act: maritime worker whose occupation of ship repairman was listed in Longshore and Harbor Workers' Compensation Act (33 USCS § 902(3)) held not precluded from being seaman under Jones Act (46 USCS Appx § 688), 116 L Ed 2d 405

Federal Employers' Liability Act (45 USCS §§ 51-60) held to create cause of action, enforceable in state court, against state-owned railroad, 116 L Ed 2d 560

Jones Act (this index)

LMRDA claims: right to jury trial held applicable to union member's LMRDA claim; § 301(a) of LMRA held to grant federal jurisdiction over member's claim that local violated international union's constitution, 116 L Ed 2d 419

Longshore and Harbor Workers' Compensation Act (this index)

OSHA: Illinois licensing statutes held preempted by OSH Act (29 USCS §§ 651 et seq.) to extent that statutes establish occupational safety and health standards for training of hazardous waste workers, 120 L Ed 2d 73

INDEX

LABOR AND EMPLOYMENT—Cont'd
Public Officers and Employees (this index)
Sanctions: Federal District Court held authorized to impose sanctions pursuant to Rule 11 of Federal Rules of Civil Procedure, even though court is later determined to lack subject matter jurisdiction, 117 L Ed 2d 280
Store owner held not to have committed unfair labor practice under § 8(a)(1) of National Labor Relations Act (29 USCS § 158(a)(1)) by barring nonemployee union organizers from parking lot, 117 L Ed 2d 79
Veterans' Reemployment Rights Act: provision of Veterans' Reemployment Rights Act (38 USCS § 2024(d)) held not to limit length of military service after which member of Armed Forces retains right to civilian reemployment, 116 L Ed 2d 578
Workers' Compensation (this index)
Workplace Hazards (this index)

LABOR MANAGEMENT RELATIONS ACT
Jury trial: right to jury trial held applicable to union member's LMRDA claim; § 301(a) of LMRA held to grant federal jurisdiction over member's claim that local violated international union's constitution, 116 L Ed 2d 419

LABOR-MANAGEMENT REPORTING AND DISCLOSURE ACT
Jury trial: right to jury trial held applicable to union member's LMRDA claim; § 301(a) of LMRA held to grant federal jurisdiction over member's claim that local violated international union's constitution, 116 L Ed 2d 419

LANDFILLS
Waste (this index)

LANDLORD AND TENANT
Rent control: mobile home rent control ordinance, viewed in context of California statute restricting termination of mobile home park tenancy, held not to constitute physical taking under Fifth Amendment, 118 L Ed 2d 153

LANGUAGE
Deportation proceedings: Equal Access to Justice Act (5 USCS § 504, 28 USCS § 2412) held not to authorize award of attorneys' fees for administrative deportation proceedings before Immigration and Naturalization Service, 116 L Ed 2d 496

INDEX

LANHAM ACT
Inherently distinctive trade dress held protectable from infringement, under trademark law (15 USCS § 1125(a)), without proof of secondary meaning, 120 L Ed 2d 615

LAW ENFORCEMENT AGENTS AND OFFICERS
Abduction: forcible abduction of Mexican citizen to United States held not to violate extradition treaty with Mexico, and thus, not to prohibit citizen's trial in Federal District Court on criminal charges, 119 L Ed 2d 441

Immunity: Secret Service agents held entitled to qualified immunity in lawsuit involving alleged unlawful arrest where agents had reasonable grounds to believe that arrestee had threatened President, 116 L Ed 2d 589

Judicial immunity: state judge held immune from 42 USCS § 1983 suit for money damages for alleged use of excessive force by police officers in bringing public defender into courtroom pursuant to judge's alleged order, 116 L Ed 2d 9

Police services: county ordinance empowering administrator to adjust public-speech permit fee based on amount of hostility likely to be created by speech's content held to violate First Amendment, 120 L Ed 2d 101

LEAFLETTING
Airport distribution: regulation prohibiting repetitive distribution of literature within airport terminals operated by public authority held to violate First Amendment, 120 L Ed 2d 669

LEASES
Rent control: mobile home rent control ordinance, viewed in context of California statute restricting termination of mobile home park tenancy, held not to constitute physical taking under Fifth Amendment, 118 L Ed 2d 153

LEAVE OF ABSENCE
Veterans' Reemployment Rights Act: provision of Veterans' Reemployment Rights Act (38 USCS § 2024(d)) held not to limit length of military service after which member of Armed Forces retains right to civilian reemployment, 116 L Ed 2d 578

LEGISLATIVE APPORTIONMENT
Apportionment and Allocation (this index)

550

INDEX

LEGISLATIVE INTENT

Deportation proceedings: Equal Access to Justice Act (5 USCS § 504, 28 USCS § 2412) held not to authorize award of attorneys' fees for administrative deportation proceedings before Immigration and Naturalization Service, 116 L Ed 2d 496

Federal Employers' Liability Act (45 USCS §§ 51-60) held to create cause of action, enforceable in state court, against state-owned railroad, 116 L Ed 2d 560

LENITY RULE

Juvenile Delinquency Act provision limiting detention to maximum term authorized for one convicted as adult held to refer to maximum sentence authorized under United States Sentencing Guidelines, 117 L Ed 2d 559

Sherman Act: photocopier manufacturer held not entitled to summary judgment dismissing federal antitrust claims as to (1) tying arrangement between parts and service, and (2) monopolization of sale of service, 119 L Ed 2d 265

LEWDNESS, INDECENCY, AND OBSCENITY

Entrapment: government held to have failed, as matter of law, to establish that individual was predisposed to illegally receive mailing of sexually explicit depictions of children and hence was not entrapped, 118 L Ed 2d 174

LICENSES AND PERMITS

Boundaries: Secretary of Army held authorized under § 10 of Rivers and Harbors Appropriation Act (33 USCS § 403) to condition approval of port construction on Alaska's disclaimer of federal-state boundary change, 118 L Ed 2d 222

Hazardous waste disposal: federal sovereign immunity held not waived as to state-imposed punitive fines under Clean Water Act (33 USCS §§ 1251 et seq.) and Resource Conservation and Recovery Act (42 USCS §§ 6901 et seq.), 118 L Ed 2d 255

OSHA: Illinois licensing statutes held preempted by OSH Act (29 USCS §§ 651 et seq.) to extent that statutes establish occupational safety and health standards for training of hazardous waste workers, 120 L Ed 2d 73

Public-speech permit fees: county ordinance empowering administrator to adjust public-speech permit fee based on amount of hostility likely to be created by speech's content held to violate First Amendment, 120 L Ed 2d 101

551

INDEX

LIENS AND ENCUMBRANCES

Bankruptcy: debtor in bankruptcy held not entitled under 11 USCS § 506(d) to strip down creditor's lien on real property to judicially determined value of collateral, 116 L Ed 2d 903

LIMITATION OF ACTIONS

Appeals: Federal Government's 30-day appeal period held to have begun to run on date of Federal District Court's order denying motion to reconsider prior order suppressing evidence in pending criminal trial, 116 L Ed 2d 1

Bankruptcy trustee held barred, after expiration of 30-day period, from contesting validity of exemption claimed by debtor under 11 USCS § 522(*l*), despite lack of colorable basis for claim, 118 L Ed 2d 280

LITERATURE

Distribution: regulation prohibiting repetitive distribution of literature within airport terminals operated by public authority held to violate First Amendment, 120 L Ed 2d 669

LOANS

Bankruptcy (this index)

LODESTAR COMPUTATION

Attorneys' fees: enhancement of attorneys' fees above lodestar, to reflect contingent fee agreement, held not permitted in awards under environmental fee-shifting statutes (33 USCS § 1365(d), 42 USCS § 6972(e)), 120 L Ed 2d 449

LOGS AND LOGGING

Timber Harvesting (this index)

LONGSHORE AND HARBOR WORKERS' COMPENSATION ACT

Forfeiture provision of Longshore and Harbor Workers' Compensation Act (33 USCS § 933(g)) held to apply where worker not then receiving or awarded compensation from employer settles third-party claim, 120 L Ed 2d 379

Maritime worker whose occupation of ship repairman was listed in Longshore and Harbor Workers' Compensation Act (33 USCS § 902(3)) held not precluded from being seaman under Jones Act (46 USCS Appx § 688), 116 L Ed 2d 405

INDEX

LONG TERM DEBTS

Bankruptcy: payments on long-term debt held to qualify for ordinary course of business exception under 11 USCS § 547(c)(2) to bankruptcy trustee's power to avoid preferential transfers, 116 L Ed 2d 514

LOW-LEVEL RADIOACTIVE WASTE POLICY AMENDMENTS ACT OF 1985

Severability: state take title provision of Low-Level Radioactive Waste Policy Amendments Act of 1985 (42 USCS § 2021e(d)(2)(C)) held to violate Tenth Amendment, but to be severable from remainder of Act, 120 L Ed 2d 120

MAIL-ORDER HOUSES

Use tax: Federal Constitution's commerce clause (Art I, § 8, cl 3), but not due process clause of Fourteenth Amendment, held to bar enforcement of North Dakota use tax against out-of-state mail-order house, 119 L Ed 2d 91

MAIL OR MAILING

Postal Service (this index)

MALICE

Cruel and unusual punishment: prisoner held able to maintain claim of cruel and unusual punishment under Federal Constitution's Eighth Amendment based on officers' excessive use of force not resulting in serious injury, 117 L Ed 2d 156

Forma pauperis: leave to proceed in forma pauperis denied, under Supreme Court Rule 39.8, for individuals whose frequent in forma pauperis petitions had been rejected without recorded dissent, 116 L Ed 2d 293

MANDAMUS

Delays: mandamus to compel Federal Court of Appeals to issue decision on second habeas corpus petition by state prisoner condemned to death, denied where state failed to object to order delaying decision, 116 L Ed 2d 669

MARITIME LAW

Jones Act (this index)
Longshore and Harbor Workers' Compensation Act (this index)
Ports and Harbors (this index)

INDEX

MASTER AND SERVANT
Labor and Employment (this index)

MATERIAL FACTS
Habeas corpus: federal habeas corpus petitioner, seeking evidentiary hearing on claim that material facts were not adequately developed in state proceedings, held generally required to show (1) cause for failure to develop facts, and (2) prejudice resulting from such failure, 118 L Ed 2d 318

MEDICAL CARE OR TREATMENT
Abortion: Pennsylvania abortion legislation held valid, except for spousal-notice provisions, under due process clause of Federal Constitution's Fourteenth Amendment, 120 L Ed 2d 674

Bivens action: federal prisoner held not required to exhaust Federal Bureau of Prisons' internal grievance procedure before initiating Bivens action solely for money damages, 117 L Ed 2d 291

Federal Tort Claims Act ban on awards of punitive damages (28 USCS § 2674) held to apply to only damages legally considered punitive under traditional common-law principles, 116 L Ed 2d 731

Hearsay evidence: admission of testimony against accused under Illinois hearsay exceptions for spontaneous declarations and medical-treatment statements held not to violate Sixth Amendment's confrontation clause, 116 L Ed 2d 848

Incompetent or Insane Persons (this index)

MEDICATION
Drugs and Narcotics (this index)

MENTAL CAPACITY OR CONDITION
Incompetent or Insane Persons (this index)

METHAMPHETAMINES
Double jeopardy held not to bar federal conspiracy prosecution where some overt acts were based on substantive offenses for which defendant was previously convicted, 118 L Ed 2d 25

MEXICO AND MEXICAN LAW
Forcible abduction of Mexican citizen to United States held not to violate extradition treaty with Mexico, and thus, not to prohibit citizen's trial in Federal District Court on criminal charges, 119 L Ed 2d 441

554

INDEX

MILITARY
Armed Forces (this index)

MILITIA
Veterans' Reemployment Rights Act: provision of Veterans'
Reemployment Rights Act (38 USCS § 2024(d)) held not
to limit length of military service after which member of
Armed Forces retains right to civilian reemployment, 116
L Ed 2d 578

MINES AND MINERALS
Boundaries: Secretary of Army held authorized under § 10 of
Rivers and Harbors Appropriation Act (33 USCS § 403) to
condition approval of port construction on Alaska's disclaimer of federal-state boundary change, 118 L Ed 2d
222
Coal-fired electric utilities: Oklahoma statute requiring coal-
fired electric utilities to burn mixture containing at least
10 percent Oklahoma-mined coal held to violate Federal
Constitution's commerce clause (Art I, § 8, cl 3), 117 L Ed
2d 1

MINORS
Children and Minors (this index)

MITIGATION OR AGGRAVATION OF PUNISHMENT
Federal Sentencing Guidelines (this index)
Florida trial judge's improper weighing in capital sentencing
hearing of aggravating factor not supported by evidence,
in violation of Eighth Amendment, held not cured by state
appellate review, 119 L Ed 2d 326
Gang membership: introduction at capital sentencing proceeding of evidence as to defendant's membership in white
racist prison gang held to violate First Amendment where
evidence had no relevance to issues in proceeding, 117 L
Ed 2d 309
Habeas corpus: rule of decisions holding aggravating circumstances unconstitutionally vague in capital sentencing proceeding held retroactively available to support federal
habeas corpus relief, 117 L Ed 2d 367
Instructions: imposition of death sentence by Florida trial
court held to violate Eighth Amendment where jury rendering advisory verdict in sentencing hearing was instructed on invalid aggravating circumstance, 120 L Ed 2d
854

MITIGATION OR AGGRAVATION OF PUNISHMENT —Cont'd

Lesser sentence: Federal Government's refusal to request lesser sentence so as to reflect accused's substantial assistance in prosecuting another person held subject to review for constitutional violations, but particular accused held to have raised no claim to such review, 118 L Ed 2d 524

Reviewing court held authorized, in appropriate circumstances, to affirm sentence in which Federal District Court's departure from Sentencing Guidelines' range is based on valid and invalid factors, 117 L Ed 2d 341

Voir dire: Illinois trial court held to violate due process by refusing to ask potential jurors, on voir dire in capital case, whether they would automatically impose death penalty if defendant was convicted, 119 L Ed 2d 492

MOBILE HOMES, TRAILER PARKS, AND TOURIST CAMPS

Rent control: mobile home rent control ordinance, viewed in context of California statute restricting termination of mobile home park tenancy, held not to constitute physical taking under Fifth Amendment, 118 L Ed 2d 153

MODIFICATION OF DECREE

Clear showing of grievous wrong evoked by new and unforeseen conditions, held not required, under Federal Civil Procedure Rule 60(b), to modify consent decree stemming from institutional reform litigation, 116 L Ed 2d 867

MONOPOLIES

Restraints of Trade, Monopolies, and Unfair Trade Practices (this index)

MUNICIPAL CORPORATIONS AND OTHER POLITICAL SUBDIVISIONS

Ordinances (this index)

Preclearance: changes in decisionmaking powers of elected members of Alabama county commissions held not to be changes with respect to voting subject to preclearance requirements of § 5 of Voting Rights Act (42 USCS § 1973c), 117 L Ed 2d 51

MUNICIPAL CORPORATIONS AND OTHER POLITICAL SUBDIVISIONS—Cont'd

Workplace hazards: 42 USCS § 1983 held not to provide remedy for municipal employee's death, because failure to train or warn about known workplace hazards does not violate Fourteenth Amendment's due process clause, 117 L Ed 2d 261

MURDER
Homicide (this index)

NAMES

Freedom of Information Act: exemption 6 of FOIA held to authorize deletion of names and other identifying information from reports of interviews with Haitian nationals returned to Haiti after attempting illegal emigration, 116 L Ed 2d 526

NARCOTICS
Drugs and Narcotics (this index)

NATIONAL FIREARMS ACT

Tax payment for making firearm held not required, under provision of National Firearms Act (26 USCS § 5821), where pistol and kit allowing conversion of pistol into firearm are packaged as unit, 119 L Ed 2d 308

NATIONAL GUARD

Veterans' Reemployment Rights Act: provision of Veterans' Reemployment Rights Act (38 USCS § 2024(d)) held not to limit length of military service after which member of Armed Forces retains right to civilian reemployment, 116 L Ed 2d 578

NATIONAL LABOR RELATIONS ACT

Unfair labor practices: store owner held not to have committed unfair labor practice under § 8(a)(1) of National Labor Relations Act (29 USCS § 158(a)(1)) by barring nonemployee union organizers from parking lot, 117 L Ed 2d 79

NATIONAL MARINE FISHERIES SERVICE

Endangered Species Act: environmental groups held to lack standing to challenge regulation interpreting § 7(a)(2) of Endangered Species Act (16 USCS § 1536(a)(2)) not to apply to actions taken in foreign nations, 119 L Ed 2d 351

INDEX

NONDOMICILIARY CORPORATIONS—Cont'd
Venue: equal protection held not violated by Montana venue rules allowing civil suit against Montana corporation in only county of principal place of business, but against foreign corporation in any county, 119 L Ed 2d 432

NONSUIT
Dismissal, Discontinuance, and Nonsuit (this index)

NORTHERN SPOTTED OWL
Timber harvesting: provision that statute meets requirements of earlier statutes on which specified pending cases involving logging and endangered spotted owl are based, held not to violate Federal Constitution's Article III, 118 L Ed 2d 73

NOTICE OR KNOWLEDGE
Abortion: Pennsylvania abortion legislation held valid, except for spousal-notice provisions, under due process clause of Federal Constitution's Fourteenth Amendment, 120 L Ed 2d 674

Appeal, Error, and Review (this index)

Habeas corpus: federal habeas corpus petitioner, seeking evidentiary hearing on claim that material facts were not adequately developed in state proceedings, held generally required to show (1) cause for failure to develop facts, and (2) prejudice resulting from such failure, 118 L Ed 2d 318

Judicial notice: dismissal of in forma pauperis action as factually frivolous under 28 USCS § 1915(d) held (1) appropriate where alleged facts are irrational or incredible, and (2) reviewable for abuse of discretion, 118 L Ed 2d 340

OBJECTIONS
Bankruptcy trustee held barred, after expiration of 30-day period, from contesting validity of exemption claimed by debtor under 11 USCS § 522(*l*), despite lack of colorable basis for claim, 118 L Ed 2d 280

OBSCENITY, LEWDNESS AND INDECENCY
Entrapment: government held to have failed, as matter of law, to establish that individual was predisposed to illegally receive mailing of sexually explicit depictions of children and hence was not entrapped, 118 L Ed 2d 174

559

INDEX

OCCUPANCY
Use, Occupancy, or Enjoyment (this index)

OCCUPATIONAL SAFETY AND HEALTH ACT
Preemption: Illinois licensing statutes held preempted by OSH Act (29 USCS §§ 651 et seq.) to extent that statutes establish occupational safety and health standards for training of hazardous waste workers, 120 L Ed 2d 73

ONE-PERSON-ONE-VOTE RULE
Apportionment of members of Congress among several states according to method of equal proportions under 2 USCS § 2a held not to violate Article I, § 2 of Federal Constitution, 118 L Ed 2d 87

OPINION OR BELIEF
Asylum: Guatemalan guerrillas' attempt to coerce Guatemalan into military service held not necessarily to constitute persecution on account of political opinion so as to make Guatemalan eligible for asylum in United States, 117 L Ed 2d 38

Gang membership: introduction at capital sentencing proceeding of evidence as to defendant's membership in white racist prison gang held to violate First Amendment where evidence had no relevance to issues in proceeding, 117 L Ed 2d 309

ORDINANCES
Cross burning: city ordinance, banning display of symbols—including burning cross—that arouse anger in others on basis of race, color, creed, religion, or gender, held facially invalid under First Amendment, 120 L Ed 2d 305

Public-speech permit fees: county ordinance empowering administrator to adjust public-speech permit fee based on amount of hostility likely to be created by speech's content held to violate First Amendment, 120 L Ed 2d 101

Rent control: mobile home rent control ordinance, viewed in context of California statute restricting termination of mobile home park tenancy, held not to constitute physical taking under Fifth Amendment, 118 L Ed 2d 153

INDEX

ORDINARY AND NECESSARY BUSINESS EXPENSES
Income tax deductions: professional expenses incurred by target corporation in course of friendly takeover held not deductible by corporation as ordinary and necessary business expenses under § 162(a) of Internal Revenue Code (26 USCS § 162(a)), 117 L Ed 2d 226

ORDINARY COURSE OF BUSINESS
Bankruptcy: payments on long-term debt held to qualify for ordinary course of business exception under 11 USCS § 547(c)(2) to bankruptcy trustee's power to avoid preferential transfers, 116 L Ed 2d 514

ORIGINAL JURISDICTION
Coal-fired electric utilities: Oklahoma statute requiring coal-fired electric utilities to burn mixture containing at least 10 percent Oklahoma-mined coal held to violate Federal Constitution's commerce clause (Art I, § 8, cl 3), 117 L Ed 2d 1

Red Cross: original federal court jurisdiction over all cases to which American National Red Cross is party held conferred by sue and be sued provision (36 USCS § 2) of Red Cross' federal corporate charter, 120 L Ed 2d 201

OSHA
Preemption: Illinois licensing statutes held preempted by OSH Act (29 USCS §§ 651 et seq.) to extent that statutes establish occupational safety and health standards for training of hazardous waste workers, 120 L Ed 2d 73

OUT-OF-STATE
Foreign State or Country (this index)

OVERBREADTH
Cross burning: city ordinance, banning display of symbols—including burning cross—that arouse anger in others on basis of race, color, creed, religion, or gender, held facially invalid under First Amendment, 120 L Ed 2d 305

OVERSEAS FEDERAL EMPLOYEES
Census: allocation of overseas federal employees to home states, for purposes of congressional reapportionment, held (1) not final agency action reviewable under APA; and (2) not unconstitutional, 120 L Ed 2d 636

INDEX

OVERT ACTS OR MATTERS
Conspiracy: double jeopardy held not to bar federal conspiracy prosecution where some overt acts were based on substantive offenses for which defendant was previously convicted, 118 L Ed 2d 25

PAIN AND SUFFERING
Cruel and unusual punishment: prisoner held able to maintain claim of cruel and unusual punishment under Federal Constitution's Eighth Amendment based on officers' excessive use of force not resulting in serious injury, 117 L Ed 2d 156

PAMPHLETS
Distribution: regulation prohibiting repetitive distribution of literature within airport terminals operated by public authority held to violate First Amendment, 120 L Ed 2d 669

PARADES
Public-speech permit fees: county ordinance empowering administrator to adjust public-speech permit fee based on amount of hostility likely to be created by speech's content held to violate First Amendment, 120 L Ed 2d 101

PARENT AND CHILD
Abortion: Pennsylvania abortion legislation held valid, except for spousal-notice provisions, under due process clause of Federal Constitution's Fourteenth Amendment, 120 L Ed 2d 674

Child Abuse or Neglect (this index)

Children and Minors (this index)

Foster care and adoption: provision of Adoption Assistance and Child Welfare Act of 1980 (42 USCS § 671(a)(15)) held not enforceable in private action under 42 USCS § 1983 or in suit directly under Act, 118 L Ed 2d 1

PARENT AND SUBSIDIARY CORPORATIONS
Taxation: Iowa business tax statute's treatment of corporation's dividends received from foreign subsidiary held to violate Federal Constitution's foreign commerce clause, 120 L Ed 2d 59

INDEX

PARKING PLACES AND LOTS

Labor unions: store owner held not to have committed unfair labor practice under § 8(a)(1) of National Labor Relations Act (29 USCS § 158(a)(1)) by barring nonemployee union organizers from parking lot, 117 L Ed 2d 79

PARTIES

Coal-fired electric utilities: Oklahoma statute requiring coal-fired electric utilities to burn mixture containing at least 10 percent Oklahoma-mined coal held to violate Federal Constitution's commerce clause (Art I, § 8, cl 3), 117 L Ed 2d 1

Endangered Species Act: environmental groups held to lack standing to challenge regulation interpreting § 7(a)(2) of Endangered Species Act (16 USCS § 1536(a)(2)) not to apply to actions taken in foreign nations, 119 L Ed 2d 351

Standing (this index)

Stock manipulation: Securities Investor Protection Corp. held unable to maintain RICO suit under 18 USCS § 1964(c) against party to scheme that allegedly disabled broker-dealers from meeting obligations to customers, 117 L Ed 2d 532

PAYMENTS

Bankruptcy: payments on long-term debt held to qualify for ordinary course of business exception under 11 USCS § 547(c)(2) to bankruptcy trustee's power to avoid preferential transfers, 116 L Ed 2d 514

Fees and Expenses (this index)

Foster care and adoption: provision of Adoption Assistance and Child Welfare Act of 1980 (42 USCS § 671(a)(15)) held not enforceable in private action under 42 USCS § 1983 or in suit directly under Act, 118 L Ed 2d 1

Son of Sam laws: New York statute, requiring that criminal's income from books or other works describing crime be escrowed and made available to victims of crime, held inconsistent with Federal Constitutions's First Amendment, 116 L Ed 2d 476

PECUNIARY INJURIES

Federal Tort Claims Act ban on awards of punitive damages (28 USCS § 2674) held to apply to only damages legally considered punitive under traditional common-law principles, 116 L Ed 2d 731

INDEX

PERSONNEL DEPARTMENT OR RECORDS

Freedom of Information Act: exemption 6 of FOIA held to authorize deletion of names and other identifying information from reports of interviews with Haitian nationals returned to Haiti after attempting illegal emigration, 116 L Ed 2d 526

PETITIONS

Elections: Illinois election laws, as construed to bar new party from running county candidates for lack of 25,000 petition signatures in each electoral district, held to violate First and Fourteenth Amendments, 116 L Ed 2d 711

PHOTOCOPIER MANUFACTURERS

Sherman Act: photocopier manufacturer held not entitled to summary judgment dismissing federal antitrust claims as to (1) tying arrangement between parts and service, and (2) monopolization of sale of service, 119 L Ed 2d 265

PHYSICAL AND MENTAL EXAMINATIONS

Hearsay evidence: admission of testimony against accused under Illinois hearsay exceptions for spontaneous declarations and medical-treatment statements held not to violate Sixth Amendment's confrontation clause, 116 L Ed 2d 848

Incompetence: California statute, requiring that criminal defendant bear burden of proving incompetence to stand trial by preponderance of evidence, held not to violate due process, 120 L Ed 2d 353

PHYSICAL PRESENCE TEST

Use tax: Federal Constitution's commerce clause (Art I, § 8, cl 3), but not due process clause of Fourteenth Amendment, held to bar enforcement of North Dakota use tax against out-of-state mail-order house, 119 L Ed 2d 91

PHYSICIANS AND SURGEONS

Abortion: Pennsylvania abortion legislation held valid, except for spousal-notice provisions, under due process clause of Federal Constitution's Fourteenth Amendment, 120 L Ed 2d 674

Incompetent or Insane Persons (this index)
Medical Care or Treatment (this index)
Physical and Mental Examinations (this index)

INDEX

PISTOLS

Tax payment for making firearm held not required, under provision of National Firearms Act (26 USCS § 5821), where pistol and kit allowing conversion of pistol into firearm are packaged as unit, 119 L Ed 2d 308

PLEA BARGAINS

Lesser sentence: Federal Government's refusal to request lesser sentence so as to reflect accused's substantial assistance in prosecuting another person held subject to review for constitutional violations, but particular accused held to have raised no claim to such review, 118 L Ed 2d 524

PLEADINGS

Forma pauperis actions: dismissal of in forma pauperis action as factually frivolous under 28 USCS § 1915(d) held (1) appropriate where alleged facts are irrational or incredible, and (2) reviewable for abuse of discretion, 118 L Ed 2d 340

Nolo contendere plea: federal habeas corpus petitioner, seeking evidentiary hearing on claim that material facts were not adequately developed in state proceedings, held generally required to show (1) cause for failure to develop facts, and (2) prejudice resulting from such failure, 118 L Ed 2d 318

Sanctions: Federal District Court held authorized to impose sanctions pursuant to Rule 11 of Federal Rules of Civil Procedure, even though court is later determined to lack subject matter jurisdiction, 117 L Ed 2d 280

POLICE
Law Enforcement Agents and Officers (this index)

POLICE POWER

Hazardous waste disposal: disposal fee imposed by Alabama on hazardous waste generated out of state, but not on waste generated in state, held to violate Federal Constitution's commerce clause (Art I, § 8, cl 3), 119 L Ed 2d 121

POLITICAL SUBDIVISIONS
Municipal Corporations and Other Political Subdivisions (this index)

POLITICS AND POLITICAL MATTERS

Apportionment of members of Congress among several states according to method of equal proportions under 2 USCS § 2a held not to violate Article I, § 2 of Federal Constitution, 118 L Ed 2d 87

Asylum: Guatemalan guerrillas' attempt to coerce Guatemalan into military service held not necessarily to constitute persecution on account of political opinion so as to make Guatemalan eligible for asylum in United States, 117 L Ed 2d 38

Elections and Voting (this index)

Nominating petitions: Illinois election laws, as construed to bar new party from running county candidates for lack of 25,000 petition signatures in each electoral district, held to violate First and Fourteenth Amendments, 116 L Ed 2d 711

Preclearance: changes in decisionmaking powers of elected members of Alabama county commissions held not to be changes with respect to voting subject to preclearance requirements of § 5 of Voting Rights Act (42 USCS § 1973c), 117 L Ed 2d 51

POLLING PLACES

Solicitation of votes: Tennessee statute prohibiting solicitation of votes and display or distribution of campaign literature within 100 feet of entrance to polling place held not to violate First and Fourteenth Amendments, 119 L Ed 2d 5

POLLUTION

Clean Water Act (this index)
Environmental Law (this index)
Hazardous Substances (this index)
Waste (this index)

POOR PERSONS

Forma Pauperis (this index)

PORNOGRAPHY

Entrapment: government held to have failed, as matter of law, to establish that individual was predisposed to illegally receive mailing of sexually explicit depictions of children and hence was not entrapped, 118 L Ed 2d 174

INDEX

PORTS AND HARBORS
Boundaries: Secretary of Army held authorized under § 10 of Rivers and Harbors Appropriation Act (33 USCS § 403) to condition approval of port construction on Alaska's disclaimer of federal-state boundary change, 118 L Ed 2d 222

Longshore and Harbor Workers' Compensation Act (this index)

POSTAL SERVICE
Entrapment: government held to have failed, as matter of law, to establish that individual was predisposed to illegally receive mailing of sexually explicit depictions of children and hence was not entrapped, 118 L Ed 2d 174

Use tax: Federal Constitution's commerce clause (Art I, § 8, cl 3), but not due process clause of Fourteenth Amendment, held to bar enforcement of North Dakota use tax against out-of-state mail-order house, 119 L Ed 2d 91

POVERTY
Forma Pauperis (this index)

PRAYER
First Amendment: inclusion of invocation and benediction by member of clergy at public secondary school graduation held forbidden by First Amendment's establishment of religion clause, 120 L Ed 2d 467

PRECEDENT
Federal Employers' Liability Act (45 USCS §§ 51-60) held to create cause of action, enforceable in state court, against state-owned railroad, 116 L Ed 2d 560

Labor unions: store owner held not to have committed unfair labor practice under § 8(a)(1) of National Labor Relations Act (29 USCS § 158(a)(1)) by barring nonemployee union organizers from parking lot, 117 L Ed 2d 79

PRECLEARANCE
Voting: changes in decisionmaking powers of elected members of Alabama county commissions held not to be changes with respect to voting subject to preclearance requirements of § 5 of Voting Rights Act (42 USCS § 1973c), 117 L Ed 2d 51

INDEX

PREEMPTION AND PREEMPTIVE RIGHTS

Airline fares: enforcement, through state consumer-protection laws, of restrictions on advertising of airline fares held preempted by provision of Airline Deregulation Act of 1978 (49 USCS Appx § 1305(a)(1)), 119 L Ed 2d 157

Cigarettes: federal cigarette labeling and advertising statutes held to preempt some but not all state-law damages claims with respect to cigarette smoking, 120 L Ed 2d 407

Jones Act: maritime worker whose occupation of ship repairman was listed in Longshore and Harbor Workers' Compensation Act (33 USCS § 902(3)) held not precluded from being seaman under Jones Act (46 USCS Appx § 688), 116 L Ed 2d 405

OSHA: Illinois licensing statutes held preempted by OSH Act (29 USCS §§ 651 et seq.) to extent that statutes establish occupational safety and health standards for training of hazardous waste workers, 120 L Ed 2d 73

PREFERENTIAL TRANSFERS

Bankruptcy: transfer of check, for purposes of determining whether transfer is voidable under 11 USCS § 547(b)(4)(A) as occurring within 90 days of bankruptcy filing, held to occur on date drawee bank honors check, 118 L Ed 2d 39

Payments on long-term debt held to qualify for ordinary course of business exception under 11 USCS § 547(c)(2) to bankruptcy trustee's power to avoid preferential transfers, 116 L Ed 2d 514

PREGNANCY

Abortion: Pennsylvania abortion legislation held valid, except for spousal-notice provisions, under due process clause of Federal Constitution's Fourteenth Amendment, 120 L Ed 2d 674

PREJUDICE

Habeas corpus: federal habeas corpus petitioner, seeking evidentiary hearing on claim that material facts were not adequately developed in state proceedings, held generally required to show (1) cause for failure to develop facts, and (2) prejudice resulting from such failure, 118 L Ed 2d 318

Speedy trial: Federal Government's negligent 8½-year delay between indictment and arrest held to violate accused's Sixth Amendment right to speedy trial despite lack of showing of actual prejudice, 120 L Ed 2d 520

INDEX

PREPONDERANCE OF EVIDENCE
Competency: California statute, requiring that criminal defendant bear burden of proving incompetence to stand trial by preponderance of evidence, held not to violate due process, 120 L Ed 2d 353

PRESENTENCE DETENTION
Credit for time served: federal sentencing credit under 18 USCS § 3585(b) for certain presentence time served held required to be computed by Attorney General after convicted federal defendant has begun to serve sentence, 117 L Ed 2d 593

PRESIDENT OF UNITED STATES
Census: allocation of overseas federal employees to home states, for purposes of congressional reapportionment, held (1) not final agency action reviewable under APA; and (2) not unconstitutional, 120 L Ed 2d 636

Threats: Secret Service agents held entitled to qualified immunity in lawsuit involving alleged unlawful arrest where agents had reasonable grounds to believe that arrestee had threatened President, 116 L Ed 2d 589

PRESS, FREEDOM OF
Freedom of Speech and Press (this index)

PRESUMPTIONS AND BURDEN OF PROOF
Battered child syndrome: introduction of evidence to prove battered child syndrome at California murder trial for allegedly killing infant, and jury instruction as to evidence's use, held not to violate due process, 116 L Ed 2d 385

Cigarette smoking: federal cigarette labeling and advertising statutes held to preempt some but not all state-law damages claims with respect to cigarette smoking, 120 L Ed 2d 407

Cross burning: city ordinance, banning display of symbols— including burning cross—that arouse anger in others on basis of race, color, creed, religion, or gender, held facially invalid under First Amendment, 120 L Ed 2d 305

Deportation: INS rule generally requiring that bond on which excludible alien is released, pending deportability determination, contain condition forbidding unauthorized employment held not facially invalid, 116 L Ed 2d 546

PRESUMPTIONS AND BURDEN OF PROOF—Cont'd

ERISA: interest in ERISA-qualified pension plan held subject to transfer restriction under applicable nonbankruptcy law, and thus excludible from property of bankruptcy estate under 11 USCS § 541(c)(2), 119 L Ed 2d 519

Habeas corpus: accused held not to have satisfied actual innocence exception so as to allow federal habeas corpus consideration of successive and abusive claims challenging Louisiana death sentence, 120 L Ed 2d 269

Incompetence: California statute, requiring that criminal defendant bear burden of proving incompetence to stand trial by preponderance of evidence, held not to violate due process, 120 L Ed 2d 353

Mitigation or aggravation of punishment: Florida trial judge's improper weighing in capital sentencing hearing of aggravating factor not supported by evidence, in violation of Eighth Amendment, held not cured by state appellate review, 119 L Ed 2d 326

Peremptory challenges: accused's objection under equal protection clause to state's race-based use of peremptory challenges prior to Supreme Court's decision in Batson v Kentucky held preserved for review by Supreme Court, 118 L Ed 2d 193

Rent control: mobile home rent control ordinance, viewed in context of California statute restricting termination of mobile home park tenancy, held not to constitute physical taking under Fifth Amendment, 118 L Ed 2d 153

Sex discrimination: damages remedy held available in sex discrimination action under Title IX of Education Amendments of 1972 (20 USCS §§ 1681-1688), 117 L Ed 2d 208

Sherman Act: photocopier manufacturer held not entitled to summary judgment dismissing federal antitrust claims as to (1) tying arrangement between parts and service, and (2) monopolization of sale of service, 119 L Ed 2d 265

PRICE FIXING

Title-search ratesetting: supervision by states of title-search ratesetting held not sufficiently active to give title insurance companies state-action immunity from federal antitrust liability, 119 L Ed 2d 410

INDEX

PRIMARY ELECTIONS
Write-in voting: Hawaii's prohibition on write-in voting held not to violate rights of state's voters under Federal Constitution's First and Fourteenth Amendments, 119 L Ed 2d 245

PRIOR ACTION OR PROCEEDING
Similar motive: showing of similar motive to develop testimony held necessary, under Federal Evidence Rule 804(b)(1), for admission of grand jury testimony of witness invoking Fifth Amendment privilege, 120 L Ed 2d 255

PRIOR CONVICTIONS
Habeas corpus: evidence held (1) sufficient to support state court grand larceny conviction, and thus (2) to require denial of federal habeas corpus relief based on insufficiency of evidence, 120 L Ed 2d 225

PRIOR RESTRAINTS
Public-speech permit fees: county ordinance empowering administrator to adjust public-speech permit fee based on amount of hostility likely to be created by speech's content held to violate First Amendment, 120 L Ed 2d 101

PRISONS AND PRISONERS
Bivens action: federal prisoner held not required to exhaust Federal Bureau of Prisons' internal grievance procedure before initiating Bivens action solely for money damages, 117 L Ed 2d 291

Consent decree: clear showing of grievous wrong evoked by new and unforeseen conditions, held not required, under Federal Civil Procedure Rule 60(b), to modify consent decree stemming from institutional reform litigation, 116 L Ed 2d 867

Credit for time served: federal sentencing credit under 18 USCS § 3585(b) for certain presentence time served held required to be computed by Attorney General after convicted federal defendant has begun to serve sentence, 117 L Ed 2d 593

Forma pauperis actions: dismissal of in forma pauperis action as factually frivolous under 28 USCS § 1915(d) held (1) appropriate where alleged facts are irrational or incredible, and (2) reviewable for abuse of discretion, 118 L Ed 2d 340

INDEX

PRISONS AND PRISONERS—Cont'd

Gang membership: introduction at capital sentencing proceeding of evidence as to defendant's membership in white racist prison gang held to violate First Amendment where evidence had no relevance to issues in proceeding, 117 L Ed 2d 309

Juvenile Delinquency Act provision limiting detention to maximum term authorized for one convicted as adult held to refer to maximum sentence authorized under United States Sentencing Guidelines, 117 L Ed 2d 559

PRIVACY

Abortion: Pennsylvania abortion legislation held valid, except for spousal-notice provisions, under due process clause of Federal Constitution's Fourteenth Amendment, 120 L Ed 2d 674

Freedom of Information Act: exemption 6 of FOIA held to authorize deletion of names and other identifying information from reports of interviews with Haitian nationals returned to Haiti after attempting illegal emigration, 116 L Ed 2d 526

PRIVATE PERSONS

Replevin: private defendants who invoke state replevin, garnishment, and attachment statutes that are declared unconstitutional, held not entitled to qualified immunity from suit under 42 USCS § 1983, 118 L Ed 2d 504

PRIVATE PROPERTY

Labor unions: store owner held not to have committed unfair labor practice under § 8(a)(1) of National Labor Relations Act (29 USCS § 158(a)(1)) by barring nonemployee union organizers from parking lot, 117 L Ed 2d 79

PRIVILEGES AND IMMUNITIES

Bankruptcy: sovereign immunity of United States held not unequivocally waived with respect to bankruptcy trustee's claim against Internal Revenue Service for monetary relief, 117 L Ed 2d 181

Default: commercial exception in Foreign Sovereign Immunities Act held to authorize Federal District Court's jurisdiction over civil suit concerning Argentina's alleged default on certain public bonds, 119 L Ed 2d 394

PRODUCTS LIABILITY

Cigarette smoking: federal cigarette labeling and advertising statutes held to preempt some but not all state-law damages claims with respect to cigarette smoking, 120 L Ed 2d 407

Red Cross: original federal court jurisdiction over all cases to which American National Red Cross is party held conferred by sue and be sued provision (36 USCS § 2) of Red Cross' federal corporate charter, 120 L Ed 2d 201

PROFITS

Son of Sam laws: New York statute, requiring that criminal's income from books or other works describing crime be escrowed and made available to victims of crime, held inconsistent with Federal Constitutions's First Amendment, 116 L Ed 2d 476

PROMOTIONS

Income tax: backpay received in settlement of claims under Title VII of Civil Rights Act of 1964 held not excludible from gross income under § 104(a)(2) of Internal Revenue Code as damages for personal injuries, 119 L Ed 2d 34

PROPERTY TAXES

Real Property Taxes (this index)

PROSECUTING ATTORNEY

Disclosure: United States Court of Appeals held to exceed its authority by imposing rule under which prosecutor must present to grand jury substantial exculpatory evidence in prosecutor's possession, 118 L Ed 2d 352

PROSPECTIVE OR RETROSPECTIVE MATTERS

Capital sentencing: rule of decisions holding aggravating circumstances unconstitutionally vague in capital sentencing proceeding held retroactively available to support federal habeas corpus relief, 117 L Ed 2d 367

Workers' compensation: state-mandated payment of workers' compensation benefits withheld under benefit coordination statute held not to violate contract clause or due process clause of Federal Constitution, 117 L Ed 2d 328

INDEX

PROTECTIONISM
County landfill: Michigan statute barring private landfill owner from accepting solid waste originating outside county in which landfill was located held to violate Federal Constitution's commerce clause (Art I, § 8, cl 3), 119 L Ed 2d 139

Hazardous waste: disposal fee imposed by Alabama on hazardous waste generated out of state, but not on waste generated in state, held to violate Federal Constitution's commerce clause (Art I, § 8, cl 3), 119 L Ed 2d 121

PROXIMATE CAUSE
Stock manipulation: Securities Investor Protection Corp. held unable to maintain RICO suit under 18 USCS § 1964(c) against party to scheme that allegedly disabled broker-dealers from meeting obligations to customers, 117 L Ed 2d 532

PSYCHIATRY
Incompetent or Insane Persons (this index)

PUBLICATIONS
Distribution: regulation prohibiting repetitive distribution of literature within airport terminals operated by public authority held to violate First Amendment, 120 L Ed 2d 669

Son of Sam laws: New York statute, requiring that criminal's income from books or other works describing crime be escrowed and made available to victims of crime, held inconsistent with Federal Constitutions's First Amendment, 116 L Ed 2d 476

PUBLIC CORRUPTION
Extortion: affirmative act of inducement by public official, such as demand, held not to be necessary element of Hobbs Act offense of extortion under color of official right (18 USCS § 1951(b)(2)), 119 L Ed 2d 57

PUBLIC DEFENDER
Excessive force: state judge held immune from 42 USCS § 1983 suit for money damages for alleged use of excessive force by police officers in bringing public defender into courtroom pursuant to judge's alleged order, 116 L Ed 2d 9

576

INDEX

PUBLIC FUNDS AND MONEY

Waste disposal: state take title provision of Low-Level Radioactive Waste Policy Amendments Act of 1985 (42 USCS § 2021e(d)(2)(C)) held to violate Tenth Amendment, but to be severable from remainder of Act, 120 L Ed 2d 120

PUBLIC HEALTH CIGARETTE SMOKING ACT OF L969

Cigarette smoking: federal cigarette labeling and advertising statutes held to preempt some but not all state-law damages claims with respect to cigarette smoking, 120 L Ed 2d 407

PUBLIC LANDS OR PROPERTY

Airport solicitations: regulation prohibiting repetitive solicitation of money within airport terminals operated by public authority held reasonable and thus not violative of First Amendment, 120 L Ed 2d 541

Literature distribution: regulation prohibiting repetitive distribution of literature within airport terminals operated by public authority held to violate First Amendment, 120 L Ed 2d 669

Public-speech permit fees: county ordinance empowering administrator to adjust public-speech permit fee based on amount of hostility likely to be created by speech's content held to violate First Amendment, 120 L Ed 2d 101

Secretary of Army held authorized under § 10 of Rivers and Harbors Appropriation Act (33 USCS § 403) to condition approval of port construction on Alaska's disclaimer of federal-state boundary change, 118 L Ed 2d 222

Timber harvesting: provision that statute meets requirements of earlier statutes on which specified pending cases involving logging and endangered spotted owl are based, held not to violate Federal Constitution's Article III, 118 L Ed 2d 73

PUBLIC OFFICERS AND EMPLOYEES

Law Enforcement Agents or Officers (this index)

Privileges and Immunities (this index)

Replevin: private defendants who invoke state replevin, garnishment, and attachment statutes that are declared unconstitutional, held not entitled to qualified immunity from suit under 42 USCS § 1983, 118 L Ed 2d 504

PUBLIC OFFICERS AND EMPLOYEES—Cont'd

Retirement benefits: Kansas' income tax on military retirement benefits, but not on state and local government retirement benefits, held inconsistent with 4 USCS § 111 prohibition against discriminatory taxes, 118 L Ed 2d 243

Workplace hazards: 42 USCS § 1983 held not to provide remedy for municipal employee's death, because failure to train or warn about known workplace hazards does not violate Fourteenth Amendment's due process clause, 117 L Ed 2d 261

PUBLIC UTILITIES

Coal-fired electric utilities: Oklahoma statute requiring coal-fired electric utilities to burn mixture containing at least 10 percent Oklahoma-mined coal held to violate Federal Constitution's commerce clause (Art I, § 8, cl 3), 117 L Ed 2d 1

PUNISHMENT

Sentence and Punishment (this index)

QUALIFIED IMMUNITY

Privileges and Immunities (this index)

QUESTIONS OF LAW AND FACT

Immunity: Secret Service agents held entitled to qualified immunity in lawsuit involving alleged unlawful arrest where agents had reasonable grounds to believe that arrestee had threatened President, 116 L Ed 2d 589

QUID PRO QUO

Extortion: affirmative act of inducement by public official, such as demand, held not to be necessary element of Hobbs Act offense of extortion under color of official right (18 USCS § 1951(b)(2)), 119 L Ed 2d 57

RACIAL DISCRIMINATION

Civil Rights and Discrimination (this index)

RACISM

Civil Rights and Discrimination (this index)

Gang membership: introduction at capital sentencing proceeding of evidence as to defendant's membership in white racist prison gang held to violate First Amendment where evidence had no relevance to issues in proceeding, 117 L Ed 2d 309

RACKETEER INFLUENCED AND CORRUPT ORGANIZATIONS ACT

Stock manipulation: Securities Investor Protection Corp. held unable to maintain RICO suit under 18 USCS § 1964(c) against party to scheme that allegedly disabled broker-dealers from meeting obligations to customers, 117 L Ed 2d 532

RADIOACTIVE WASTE DISPOSAL

Waste disposal: state take title provision of Low-Level Radioactive Waste Policy Amendments Act of 1985 (42 USCS § 2021e(d)(2)(C)) held to violate Tenth Amendment, but to be severable from remainder of Act, 120 L Ed 2d 120

RAIL PASSENGER SERVICE ACT OF 1970

Conveyance of track: Interstate Commerce Commission held to have authority, under 45 USCS § 562(d)(1), to require conveyance of track from railroad to Amtrak for purpose of reconveying track to second railroad, 118 L Ed 2d 52

RAILROADS

Acquisition of property: Interstate Commerce Commission held to have authority, under 45 USCS § 562(d)(1), to require conveyance of track from railroad to Amtrak for purpose of reconveying track to second railroad, 118 L Ed 2d 52

Federal Employers' Liability Act (45 USCS §§ 51-60) held to create cause of action, enforceable in state court, against state-owned railroad, 116 L Ed 2d 560

RALLIES

Public-speech permit fees: county ordinance empowering administrator to adjust public-speech permit fee based on amount of hostility likely to be created by speech's content held to violate First Amendment, 120 L Ed 2d 101

RAPE

Hearsay evidence: admission of testimony against accused under Illinois hearsay exceptions for spontaneous declarations and medical-treatment statements held not to violate Sixth Amendment's confrontation clause, 116 L Ed 2d 848

RATES AND CHARGES

Fees and Expenses (this index)

INDEX

RATESETTING

Title-search ratesetting: supervision by states of title-search ratesetting held not sufficiently active to give title insurance companies state-action immunity from federal antitrust liability, 119 L Ed 2d 410

REAL PROPERTY TAXES

Equal protection held not violated by California Constitution's real property tax system which generally assesses property on value at time of acquisition, rather than on current value, 120 L Ed 2d 1

Reservation land: Indian General Allotment Act of 1887 (25 USCS §§ 331 et seq.) held (1) to permit county ad valorem tax on fee-patented reservation land, but (2) not to allow county excise tax on sales of such land, 116 L Ed 2d 687

Taxpayers' actions: equal protection held not violated by California Constitution's real property tax system which generally assesses property on value at time of acquisition, rather than on current value, 120 L Ed 2d 1

REAPPORTIONMENT

Apportionment and Allocation (this index)

REASONABLE DOUBT

Habeas corpus: evidence held (1) sufficient to support state court grand larceny conviction, and thus (2) to require denial of federal habeas corpus relief based on insufficiency of evidence, 120 L Ed 2d 225

REASONABLE EFFORTS CLAUSE

Foster care and adoption: provision of Adoption Assistance and Child Welfare Act of 1980 (42 USCS § 671(a)(15)) held not enforceable in private action under 42 USCS § 1983 or in suit directly under Act, 118 L Ed 2d 1

REBATES

Refunds and Rebates (this index)

REBUTTAL

First Amendment: introduction at capital sentencing proceeding of evidence as to defendant's membership in white racist prison gang held to violate First Amendment where evidence had no relevance to issues in proceeding, 117 L Ed 2d 309

RECONSIDERATION
Appeals: Federal Government's 30-day appeal period held to have begun to run on date of Federal District Court's order denying motion to reconsider prior order suppressing evidence in pending criminal trial, 116 L Ed 2d 1

RECORDS, RECORDKEEPING, AND REPORTS
Abortion: Pennsylvania abortion legislation held valid, except for spousal-notice provisions, under due process clause of Federal Constitution's Fourteenth Amendment, 120 L Ed 2d 674

Freedom of Information Act: exemption 6 of FOIA held to authorize deletion of names and other identifying information from reports of interviews with Haitian nationals returned to Haiti after attempting illegal emigration, 116 L Ed 2d 526

RECRUITMENT
Conscription: Guatemalan guerrillas' attempt to coerce Guatemalan into military service held not necessarily to constitute persecution on account of political opinion so as to make Guatemalan eligible for asylum in United States, 117 L Ed 2d 38

RED CROSS
Jurisdiction: original federal court jurisdiction over all cases to which American National Red Cross is party held conferred by sue and be sued provision (36 USCS § 2) of Red Cross' federal corporate charter, 120 L Ed 2d 201

REEMPLOYMENT
Labor and Employment (this index)

REFUGEES AND ASYLEES
Deportation or Exclusion of Aliens (this index)

REFUNDS AND REBATES
Income tax: backpay received in settlement of claims under Title VII of Civil Rights Act of 1964 held not excludible from gross income under § 104(a)(2) of Internal Revenue Code as damages for personal injuries, 119 L Ed 2d 34

Property taxes: equal protection held not violated by California Constitution's real property tax system which generally assesses property on value at time of acquisition, rather than on current value, 120 L Ed 2d 1

INDEX

REMOVAL OF ACTIONS
Red Cross: original federal court jurisdiction over all cases to which American National Red Cross is party held conferred by sue and be sued provision (36 USCS § 2) of Red Cross' federal corporate charter, 120 L Ed 2d 201

RENT CONTROL ORDINANCES
Mobile home rent control ordinance, viewed in context of California statute restricting termination of mobile home park tenancy, held not to constitute physical taking under Fifth Amendment, 118 L Ed 2d 153

REOPENING
Deportation proceedings: Attorney General's denial of alien's motion to reopen deportation proceedings held not abuse of discretion, 116 L Ed 2d 823

REORGANIZATION
Taxation: trustee liquidating and distributing property as part of plan under Chapter 11 of Bankruptcy Code held required, as to income attributable to property, to file federal income tax returns and pay tax, 117 L Ed 2d 196

REPLEVIN
Private defendants who invoke state replevin, garnishment, and attachment statutes that are declared unconstitutional, held not entitled to qualified immunity from suit under 42 USCS § 1983, 118 L Ed 2d 504

REPORTS
Records, Recordkeeping, and Reports (this index)

REPUBLICAN FORM OF GOVERNMENT
Waste disposal: state take title provision of Low-Level Radioactive Waste Policy Amendments Act of 1985 (42 USCS § 2021e(d)(2)(C)) held to violate Tenth Amendment, but to be severable from remainder of Act, 120 L Ed 2d 120

REPUTATION
First Amendment: introduction at capital sentencing proceeding of evidence as to defendant's membership in white racist prison gang held to violate First Amendment where evidence had no relevance to issues in proceeding, 117 L Ed 2d 309

INDEX

RESERVATION LANDS

Taxation: Indian General Allotment Act of 1887 (25 USCS §§ 331 et seq.) held (1) to permit county ad valorem tax on fee-patented reservation land, but (2) not to allow county excise tax on sales of such land, 116 L Ed 2d 687

RESERVE MILITARY FORCES

Veterans' Reemployment Rights Act: provision of Veterans' Reemployment Rights Act (38 USCS § 2024(d)) held not to limit length of military service after which member of Armed Forces retains right to civilian reemployment, 116 L Ed 2d 578

RESIDENCE

Domicile and Residence (this index)

RESOURCE CONSERVATION AND RECOVERY ACT

Sovereign immunity: federal sovereign immunity held not waived as to state-imposed punitive fines under Clean Water Act (33 USCS §§ 1251 et seq.) and Resource Conservation and Recovery Act (42 USCS §§ 6901 et seq.), 118 L Ed 2d 255

RESTAURANTS AND EATING PLACES

Inherently distinctive trade dress held protectable from infringement, under trademark law (15 USCS § 1125(a)), without proof of secondary meaning, 120 L Ed 2d 615

RESTRAINTS OF TRADE, MONOPOLIES, AND UNFAIR TRADE PRACTICES

Inherently distinctive trade dress held protectable from infringement, under trademark law (15 USCS § 1125(a)), without proof of secondary meaning, 120 L Ed 2d 615

Sherman Act: photocopier manufacturer held not entitled to summary judgment dismissing federal antitrust claims as to (1) tying arrangement between parts and service, and (2) monopolization of sale of service, 119 L Ed 2d 265

Title-search ratesetting: supervision by states of title-search ratesetting held not sufficiently active to give title insurance companies state-action immunity from federal antitrust liability, 119 L Ed 2d 410

RETAILERS
Use tax: Federal Constitution's commerce clause (Art I, § 8, cl 3), but not due process clause of Fourteenth Amendment, held to bar enforcement of North Dakota use tax against out-of-state mail-order house, 119 L Ed 2d 91

RETIREMENT BENEFITS
Pensions and Retirement Benefits (this index)

RETROACTIVITY
Prospective or Retrospective Matters (this index)

REVIEW
Appeal, Error, and Review (this index)

RICO
Stock manipulation: Securities Investor Protection Corp. held unable to maintain RICO suit under 18 USCS § 1964(c) against party to scheme that allegedly disabled broker-dealers from meeting obligations to customers, 117 L Ed 2d 532

RIVERS AND HARBORS APPROPRIATION ACT
Boundaries: Secretary of Army held authorized under § 10 of Rivers and Harbors Appropriation Act (33 USCS § 403) to condition approval of port construction on Alaska's disclaimer of federal-state boundary change, 118 L Ed 2d 222

RIVERS AND STREAMS
Boundaries: Secretary of Army held authorized under § 10 of Rivers and Harbors Appropriation Act (33 USCS § 403) to condition approval of port construction on Alaska's disclaimer of federal-state boundary change, 118 L Ed 2d 222
Discharge permits: EPA's issuance of discharge permit to sewage plant, based on finding that discharges would not cause detectable violation of downstream state's water quality standards, held authorized by Clean Water Act, 117 L Ed 2d 239

ROE V WADE
Pennsylvania abortion legislation held valid, except for spousal-notice provisions, under due process clause of Federal Constitution's Fourteenth Amendment, 120 L Ed 2d 674

INDEX

RULES OF APPELLATE PROCEDURE

Federal Government's 30-day appeal period held to have begun to run on date of Federal District Court's order denying motion to reconsider prior order suppressing evidence in pending criminal trial, 116 L Ed 2d 1

Notice: informal brief filed in Federal Court of Appeals held effective as notice of appeal under Rule 3 of Federal Rules of Appellate Procedure, if filing of brief is timely and conveys information required by Rule 3, 116 L Ed 2d 678

RULES OF CIVIL PROCEDURE

Consent decree: clear showing of grievous wrong evoked by new and unforeseen conditions, held not required, under Federal Civil Procedure Rule 60(b), to modify consent decree stemming from institutional reform litigation, 116 L Ed 2d 867

Sanctions: Federal District Court held authorized to impose sanctions pursuant to Rule 11 of Federal Rules of Civil Procedure, even though court is later determined to lack subject matter jurisdiction, 117 L Ed 2d 280

Sherman Act: photocopier manufacturer held not entitled to summary judgment dismissing federal antitrust claims as to (1) tying arrangement between parts and service, and (2) monopolization of sale of service, 119 L Ed 2d 265

RULES OF EVIDENCE
Federal Rules of Evidence (this index)

RULES OF SUPREME COURT
Supreme Court Rules (this index)

SADISM

Cruel and unusual punishment: prisoner held able to maintain claim of cruel and unusual punishment under Federal Constitution's Eighth Amendment based on officers' excessive use of force not resulting in serious injury, 117 L Ed 2d 156

SAFETY
Health and Safety (this index)

SALARIES
Compensation (this index)

586

INDEX

SALE OR TRANSFER OF PROPERTY

Bankruptcy: transfer of check, for purposes of determining whether transfer is voidable under 11 USCS § 547(b)(4)(A) as occurring within 90 days of bankruptcy filing, held to occur on date drawee bank honors check, 118 L Ed 2d 39

County landfill: Michigan statute barring private landfill owner from accepting solid waste originating outside county in which landfill was located held to violate Federal Constitution's commerce clause (Art I, § 8, cl 3), 119 L Ed 2d 139

Eminent domain: South Carolina court held to have applied wrong standard in determining whether state beachfront management statute, by barring construction, effected taking of property under Fifth Amendment, 120 L Ed 2d 798

ERISA: interest in ERISA-qualified pension plan held subject to transfer restriction under applicable nonbankruptcy law, and thus excludible from property of bankruptcy estate under 11 USCS § 541(c)(2), 119 L Ed 2d 519

Hazardous waste: disposal fee imposed by Alabama on hazardous waste generated out of state, but not on waste generated in state, held to violate Federal Constitution's commerce clause (Art I, § 8, cl 3), 119 L Ed 2d 121

Income tax: state held not prohibited, under 15 USCS § 381(a), from imposing tax on gum manufacturer's income, where manufacturer's in-state activities include replacement, supply, and storage of gum, 120 L Ed 2d 174

Mail-order use tax: Federal Constitution's commerce clause (Art I, § 8, cl 3), but not due process clause of Fourteenth Amendment, held to bar enforcement of North Dakota use tax against out-of-state mail-order house, 119 L Ed 2d 91

Preferential Transfers (this index)

Railroads: Interstate Commerce Commission held to have authority, under 45 USCS § 562(d)(1), to require conveyance of track from railroad to Amtrak for purpose of reconveying track to second railroad, 118 L Ed 2d 52

Sherman Act: Sherman Act: photocopier manufacturer held not entitled to summary judgment dismissing federal antitrust claims as to (1) tying arrangement between parts and service, and (2) monopolization of sale of service, 119 L Ed 2d 265

SALE OR TRANSFER OF PROPERTY—Cont'd
Taxation
- Indian General Allotment Act of 1887 (25 USCS §§ 331 et seq.) held (1) to permit county ad valorem tax on fee-patented reservation land, but (2) not to allow county excise tax on sales of such land, 116 L Ed 2d 687
- mail-order use tax: Federal Constitution's commerce clause (Art I, § 8, cl 3), but not due process clause of Fourteenth Amendment, held to bar enforcement of North Dakota use tax against out-of-state mail-order house, 119 L Ed 2d 91
- sales and use tax: Federal Constitution's commerce clause (Art I, § 8, cl 3), but not due process clause of Fourteenth Amendment, held to bar enforcement of North Dakota use tax against out-of-state mail-order house, 119 L Ed 2d 91
- unitary business principle held to (1) govern states' federal constitutional power to tax nondomiciliary corporations' income, and (2) prevent state's taxation of gain on particular stock sale, 119 L Ed 2d 533

SALES AND USE TAX
Mail order: Federal Constitution's commerce clause (Art I, § 8, cl 3), but not due process clause of Fourteenth Amendment, held to bar enforcement of North Dakota use tax against out-of-state mail-order house, 119 L Ed 2d 91

SANITARY LANDFILLS
Waste (this index)

SAVING CLAUSE
Coal-fired electric utilities: Oklahoma statute requiring coal-fired electric utilities to burn mixture containing at least 10 percent Oklahoma-mined coal held to violate Federal Constitution's commerce clause (Art I, § 8, cl 3), 117 L Ed 2d 1

SCHOOL BUSES
Desegregation: federal court in ongoing school desegregation case held to have discretion to order incremental withdrawal of supervision over Georgia school district, 118 L Ed 2d 108

INDEX

SCHOOLS AND EDUCATION

OSHA: Illinois licensing statutes held preempted by OSH Act (29 USCS §§ 651 et seq.) to extent that statutes establish occupational safety and health standards for training of hazardous waste workers, 120 L Ed 2d 73

Religious freedom: inclusion of invocation and benediction by member of clergy at public secondary school graduation held forbidden by First Amendment's establishment of religion clause, 120 L Ed 2d 467

Segregation and Desegregation (this index)

Sex discrimination: damages remedy held available in sex discrimination action under Title IX of Education Amendments of 1972 (20 USCS §§ 1681-1688), 117 L Ed 2d 208

Teachers and Instructors (this index)

SEAMEN

Jones Act (this index)

SEARCH AND SEIZURE

Appeals: Federal Government's 30-day appeal period held to have begun to run on date of Federal District Court's order denying motion to reconsider prior order suppressing evidence in pending criminal trial, 116 L Ed 2d 1

Habeas corpus: evidence held (1) sufficient to support state court grand larceny conviction, and thus (2) to require denial of federal habeas corpus relief based on insufficiency of evidence, 120 L Ed 2d 225

Immunity: Secret Service agents held entitled to qualified immunity in lawsuit involving alleged unlawful arrest where agents had reasonable grounds to believe that arrestee had threatened President, 116 L Ed 2d 589

SECONDARY MEANING

Trade dress infringement: inherently distinctive trade dress held protectable from infringement, under trademark law (15 USCS § 1125(a)), without proof of secondary meaning, 120 L Ed 2d 615

SECRETARY OF COMMERCE

Census: allocation of overseas federal employees to home states, for purposes of congressional reapportionment, held (1) not final agency action reviewable under APA; and (2) not unconstitutional, 120 L Ed 2d 636

SECRETARY OF INTERIOR

Endangered Species Act: environmental groups held to lack standing to challenge regulation interpreting § 7(a)(2) of Endangered Species Act (16 USCS § 1536(a)(2)) not to apply to actions taken in foreign nations, 119 L Ed 2d 351

SECRETS AND SECRECY

Freedom of Information Act: exemption 6 of FOIA held to authorize deletion of names and other identifying information from reports of interviews with Haitian nationals returned to Haiti after attempting illegal emigration, 116 L Ed 2d 526

SECRET SERVICE

Immunity: Secret Service agents held entitled to qualified immunity in lawsuit involving alleged unlawful arrest where agents had reasonable grounds to believe that arrestee had threatened President, 116 L Ed 2d 589

SECTARIAN PRAYERS

Schools and education: inclusion of invocation and benediction by member of clergy at public secondary school graduation held forbidden by First Amendment's establishment of religion clause, 120 L Ed 2d 467

SECURITIES REGULATION

Stock manipulation: Securities Investor Protection Corp. held unable to maintain RICO suit under 18 USCS § 1964(c) against party to scheme that allegedly disabled broker-dealers from meeting obligations to customers, 117 L Ed 2d 532

SEGREGATION AND DESEGREGATION

Colleges and universities: several aspects of Mississippi's public university system held suspect for purposes of determining whether state had complied with its duty to desegregate, 120 L Ed 2d 575

Federal court in ongoing school desegregation case held to have discretion to order incremental withdrawal of supervision over Georgia school district, 118 L Ed 2d 108

SEIZURE

Search and Seizure (this index)

INDEX

SELF-INCRIMINATION
Similar motive: showing of similar motive to develop testimony held necessary, under Federal Evidence Rule 804(b)(1), for admission of grand jury testimony of witness invoking Fifth Amendment privilege, 120 L Ed 2d 255

SENTENCE AND PUNISHMENT
Capital Offenses and Punishment (this index)
Credit for time served: federal sentencing credit under 18 USCS § 3585(b) for certain presentence time served held required to be computed by Attorney General after convicted federal defendant has begun to serve sentence, 117 L Ed 2d 593
Cruel and Unusual Punishment (this index)
Federal Sentencing Guidelines (this index)
Fines, Forfeitures, and Penalties (this index)
Lenity Rule (this index)
Lesser sentence: Federal Government's refusal to request lesser sentence so as to reflect accused's substantial assistance in prosecuting another person held subject to review for constitutional violations, but particular accused held to have raised no claim to such review, 118 L Ed 2d 524
Mentally ill persons: Louisiana statute, permitting indefinite detention of insanity acquittees who are not mentally ill but who do not prove they would not be dangerous, held to violate Fourteenth Amendment's due process clause, 118 L Ed 2d 437
Mitigation or Aggravation of Punishment (this index)
Peremptory challenges: accused's objection under equal protection clause to state's race-based use of peremptory challenges prior to Supreme Court's decision in Batson v Kentucky held preserved for review by Supreme Court, 118 L Ed 2d 193
Prisons and Prisoners (this index)

SENTENCING GUIDELINES
Federal Sentencing Guidelines (this index)

SENTENCING REFORM ACT
Federal Sentencing Guidelines (this index)

SEPARATION OF POWERS
Sex discrimination: damages remedy held available in sex discrimination action under Title IX of Education Amendments of 1972 (20 USCS §§ 1681-1688), 117 L Ed 2d 208

INDEX

SETTLEMENT
Longshore and Harbor Workers' Compensation Act: forfeiture provision of Longshore and Harbor Workers' Compensation Act (33 USCS § 933(g)) held to apply where worker not then receiving or awarded compensation from employer settles third-party claim, 120 L Ed 2d 379

SEVENTH AMENDMENT
Jury and Jury Trial (this index)

SEVERABILITY
Waste disposal: state take title provision of Low-Level Radioactive Waste Policy Amendments Act of 1985 (42 USCS § 2021e(d)(2)(C)) held to violate Tenth Amendment, but to be severable from remainder of Act, 120 L Ed 2d 120

SEVERANCE TAX
Coal-fired electric utilities: Oklahoma statute requiring coal-fired electric utilities to burn mixture containing at least 10 percent Oklahoma-mined coal held to violate Federal Constitution's commerce clause (Art I, § 8, cl 3), 117 L Ed 2d 1
Hazardous waste disposal: disposal fee imposed by Alabama on hazardous waste generated out of state, but not on waste generated in state, held to violate Federal Constitution's commerce clause (Art I, § 8, cl 3), 119 L Ed 2d 121

SEWAGE TREATMENT PLANTS
Discharge permits: EPA's issuance of discharge permit to sewage plant, based on finding that discharges would not cause detectable violation of downstream state's water quality standards, held authorized by Clean Water Act, 117 L Ed 2d 239

SEX DISCRIMINATION
Civil Rights and Discrimination (this index)

SEXUAL ABUSE
Child Abuse or Neglect (this index)
Diversity jurisdiction: domestic relations exception to federal courts' diversity jurisdiction held inapplicable to woman's child-abuse tort claim against her former husband and his female companion, 119 L Ed 2d 468

SEXUAL HARASSMENT
Damages remedy held available in sex discrimination action
under Title IX of Education Amendments of 1972 (20
USCS §§ 1681-1688), 117 L Ed 2d 208

SEXUALLY EXPLICIT MATERIALS
Entrapment: government held to have failed, as matter of law,
to establish that individual was predisposed to illegally
receive mailing of sexually explicit depictions of children
and hence was not entrapped, 118 L Ed 2d 174

SHERMAN ACT
Photocopier manufacturer held not entitled to summary judgment dismissing federal antitrust claims as to (1) tying
arrangement between parts and service, and (2) monopolization of sale of service, 119 L Ed 2d 265

SHIPS AND SHIPPING
Jones Act (this index)
Longshore and Harbor Workers' Compensation Act (this
index)

SHOPPING CENTERS
Labor unions: store owner held not to have committed unfair
labor practice under § 8(a)(1) of National Labor Relations
Act (29 USCS § 158(a)(1)) by barring nonemployee union
organizers from parking lot, 117 L Ed 2d 79

SHORT TERM DEBTS
Bankruptcy: payments on long-term debt held to qualify for
ordinary course of business exception under 11 USCS
§ 547(c)(2) to bankruptcy trustee's power to avoid preferential transfers, 116 L Ed 2d 514

SIGNATURES
Nominating petitions: Illinois election laws, as construed to
bar new party from running county candidates for lack of
25,000 petition signatures in each electoral district, held
to violate First and Fourteenth Amendments, 116 L Ed 2d
711

SIGNS
Labor unions: store owner held not to have committed unfair
labor practice under § 8(a)(1) of National Labor Relations
Act (29 USCS § 158(a)(1)) by barring nonemployee union
organizers from parking lot, 117 L Ed 2d 79

593

INDEX

SIMILAR MOTIVES

Fifth Amendment: showing of similar motive to develop testimony held necessary, under Federal Evidence Rule 804(b)(1), for admission of grand jury testimony of witness invoking Fifth Amendment privilege, 120 L Ed 2d 255

SIXTH AMENDMENT

Antipsychotic drugs: Nevada court's judgment upholding conviction reversed and remanded, where defendant claimed that forced administration of antipsychotic drug during trial violated rights under Sixth and Fourteenth Amendments, 118 L Ed 2d 479

Federal Government's negligent 8½-year delay between indictment and arrest held to violate accused's Sixth Amendment right to speedy trial despite lack of showing of actual prejudice, 120 L Ed 2d 520

Hearsay evidence: admission of testimony against accused under Illinois hearsay exceptions for spontaneous declarations and medical-treatment statements held not to violate Sixth Amendment's confrontation clause, 116 L Ed 2d 848

Jury and Jury Trial (this index)

SMOKING

Preemption: federal cigarette labeling and advertising statutes held to preempt some but not all state-law damages claims with respect to cigarette smoking, 120 L Ed 2d 407

SOFTWARE PROGRAM

Mail order: Federal Constitution's commerce clause (Art I, § 8, cl 3), but not due process clause of Fourteenth Amendment, held to bar enforcement of North Dakota use tax against out-of-state mail-order house, 119 L Ed 2d 91

SOLICITATION OF BUSINESS

Income tax: state held not prohibited, under 15 USCS § 381(a), from imposing tax on gum manufacturer's income, where manufacturer's in-state activities include replacement, supply, and storage of gum, 120 L Ed 2d 174

SOLICITATION OF MONEY

Airport terminals: regulation prohibiting repetitive solicitation of money within airport terminals operated by public authority held reasonable and thus not violative of First Amendment, 120 L Ed 2d 541

INDEX

SOLICITATION OF VOTES
Polling places: Tennessee statute prohibiting solicitation of votes and display or distribution of campaign literature within 100 feet of entrance to polling place held not to violate First and Fourteenth Amendments, 119 L Ed 2d 5

SOLID WASTE
Waste (this index)

SOLID WASTE DISPOSAL ACT
Attorneys' fees: enhancement of attorneys' fees above lodestar, to reflect contingent fee agreement, held not permitted in awards under environmental fee-shifting statutes (33 USCS § 1365(d), 42 USCS § 6972(e)), 120 L Ed 2d 449

SON OF SAM LAWS
New York statute, requiring that criminal's income from books or other works describing crime be escrowed and made available to victims of crime, held inconsistent with Federal Constitutions's First Amendment, 116 L Ed 2d 476

SOURCE OF STRENGTH REGULATION
Bankruptcy: Federal District Court held not to have authority, in bankruptcy case, to enjoin Federal Reserve Board proceedings against debtor bank holding company for alleged banking law violations, 116 L Ed 2d 358

SOVEREIGN IMMUNITY
Bankruptcy sovereign immunity of United States held not unequivocally waived with respect to bankruptcy trustee's claim against Internal Revenue Service for monetary relief, 117 L Ed 2d 181

Deportation proceedings: Equal Access to Justice Act (5 USCS § 504, 28 USCS § 2412) held not to authorize award of attorneys' fees for administrative deportation proceedings before Immigration and Naturalization Service, 116 L Ed 2d 496

Pollution: federal sovereign immunity held not waived as to state-imposed punitive fines under Clean Water Act (33 USCS §§ 1251 et seq.) and Resource Conservation and Recovery Act (42 USCS §§ 6901 et seq.), 118 L Ed 2d 255

Retirement benefits: Kansas' income tax on military retirement benefits, but not on state and local government retirement benefits, held inconsistent with 4 USCS § 111 prohibition against discriminatory taxes, 118 L Ed 2d 243

SOVEREIGN IMMUNITY—Cont'd

State officials held subject to personal liability for damages under 42 USCS § 1983 based on official acts, where § 1983 actions were brought against officials in their individual capacities, 116 L Ed 2d 301

SOVEREIGNTY

Waste disposal: state take title provision of Low-Level Radioactive Waste Policy Amendments Act of 1985 (42 USCS § 2021e(d)(2)(C)) held to violate Tenth Amendment, but to be severable from remainder of Act, 120 L Ed 2d 120

SPEECH AND PRESS, FREEDOM OF

Freedom of Speech and Press (this index)

SPEEDY TRIAL

Federal Government's negligent 8½-year delay between indictment and arrest held to violate accused's Sixth Amendment right to speedy trial despite lack of showing of actual prejudice, 120 L Ed 2d 520

SPENDING CLAUSE

Waste disposal: state take title provision of Low-Level Radioactive Waste Policy Amendments Act of 1985 (42 USCS § 2021e(d)(2)(C)) held to violate Tenth Amendment, but to be severable from remainder of Act, 120 L Ed 2d 120

SPENDTHRIFT TRUSTS

ERISA: interest in ERISA-qualified pension plan held subject to transfer restriction under applicable nonbankruptcy law, and thus excludible from property of bankruptcy estate under 11 USCS § 541(c)(2), 119 L Ed 2d 519

SPONTANEOUS DECLARATIONS

Hearsay evidence: admission of testimony against accused under Illinois hearsay exceptions for spontaneous declarations and medical-treatment statements held not to violate Sixth Amendment's confrontation clause, 116 L Ed 2d 848

SPOTTED OWL

Timber harvesting: provision that statute meets requirements of earlier statutes on which specified pending cases involving logging and endangered spotted owl are based, held not to violate Federal Constitution's Article III, 118 L Ed 2d 73

INDEX

SPOUSES

Abortion: Pennsylvania abortion legislation held valid, except for spousal-notice provisions, under due process clause of Federal Constitution's Fourteenth Amendment, 120 L Ed 2d 674

Diversity jurisdiction: domestic relations exception to federal courts' diversity jurisdiction held inapplicable to woman's child-abuse tort claim against her former husband and his female companion, 119 L Ed 2d 468

STANDING

Census: allocation of overseas federal employees to home states, for purposes of congressional reapportionment, held (1) not final agency action reviewable under APA; and (2) not unconstitutional, 120 L Ed 2d 636

Endangered Species Act: environmental groups held to lack standing to challenge regulation interpreting § 7(a)(2) of Endangered Species Act (16 USCS § 1536(a)(2)) not to apply to actions taken in foreign nations, 119 L Ed 2d 351

STARE DECISIS

Precedent (this index)

STATE ACTION

Immunity: state officials held subject to personal liability for damages under 42 USCS § 1983 based on official acts, where § 1983 actions were brought against officials in their individual capacities, 116 L Ed 2d 301

Peremptory challenges: Fourteenth Amendment's equal protection clause held to prohibit Georgia criminal defendants from engaging in purposeful racial discrimination in exercise of peremptory challenges of potential jurors, 120 L Ed 2d 33

Title-search ratesetting: supervision by states of title-search ratesetting held not sufficiently active to give title insurance companies state-action immunity from federal antitrust liability, 119 L Ed 2d 410

STATE OF MIND

Cruel and unusual punishment: prisoner held able to maintain claim of cruel and unusual punishment under Federal Constitution's Eighth Amendment based on officers' excessive use of force not resulting in serious injury, 117 L Ed 2d 156

INDEX

STATES

Coal-fired electric utilities: Oklahoma statute requiring coal-fired electric utilities to burn mixture containing at least 10 percent Oklahoma-mined coal held to violate Federal Constitution's commerce clause (Art I, § 8, cl 3), 117 L Ed 2d 1

Federal Employers' Liability Act (45 USCS §§ 51-60) held to create cause of action, enforceable in state court, against state-owned railroad, 116 L Ed 2d 560

Waste disposal: state take title provision of Low-Level Radioactive Waste Policy Amendments Act of 1985 (42 USCS § 2021e(d)(2)(C)) held to violate Tenth Amendment, but to be severable from remainder of Act, 120 L Ed 2d 120

STAY

Bankruptcy: Federal District Court held not to have authority, in bankruptcy case, to enjoin Federal Reserve Board proceedings against debtor bank holding company for alleged banking law violations, 116 L Ed 2d 358

Delays: mandamus to compel Federal Court of Appeals to issue decision on second habeas corpus petition by state prisoner condemned to death, denied where state failed to object to order delaying decision, 116 L Ed 2d 669

Execution or sentence

– exculpatory evidence: application for stay of execution denied where Federal District Court found that alleged exculpatory evidence produced by defense did not amount to colorable claim of innocence, 119 L Ed 2d 1

– method of execution: application to vacate stay of accused's execution by cyanide gas in California granted by Supreme Court, where accused had not challenged method of execution in prior habeas corpus petitions, 118 L Ed 2d 293

STOCK AND STOCKHOLDERS

Stock manipulation: Securities Investor Protection Corp. held unable to maintain RICO suit under 18 USCS § 1964(c) against party to scheme that allegedly disabled broker-dealers from meeting obligations to customers, 117 L Ed 2d 532

Taxation: unitary business principle held to (1) govern states' federal constitutional power to tax nondomiciliary corporations' income, and (2) prevent state's taxation of gain on particular stock sale, 119 L Ed 2d 533

INDEX

SUBMERGED LANDS ACT

Boundaries: and Harbors Appropriation Act (33 USCS § 403) to condition approval of port construction on Alaska's disclaimer of federal-state boundary change, 118 L Ed 2d 222

SUBROGATION

Stock manipulation: Securities Investor Protection Corp. held unable to maintain RICO suit under 18 USCS § 1964(c) against party to scheme that allegedly disabled broker-dealers from meeting obligations to customers, 117 L Ed 2d 532

SUBSIDIARY CORPORATIONS

Taxation: Iowa business tax statute's treatment of corporation's dividends received from foreign subsidiary held to violate Federal Constitution's foreign commerce clause, 120 L Ed 2d 59

SUE AND BE SUED

Red Cross: original federal court jurisdiction over all cases to which American National Red Cross is party held conferred by sue and be sued provision (36 USCS § 2) of Red Cross' federal corporate charter, 120 L Ed 2d 201

SUMMARY JUDGMENT

Sherman Act: photocopier manufacturer held not entitled to summary judgment dismissing federal antitrust claims as to (1) tying arrangement between parts and service, and (2) monopolization of sale of service, 119 L Ed 2d 265

SUPPRESSION OF EVIDENCE

Appeals: Federal Government's 30-day appeal period held to have begun to run on date of Federal District Court's order denying motion to reconsider prior order suppressing evidence in pending criminal trial, 116 L Ed 2d 1

SUPREMACY CLAUSE

Federal Employers' Liability Act (45 USCS §§ 51-60) held to create cause of action, enforceable in state court, against state-owned railroad, 116 L Ed 2d 560
Preemption and Preemptive Rights (this index)

INDEX

SUPREME COURT RULES

Cross burning: city ordinance, banning display of symbols— including burning cross—that arouse anger in others on basis of race, color, creed, religion, or gender, held facially invalid under First Amendment, 120 L Ed 2d 305

Forma pauperis: leave to proceed in forma pauperis denied, under Supreme Court Rule 39.8, for individuals whose frequent in forma pauperis petitions had been rejected without recorded dissent, 116 L Ed 2d 293

Mandamus to compel Federal Court of Appeals to issue decision on second habeas corpus petition by state prisoner condemned to death, denied where state failed to object to order delaying decision, 116 L Ed 2d 669

Rent control: mobile home rent control ordinance, viewed in context of California statute restricting termination of mobile home park tenancy, held not to constitute physical taking under Fifth Amendment, 118 L Ed 2d 153

SURCHARGES

Airline fares: enforcement, through state consumer-protection laws, of restrictions on advertising of airline fares held preempted by provision of Airline Deregulation Act of 1978 (49 USCS Appx § 1305(a)(1)), 119 L Ed 2d 157

Waste disposal: state take title provision of Low-Level Radioactive Waste Policy Amendments Act of 1985 (42 USCS § 2021e(d)(2)(C)) held to violate Tenth Amendment, but to be severable from remainder of Act, 120 L Ed 2d 120

SYMBOLS

First Amendment: city ordinance, banning display of symbols —including burning cross—that arouse anger in others on basis of race, color, creed, religion, or gender, held facially invalid under First Amendment, 120 L Ed 2d 305

TAKEOVERS

Income tax deductions: professional expenses incurred by target corporation in course of friendly takeover held not deductible by corporation as ordinary and necessary business expenses under § 162(a) of Internal Revenue Code (26 USCS § 162(a)), 117 L Ed 2d 226

INDEX

TAKINGS CLAUSE

Rent control: mobile home rent control ordinance, viewed in context of California statute restricting termination of mobile home park tenancy, held not to constitute physical taking under Fifth Amendment, 118 L Ed 2d 153

South Carolina court held to have applied wrong standard in determining whether state beachfront management statute, by barring construction, effected taking of property under Fifth Amendment, 120 L Ed 2d 798

TAXATION

Ad valorem tax: Indian General Allotment Act of 1887 (25 USCS §§ 331 et seq.) held (1) to permit county ad valorem tax on fee-patented reservation land, but (2) not to allow county excise tax on sales of such land, 116 L Ed 2d 687

Airline fares: enforcement, through state consumer-protection laws, of restrictions on advertising of airline fares held preempted by provision of Airline Deregulation Act of 1978 (49 USCS Appx § 1305(a)(1)), 119 L Ed 2d 157

Bankruptcy (this index)

Damage awards: backpay received in settlement of claims under Title VII of Civil Rights Act of 1964 held not excludible from gross income under § 104(a)(2) of Internal Revenue Code as damages for personal injuries, 119 L Ed 2d 34

Deductions: professional expenses incurred by target corporation in course of friendly takeover held not deductible by corporation as ordinary and necessary business expenses under § 162(a) of Internal Revenue Code (26 USCS § 162(a)), 117 L Ed 2d 226

Dividends: Iowa business tax statute's treatment of corporation's dividends received from foreign subsidiary held to violate Federal Constitution's foreign commerce clause, 120 L Ed 2d 59

Excise taxes: Indian General Allotment Act of 1887 (25 USCS §§ 331 et seq.) held (1) to permit county ad valorem tax on fee-patented reservation land, but (2) not to allow county excise tax on sales of such land, 116 L Ed 2d 687

Income Tax (this index)

Mail-order use tax: Federal Constitution's commerce clause (Art I, § 8, cl 3), but not due process clause of Fourteenth Amendment, held to bar enforcement of North Dakota use tax against out-of-state mail-order house, 119 L Ed 2d 91

INDEX

TAXATION—Cont'd

Real Property Taxes (this index)

Retirement benefits: Kansas' income tax on military retirement benefits, but not on state and local government retirement benefits, held inconsistent with 4 USCS § 111 prohibition against discriminatory taxes, 118 L Ed 2d 243

Sale or Transfer of Property (this index)

Sales and use tax: Federal Constitution's commerce clause (Art I, § 8, cl 3), but not due process clause of Fourteenth Amendment, held to bar enforcement of North Dakota use tax against out-of-state mail-order house, 119 L Ed 2d 91

Severance Tax (this index)

Unitary business principle held to (1) govern states' federal constitutional power to tax nondomiciliary corporations' income, and (2) prevent state's taxation of gain on particular stock sale, 119 L Ed 2d 533

Weapons and firearms: tax payment for making firearm held not required, under provision of National Firearms Act (26 USCS § 5821), where pistol and kit allowing conversion of pistol into firearm are packaged as unit, 119 L Ed 2d 308

TAXPAYERS' ACTIONS

Real property: equal protection held not violated by California Constitution's real property tax system which generally assesses property on value at time of acquisition, rather than on current value, 120 L Ed 2d 1

TEACHERS AND INSTRUCTORS

Desegregation: federal court in ongoing school desegregation case held to have discretion to order incremental withdrawal of supervision over Georgia school district, 118 L Ed 2d 108

Sex discrimination: damages remedy held available in sex discrimination action under Title IX of Education Amendments of 1972 (20 USCS §§ 1681-1688), 117 L Ed 2d 208

TENANT

Landlord and Tenant (this index)

INDEX

TENTH AMENDMENT

Waste disposal: state take title provision of Low-Level Radioactive Waste Policy Amendments Act of 1985 (42 USCS § 2021e(d)(2)(C)) held to violate Tenth Amendment, but to be severable from remainder of Act, 120 L Ed 2d 120

THEISTIC PRAYERS

Schools and education: inclusion of invocation and benediction by member of clergy at public secondary school graduation held forbidden by First Amendment's establishment of religion clause, 120 L Ed 2d 467

THIRD PARTIES

Longshore and Harbor Workers' Compensation Act: forfeiture provision of Longshore and Harbor Workers' Compensation Act (33 USCS § 933(g)) held to apply where worker not then receiving or awarded compensation from employer settles third-party claim, 120 L Ed 2d 379

THREATS

Cross burning: city ordinance, banning display of symbols—including burning cross—that arouse anger in others on basis of race, color, creed, religion, or gender, held facially invalid under First Amendment, 120 L Ed 2d 305

Secret Service agents held entitled to qualified immunity in lawsuit involving alleged unlawful arrest where agents had reasonable grounds to believe that arrestee had threatened President, 116 L Ed 2d 589

TIMBER HARVESTING

Statutes: provision that statute meets requirements of earlier statutes on which specified pending cases involving logging and endangered spotted owl are based, held not to violate Federal Constitution's Article III, 118 L Ed 2d 73

TIME OR DATE

Appeals: Federal Government's 30-day appeal period held to have begun to run on date of Federal District Court's order denying motion to reconsider prior order suppressing evidence in pending criminal trial, 116 L Ed 2d 1

Bankruptcy: transfer of check, for purposes of determining whether transfer is voidable under 11 USCS § 547(b)(4)(A) as occurring within 90 days of bankruptcy filing, held to occur on date drawee bank honors check, 118 L Ed 2d 39

INDEX

TIME OR DATE—Cont'd

Credit for time served: federal sentencing credit under 18 USCS § 3585(b) for certain presentence time served held required to be computed by Attorney General after convicted federal defendant has begun to serve sentence, 117 L Ed 2d 593

Juvenile Delinquency Act provision limiting detention to maximum term authorized for one convicted as adult held to refer to maximum sentence authorized under United States Sentencing Guidelines, 117 L Ed 2d 559

Limitation of Actions (this index)

Notice of appeal: informal brief filed in Federal Court of Appeals held effective as notice of appeal under Rule 3 of Federal Rules of Appellate Procedure, if filing of brief is timely and conveys information required by Rule 3, 116 L Ed 2d 678

Veterans' Reemployment Rights Act: provision of Veterans' Reemployment Rights Act (38 USCS § 2024(d)) held not to limit length of military service after which member of Armed Forces retains right to civilian reemployment, 116 L Ed 2d 578

TITLE

Waste disposal: state take title provision of Low-Level Radioactive Waste Policy Amendments Act of 1985 (42 USCS § 2021e(d)(2)(C)) held to violate Tenth Amendment, but to be severable from remainder of Act, 120 L Ed 2d 120

TITLE INSURANCE

Ratesetting: supervision by states of title-search ratesetting held not sufficiently active to give title insurance companies state-action immunity from federal antitrust liability, 119 L Ed 2d 410

TOBACCO AND TOBACCO PRODUCTS

Preemption: federal cigarette labeling and advertising statutes held to preempt some but not all state-law damages claims with respect to cigarette smoking, 120 L Ed 2d 407

TOLLING PERIOD

Appeals: Federal Government's 30-day appeal period held to have begun to run on date of Federal District Court's order denying motion to reconsider prior order suppressing evidence in pending criminal trial, 116 L Ed 2d 1

TRACKAGE RIGHTS

Interstate Commerce Commission held to have authority, under 45 USCS § 562(d)(1), to require conveyance of track from railroad to Amtrak for purpose of reconveying track to second railroad, 118 L Ed 2d 52

TRADE DRESS INFRINGEMENT

Inherently distinctive trade dress held protectable from infringement, under trademark law (15 USCS § 1125(a)), without proof of secondary meaning, 120 L Ed 2d 615

TRAINING

As to education in general. **Schools and Education** (this index)

OSHA: Illinois licensing statutes held preempted by OSH Act (29 USCS §§ 651 et seq.) to extent that statutes establish occupational safety and health standards for training of hazardous waste workers, 120 L Ed 2d 73

Workplace hazards: 42 USCS § 1983 held not to provide remedy for municipal employee's death, because failure to train or warn about known workplace hazards does not violate Fourteenth Amendment's due process clause, 117 L Ed 2d 261

TRANSCRIPTS

Disclosure: United States Court of Appeals held to exceed its authority by imposing rule under which prosecutor must present to grand jury substantial exculpatory evidence in prosecutor's possession, 118 L Ed 2d 352

TRANSFER OF PROPERTY

Sale or Transfer of Property (this index)

TRANSLATIONS

Habeas corpus: federal habeas corpus petitioner, seeking evidentiary hearing on claim that material facts were not adequately developed in state proceedings, held generally required to show (1) cause for failure to develop facts, and (2) prejudice resulting from such failure, 118 L Ed 2d 318

TRANSPORTATION

Common Carriers (this index)

Desegregation: federal court in ongoing school desegregation case held to have discretion to order incremental withdrawal of supervision over Georgia school district, 118 L Ed 2d 108

Railroads (this index)

INDEX

TREATIES

Abduction: forcible abduction of Mexican citizen to United States held not to violate extradition treaty with Mexico, and thus, not to prohibit citizen's trial in Federal District Court on criminal charges, 119 L Ed 2d 441

TRESPASS

Labor unions: store owner held not to have committed unfair labor practice under § 8(a)(1) of National Labor Relations Act (29 USCS § 158(a)(1)) by barring nonemployee union organizers from parking lot, 117 L Ed 2d 79

TRIAL

Speedy Trial (this index)

TRUSTS AND TRUSTEES

Bankruptcy trustee. **Bankruptcy** (this index)

Spendthrift trusts: interest in ERISA-qualified pension plan held subject to transfer restriction under applicable non-bankruptcy law, and thus excludible from property of bankruptcy estate under 11 USCS § 541(c)(2), 119 L Ed 2d 519

Taxation: Indian General Allotment Act of 1887 (25 USCS §§ 331 et seq.) held (1) to permit county ad valorem tax on fee-patented reservation land, but (2) not to allow county excise tax on sales of such land, 116 L Ed 2d 687

TYING ARRANGEMENTS

Sherman Act: photocopier manufacturer held not entitled to summary judgment dismissing federal antitrust claims as to (1) tying arrangement between parts and service, and (2) monopolization of sale of service, 119 L Ed 2d 265

UNFAIR LABOR PRACTICES

Store owner held not to have committed unfair labor practice under § 8(a)(1) of National Labor Relations Act (29 USCS § 158(a)(1)) by barring nonemployee union organizers from parking lot, 117 L Ed 2d 79

UNFAIR TRADE PRACTICES

Restraints of Trade, Monopolies, and Unfair Trade Practices (this index)

UNIFORM DIVISION OF INCOME FOR TAX PURPOSES ACT

Taxation: unitary business principle held to (1) govern states' federal constitutional power to tax nondomiciliary corporations' income, and (2) prevent state's taxation of gain on particular stock sale, 119 L Ed 2d 533

UNIONS

Collective Bargaining (this index)
Labor and Employment (this index)

UNITARY BUSINESS PRINCIPLE

Iowa business tax statute's treatment of corporation's dividends received from foreign subsidiary held to violate Federal Constitution's foreign commerce clause, 120 L Ed 2d 59

Unitary business principle held to (1) govern states' federal constitutional power to tax nondomiciliary corporations' income, and (2) prevent state's taxation of gain on particular stock sale, 119 L Ed 2d 533

UNITARY SCHOOL SYSTEM

Desegregation: federal court in ongoing school desegregation case held to have discretion to order incremental withdrawal of supervision over Georgia school district, 118 L Ed 2d 108

UNIVERSITIES

Schools and Education (this index)

USE, OCCUPANCY, OR ENJOYMENT

Eminent domain: South Carolina court held to have applied wrong standard in determining whether state beachfront management statute, by barring construction, effected taking of property under Fifth Amendment, 120 L Ed 2d 798

USE TAX

Commerce clause: Federal Constitution's commerce clause (Art I, § 8, cl 3), but not due process clause of Fourteenth Amendment, held to bar enforcement of North Dakota use tax against out-of-state mail-order house, 119 L Ed 2d 91

INDEX

UTILITIES

Coal-fired electric utilities: Oklahoma statute requiring coal-fired electric utilities to burn mixture containing at least 10 percent Oklahoma-mined coal held to violate Federal Constitution's commerce clause (Art I, § 8, cl 3), 117 L Ed 2d 1

VACATION PAY

Income tax: backpay received in settlement of claims under Title VII of Civil Rights Act of 1964 held not excludible from gross income under § 104(a)(2) of Internal Revenue Code as damages for personal injuries, 119 L Ed 2d 34

VAGUENESS

Certainty and Definiteness (this index)

VALUE AND VALUATION

Bankruptcy: debtor in bankruptcy held not entitled under 11 USCS § 506(d) to strip down creditor's lien on real property to judicially determined value of collateral, 116 L Ed 2d 903

Eminent domain: South Carolina court held to have applied wrong standard in determining whether state beachfront management statute, by barring construction, effected taking of property under Fifth Amendment, 120 L Ed 2d 798

Property taxes: equal protection held not violated by California Constitution's real property tax system which generally assesses property on value at time of acquisition, rather than on current value, 120 L Ed 2d 1

VENUE

Equal protection held not violated by Montana venue rules allowing civil suit against Montana corporation in only county of principal place of business, but against foreign corporation in any county, 119 L Ed 2d 432

VERDICT

Due process held not to require that general guilty verdict on federal multiple conspiracy charge be set aside if evidence is inadequate to support conviction as to one object, 116 L Ed 2d 371

INDEX

VETERANS' REEMPLOYMENT RIGHTS ACT
Length of service: Provision of Veterans' Reemployment Rights Act (38 USCS § 2024(d)) held not to limit length of military service after which member of Armed Forces retains right to civilian reemployment, 116 L Ed 2d 578

VICTIMS
Son of Sam laws: New York statute, requiring that criminal's income from books or other works describing crime be escrowed and made available to victims of crime, held inconsistent with Federal Constitutions's First Amendment, 116 L Ed 2d 476

VIOLENCE OR FORCE
Duress or Coercion (this index)

VOIR DIRE
Death penalty: Illinois trial court held to violate due process by refusing to ask potential jurors, on voir dire in capital case, whether they would automatically impose death penalty if defendant was convicted, 119 L Ed 2d 492

VOLUNTARINESS
Duress or Coercion (this index)

VOTES AND VOTING
Elections and Voting (this index)

VOTING RIGHTS ACTS
Preclearance: changes in decisionmaking powers of elected members of Alabama county commissions held not to be changes with respect to voting subject to preclearance requirements of § 5 of Voting Rights Act (42 USCS § 1973c), 117 L Ed 2d 51

WAGES
Compensation (this index)

WAIVER
Aggravating circumstances: Florida trial judge's improper weighing in capital sentencing hearing of aggravating factor not supported by evidence, in violation of Eighth Amendment, held not cured by state appellate review, 119 L Ed 2d 326

609

INDEX

WARRANTS

Immunity: Secret Service agents held entitled to qualified immunity in lawsuit involving alleged unlawful arrest where agents had reasonable grounds to believe that arrestee had threatened President, 116 L Ed 2d 589

WASTE

Clean Water Act (this index)

Counties: Michigan statute barring private landfill owner from accepting solid waste originating outside county in which landfill was located held to violate Federal Constitution's commerce clause (Art I, § 8, cl 3), 119 L Ed 2d 139

Hazardous Substances (this index)

WATER POLLUTION

Clean Water Act (this index)

Environmental Law (this index)

WEAPONS AND FIREARMS

Tax payment for making firearm held not required, under provision of National Firearms Act (26 USCS § 5821), where pistol and kit allowing conversion of pistol into firearm are packaged as unit, 119 L Ed 2d 308

WILDLIFE CONSERVATION

Endangered Species Act: environmental groups held to lack standing to challenge regulation interpreting § 7(a)(2) of Endangered Species Act (16 USCS § 1536(a)(2)) not to apply to actions taken in foreign nations, 119 L Ed 2d 351

Environmental Law (this index)

Timber harvesting: provision that statute meets requirements of earlier statutes on which specified pending cases involving logging and endangered spotted owl are based, held not to violate Federal Constitution's Article III, 118 L Ed 2d 73

WILLFUL ACTS

Intentional, Willful, or Wanton Acts (this index)

WITHERSPOON ISSUES OR RULE

Death penalty: Illinois trial court held to violate due process by refusing to ask potential jurors, on voir dire in capital case, whether they would automatically impose death penalty if defendant was convicted, 119 L Ed 2d 492

INDEX

WITNESSES
Evidence (this index)

Hearsay evidence: admission of testimony against accused under Illinois hearsay exceptions for spontaneous declarations and medical-treatment statements held not to violate Sixth Amendment's confrontation clause, 116 L Ed 2d 848

WIVES
Spouses (this index)

WORDS AND PHRASES

Adversary adjudication: Equal Access to Justice Act (5 USCS § 504, 28 USCS § 2412) held not to authorize award of attorneys' fees for administrative deportation proceedings before Immigration and Naturalization Service, 116 L Ed 2d 496

Allowed secured claim: debtor in bankruptcy held not entitled under 11 USCS § 506(d) to strip down creditor's lien on real property to judicially determined value of collateral, 116 L Ed 2d 903

Creditor: trustee liquidating and distributing property as part of plan under Chapter 11 of Bankruptcy Code held required, as to income attributable to property, to file federal income tax returns and pay tax, 117 L Ed 2d 196

Employee: ERISA provision (29 USCS § 1002(6)) defining employee as any individual employed by an employer, held to incorporate traditional agency-law criteria for identifying master-servant relationships, 117 L Ed 2d 581

Employee: maritime worker whose occupation of ship repairman was listed in Longshore and Harbor Workers' Compensation Act (33 USCS § 902(3)) held not precluded from being seaman under Jones Act (46 USCS Appx § 688), 116 L Ed 2d 405

Extortion: affirmative act of inducement by public official, such as demand, held not to be necessary element of Hobbs Act offense of extortion under color of official right (18 USCS § 1951(b)(2)), 119 L Ed 2d 57

Fiduciary: trustee liquidating and distributing property as part of plan under Chapter 11 of Bankruptcy Code held required, as to income attributable to property, to file federal income tax returns and pay tax, 117 L Ed 2d 196

INDEX

WORDS AND PHRASES—Cont'd

Making: tax payment for making firearm held not required, under provision of National Firearms Act (26 USCS § 5821), where pistol and kit allowing conversion of pistol into firearm are packaged as unit, 119 L Ed 2d 308

Medical emergency: Pennsylvania abortion legislation held valid, except for spousal-notice provisions, under due process clause of Federal Constitution's Fourteenth Amendment, 120 L Ed 2d 674

Participant: ERISA provision (29 USCS § 1002(6)) defining employee as any individual employed by an employer, held to incorporate traditional agency-law criteria for identifying master-servant relationships, 117 L Ed 2d 581

Person: federal sovereign immunity held not waived as to state-imposed punitive fines under Clean Water Act (33 USCS §§ 1251 et seq.) and Resource Conservation and Recovery Act (42 USCS §§ 6901 et seq.), 118 L Ed 2d 255

Punitive damages: Federal Tort Claims Act ban on awards of punitive damages (28 USCS § 2674) held to apply to only damages legally considered punitive under traditional common-law principles, 116 L Ed 2d 731

Regular or systematic solicitation: Federal Constitution's commerce clause (Art I, § 8, cl 3), but not due process clause of Fourteenth Amendment, held to bar enforcement of North Dakota use tax against out-of-state mail-order house, 119 L Ed 2d 91

WORKERS' COMPENSATION

Federal Employers' Liability Act (45 USCS §§ 51-60) held to create cause of action, enforceable in state court, against state-owned railroad, 116 L Ed 2d 560

Jones Act (this index)

Longshore and Harbor Workers' Compensation Act (this index)

State-mandated payment of workers' compensation benefits withheld under benefit coordination statute held not to violate contract clause or due process clause of Federal Constitution, 117 L Ed 2d 328

WORKPLACE HAZARDS

Due process: 42 USCS § 1983 held not to provide remedy for municipal employee's death, because failure to train or warn about known workplace hazards does not violate

613

WORKPLACE HAZARDS—Cont'd

Fourteenth Amendment's due process clause, 117 L Ed 2d 261

OSHA: Illinois licensing statutes held preempted by OSH Act (29 USCS §§ 651 et seq.) to extent that statutes establish occupational safety and health standards for training of hazardous waste workers, 120 L Ed 2d 73

WRITE-IN CANDIDATES AND VOTES

Hawaii's prohibition on write-in voting held not to violate rights of state's voters under Federal Constitution's First and Fourteenth Amendments, 119 L Ed 2d 245

WRONGFUL DEATH

Federal Tort Claims Act ban on awards of punitive damages (28 USCS § 2674) held to apply to only damages legally considered punitive under traditional common-law principles, 116 L Ed 2d 731